MACMILLAN/McGRAW-HILL

Mathematics in Action

Audrey L. Jackson   Martin L. Johnson   Steven J. Leinwand
Richard D. Lodholz   Gary L. Musser   Walter G. Secada

MACMILLAN/McGRAW-HILL SCHOOL PUBLISHING COMPANY
New York   Columbus

CONSULTANTS

MULTICULTURAL AND EDUCATIONAL CONSULTANTS

Rim An

Marcia Ascher

Elsie Babcock

Vicki Chan

Dr. Alejandro Gallard

Zelda Gold

Jerilyn Grignon

Earlene Hall

Susan Lair

Dr. Barbara Merino

Carol Mitchell

James R. Murphy

Gail Lowe Parrino

Yolanda Rodriguez

Claudia Zaslavsky

ASSESSMENT CONSULTANT

Michael Priestley

COOPERATIVE LEARNING CONSULTANT

Liana Nan Graves

ACKNOWLEDGMENTS

The publisher gratefully acknowledges permission to reprint the following copyrighted material:

Chart of "Tallest Trees Found in the United States." Excerpted from AMERICAN FORESTS MAGAZINE, a publication of the American Forestry Association, 1516 P Street N.W., Washington, D.C. 20005. Used by permission.

"Olympic Swimming—100-Meter Freestyle Records," from THE WORLD ALMANAC, 1989. Copyright © Newspaper Enterprise Association. New York, N.Y. 10166. Used by permission.

COVER DESIGN Designframe Inc. **COVER PHOTOGRAPHY** Pete McArthur

ILLUSTRATION Ray Alma; 447 • Phil Anderson; 6, 7 • George Baquero; 77, 306, 318, 319, 419, 434, 505 • Rick Berlin; 230, 304, 305, 308 • Rose Mary Berlin; 286, 287 • Craig Berman; 136, 137 • Lloyd Birmingham; 162, 228, 237 • Rick Brown; 2, 3 • Circa 86, Inc.; 173, 215, 216 • William Colrus; 93 • Jack E. Davis; 26, 27 • Bruce Day; 144, 150, 151, 406, 407 • Jim Deigan; 272, 273 • Steve DeStefano; 222 • Cathy Diefendorf; 310, 311, 390 • Bert Dodson; 366, 367, 418 • Eldon Doty; 60, 61, 87, 110, 111, 217, 337, 408, 409, 438, 439, 471, 484 • Leslie Dunlap; 444, 496 • Steve Duquette; 234, 235 • Julie Durell; 490 • Richard Erickson; 256, 257 • Kim Wilson Eversz; 102, 103 • Barbara Friedman; 156, 157, 279 • Donald Gambino; 39, 121, 331 • Ignacio Gomez; 178, 179, 260, 261, 268, 269 • Gershom Griffith; 362, 388 • Patricia Gural-Hinton; 324, 325 • Marika Hahn; 364 bottom • Meryl Henderson; 116 • Al Hering; 206 • Dennis Hockerman; 196, 197, 276, 277 • Marilyn Janovitz; 176, 177 • Terry Kovalcik; 148, 149, 262, 263 • Ron Le Hew; 194, 195 • Jeff Lewin; 322 • Benton Mahan; 383 • Wallop Manyum; 22, 23 • Ginidir Marshall; 203 • Claude Martinot; 356, 357 • Bill Mayer; 488, 489 • Kimble Mead; 232, 233 • Patrick Merrell; 72, 73, 90, 91, 108, 109, 146, 147 • Mike Quon Design Office, Inc.; 142, 143, 220, 221, 320, 321 • MKR Design; Handmade props • Leo Monahan; 1 • Sal Murdocca; 96, 97, 352, 353 • Ann Neumann; 326 • Patrick O'Chapin; 12, 13, 58, 59 • Hima Pamoedjo; 104, 177 right, 186, 202, 203, 258, 259, 289, 354, 355, 364 top, 502, 516 • Alex Pietersen; 207 • Jan Pyk; 392, 393 • Marcy Dunn Ramsey; 515 • Chris Reed; 64, 65 • Suzanne Roz; 16, 17 • Phil Scheuer; 8, 9, 412, 413, 478, 479 • Bob Shein; 358, 476 • David Sheldon; 192, 314, 315 • Blanche Sims; 188, 189 • Terry Sirrell; 190, 191 • Steve Smallwood; 365 • Joel Snyder; 131, 217, 255 • Peter Spacek; 448, 449 • Leslie Stall; 404 • Arvis Stewart; 134 • Wayne Anthony Still; 270 • George Ulrich; 337 • Vantage Art, Inc.; 328 • Joe Veno; 24, 25 • Josie Yee; 159, 328, 415, 453, 455 • Rusty Zabransky; 36, 74, 118, 160, 204, 242, 288, 289, 348, 370, 416, 458, 502 • Ron Zalme; 4, 5, 138, 217, 346, 442, 446, 494 • Jerry Zimmerman; 34, 35, 100, 101, 398, 399 • Robert Zimmerman; 394, 395 • **CONTENTS:** Don Baker

PHOTOGRAPHY *African Textiles*, Crescent Books/Courtesy of the Trustees of the British Museum, 256-257 bkgnd border • Allstock/© John Marshall, 51-52 bkgnd; © Brian Stablyk, 394-395 bkgnd; Greg Vaughn, 430-431MB; © Zefa, 64-65 bkgnd • The Bettmann Archive, 152ML, 153ML • Bettmann Newsphotos/UPI, 152ML, BL • Rudy Von Briel, 28 • The British Museum, 10BL, 10-11BL, 11TR • Bruce Coleman, Inc/A.J. Deane, 185; Frank Oberle, 373B; Dr. David Schwimmer, 160 • DDB Stock Photo/D. Donne Bryant, 175C; © Carolyn Kerson, 120L • Esto Photographics/Jeff Goldberg, 329 • Folio, Inc./John Keith, 324R; Jerry Mesmer, 372; Al Messerschmidt, 486; Richard Quataert, 88-89 • FPG International, 68; E.A. McGee, 370T; Gerald L. French, 94 • Fundamental Photographs/Richard Megna, 461 • The Granger Collection, 218T • Grant Heilman/Runk Schoenberger, 38; Barry L. Runk, 274, 288T • Scott Harvey for MMSD, 20TL, 21T, 38C, 97B, 188L, 302-303T strip • Michal Heron, 54, 281, 284, 285, 386, 387, 397, 400, 433, 454, 456 • The Image Bank/T.I. Baker, 244; Gary Cralle, 10-11BR, BL across gutter, 275; Mel DiGiacomo, 492R; Geoffrey Gove, 356-357 bkgnd; © Bill Hickey, 153T; Gerard Mathieu, 324B; Roger Miller, 492; Co Rentmeester, 345; Weinberg-Clark, 325; A.T. Willett, 493 • The Image Works/Mark Antman, 474 • International Stock Photography Ltd./Richard Pharaoh, 39T • Jerry Jacka, 75T • Ken Karp for MMSD, 189T • The Kentucky Quilt Project/Cuesta Benberry, 302BL • Lee Boltin, 10-11CR, CL, across gutter • Magnum Photos/Marilyn Silverstone, 520R • Maine Scene/Alan Carey, 14BL; Morgan Hebard Jr., 15L; Ron Monteleon, 14TL, 15R; Marjorie Nietz, 14C; Andy Payson, 14TR; Mark Picard, 14BR • Lawrence Migdale, 68R • Monkmeyer Press/Nancy Lehmann, 317C • Odyssey/Chicago/Robert Frerck, 218-219 • Warren Ogden, 31, 68L, 161BR • Stephen Ogilvy, 18, 19, 30, 53, 66, 94, 113, 267, 396, 415, 436, 457, 482, 483, 502, 503 • Omni-Photo Communications/Ken Karp, 39, 54, 76, 112, 154, 155, 159, 182, 205, 322, 410, 411, 414, 416, 417, 441; John Lei, 49, 52, 95, 106, 158, 226, 227, 238, 239, 266, 344, 401, 432, 440, 452, 455, 459, 500, 501 • Pacific Stock/Kyle Rothenburg, 430-431 bkgnd • Peter Arnold, Inc./Harvey Lloyd, 257B • Photo Edit/Robert Brenner, 481; Tony Freeman, 183; John Neubauer, 88L; Alan Odie, 280 • Photo Researchers/Richard Dranitzke, 384-385M; M.H. English, 350; Explorer, 317R; Jacana, 204B; Kent & Donna Dannen, 204T; Tom McHugh, 161, 203; Lawrence Migdale, 316C; John Moss, 132BL; Hans Namuth, 482; J.H. Robinson, 181; Gianni Tortoli, 385BR • Picturesque/© Will & Demi McIntyre, 120R • Rainbow/Larry Brownstein, 63; Dan McCoy, 160, 312BL; Hank Morgan, 360 • Photori/Mauritius, 402B; Leonard Rue, 403 • The Picture Cube/© Scott Berner, 303BL • Picturesque/Will & Demi McIntyre, 472L, 473BR, T • © Carl Purcell, 132-133 • Research Plus, 288 • Kurt Anderson, 119; Gene Anthony, 37; Franklin Avery, 75; Laurence Bartone, 37, 133, 161, 219, 243, 289, 328, 371, 417, 459, 503; Lawrence Migdale, 89; Karen Rantzman, 205; John Running, 330 • Joseph Sachs, 118, 458 • San Francisco Craft & Folk Art Museum/Emma Hall, 303BR • Shostal/Superstock/David Forbert, 313; August Upitis, 312TC • Elliott Varner Smith, 282 • Smithsonian Institution Bureau of American Ethnology, 51T • Starlight/NASA JSC, 224; Roger Ressmeyer, 225 • Stock Boston/© Fredrik D. Bodin, 302-303 bkgnd • The Stock Market/G. Anderson, 520; Peter Beck, 307; Steve Elmore, 520C; David Frazier, 329; Michael Furman, 370B; P. Robert Garvey, 88-89; Ted Horowitz, 458; K. Iwaski, 290; © Tom McCarthy, 302-303BM; Roy Morsch, 76, 373T; Dave Wilheim, 373M • University of California/Bancroft Library, 473BL • University of Pennsylvania, Object #21444, 430L • Viesti Associates, Inc./Dan Barba, 20; Larry Kolvoord, 21; Skye Mason, 33 inset, 368; Ginny Ganong Nichols, 32, 62L, 71, 98, 114, 140, 141, 198, 199, 240, 241; Courtesy of The Fernbank Science Center, Atlanta, Georgia, 369, 402L, 450L, 451T, 480, 498; Ken Ross, 70, 115, 266, 316L, 450R, 451B, 499; Kevin Vandivier, 33T; Joe Viesti, 62R, 317L • Bill Waltzer, 75 • WestLight/Craig Aurness, 67; © Digital Art, 488-489 bkgnd; © Lois Ellen Frank, 10-11 bkgnd; Richard Fukuhara, 342-343 bkgnd; © Chuck O'Rear, 4-5 bkgnd; Robert Young Pelton, 6-7 bkgnd; Bill Ross, 324M; Adam Smith Productions, 8-9 bkgnd; H.D. Thoreau, 330T • Woodfin Camp & Associates, Inc./John Blaustein, 312TL; Robert Frerck, 283; David Alan Harvey, 174-175; Kal Muller, 256-257 bkgnd; Mireilli Vantier, 472-473 bkgnd • **CONTENTS:** Tony Freeman, vii • Ken Karp, iiiB • Larry Kolvoard, vT • John Lei, iiiT • Ginny Ganong Nichols, iv • Stephen Ogilvy, ix • Omni-Photo Communications/Ken Karp, viiiT&B • Ginny Ganong Nichols, Viesti Associates, Inc., vB, vi, x

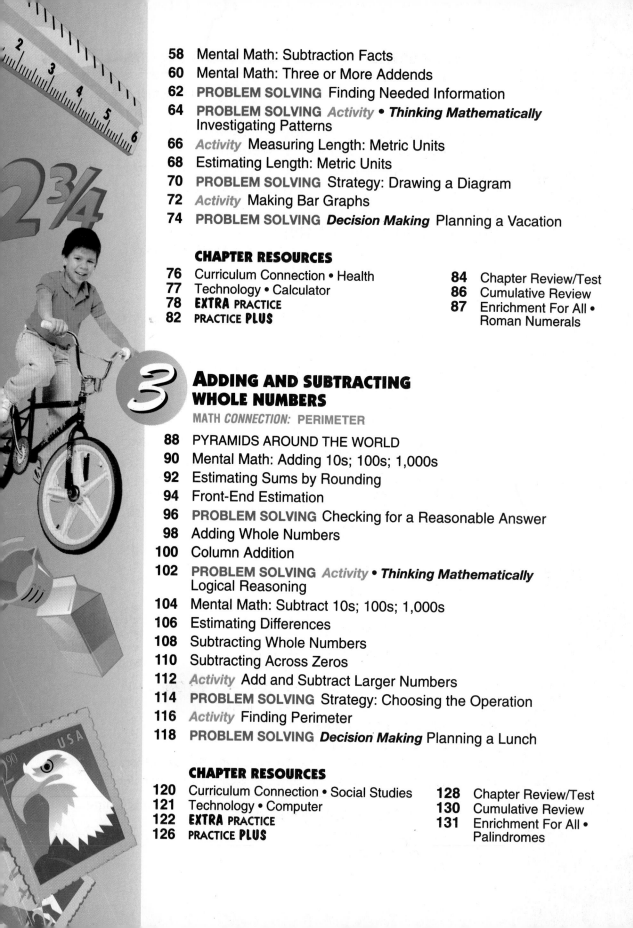

3 ADDING AND SUBTRACTING WHOLE NUMBERS

MATH *CONNECTION:* PERIMETER

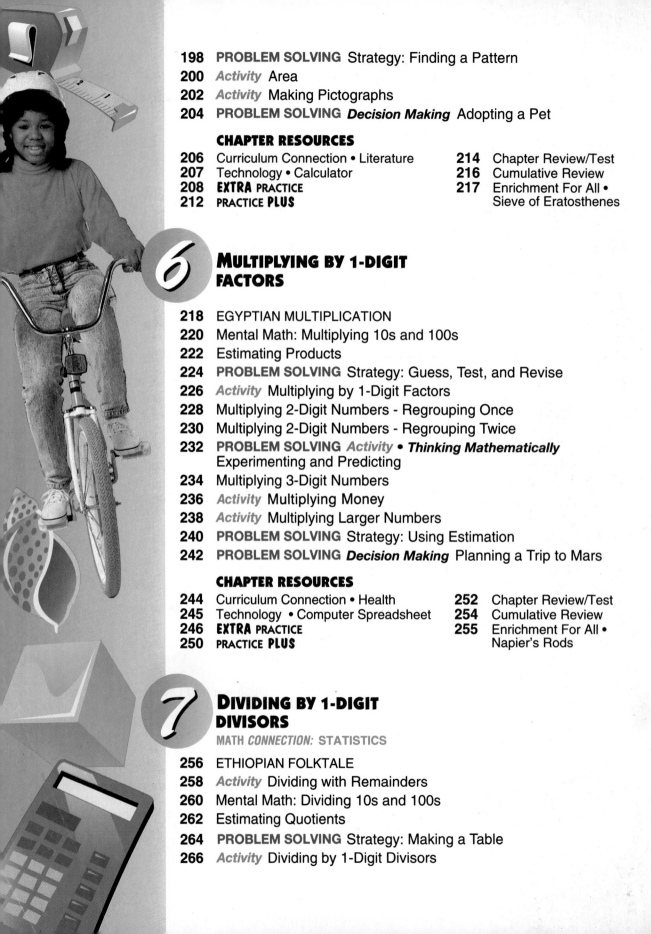

6 MULTIPLYING BY 1-DIGIT FACTORS

7 DIVIDING BY 1-DIGIT DIVISORS

MATH *CONNECTION:* STATISTICS

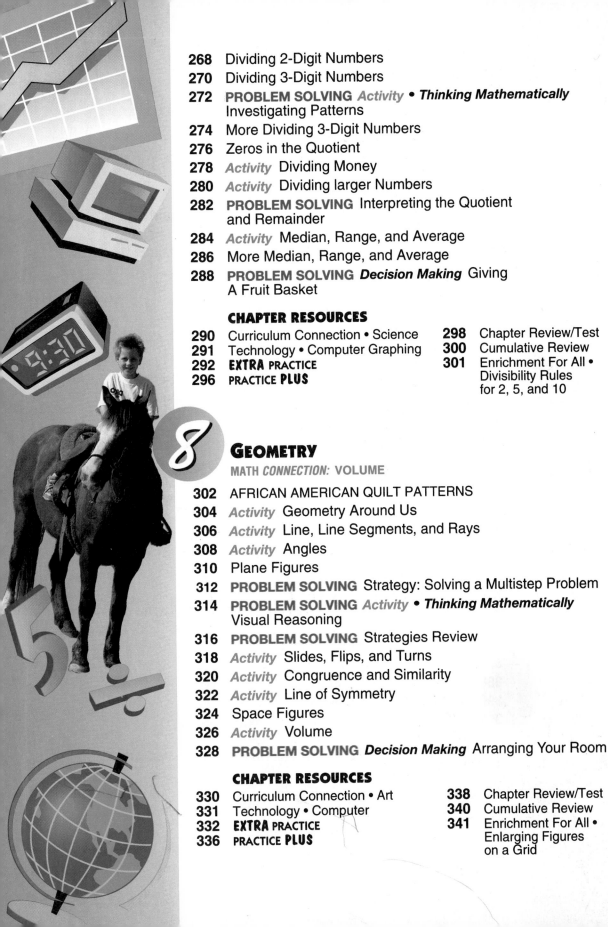

8 GEOMETRY

MATH *CONNECTION:* VOLUME

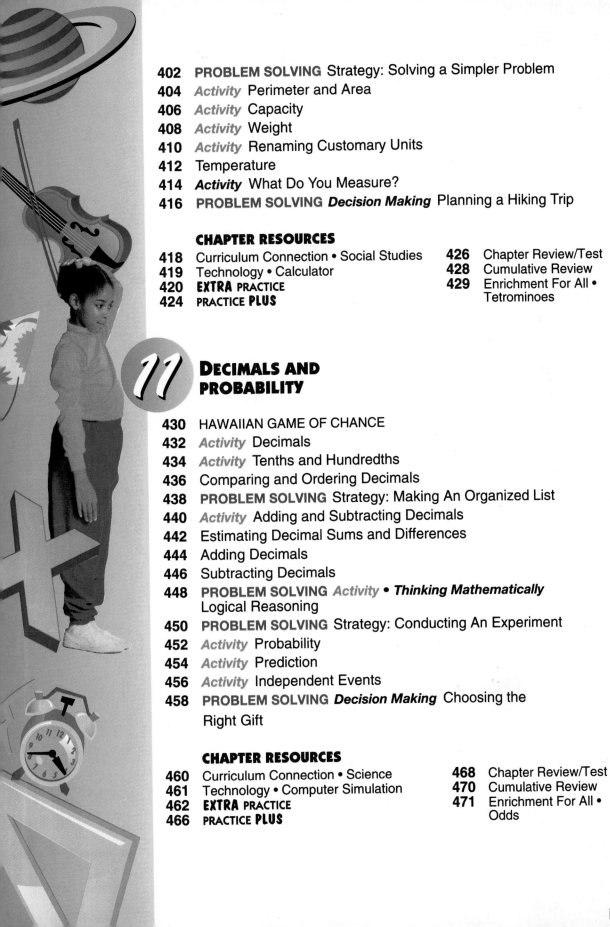

11 DECIMALS AND PROBABILITY

12 MULTIPLYING AND DIVIDING BY 2-DIGIT NUMBERS

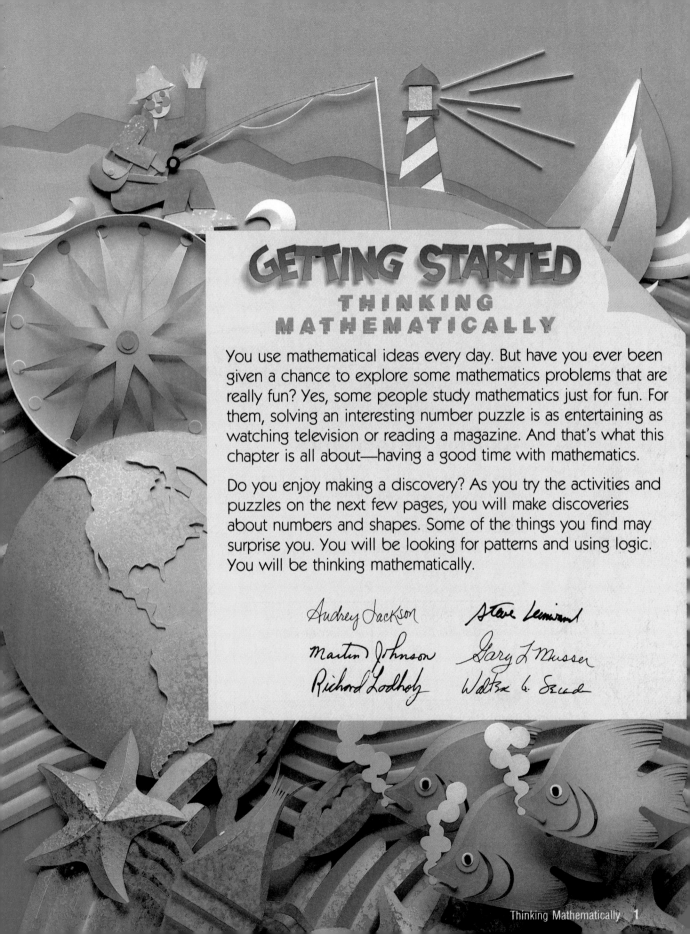

GETTING STARTED

THINKING MATHEMATICALLY

You use mathematical ideas every day. But have you ever been given a chance to explore some mathematics problems that are really fun? Yes, some people study mathematics just for fun. For them, solving an interesting number puzzle is as entertaining as watching television or reading a magazine. And that's what this chapter is all about—having a good time with mathematics.

Do you enjoy making a discovery? As you try the activities and puzzles on the next few pages, you will make discoveries about numbers and shapes. Some of the things you find may surprise you. You will be looking for patterns and using logic. You will be thinking mathematically.

Audrey Jackson

Martin Johnson

Richard Lodholz

Steve Leinwand

Gary L. Musser

Walter G. Secada

School Store

PENCILS 5¢ each
PENS 8¢ each
ERASERS 10¢ each

NO MORE THAN 3 OF EACH ITEM TO A CUSTOMER.

Applying Mathematics

You use mathematics to solve problems all the time. Think about buying and selling items in a school store.

Suppose you are running the school store. Copy and complete the following order forms from other students.

1.

School Store
Order Form

#	Item	Cost
2	Pencils	_____
3	Erasers	_____
Total Cost		_____

2.

School Store
Order Form

#	Item	Cost
1	Pencil	_____
3	Pens	_____
2	Erasers	_____
Total Cost		_____

3.

School Store
Order Form

#	Item	Cost
3	Pens	_____
3	Pencils	_____
Total Cost		_____

4. Make up your own order and find its cost.

5. A friend of yours spent exactly 30¢ in the store. What possible purchases could your friend have made?

6. Can you spend exactly 50¢? Why or why not?

Suppose you are the clerk in the school store. Solve the following problems.

7. Mike pays for 1 pencil, 3 pens, and 1 eraser with 2 quarters.
   How much does Mike spend?
   How much change does Mike get?
   What coins would you give him to make the change?

8. Alissa buys one of each item with a dollar.
   How much does she spend?
   How much change does she get?
   What coins would you give her to make the change?

9. Lonnie needs 3 pencils and 2 pens. He has a quarter. What problem does Lonnie face?
   What can Lonnie do to solve his problem?

Now suppose you are a customer in the store.

10. What is the greatest amount you could spend at one time in the school store? (*Hint:* Remember the sign.)

11. List all the different orders you can make of 3 or more items that have a total cost of 25¢ or less.

12. Suppose you had exactly 26¢. Could you spend the 26¢ exactly in the school store? How? Is there more than one way to spend exactly 26¢ in the store? What other ways could you spend exactly 26¢?

Using Number Concepts

First, make a set of 9 playing cards, one card for each of the numbers 1 to 9. Use blank cards or cut sheets of paper into 9 equal-sized pieces.

| 1 | 2 | 3 | 4 | 5 | 6 | 7 | 8 | 9 |

Next, on another sheet of paper, draw a board like the one at the right. The spaces should be about the same size as your cards.

Play the games.

1. Pick any 4 of your cards. Place them on your board so that you get the greatest sum. How did you arrange the numbers you picked?

2. Now pick the 4 cards that would give you the greatest sum. How would you arrange these cards? What is the greatest possible sum?

3. Pick the 4 cards that would give you the least possible sum. How would you arrange these cards? What is the least possible sum?

4. Can you use 4 cards to get a sum of exactly 75 in this game?

How many different ways can you get 75 using 4 cards?
How many different ways can you get 75 using 3 cards?

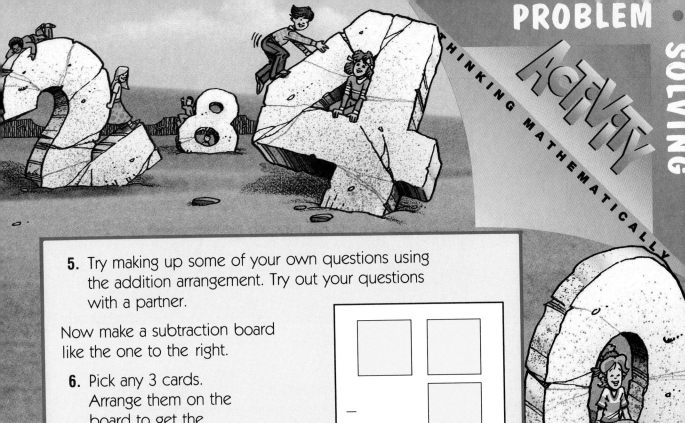

5. Try making up some of your own questions using the addition arrangement. Try out your questions with a partner.

Now make a subtraction board like the one to the right.

6. Pick any 3 cards. Arrange them on the board to get the greatest possible difference.

7. Use these same 3 cards to get the least possible difference.

8. Which 3 cards would you pick to get a difference closest to 10? What is the difference? Is there another way?

9. Discuss your reasoning on Problems 6, 7, and 8 with a partner.

10. Now pick the 3 cards that will give you the greatest possible difference. What is this difference? How do you know that it is the greatest possible difference?

11. Pick the 3 cards that will give you the least possible difference. What is this difference? How do you know that it is the least possible difference?

12. Make up your own questions using the subtraction arrangement. Try them out with a partner.

Visual Reasoning

Cut out two identical squares from two sheets of different-colored paper. Then fold each square in half to make a triangle and cut along the fold. You should have four triangles—two of each color.

Now experiment with your triangles. Put them together to make a rectangle. Then move the triangles around to make another rectangle with a different design. Each time you create a new design, draw a picture of it. For example:

Be careful.   and   are not different designs.

You can make the design on the second rectangle simply by turning the first rectangle.

1. Work with a partner. Compare your designs. Did you both find the same designs? Can you find other designs working together?

2. How many different rectangular designs can you make?

3. What other shapes and designs can each of you make using your four triangles? Do you have to decide on some rules for how to arrange the triangles?

4. Work with your partner and use all eight of your triangles to create shapes and designs. See what you can discover. Do you think you will make more shapes and designs than you did with four triangles? Why?

Measuring

Here is a funny-looking ruler. It is 8 units long, but it has only three marks.

8 units

1			5	6	

Suppose you may use the ruler only once for each length you measure. How can you measure any length from 1 to 8 units?

For example, to measure 1 unit you can use the part from the end of the ruler to the 1.

1. Which part can you use to measure 5 units? 6 units? 8 units?

To measure 4 units you can use the part from 1 to 5

2. Which part can you use to measure 2 units? 3 units?

Suppose you have another ruler, 10 units long.

10 units

?

You want to be able to measure all lengths from 1 to 10 units. What is the least number of marks you need to make on the ruler?

Copy the ruler and the number grid. Each time you put a mark on the ruler, use the grid to cross off the lengths you can measure.

1	2	3	4	5	6	7	8	9	10

3. If you make a mark at 1 unit, which lengths can you measure?

4. Suppose you make another mark at 4 units. Now which other lengths can you measure?

5. Which lengths are left for you to measure?

6. Where will you put the next mark? Which lengths can you measure?

7. Do you need another mark? If so, where will you put it? How many marks did you use in all?

8. Can you find a different set of marks that will also work? What are the marks?

MONDAY, MONDAY

WE BOTH HAVE BASEBALL PRACTICE ON THURSDAY. IT'S OUR FAVORITE DAY!

Collecting and Interpreting Data

GETTING STARTED

Some days are more popular than others. For example, Saturday is much more popular than Monday.

1. Why do you think this is true?

2. What is your favorite day of the week? Why?

3. Guess which day or days will be more popular with the students in your class. Which day or days will be least popular?

COLLECTING AND DISPLAYING DATA

A better way to answer these questions is to collect some actual data.

4. Take a class survey. Ask each student his or her favorite day. Then ask about the least favorite day. Use tally marks to record the answers. Copy the survey form below or design your own.

5. Total your results.

	FAVORITE DAY		LEAST FAVORITE DAY	
	Tally	Total	Tally	Total
Monday				
Tuesday				
Wednesday				
Thursday				
Friday				
Saturday				
Sunday				

I LOVE SUNDAYS BEST 'CAUSE OF SUNDAY DINNER!

DISPLAYING DATA

6. Use the data in your table. Copy and complete the two bar graphs below.

FAVORITE DAY

Number of Students

Mon. Tues. Wed. Thurs. Fri. Sat. Sun.

LEAST FAVORITE DAY

Number of Students

Mon. Tues. Wed. Thurs. Fri. Sat. Sun.

ANALYZING DATA

7. What do the bar graphs show you? What are the results of your survey?

8. Which day was the second favorite? Was it a close second? What does this tell you?

9. Were your own favorite and least favorite days the same as the survey results? Were your guesses about the other students' choices correct?

10. Can you think of some ways to use what you learned from this survey?

MONEY *around the* WORLD

Every day in every part of the world, money changes hands. But money doesn't always mean coins and bills.

Objects of value, such as beads, cloth, or shells, have often been used as money. In the Santa Cruz Islands in the Pacific Ocean east of Australia, people made money coils out of fibers and feathers. Until a few hundred years ago, payments in Mexico could be made with cacao beans.

FEATHER MONEY FROM SANTA CRUZ ISLANDS

People in China, Thailand, and India have used cowrie shells as money. Among many African cultures, cowrie shells were the most popular form of money for centuries. In eastern Africa, where salt was scarce, it was made into bars and used for money.

▼ COWRIE SHELLS

▲ SALT BAR FROM ETHIOPIA

In other parts of Africa, metals were valuable. They were made into objects used as money. The Kissi of Liberia and Sierra Leone used twisted pieces of iron, which became known as Kissi "pennies." The Ibo of Nigeria used copper bracelets as money. The Bushoong of the Zaire region of central Africa used copper knives.

◄ COPPER BRACELET FROM NIGERIA

1. Think about the different kinds of money listed here. Why do you think they were used by the different cultures?

◄ KISSI PENNY

2. Suppose you were going to pick a classroom object to use as money. What would you choose? What would make the object valuable to others?

◄ CACAO BEANS

Building Tens and Hundreds

Mr. Massaro lays tile. He keeps his tiles in:

 Squares of 100   Strips of 10   □ Single tiles

He has these tiles left from his last job. How many tiles does he have?

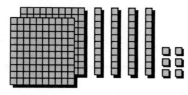

WORKING TOGETHER

1. Use your **place-value** models to show how many tiles Mr. Massaro has.

2. Record on a place-value chart how many of each model you used.

Hundreds	Tens	Ones
■	■	■

3. Complete: ■ hundreds ■ tens ■ ones

4. How many tiles does Mr. Massaro have? Write the number.

5. Read the number aloud. Then write the number in words.

Mr. Massaro has 12 strips of white tiles.

6. Use your place-value models to show this. Write how many of each model you used.

   ■ hundreds ■ tens ■ ones

7. Regroup your models to show hundreds. Tell how you did this.

   ■ hundreds ■ tens ■ ones

8. Write how many of each model you have now.

9. How many white tiles does Mr. Massaro have? Write the number.

10. Read the number aloud. Then write the number in words.

SHARING IDEAS

11. How does place value help you read and write numbers?

12. How is regrouping tens as hundreds the same as regrouping ones as tens?

PRACTICE

Write the number.

13.

14.

15. 7 tens 4 ones

16. three hundred twenty

17. 16 tens 5 ones

Write the word name.

18. 216

19. 705

20. 9 hundreds 6 tens

Regroup.

21. 3 hundreds 3 tens 14 ones = 3 hundreds ■ tens ■ ones

22. 18 tens 9 ones = ■ hundred ■ tens 9 ones

23. 2 hundreds 9 tens 17 ones = 3 hundreds ■ tens ■ ones

Solve.

24. Gene has 5 squares and 6 strips of yellow tiles. He also has 4 single yellow tiles. How many yellow tiles does he have?

25. Kerry has 4 squares and 2 strips of blue tiles. How many blue tiles does she have?

26. Rearrange the digits 5, 7, and 8 to make as many different three-digit numbers as you can.

Critical Thinking

27. Joshua regrouped 1 hundred 2 tens 4 ones as 12 tens 4 ones. Tell how he did this.

Thousands

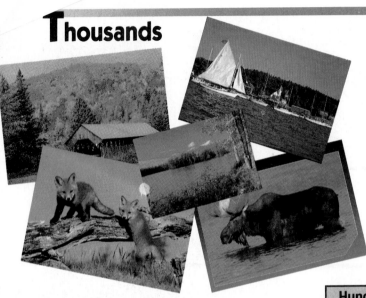

A. Jacques owns the Crafty Card store. He sells postcards in boxes of 100, in sets of 10, and as singles. During one week Jacques sells 12 boxes, 4 sets, and 6 single cards. How many postcards does he sell?

You can record what Jacques sells on a place-value chart.

Hundreds	Tens	Ones
12	4	6

Think: 10 hundreds = 1 thousand

Regroup the hundreds to show thousands.

Thousands	Hundreds	Tens	Ones
1	2	4	6

You read this as one thousand, two hundred forty-six. Jacques sells 1,246 postcards.

B. The value of a digit depends on its place in a number.

The value of the 1 in the ten-thousands place is 10,000.

Thousands Period			Ones Period		
H	T	O	H	T	O
	1	0	5	7	3

1. What is the value of the 5? How do you know?

2. In which place is the 0? What does this mean?

You can use these values to write the number in **expanded form:** 10,000 + 500 + 70 + 3.

You read 10,573 as ten thousand, five hundred seventy-three.

3. Where do you place a comma when you write a number? Why?

Place Value						Number	Word Name
Thousands Period			Ones Period				
H	T	O	H	T	O		
4. ■	■	■	■	■	■	398,028	5. ■
	6	3	7	4	5	6. ■	7. ■
8.		■	■	■	■	8,571	9. ■

Write the number.

10. 5,000 + 900 + 20 + 9   **11.** 6,000 + 70 + 1

12. one thousand, four hundred two

P**RACTICE**

Name the place and the value of the digit 5 in the number.

13. 6,415   **14.** 5,146   **15.** 1,564   **16.** 451   **17.** 54,614

Write the number in expanded form.

18. 210   **19.** 9,999   **20.** 65   **21.** 4,028   **22.** 100,702

Write the word name.

23. 61,032   **24.** 5,460   **25.** 204,204   **26.** 913,722

Write the number.

27. eight hundred twenty-five thousand, four hundred twenty-one

28. 4,000 + 200 + 60 + 5   **29.** nine hundred thousand, one

30. 5 ten thousands 9 thousands 2 hundreds 8 ones

Solve.

31. Last week Jacques sold 8,641 postcards. Write this number in expanded form.

32. During one month he sold one hundred sixty-three thousand, nine hundred forty-five cards. Write this number.

Millions

A. The counter in the sign at the main store of Fred's Fast Food chain shows the number of meals served. What number will show when one more meal is served?

The counter is like a place-value chart.

After one more meal is served, 10 hundred thousand meals will have been served.

Millions Period			Thousands Period			Ones Period		
H	T	O	H	T	O	H	T	O
			9	9	9	9	9	9

Think: 10 hundred thousand = 1 million

When one more meal is served, the counter will show 1,000,000.

1. What is the greatest possible number you can write in the place-value chart above? How do you know?

2. Write this number in words.

B. You can use what you learned about place value to read and write greater numbers.

Read: seven hundred nine million, forty-eight thousand, three hundred twenty

Millions Period			Thousands Period			Ones Period		
H	T	O	H	T	O	H	T	O
7	0	9	0	4	8	3	2	0

Write: 709,048,320

3. In which place is the 7? What is its value?

4. What number is 10,000 greater? 1,000,000 greater?

TRY OUT Write the letter of the correct answer. Match the number to the clue.

5. 10,032,850

6. 31,208,050

7. 13,208,050

a. The 3 is in the one millions place.

b. The value of the 3 is 30,000.

c. There are 3 thousands.

d. There are 3 ten millions.

PRACTICE

Write the digit in the ten-thousands place
and in the ten-millions place.

8. 534,509,390   **9.** 67,272,388   **10.** 48,078,010   **11.** 206,923,200

12. 45,528,200   **13.** 137,175,438   **14.** 29,713,010   **15.** 305,708,403

Write the number.

16. forty million, three hundred two thousand, one hundred ten

17. sixteen million, thirty thousand, nine hundred fourteen

18. one hundred ninety million, six hundred forty-five

19. two hundred five million, thirty thousand, eleven

20. 3 ten millions, 4 millions, 2 ten thousands, 9 tens, 8 ones

21. 100 greater than 3,451

22. 1,000 less than 3,674,261

23. 10,000,000 less than 276,892,371

24. 1,000,000 greater than 14,567,890

25. 100,000,000 greater than 434,275,211

26. 1,000,000 less than 1,789,204

27. What number is 100,000 greater than 99,999,999? In which places did the digits change?

Solve.

28. Tio's Taco Tower has sold 34,639,751 tacos. In what place is the 4 in the number?

29. There are 32,645 Paula's Pita Palaces across the country. What is the value of the 3 in the number?

CALCULATOR

1. Tell how 5,861,000 was changed to 5,961,000 on the display.

2. How would you then change it to 5,951,000?

3. How would you then change it to 6,951,000?

4. How would you then change it back to 5,861,000?

How Big Is a Hundred Million?

How tall would a stack of 100,000,000 sheets of paper be? Would it be as tall as your school? as tall as a mountain?

You can use what you know about numbers to estimate the height of the stack.

WORKING TOGETHER

Make a stack of 100 sheets of paper.

1. What object in your classroom is about this tall?

2. How many stacks of 100 do you need to make a stack of 1,000?

3. How would you estimate the height of a stack of 1,000 sheets of paper? What object in your classroom is about this tall?

4. How could you estimate the height of a stack of 10,000 sheets of paper? of 100,000 sheets? of 1,000,000 sheets?

5. How do your estimates compare with your height?
   with the height of your classroom?
   with the height of your school?

6. Estimate the height of 100,000,000 sheets of paper. Tell how you made the estimate. Can you think of something this tall?

SHARING IDEAS

7. How did you use place value to help you estimate?

8. Compare your method for estimating the heights of the stacks with those of others. How were the methods the same? How were they different?

ON YOUR OWN

Choose at least one activity. You may wish to try more than one.

9. About how many pages are in all the books in your school or neighborhood library? How did you find this number?

10. Estimate how long it would take you to count to 100,000,000. How did you make this estimate?

11. About how many steps do you take to get to school? 100? 1,000? 1,000,000? Tell how you estimated this number.

12. Look in newspapers and magazines for large numbers. Write about how you think these large numbers were counted.

PROBLEM SOLVING

Using the Five-Step Process

Anna has signed up for classes to learn how to read and write Chinese. She has $10.00. She needs to buy an ink stick for $3.99, a writing brush for $2.99, and practice books for $1.99. Will Anna have enough money to pay for these?

Study how the five-step process is used to solve this problem.

UNDERSTAND	
What do I know?	I know that Anna has $10.00 and that the items she wants to buy cost $3.99, $2.99, and $1.99.
What do I need to find out?	I need to find out whether Anna has enough money to buy the items.

PLAN	
What can I do?	I can estimate the total cost and compare it with the money she has.

TRY	
Let me try my plan.	***Think:*** $3.99 is about $4. $2.99 is about $3. $1.99 is about $2. $4 + $3 + $2 = $9 The total cost is less than $10.00. Anna has enough money.

CHECK	
Did I answer the question?	Yes. Anna has enough money.
Does my answer make sense?	Yes. When I estimated I used prices a little greater than the real cost of the items.

EXTEND	
What have I learned?	I learned that I can solve some problems by estimating.

Remember:
What do I know?
What do I need to find out?
What can I do?
Did I answer the question?
What have I learned?

PRACTICE

Apply what you have learned about the five-step process to solve the problem.

1. Anna wants to buy a tape of Chinese folk songs for $4.99, a Chinese ink well for $8.98, and a Chinese storybook for $1.99. Is $15.00 enough to pay for them?

2. There are 15 students in Anna's class. Of them, 9 know how to count from one to ten in Chinese. How many students do not know how to count from one to ten in Chinese?

3. Olivia learned 9 Chinese words today and 7 Chinese words yesterday. How many Chinese words did she learn in all?

4. Ramón had 8 writing brushes. He bought 6 more brushes. How many writing brushes does he have now?

5. Wei-Sen saw 9 friends at school in the morning and 8 different friends in the afternoon. How many friends did he see that day?

6. Ms. Chin has 9 students in her morning class. She has only 6 students in her afternoon class. How many more students does she have in the morning?

Counting Money

A. Kenata has a half dollar, a quarter, 2 nickels, and 4 pennies. Can she buy the notebook? First Kenata needs to know how much she has. She can count to find the amount.

Think: 50¢ 75¢ 80¢ 85¢ 86¢ 87¢ 88¢ 89¢

Kenata has 89¢. She can buy the notebook.

1. How does Kenata know she can buy the notebook?

2. What coins can she use to pay the exact price?

3. What is another way you could pay the exact price?

B. Jan has one each of these bills.

| ten-dollar bill | five-dollar bill | one-dollar bill |
| $10.00 | $5.00 | $1.00 |

4. How much money does Jan have?

5. **What if** Jan also had 2 quarters, 3 dimes, and 2 pennies? How much money would she have in all?

TRY OUT   Write the amount.

6.

7. 1 nickel, 4 pennies

8. 1 quarter, 2 dimes, 3 nickels

9. 3 five-dollar bills, 2 quarters, 3 dimes

---

half dollar
50¢
$.50

quarter
25¢
$.25

dime
10¢
$.10

nickel
5¢
$.05

penny
1¢
$.01

PRACTICE

Write the amount. Write amounts less than 1 dollar in two ways.

10.

11.

12. 1 half dollar,
2 nickels,
3 pennies

13. 2 one-dollar bills,
1 quarter, 2 dimes,
6 pennies

14. 1 ten-dollar bill,
1 five-dollar bill,
1 nickel

Name the bills and coins needed to make the amount.

15. $1.10, with 11 coins

16. $1.42, with 1 bill and 9 coins

Solve.

17. Alice buys 3 postcards for 75¢. She gives the clerk 4 coins. She does not get any change. What coins does she give the clerk?

18. Lucy buys a glass of orange juice for 85¢. Are 3 dimes and a half dollar enough to pay for it?

19. Jaime sees a sweater for $18.00. He says, "I have 5 bills. That is just enough to buy it." What bills does Jaime have?

20. *Write a problem* about money using the following information: Adam has a five-dollar bill, 2 quarters, and 1 penny.

Critical Thinking

21. Erik is buying a book that costs $7.29. He wants to give the clerk the exact amount using the fewest coins and bills. Which coins and bills should Erik give the clerk? How did you find your answer?

Making Change

Millie works in a restaurant. A customer pays her $3.00 for a meal that costs $2.49. Millie counts out loud as she gives change.

Millie counts: $2.49 $2.50 $2.75 $3.00

Millie gives:

1. Why does Millie begin counting at $2.49 and stop counting at $3.00?

2. How much change does Millie give to the customer?

3. How could Millie have given change using only 2 coins?

Suppose the customer handed Millie a $5 bill.

4. Tell how Millie would count out the change.

5. How much change would Millie give?

TRY OUT   Name the coins and bills given as change.

6. Cost: $3.48
   Amount given: $5.00

7. Cost: $.37
   Amount given: $1.00

8. Cost: $7.34
   Amount given: $10.00

PRACTICE

Name the coins and bills given as change. Tell how much change would be given.

9. Cost: $.65
Amount given:
$1.00

10. Cost: $.83
Amount given:
$1.00

11. Cost: $.39
Amount given:
$1.00

12. Cost: $1.19
Amount given:
$2.00

13. Cost: $3.59
Amount given:
$5.00

14. Cost: $2.64
Amount given:
$10.00

15. Cost: $9.55
Amount given:
$20.00

16. Cost: $4.29
Amount given:
$5.00

17. Cost: $5.81
Amount given:
$20.00

Solve.

18. Ed buys a pear for 35¢. He gives the clerk a dollar. There are no quarters in the cash register. How can the clerk give him his change?

19. Arlette buys a meal that costs $4.16. She gives Millie $5.00. What change should Arlette receive?

20. **Write a problem** about a purchase made by Leo and the change he received. Leo has $10.00.

Critical Thinking   Find the amount given. Tell how you found it.

21. Cost: $3.98
Change: 2 pennies, 1 one-dollar bill
Amount given: ■

22. Cost: $1.78
Change: 2 pennies, 2 dimes
Amount given: ■

LOGICAL REASONING

Carl has twice as many coins as Gertie. Gertie's coins are worth twice as much as Carl's. Carl's coins are worth $.40. Gertie has 4 coins. They have no quarters. What coins does Carl have? What coins does Gertie have?

Spying by

375

Logical Reasoning

Number Spy is a game for two players. One player is the Codemaker. The other player is the Number Spy.

The Codemaker chooses a 3-digit number that does not repeat any digits. The Number Spy uses logical reasoning to find the secret number.

Each turn, the Number Spy guesses a 3-digit number. The Codemaker compares the guess with the secret number and gives a clue. The clue tells:

- how many of the digits are in the secret number, and
- how many of the digits are in the correct position.

Kate and Marty play Number Spy. Marty is the Codemaker. Kate is the Number Spy.

The chart on the next page describes their game. The third column shows how Kate uses reasoning to find the secret number.

NUMBERS

one digit, no places.

Kate's Guess	Marty's Clue	Kate's Reasoning
375	1 digit, no places	There is a 3 or a 7 or a 5 in the number.
786	no digits, no places	There is no 7, 8, or 6. There must be a 3 or a 5.
123	1 digit, no places	There could be a 1, 2, or 3.
125	no digits, no places	The 3 must be correct. There is no 1, 2, or 5. The only other possible digits are 0, 4, and 9.
349	3 digits, 1 place	I was right about the digits. Now I'll get the places.
394	3 digits, no places	The 3 can't be first.
493	3 digits, 1 place	Closer! I'll try switching the last two numbers.
439	3 digits, 3 places	Got it!

1. Before you begin playing, practice giving correct clues. Suppose the secret number is 682. What clue would you give for each of these guesses?
   a. 931   **b.** 614   **c.** 827

   d. 862   **e.** 801

2. Try playing Number Spy with a partner. Switch roles after each round. When you are the Spy, write the digits 0–9 on a piece of paper. Cross out digits when you know they are not in the secret number.

Comparing and Ordering Numbers

A. Phyllis and Alex are marathon runners. Last year Phyllis ran 1,932 miles and Alex ran 1,682 miles. Who ran the greater distance last year?

Compare the numbers to solve the problem.

Step 1	Step 2
Line up the ones. Begin at the left and compare to find the first place where the digits are different.	**Compare the digits.**
1, **9** 3 2 1, **6** 8 2	**9 > 6 or 6 < 9** *Think:* 900 > 600 600 < 900

So 1,932 > 1,682 or 1,682 < 1,932.
Phyllis ran the greater distance.

1. Why don't you need to compare the digits in the tens places?

2. Compare 3,459 and 876. Which is greater? How do you know?

3. Compare $803.46 and $807.01. Which is less? How do you know?

B. You can compare $874; $8,742; $87; and $847 to order them from least to greatest.

Step 1	Step 2	Step 3
Line up the ones.	**Compare the other numbers.**	**Order the numbers from least to greatest.**
$ 874 → $8,742 $ 87 ← *The number with the fewest digits is the least.* $ 847 *The number with the most digits is the greatest.*	$8**74** $8**47** *Think:* 7 > 4. So $874 > $847.	$87; $847; $874; $8,742

4. Tell how you would order the numbers from greatest to least.

TRY OUT

Compare. Use >, <, or =.

5. $21.36 ● $24.92 **6.** 7,451 ● 989 **7.** 12,131 ● 13,121

Write in order from greatest to least.

8. 881; 1,857; 5,281; 2,181 **9.** 432; 1,002; 39; 986

PRACTICE

Compare. Use >, <, or =.

10. 982 ● 321 **11.** 758 ● 1,298 **12.** $19.62 ● $18.62

13. $11.09 ● $10.90 **14.** 8,621 ● 2,394 **15.** 4,979 ● 4,991

16. 10,365 ● 8,365 **17.** 11,091 ● 11,901 **18.** 97,000 ● 79,999

Write in order from least to greatest.

19. 89; 1,361; 782; 4,321 **20.** 1,051; 269; 3,468; 892

21. 6,520; 520; 25; 652 **22.** $28.50, $8.50, $25.80, $19.90

Write in order from greatest to least.

23. 58, 97, 103, 49 **24.** 1,321; 3,211; 1,231; 1,123

25. $1.29; $12.90; $10.29; $1.92 **26.** 5,116; 516; 5,616; 561

Mixed Applications

27. In golf the lowest score wins. Rank these players' scores from first to fourth: Randy, 98; Debby, 87; Lucy, 93; Tad, 79.

28. In bowling the highest score wins. Which player won? May, 135; Luigi, 198; Agnes, 203; Phil, 145.

29. Jim buys a set of three golf balls for $3.75. He gives the clerk $5.00. What change does he receive?

Mixed Review

Write the number.

30. five hundred twenty-eight **31.** 900 + 90 + 8 **32.** four thousand, two

EXTRA PRACTICE, page 42

Rounding Numbers

A. Last year 62 students went to computer class. This year 69 students went. About how many students went each year?

You can round numbers to estimate about how many.

Round 62 to the nearest ten.   **Round 69 to the nearest ten.**

60   61   62   63   64   65   66   67   68   69   70

Think: 62 is between 60 and 70.   ***Think:*** 69 is between 60 and 70.
         62 is closer to 60 than to 70.   69 is closer to 70 than to 60.
         Round down.   Round up.

62 rounded to the nearest ten is 60.   69 rounded to the nearest ten is 70.
About 60 students went last year.   About 70 students went this year.

1. What is 64 rounded to the nearest ten?

When a number is halfway between two numbers, round up to the greater number.

2. What is 65 rounded to the nearest ten?

B. You can round numbers without using a number line.

Round 247 to the nearest hundred.

Step 1	Step 2	Step 3
Find the place to which you are rounding.	Look at the digit to the right of that place.	If it is 5 or greater, round up. If it is less than 5, round down. **Think:** 4 < 5 Round down.
247	2**4**7	247 → 200

So 247 rounded to the nearest hundred is 200.

3. What is 247 rounded to the nearest ten? How did you round?

4. What is 1,578 rounded to the nearest thousand? How did you round?

5. Round $32.78 to the nearest ten dollars. How did you round?

TRY OUT Write the number.

6. Round 678 to the nearest hundred.

7. Round 1,323 to the nearest thousand.

8. Round $51.78 to the nearest dollar.

9. Round $55.00 to the nearest ten dollars.

PRACTICE

Round to the nearest ten or ten cents.

10. $.37 **11.** 42 **12.** $1.68 **13.** 25 **14.** 99 **15.** 328

Round to the nearest hundred or dollar.

16. $1.53 **17.** 241 **18.** $65.92 **19.** 367 **20.** 1,233 **21.** 78

Round to the nearest thousand or ten dollars.

22. 1,200 **23.** $38.42 **24.** 6,938 **25.** $92.99 **26.** 5,630 **27.** 3,501

Critical Thinking

28. Which of these numbers would round to 700 if rounded to the nearest hundred? Why?

 634   734   658   758   690   750   599

Mixed Applications

Solve. You will need to use the Databank on page 517 for Problems 31 and 32.

29. Mary spends $14.65 on computer disks. Count up to find her change from $20.00.

30. Jim buys 1,348 computer disks. How many disks to the nearest hundred does he buy?

31. During 1990 which computer company had the greatest profits? the least profits?

32. Order the companies from least to greatest according to their profits in 1991.

Mixed Review

Write in expanded form.

33. five hundred two **34.** 6,487 **35.** 3,092 **36.** 10,111

✓ UNDERSTAND
✓ PLAN
✓ TRY
CHECK
✓ EXTEND

Strategy: Using Number Sense

Ari and Keesha want to know about how many students can be seated in the school lunchroom. About 25? 150? 500? They can use *number sense* to choose the answer.

Keesha knows that there are about 25 students in her class. She also knows that all students in the third and fourth grades eat together in the lunchroom.

The lunchroom seats more than 25 people.

The lunchroom seats less than 500 people.

Ari knows that there are about 500 students in the school. They cannot all eat together in the lunchroom.

So the lunchroom seats about 150 students.

1. **What if** every seat in a major league baseball stadium were filled? About how many people would be watching the game? How do you know?
   a. 40   **b.** 400   **c.** 40,000

2. How can you use number sense to solve problems like the ones above?

PRACTICE

Write the letter of the greatest possible answer.

3. About how many people can fit in a car?
   a. 5   **b.** 25   **c.** 50

4. About how many office workers can fit in an elevator?
   a. 5   **b.** 20   **c.** 200

5. About how many shoppers can ride on an escalator at the same time?
   a. 5   **b.** 50   **c.** 500

6. About how many children can ride on a merry-go-round?
   a. 5   **b.** 50   **c.** 500

7. About how many passengers can fly on a large jet?
   a. 5   **b.** 25   **c.** 400

8. About how many riders can sit on a bus?
   a. 2   **b.** 50   **c.** 200

9. About how much money does a fourth-grader's lunch cost?
   a. $2   **b.** $20   **c.** $200

10. About how much does it cost to buy 2 notebooks?
   a. $.30   **b.** $3.00   **c.** $30.00

11. About how much money should you save if you want to buy a bicycle?
   a. $6.00   **b.** $60.00   **c.** $600

12. About how much does a complete videogame system cost?
   a. $.80   **b.** $8.00   **c.** $80.00

EXTRA PRACTICE, page 43

Activity

Using Tables

Erin is ordering records, cassettes, and compact discs for her store. She needs to know which type of recording is bought most often. This table shows last month's record sales for the three most popular groups.

Group	Record Sales
Broken Rocks	113
Up Beat	109
Music Masters	88

WORKING TOGETHER

The Broken Rocks also sold 345 cassettes and 213 compact discs. Up Beat sold 536 cassettes and 510 compact discs. Music Masters sold 423 cassettes and 315 compact discs.

Group	Number Sold		

1. Complete this table to show how many records, cassettes, and compact discs of each group were sold.

2. How did you label the column headings and list the groups?

3. How did this help you complete the table?

4. Which type of recording is bought most often?

SHARING IDEAS

5. Compare your table with those of others. How are the tables the same? How are they different?

6. Are there other ways to organize the data? How?

7. Which group is the most popular? How do you know?

8. Why is a table a useful way to record data? What makes the data easy to read?

PRACTICE

Use the table to answer
Problems 9–13.

9. How are the prices organized?

10. The two most expensive
    compact discs sell for $16.99
    and $20.99. Copy and
    complete the table to show
    these prices.

Code	Record Albums	Cassettes	Compact Discs
			Price
A	$3.99	$3.99	$8.99
B	$6.99	$6.99	$10.99
C	$8.99	$8.99	$14.99
D	$11.99	■	■
E	$14.99	$14.99	■

11. Look at the prices of records
    and cassettes. What might be the price of a code
    D cassette? How do you know?

12. Pablo has $10. What is the most expensive
    compact disc he can buy?

13. Sara wants to buy a code C record.
    Is $10 enough? How do you know?

14. The Inwood branch of the public library has
    215 pop, 79 jazz, and 174 classical record
    albums. There are 187 pop, 102 jazz, and 241
    classical record albums at the Elmsford
    branch. The Shore branch has 256 pop,
    163 jazz, and 204 classical record albums.
    Make a table to show this data. Compare
    your table with those of others.

15. Ask other students to name their favorite
    type of music. Then ask them to name their
    favorite recording artist. Make a table to
    show their responses. Compare your
    table with those of others.

Mixed Review

Compare. Use >, <, or =.

16. 867 ● 483   17. 78 ● 102   18. 45¢ ● $.45   19. 367 ● 365

Round to the nearest 10 or $.10.

20. 55   21. 81   22. 78   23. $.44

EXTRA PRACTICE, page 43

DECISION MAKING

Problem Solving: Choosing a Job to Earn Money

SITUATION

Laura needs $60 to buy a bicycle. She asks three friends how they have earned money.

PROBLEM

Which job is best for Laura?

DATA

Joey—did yard work (mowing, raking, weeding)

Time spent: 4 hours for each yard. Weekend days only. Nice days only.
Equipment: rake, lawn mower, trash bags — provided by lawn owner
Earnings: $10 per yard
Note: Jobs are not steady. Must find new jobs each week.

Ben—had lemonade stand

Time spent: Worked when he wanted, usually on warm day. Up to 6 hours on weekend days and 2 hours after school.
Equipment: table, pitcher, cups, ice, lemonade, sign
Earnings: $1–$5 each hour
Note: Liked being his own boss.

Rita — walked dogs

Time spent: half hour twice a day (before and after school) 5 days a week
Earnings: $2 for each dog each day
Note: work is steady, but lots of responsibility

USING THE DATA

1. Walking one dog, Laura will make $2 each day. How much will she make in a week? How many weeks will it take Laura to make $60?

2. How many yards must Laura do to make $60? At two yards a week, how many weeks will it take her to earn $60?

3. If Laura makes $5 an hour selling lemonade, how much can she make in 1 weekday? in 5 weekdays?

4. If Laura makes only $1 an hour selling lemonade, how much can she make in 1 weekday? in 5 weekdays?

5. At $5 an hour, how long would it take Laura to make $60 selling lemonade? At $1 an hour, how long would it take her to make $60?

MAKING DECISIONS

6. What things should Laura consider about each job before deciding which one is right for her?

7. At which job can Laura earn the most money in the least time?

8. Can Laura be sure she will make $5 an hour selling lemonade? Why or why not?

9. At which job can Laura be sure of the amount she will earn? Why?

10. *What if* Laura walks two or three dogs a day? How would this change the time it takes her to earn $60?

11. *What if* Laura's parents lend her money to start her lemonade stand? How would this change the time it takes her to earn $60?

12. Which job would you choose? Why?

Math and Social Studies

The national calendar of the United States is a **solar calendar**. The length of a year is based on the time it takes the earth to travel around the sun: 365 days, 5 hours, 48 minutes, and 46 seconds. We round to the nearest day. So our calendar year is 365 days long. The extra time is made up by adding a day every fourth year. This is called a leap year.

The Islamic calendar is a **lunar calendar**. It is based on the time it takes the moon to go from new to full and back to new. This takes between 29 and 30 days. So the months are either 29 or 30 days long. There are 12 months in a year, and 354 days in a regular year.

How many more days are in the solar year than in an Islamic year?

Think: You know that 354 is 1 ten and 1 less than 365. You could also count on from 354.

There are 11 more days in the solar year than in the Islamic year.

ACTIVITIES

1. The Jewish calendar is a **luni-solar calendar**. What do you think this means? Find out how many days and months are in a year on this calendar.

2. Find out about calendars in other cultures, such as those of the North American Indians, the Chinese, or the Maya. In a report to the class explain how these calendars compare to our national calendar.

Computer: Patterns

The pattern below is formed using four different positions of one shape.

A ▷ ∀ ◁
1   2   3   4

▷ ∀ A ◁ ▷ ∀ A ◁ ▷

The part of the pattern that repeats is called the **rule**.

1. What is the rule for this pattern?

2. How would you describe this pattern?

3. What is the number of the shape that comes next in the pattern?

You can use a computer to explore patterns.

AT THE COMPUTER

Run the computer program called PATTERN 4.
Work with a partner.

4. Have the computer make a pattern. Choose the number of the shape that will complete the pattern.

5. Give the rule for the pattern. Then describe it in your own words to your partner.

6. Complete several more patterns and give their rules.

7. Now use the program to make your own patterns. Take turns creating your own rule of either three or four figures. Then have the computer make a pattern using your rule. Have your partner complete the pattern and give the rule.

8. Make a new rule. Challenge your partner to give the number of the seventh shape in the pattern. Then use the computer to check.

9. Why is a computer helpful in exploring patterns?

EXTRA PRACTICE

Building Tens and Hundreds, page 13 ....

Write the number.

1. 8 tens 7 ones   **2.** four hundred fifty   **3.** 19 tens 6 ones

4. two hundred five   **5.** 10 tens 9 ones   **6.** 12 tens 1 one

Regroup.

7. 5 hundreds 4 tens 17 ones = 5 hundreds ■ tens ■ ones

8. 15 tens 8 ones = ■ hundred ■ tens 8 ones

9. 3 hundreds 8 tens 28 ones = 4 hundreds ■ tens ■ ones

Thousands, page 15 ....

Name the place and value of the digit 7 in the number.

1. 4,987   **2.** 61,374   **3.** 2,713   **4.** 17,183

Write the word name.

5. 21,073   **6.** 6,000 + 100 + 50   **7.** 309,209

Write the number.

8. 3,000 + 400 + 50 + 3   **9.** sixty-four thousand, four

10. 8 hundred thousands 7 thousands 4 hundreds 2 ones

Millions, page 17 ....

Write the digit in the one thousands place and in the one
millions place.

1. 637,149,875   **2.** 53,140,685   **3.** 80,656,030

4. 25,017,300   **5.** 240,372,311   **6.** 409,308,205

Write the number.

7. thirty million, two hundred five
thousand, two hundred twelve

8. fourteen million, twenty
thousand, eight hundred ten

9. 4 ten millions 2 millions 5 ten thousands 6 tens 2 ones

Problem Solving: Using the Five-Step Process, page 21 ....

Solve. Use the five-step process.

1. Gary wants to buy a pair of socks for $3.99, a package of wristbands for $1.99, and a cap for $5.99. Is $10 enough money to pay for these items?

2. There are 17 students in gym class. Eight students have finished their warm-up exercises. How many students have not finished their warm-up exercises?

3. Karla had 6 pennies. She found 8 more. How many pennies does she have now?

4. Mr. and Mrs. Anderson have 6 mollies and 5 guppies. How many fish do they have?

5. Frankie has 8 pages to read in his reading book and 5 pages to read in his social studies book. How many pages does he have to read?

6. Kevin has 15 stamps in his collection. Wanda has 9 stamps in her collection. How many more stamps does Kevin have than Wanda?

Counting Money, page 23 ....

Write the amount. Write amounts less than 1 dollar in two ways.

1. 2 quarters, 4 nickels, 7 pennies

2. 3 one-dollar bills, 3 quarters, 1 dime, 8 pennies

3. 2 ten-dollar bills, 1 five-dollar bill, 1 penny

4. 1 quarter, 4 dimes, 4 nickels, 4 pennies

5. 6 quarters, 5 dimes, 3 nickels, 9 pennies

6. 1 twenty-dollar bill, 2 five-dollar bills, 3 quarters

Name the bills and coins needed to make the amount.

7. $1.30 with 13 coins

8. $1.32 with 1 bill and 4 coins

9. $1.75 with 7 coins

10. $12.21 with 3 bills and 3 coins

11. $1.89 with 1 bill and 17 coins

12. $20.40 with 3 bills and 7 coins

EXTRA PRACTICE

Making Change, page 25..
Name the coins and bills given as change. Tell how much change would be given.

1. Cost: $.35
Amount given:
$1.00

2. Cost: $.74
Amount given:
$1.00

3. Cost: $1.24
Amount given:
$2.00

4. Cost: $2.89
Amount given:
$5.00

5. Cost: $2.15
Amount given:
$10.00

6. Cost: $4.64
Amount given:
$20.00

Comparing and Ordering Numbers, page 29......................................
Compare. Use >, <, or =.

1. 357 ● 253

2. 657 ● 2,175

3. $15.75 ● $12.57

4. $11.07 ● $10.10

5. 6,753 ● 3,789

6. 5,875 ● 5,987

Write in order from least to greatest.

7. 63; 1,255; 876; 2,309

8. 2,073; 409; 3,730; 794

9. $17.35; $7.35; $13.75; $11.73

10. $6.66, $16.21, $2.94, $9.30

Write in order from greatest to least.

11. $.35, $.76, $1.09, $.45

12. 529; 5,290; 5,092; 592

13. 1,416; 4,161; 1,136; 1,316

14. $7.38, $8.37, $7.57, $7.34

Rounding Numbers, page 31..
Round to the nearest ten or ten cents.

1. $.43   **2.** 89   **3.** $1.47   **4.** 35   **5.** 98   **6.** 472

Round to the nearest hundred or one dollar.

7. $1.59   **8.** 312   **9.** $75.83   **10.** 489   **11.** 1,341   **12.** 89

Round to the nearest thousand or ten dollars.

13. 1,100   **14.** $47.39   **15.** 4,818   **16.** $81.89   **17.** 3,610   **18.** 4,502

Problem Solving: Using Number Sense, page 33.............................

Write the letter of the greatest possible answer.

1. About how many grapes are in a bunch?

   a. 5   **b.** 30   **c.** 500

2. About how many pencils can fit in a pencil case?

   a. 10   **b.** 60   **c.** 150

3. About how many pages are in a notebook?

   a. 5   **b.** 10   **c.** 50

4. About how many colors are in a rainbow?

   a. 7   **b.** 32   **c.** 100

5. About how many lines are on a loose-leaf page?

   a. 5   **b.** 30   **c.** 200

6. About how many bananas are in a bunch?

   a. 6   **b.** 60   **c.** 160

7. About how many peas are there in a pod?

   a. 6   **b.** 32   **c.** 68

8. About how many children can ride on a school bus?

   a. 15   **b.** 60   **c.** 150

Using Tables, page 35 ....

Use the table to answer Problems 1–5.

1. How are the prices organized?

2. Look at the prices of the Top-40 and Rock albums. What might be the price of a Code D rock album? How do you know?

3. The two most expensive oldies albums sell for $14.99 and $24.99. Complete the table to show these prices.

	ALBUM PRICES		
Code	Top-40	Rock	Oldies
A	$7.99	$7.99	$8.99
B	$8.99	$8.99	$11.99
C	$10.99	$10.99	$12.99
D	$12.99	■	■
E	$15.99	$15.99	■

4. Christa has $10. What is the most expensive Rock album she can buy?

5. Rob wants to buy a Code C Top-40 album. Is $10 enough? How do you know?

Understanding Numbers and Money   **43**

PRACTICE PLUS

KEY SKILL: MILLIONS (Use after page 17.)

Level A . . . .

Write the digit in the ten thousands place.

1. 978,566   **2.** 64,830   **3.** 1,845,322   **4.** 29,763,076

Write the number.

5. six hundred thousand, twelve

6. four hundred thousand, five hundred seven

7. one million, two hundred ninety-one thousand, forty-two

8. ten million, sixty-seven thousand, three hundred forty

9. Ron's Rib Ranch has sold 54,879,310 ribs. In what place is the 4 in the number?

Level B . . . .

Write the digit in the ten millions place.

10. 310,430,780   **11.** 23,708,765   **12.** 134,956,743   **13.** 206,906,554

Write the number.

14. thirty million, two hundred three thousand, four hundred one

15. 9 hundred millions 6 hundred thousands 4 hundreds 3 tens

16. 6,000,000 + 30,000 + 800 + 40 + 9

17. 200,000,000 + 30,000,000 + 100,000 + 90

18. Sandy's Salad Bar sold 1,045,879 salads last year. What is the value of the 4 in the number?

Level C . . . .

Write the number.

19. one million greater than 13,678,987

20. ten thousand less than 846,999,560

21. 100,000,000 greater than 608,966,000

22. 10,000,000 less than 947,037,576

23. Harry's Hot Dog House sold 345,876,904 hot dogs. What is the value of the 3 in the number?

KEY SKILL: ROUNDING NUMBERS (Use after page 31.)

Level A

Round to the nearest ten or ten cents.

1. 22   **2.** 37   **3.** 65   **4.** $.51   **5.** $.14

Round to the nearest hundred or dollar.

6. $1.13   **7.** 250   **8.** $7.83   **9.** 926   **10.** 482

11. Last month 156 people went to the Computer Fair. How many people went, rounded to the nearest ten?

Level B

Round to the nearest ten or ten cents.

12. 88   **13.** 114   **14.** $8.46   **15.** 4,872   **16.** $23.58

Round to the nearest thousand or ten dollars.

17. 7,391   **18.** $85.78   **19.** 5,312   **20.** 2,764   **21.** $14.99

22. There are 2,065 software packages on display at the fair. How many packages are on display, rounded to the nearest hundred?

Level C

Round to the nearest hundred or dollar.

23. $81.58   **24.** 3,427   **25.** 7,611   **26.** 11,883   **27.** $410.39

Round to the nearest thousand or ten dollars.

28. 5,678   **29.** 91,023   **30.** $492.89   **31.** 629,346   **32.** 19,903

33. Which of these numbers would round to 1,600 if rounded to the nearest hundred?

1,541   1,651   1,574   1,599   1,700   1,629   1,612

34. Kerry spent $132.89 on computer disks. How much did he spend to the nearest ten dollars?

CHAPTER REVIEW/TEST

LANGUAGE AND MATHEMATICS

Complete the sentences. Use the words in the chart.

1. 14 tens 7 ones may be ■ as 1 hundred 4 tens and 7 ones.

2. The ■ of the 6 in the number 6,805 is 6,000.

3. 839, ■ to the nearest hundred, is 800.

CONCEPTS AND SKILLS

Write the word name.

4. 609

5. 51,024

Write the number.

6. 8 hundreds 4 tens 3 ones

Write the number in expanded form.

7. three hundred ninety-one thousand, two hundred

8. 713

Write the amount.

9. 1 half dollar, 1 quarter, 2 nickels, 2 pennies

Name the coins and bills given as change.

10. Cost: $6.29; Amount given: $20.00

Compare. Use >, <, or =.

11. 565 ● 655

Write in order from greatest to least.

12. $34.00; $9.72; $82.70; $96.56

Round to the nearest 1,000 or $10.00.

13. 2,540

14. $43.98

15. 1,921

Use the table to answer problems 16 and 17.

16. Look at the prices of the different kinds of videos. What might be the price of a music video rented on Tuesday? How do you know?

17. Is $7 enough to rent two dramas?

COST OF RENTING VIDEO CASSETTES

Type of Video	Regular Price	Tuesday (Discount Day)
Music	$4.99	■
Drama	$4.99	$3.99
Cartoons	$3.99	$2.99

Critical Thinking

18. Karen pays $8.37 for a kite. She uses the fewest coins and bills possible. Which coins and bills does she use?

Mixed Applications

19. Lisa has 34¢, Adam has 17¢, Josh has 12¢, and Mara has 22¢. Which is closest to their total amount of money?
a. 80¢ **b.** 50¢ **c.** $5.00

20. If someone sits in each seat in the local theater, about how many people are watching the movie?
a. 25 **b.** 250 **c.** 2,000

PERFORMANCE ASSESSMENT

Work with your group to solve this problem.

Suppose your group is helping the school librarian keep records of books purchased for the school library. This list shows the title, number of pages, and price of four books.

Title	Number of Pages	Price
A Treasury of Children's Literature	640	$39.95
World Atlas	244	$72.50
School Dictionary	965	$13.95
Birdfeeding Handbook	188	$ 6.75

Round the number of pages in each book to the nearest ten and round the price of each book to the nearest dollar. Then, make a table that lists the books in order by number of pages, from greatest to least, and make another table that lists the books in order by price, from least expensive to most expensive.

1. *Think about:*
   - how to round the numbers and the prices
   - how to make tables to present the books in order

2. Write two statements comparing the number of pages in the books and two statements comparing the price of the books.

CUMULATIVE REVIEW

Choose the letter of the correct answer.

1. Choose the word name for 203.

   a. two hundred thirty
   b. twenty three hundred
   c. two hundred three
   d. not given

2. Choose the number for six million one.

   a. 600,001   **c.** 60,000,001
   b. 6,000,001   **d.** not given

3. Which is 1,000 greater than 64,123?

   a. 65,123   **c.** 63,123
   b. 54,123   **d.** not given

4. How much is 1 quarter, 2 nickels?

   a. 27¢   **c.** 35¢
   b. 30¢   **d.** not given

5. Compare: 80,015 ● 80,510

   a. <   **c.** =
   b. >   **d.** not given

6. Compare: $4.52 ● $4.03

   a. <   **c.** =
   b. >   **d.** not given

7. Cost: $.68   Given: $.70
   What is the change?

   a. 2 pennies   **c.** 2 nickels
   b. 3 pennies   **d.** not given

8. How much is 4 one-dollar bills, 4 nickels, 4 pennies?

   a. $4.19   **c.** $4.44
   b. $4.24   **d.** $4.49

9. Round 72 to the nearest ten.

   a. 60   **c.** 75
   b. 70   **d.** 80

10. Round 879 to the nearest hundred.

    a. 900   **c.** 870
    b. 880   **d.** 800

11. What is the expanded form for two hundred one?

    a. $200 + 10 + 1$
    b. $200 + 10$
    c. $200 + 1$
    d. not given

12. What is the value of 4 in 1,432?

    a. 4   **c.** 400
    b. 40   **d.** not given

13. Choose the greatest number.

    a. 538   **c.** 3,158
    b. 851   **d.** 3,518

14. Which is greater than $.59?

    a. 1 half dollar   **c.** 3 quarters
    b. 2 dimes   **d.** 6 nickels

ENRICHMENT FOR ALL

THE ABACUS

The abacus is an ancient counting board. Each column of beads stands for a place value.

A number is shown by pushing beads to the crossbar.
Each pushed-up bead below the crossbar is 1.
Each pushed-down bead above the crossbar is 5.
Add to find the digit in each place.

Thousands Hundreds Tens Ones

crossbar

$$\begin{array}{r} 5 \\ +1 \\ \hline 6 \end{array}$$

8 0 3 6

The abacus above shows the number 8,036.

1. How is 6 shown in the ones place?

2. How is 0 shown in the hundreds place?

3. **What if** you want to show the number 8,536? Which bead would you move?

4. Which beads would you move to show the number 8,076?

Write the number shown on the abacus.

5.

6.

7.

8.

9.

Draw a picture to show the number on an abacus.

10. 457 11. 3,604 12. 200,543 13. 2,076,098

NATIVE AMERICAN SIGN LANGUAGE

Have you ever seen anyone make a gesture instead of using words? Perhaps the person waved a hand instead of saying hello. You may have seen hearing-impaired people communicate with a special system of gestures. People all over the world use different kinds of gestures and signals to make themselves understood.

Before Europeans arrived on this continent, many Native American groups had created sign languages. There were hundreds of languages spoken among the groups. Each sign language contained thousands of signs. They included signs for words and numbers. People who spoke different languages were able to communicate by using a common language of signs.

Great Plains

The most advanced system of sign language developed in the Great Plains region of the United States. The Indians of the Plains traveled in search of buffalo and met many people who spoke a variety of languages. The Kiowa were the most skillful in using the sign language.

The Plains Indians also used symbols to record important events. They drew or painted the symbols on buffalo hides to make a Winter Count.

1 What is the rule for adding a 1 to each number in this system of sign language?

2 Discuss hand signs and other gestures you know. Take turns demonstrating gestures and explaining their meanings. Try having conversations using only signs.

3 Work with a partner. Invent a different system of signs for the numbers 1 to 10. Describe the rules you used.

50

USING ADDITION AND SUBTRACTION FACTS

MATH *CONNECTIONS*: Algebra • Measurement • Statistics

ACTiViTy

Informal Algebra: Meaning of Addition and Subtraction

This activity will help you learn about the properties of addition and subtraction.

WORKING TOGETHER

1. Pick any two numbers from 0 to 9. Write two word sentences using these numbers.

2. Ask an addition question.

   Write the number sentence that answers the question.

3. Ask a subtraction question that uses the sum.

   Write the number sentence that answers the question.

4. Ask a subtraction question to compare the numbers.

   Write the number sentence.

Example

Think: 9 and 6
I have 9 red cars.
You have 6 blue cars.

How many cars are there in all?

$$9 + 6 = 15$$

$$\begin{array}{r} 9 \leftarrow \textbf{addend} \\ + \ 6 \leftarrow \textbf{addend} \\ \hline 15 \leftarrow \textbf{sum} \end{array}$$

There are 15 cars in all.

If there are 9 red cars, how many blue cars are there?

$$15 - 9 = 6$$

$$\begin{array}{r} 15 \\ - \ 9 \\ \hline 6 \leftarrow \textbf{difference} \end{array}$$

There are 6 blue cars.

How many more red cars are there than blue cars?

$$9 - 6 = 3$$

There are 3 more red cars than blue cars.

5. Now pick another pair of numbers and do this activity again. Stop when you have completed the activity for four pairs of numbers.

6. Look at the addition question given in the example. Can you write another number sentence to answer this question? If so, write it.

7. Can you ask another subtraction question that uses the numbers in the example? If so, write it and the number sentence to answer it.

SHARING IDEAS

8. How do your questions and number sentences compare with those of others?

9. How do your questions and number sentences show that addition and subtraction are opposites?

10. If you change the order of the addends, does the sum change? How do you know?

11. What is the sum when you add 0 to a number?

12. What is the difference when you subtract 0 from a number? when you subtract a number from itself?

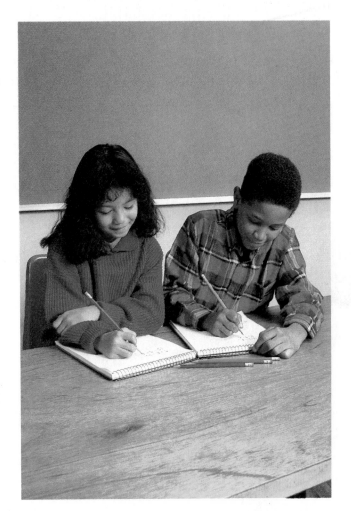

PRACTICE

Add or subtract.

13. $\begin{array}{r} 0 \\ +1 \\ \hline \end{array}$ **14.** $\begin{array}{r} 5 \\ -0 \\ \hline \end{array}$ **15.** $\begin{array}{r} 2 \\ +8 \\ \hline \end{array}$ **16.** $\begin{array}{r} 10 \\ -8 \\ \hline \end{array}$ **17.** $\begin{array}{r} 4 \\ -4 \\ \hline \end{array}$ **18.** $\begin{array}{r} 5 \\ +2 \\ \hline \end{array}$ **19.** $\begin{array}{r} 1 \\ +7 \\ \hline \end{array}$

20. $8 - 7$ **21.** $2 + 7$ **22.** $6 + 6$ **23.** $4 + 5$ **24.** $13 - 4$

25. $9 - \blacksquare = 9$ **26.** $\blacksquare + 5 = 5$ **27.** $3 - \blacksquare = 0$ **28.** $6 + \blacksquare = 3 + 6$

29. $\blacksquare + 0 = 2$ **30.** $4 - \blacksquare = 4$ **31.** $\blacksquare - 0 = 0$ **32.** $9 + 1 = \blacksquare + 9$

33. How much more than 3 is 6?   **34.** 9 and 5 more equals what number?

Informal Algebra: Fact Families

Angie and Rhoda are using a spinner to learn about fact families. They take turns spinning. On the first round Angie spins a 4 and an 8. The girls use the numbers to write the fact family.

Angie records the related addition sentences on a chart.

Rhoda records the related subtraction sentences on another chart.

Addend	+	Addend	=	Sum or Total
4	+	8	=	12
8	+	4	=	12

Total	−	Number Taken Away	=	Number Left
12	−	8	=	4
12	−	4	=	8

WORKING TOGETHER

Copy the charts above.

1. The number sentences on both charts belong to the same fact family. Tell how they are related.

2. **What if** Angie spins a 7 and a 0? Write the related number sentences that make up the fact family on your charts.

3. **What if** Rhoda spins a 2 and a 2? Write the related number sentences on your charts.

Use a spinner and repeat this activity four more times. See how many related number sentences you can write. Record them on your charts.

4. Did you write the same number of related sentences for every fact family? Why or why not?

SHARING IDEAS

5. Compare your charts with those of other students. How are they the same? How are they different?

6. How did the addition and subtraction properties help you write fact families?

PRACTICE

Find the sum or difference. Write the related number
sentences that make up the fact family.

7. 5 $+3$	**8.** 11 -8	**9.** 11 -9	**10.** 8 $+7$	**11.** 16 -9	**12.** 7 $+7$

13. $10 - 5$ **14.** $9 + 8$ **15.** $0 + 3$ **16.** $10 - 4$ **17.** $6 - 6$

Write the fact families for the set of numbers.

18. 6, 2, 8   **19.** 5, 1, 6   **20.** 0, 9, 9   **21.** 4, 4, 8   **22.** 3, 7, 10

Complete the fact. Find the missing number.

23. $8 + \blacksquare = 14$ **24.** $6 - \blacksquare = 4$ **25.** $\blacksquare + 5 = 8$ **26.** $9 + \blacksquare = 18$

27. $\blacksquare + 5 = 11$ **28.** $1 + \blacksquare = 1$ **29.** $\blacksquare - 2 = 7$ **30.** $17 - \blacksquare = 9$

Critical Thinking

Look at each set of numbers. Can you write a fact family?
Why or why not?

31. 0, 7, 8   **32.** 1, 2, 3   **33.** 3, 3, 3   **34.** 9, 1, 10

Mixed Applications

35. Tom and Leah have the same
number of fruits. Tom has 6 plums
and 9 mangos. Leah has 6 mangos
and some plums. How many plums
does she have?

36. Alma ordered 2 pounds of
pecans by mail from Georgia.
She used all of them to make a
pecan pie. How many pounds
of pecans did Alma have left?

37. Fizzville is 9 miles from Beat
City. Alec rides the bus from
Beat City for 5 miles. How
much farther is it to Fizzville?

38. Joe collected 1,213 bottle caps
from all over the world. How
many bottle caps did he collect
to the nearest thousand?

Mixed Review

Round to the nearest ten or ten dollars.

39. 67   **40.** $29.85   **41.** 691   **42.** 7,555   **43.** $8.81

Mental Math: Addition Facts

Jason, Robert, and Joyce use mental math to help them learn addition facts.

A. To find 7 + 4, Jason uses **counting on.**

7 + 4 = ■

Think: Start at 7. Count on 4 more.
Count: 8, 9, 10, 11

So 7 + 4 = 11.

1. How can you use counting on to find 8 + 5? What is the sum?

2. Use counting on to find 3 + 9. How would changing the order of addends make it easier to count on?

B. Joyce and Robert use **doubles** to find 5 + 6.

5 + 6 = ■

Joyce thinks:
5 + 5 = 10.
I know that 6 is 1 more than 5.
5 + 5 + 1 = 11
So 5 + 6 = 11.

Robert thinks:
6 + 6 = 12.
I know that 5 is 1 less than 6.
6 + 6 − 1 = 11
So 5 + 6 = 11.

3. Use doubles to find 7 + 6.

C. Jason said that he could make a 10 to help him find 9 + 3.

$$\begin{array}{r} 9 \\ +\ 3 \\ \hline \end{array}$$

Think: I add 1 to 9 to make 10.
I take away 1 from 3 to make 2.

$$\begin{array}{r} 10 \\ +\ 2 \\ \hline 12 \end{array}$$

Since 10 + 2 = 12, Jason knows that 9 + 3 = 12.

4. Use this method to find 4 + 9.

TRY OUT   Add. Use mental math.

5. 9 + 4   **6.** 5 + 4   **7.** 4 + 7   **8.** 2 + 5

PRACTICE

Add. Use mental math.

9. 3 +3	**10.** 7 +7	**11.** 0 +2	**12.** 8 +6	**13.** 5 +8	**14.** 3 +6
15. 4 +3	**16.** 7 +8	**17.** 7 +1	**18.** 8 +8	**19.** 8 +0	**20.** 6 +7

21. 2 + 3   **22.** 8 + 2   **23.** 2 + 4   **24.** 1 + 8   **25.** 5 + 7

26. 0 + 4   **27.** 6 + 3   **28.** 5 + 5   **29.** 5 + 9   **30.** 9 + 9

31. What is 4 plus 2?   **32.** What is the sum of 9 + 7?

33. 4 plus 8 is what number?   **34.** What is 7 and 5 more?

Critical Thinking

35. Tell how you could use what you know about
adding doubles to help you find 6 + 8.

Mixed Applications

36. José's grandparents send him 7 stamps from
Spain and 9 stamps from France. How many
stamps does José get?

37. It is 5,663 miles from Paris to Los Angeles and
5,477 miles from Tokyo to Los Angeles. Which
of these cities is closer to Los Angeles?

38. *Write a problem* for this fact: 3 + 4 = 7. Trade
problems with other students and solve.

Mixed Review

Name the place and the value of the digit 4 in the number.

39. 409   **40.** 42,500   **41.** 491,999   **42.** 34,860   **43.** 574

Mental Math: Subtraction Facts

Using mental math helped Joyce, Robert, and Jason learn addition facts. They decided to use mental math to help them learn subtraction facts.

A. To find 12 − 4, Robert uses **counting back.**

12 − 4 = ■

Think: Start at 12. Count back 4.
Count: 11, 10, 9, 8

So 12 − 4 = 8.

1. How can you use counting back to find 14 − 5? What is the difference?

B. Joyce subtracts from 10 and then adds to find the difference.

11 − 6 = ■   *Think:*
$$\begin{array}{rr} 10 - 6 = & 4 \\ +\ 1 & +\,1 \\ \hline 11 - 6 = & 5 \end{array}$$

2. Use this method to find 13 − 9.

C. Jason uses related facts to help him find the difference.

$$\begin{array}{r} 9 \\ -\ 4 \\ \hline \end{array}$$
Think: Since 5 + 4 = 9, then 9 − 4 = 5.

3. Use a related fact to find 12 − 6.

TRY OUT   Subtract. Use mental math.

4. 7 − 3   **5.** 13 − 5   **6.** 11 − 7   **7.** 10 − 2

PRACTICE

Subtract. Use mental math.

8. $\begin{array}{r} 10 \\ -\ 1 \\ \hline \end{array}$ 9. $\begin{array}{r} 13 \\ -\ 6 \\ \hline \end{array}$ 10. $\begin{array}{r} 12 \\ -\ 5 \\ \hline \end{array}$ 11. $\begin{array}{r} 14 \\ -\ 8 \\ \hline \end{array}$ 12. $\begin{array}{r} 8 \\ -\ 8 \\ \hline \end{array}$ 13. $\begin{array}{r} 11 \\ -\ 5 \\ \hline \end{array}$

14. $\begin{array}{r} 9 \\ -\ 8 \\ \hline \end{array}$ 15. $\begin{array}{r} 18 \\ -\ 9 \\ \hline \end{array}$ 16. $\begin{array}{r} 9 \\ -\ 3 \\ \hline \end{array}$ 17. $\begin{array}{r} 7 \\ -\ 2 \\ \hline \end{array}$ 18. $\begin{array}{r} 14 \\ -\ 6 \\ \hline \end{array}$ 19. $\begin{array}{r} 16 \\ -\ 9 \\ \hline \end{array}$

20. $6 - 4$ 21. $8 - 1$ 22. $12 - 3$ 23. $14 - 9$ 24. $12 - 7$

25. $12 - 9$ 26. $10 - 7$ 27. $16 - 8$ 28. $9 - 7$ 29. $13 - 8$

30. 4 less than 11

31. the difference between 15 and 8

32. 5 take away 3

33. 13 is how many more than 7?

Mixed Applications

34. Jeff travels 8 miles from his house to the beach. He travels 3 miles from the beach to his friend Wendy's house. How many miles does Jeff travel?

35. The depth of the water at the docks is 7 feet at low tide. At high tide the depth is 15 feet. How many feet does the water rise?

36. Marsha found 7 shells by the seashore. Leon found 5 shells. How many more shells did Marsha find than Leon?

37. *Write a problem* for this fact: $7 - 4 = 3$. Trade problems with other students and solve.

CHALLENGE

The ones digit of an even number is 0, 2, 4, 6, or 8. The ones digit of an odd number is 1, 3, 5, 7, or 9.

1. Pick two even numbers. Add them.

2. Pick two odd numbers. Add them.

3. Pick an even number and an odd number. Add them.

4. Repeat Steps 1–3 five times.

5. Compare your sums. What does this tell you about adding even and odd numbers?

Mental Math: Three or More Addends

A. Diego and Susan group addends in different ways to help them find sums.

Add: 4 + 3 + 2

Diego found the sum this way.

$$(4 + 3) + 2 = \blacksquare$$
$$7 \quad + 2 = 9$$

Susan found the sum this way.

$$4 + (3 + 2) = \blacksquare$$
$$4 + \quad 5 \quad = 9$$

Parentheses show how they grouped the addends.

1. Does changing the way you group addends change the sum? Tell why.

2. How could you group the addends to find 5 + 2 + 4 in two ways?

B. You can group addends differently to help you add mentally.

Add: 3 + 6 + 7

Susan found the sum by making a 10.

$$\begin{aligned} 3 \\ 6 \\ + 7 \end{aligned} \quad 10$$

Think: Look for sums of 10.
3 + 7 = 10; 10 + 6 = 16

So 3 + 6 + 7 = 16.

3. Find the sum of 2 + 4 + 8 + 4 by making a 10.

TRY OUT Write the letter of the correct answer.
Find the sum. Use mental math.

4. 9 + 1 + 3   **a.** 91   **b.** 10   **c.** 13   **d.** 9

5. 6 + 1 + 6   **a.** 13   **b.** 12   **c.** 11   **d.** 7

6. 5 + 4 + 5   **a.** 50   **b.** 5   **c.** 10   **d.** 14

7. 9 + 6 + 3   **a.** 9   **b.** 19   **c.** 18   **d.** 15

PRACTICE

Find the sum. Use mental math.

8.	9.	10.	11.	12.	13.
8	3	5	6	7	9
7	6	4	2	9	2
+ 3	+ 5	+ 8	+ 7	+ 1	+ 8

14.	15.	16.	17.	18.	19.
1	6	2	8	6	1
4	7	3	2	3	7
+ 5	+ 8	5	1	4	9
		+ 4	+ 5	+ 2	+ 3

20. $5 + 3 + 6$ **21.** $2 + 8 + 3$ **22.** $4 + 7 + 6$ **23.** $9 + 2 + 8$

24. $1 + 1 + 4 + 5$ **25.** $5 + 3 + 2 + 4$ **26.** $5 + 3 + 3 + 5$

Find the missing addend.

27. $(4 + 5) + 6 = 5 + (\blacksquare + 6)$ **28.** $8 + (2 + \blacksquare) = 2 + (6 + 8)$

Mixed Applications

29. Joanne spent 5 hours on the beach on Monday, 5 hours on Tuesday, and 3 hours on Wednesday. How many hours did she spend on the beach?

30. Ken is flying on an 8-hour flight from Seattle to Honolulu. He has already been flying for 3 hours. How many more hours does he have to fly?

31. Jean has 3 leis. Nora has 5 leis. The twins have 4 leis each. How many leis do the sisters have in total?

32. An airline has 472 dinners ready for the next flight out. How many dinners are there to the nearest hundred?

CHALLENGE

Find the answer. Do the work in parentheses first.

1. $(9 - 3) + 6$ **2.** $3 + (7 - 5)$ **3.** $8 - (4 + 3)$

4. $(4 + 5) + 3$ **5.** $7 + (8 - 2)$ **6.** $18 - (7 + 2)$

7. Which of the exercises would have different answers if you moved the parentheses?

Finding Needed Information

Jimmy and his family are driving to the Menominee Nation Powwow near Keshena, Wisconsin. They have been on the road for 2 days. Jimmy wants to find out how many days the trip will last.

1. What information does Jimmy know?

2. What does he need to find out?

Sometimes you do not have enough information to solve a problem. You need to look up additional information.

3. What additional information does Jimmy need?

Jimmy studied a map and figured out that it will take 4 more days to get to Keshena.

4. Does he have enough information now?

5. How many days will the trip take?

6. Jimmy's mother says he can go to the Menominee Logging Museum every day it rains during the powwow. What information does he need to solve the problem? Can he find it now?

7. Why is it important to list all the information needed to solve a problem?

PRACTICE

Solve. Use mental math, or paper and pencil. If there is
not enough information, write what is needed.

8. Jimmy is buying a poster at the Logging Museum gift
   shop. The poster costs $8.98. How much change should
   he get?

9. Michael sees a herd of deer in the
   Menominee Indian Reservation. He counts
   17 deer. Then 8 run away. How many
   deer are left?

10. Jimmy went fishing and caught 15
    wall-eyed pike. How many more pike
    than Jimmy did Jimmy's mother catch?

11. Other people from Jimmy's town
    were at the powwow. Of
    them, 9 took part in the
    traditional storytelling, 8 in
    the dance competition, and
    4 in fishing contests. How
    many people from Jimmy's
    town took part in all of
    these powwow activities?

Strategies and Skills Review

Solve. You may need to use the Databank on page 517.

12. Jimmy and his sister hiked for 2 hours with only a 10-minute
    rest. Did they walk about 5 miles? 15 miles? 25 miles?

13. About how much more rain falls in Fairbanks, Alaska, than
    in Los Angeles, California, in a year?

14. Jimmy's father bought a package of frankfurters and 6 ears
    of corn for dinner. Did he spend about $5? $10? $50?

15. *Write a problem.* Leave out one piece of information needed
    to solve the problem. Ask others to tell what additional information
    is needed and how it can be found.

COUNTDOWN

Investigating Patterns

A. You can use the ⟨=⟩ key on a calculator to repeat calculations. You know that $5 + 5 + 5 + 5 = 20$.

What is the result when you enter this series on a calculator?

⟨5⟩ ⟨+⟩ ⟨5⟩ ⟨=⟩ ⟨=⟩ ⟨=⟩

Each time you press the ⟨=⟩ key, you add 5. The ⟨=⟩ key makes it easy to do repeated addition.

1. How could you use the ⟨=⟩ key to help you find the cost of six $6.85 records? Try it.

B. You can also use a calculator for repeated subtraction. Suppose you won a $300 prize. How many $43 video games could you buy?

You could subtract the cost of one game at a time:

⟨3⟩⟨0⟩⟨0⟩⟨−⟩⟨4⟩⟨3⟩⟨=⟩⟨−⟩⟨4⟩⟨3⟩⟨=⟩ and so on.

Or you could use constant subtraction:

⟨3⟩⟨0⟩⟨0⟩⟨−⟩⟨4⟩⟨3⟩⟨=⟩⟨=⟩⟨=⟩⟨=⟩ and so on.

2. How do you know when you have your answer?

Many problems can be solved using repeated addition or subtraction. Can you find more than one way to find each answer?

3. Suppose you have $35. How many $7.98 cassette tapes can you buy?

4. One class has raised $250 by selling cases of pens for $15.50 each. How many more cases of pens does the class need to sell to reach its goal of $325?

5. How many 5-minute pinball games can you play in 1 hour (1 hour = 60 minutes)? Would $2.75 be enough to play that many games if each game cost 25 cents?

C. Do you remember what to do when you make a mistake entering a number on a calculator? You should use the $\boxed{C}$ key. Try this experiment:

What if you want to add 37 and 98? Press the following keys:

$\boxed{3}$ $\boxed{7}$ $\boxed{+}$ $\boxed{9}$ $\boxed{9}$

Now press $\boxed{C}$ once. When you press this key once, it erases only the last number you entered. You will see 0 in the display. This tells you that you have erased the 99. Now enter $\boxed{+}$ $\boxed{9}$ $\boxed{8}$ and press $\boxed{=}$.

What if you want to add 54 and 89? Press the following keys:

$\boxed{5}$ $\boxed{4}$ $\boxed{-}$ $\boxed{8}$ $\boxed{9}$

If you press $\boxed{C}$ once, you will erase only the 89, not the subtraction. Now press $\boxed{C}$ twice. When you press this key twice, it erases everything you have done. Then start again.

6. What happens when you enter $\boxed{7}$ $\boxed{8}$ $\boxed{+}$ and then press $\boxed{C}$ once? What happens when you enter $\boxed{7}$ $\boxed{8}$ $\boxed{+}$ $\boxed{3}$ $\boxed{2}$ and then press $\boxed{C}$ once?

7. Here's a calculator puzzle. Use only these keys.

$\boxed{0}$, $\boxed{1}$, $\boxed{+}$, $\boxed{-}$, $\boxed{=}$

Can you get 135 in the display? How? Can you find the method that uses the fewest keystrokes?

8. Can you get the display to show 478 using the same keys? Can you find the method that uses the fewest keystrokes?

ACTIVITY

Measuring Length: Metric Units

WORKING TOGETHER

Use the width of the tip of your
index finger to measure the length
of this crayon.

1. How many fingertips long is the crayon?

2. Compare your measurement with those of other
   students. Are they the same? Why or why not?

The width of the tip of your index finger is about 1 centimeter.
The **centimeter (cm)** is a metric unit of length.

You can use a centimeter
ruler to measure short lengths.

> Be sure to line up the
> left end of the crayon
> with the left end of
> the scale on the ruler.

3. Use a centimeter ruler to
   .measure the length of the
   crayon.

4. What is the length of the
   crayon to the nearest
   centimeter?

5. Use the tip of your index finger to measure
   the length of your desk. Compare your
   measurement with those of others. Are they
   the same? Why or why not?

6. Use a centimeter ruler to measure the length
   of your desk. Compare your measurements
   with those of others. Are they the same?
   Why or why not?

Use a centimeter ruler to measure the following.
Compare your measurements with those of others.

7. the length of your math book

8. the height of your desk

9. Why do you think it is better to use a centimeter ruler than the width of your finger to measure length?

10. What is meant by "measuring to the nearest centimeter"?

PRACTICE

Copy and complete this chart. Estimate. Then use your centimeter ruler to measure.

	Object	Estimate	Measurement
11.	Width of your math book	■	■
12.	Width of your shoe	■	■
13.	Depth of a windowsill	■	■
14.	Height of your chair	■	■

15. Choose three more objects to measure. Record your work on your chart.

Use your centimeter ruler. Draw lines with the following lengths:

16. 6 cm   **17.** 11 cm   **18.** 1 cm   **19.** 10 cm

Critical Thinking

20. You use centimeters to measure the width, length, height, or depth of an object. How are these measurements the same? How are they different?

Mixed Applications

Solve. You will need to use the Databank on page 517.

21. The Sears Tower in Chicago and the World Trade Center in New York are both 110 stories tall. Which one is taller?

22. *Write a problem* using the information in the Databank. Solve your problem. Trade problems with other students and solve them.

son
TEL
REE

Estimating Length: Metric Units

The **decimeter (dm),** the **meter (m),** and the **kilometer (km)** are other metric units used to measure length and distance.

The width of a cassette tape is about 1 decimeter.

The width of a door is about 1 meter.

A kilometer is about how far you might walk in 20 minutes.

This chart shows how the units are related.

10 centimeters (cm)	= 1 decimeter (dm)
10 decimeters (dm)	= 1 meter (m)
100 centimeters (cm)	= 1 meter (m)
1,000 meters (m)	= 1 kilometer (km)

Tell whether you would use m, cm, dm, or km to measure:

1. the distance from Dallas, Texas, to Chicago, Illinois

2. the width of your desk

3. the height of a building

4. How did you decide which unit to use to measure each?

TRY OUT
Write the letter of the correct answer. Would you use cm, dm, m, or km to measure?

5. the length of a key   **a.** cm   **b.** dm   **c.** m   **d.** km

6. the distance across a state   **a.** cm   **b.** dm   **c.** m   **d.** km

7. the width of a napkin   **a.** cm   **b.** dm   **c.** m   **d.** km

8. the length of a swimming pool   **a.** cm   **b.** dm   **c.** m   **d.** km

PRACTICE

Tell whether you would use cm, dm, m, or km to measure.

9. the height of a house   10. the length of a car

11. the length of a worm   12. the distance across a lake

Write the letter of the best estimate.

13. the distance a car travels in an hour   **a.** 60 dm   **b.** 60 m   **c.** 60 km

14. the length of your thumb   **a.** 2 cm   **b.** 2 dm   **c.** 2 m

15. the width of a chair   **a.** 6 cm   **b.** 6 dm   **c.** 6 m

16. the height of a flagpole   **a.** 3 dm   **b.** 3 m   **c.** 3 km

Complete the chart. Use the units given.

Object	Estimate	Actual Measure
Length of your arm (cm)	17. ■	18. ■
Distance around your head (dm)	19. ■	20. ■
Length of your classroom (m)	21. ■	22. ■

Mixed Applications

23. Judy hiked 4 km on Sunday, 3 km on Monday, 5 km on Tuesday, and 6 km on Wednesday. How many km did she hike in all?

24. An oak tree can grow more than ten times the height of an adult. Which metric unit would be the best to use to measure the height of an oak tree?

25. The city of Troy is 9 km north of my home. The city of Lester is 7 km south of my home. How far is it from Troy to Lester?

26. A highway sign shows that it is 9 km north to Troy and 18 km north to Ashby. How far is it from Troy to Ashby?

PROBLEM SOLVING

Strategy: Drawing a Diagram

Helen is on a camping trip with her family. She and her brother, Hal, are going to cut a log into 4 pieces to use for firewood. How many cuts do they need to make?

1. What information do you know?

2. What do you need to find out?

Sometimes it helps to draw a diagram to understand the problem better.

3. Draw a diagram of a log. Show how to cut it into 4 pieces. How many cuts are needed?

4. If you had not drawn a diagram of the log, would your answer have been different?

5. *What if* they wanted to cut the log into 8 pieces? How many cuts would they need to make? Draw a diagram and count the number of cuts.

6. How does drawing a diagram help you solve problems like this?

PRACTICE

Draw a diagram to help you solve the problem.

7. Helen is using a red ribbon to mark the boundary of the campsite. She cuts the ribbon into 6 pieces. How many cuts does she need to make?

8. Four cars are parked bumper to bumper. How many bumpers are touching?

9. A farmer builds a 100-foot fence to separate her farm from the campground. She puts posts into the ground every 10 feet. How many posts does she need in order to build her fence?

10. Hal is riding in the family car to the campsite. He notices that 1 telephone wire is always strung between 2 poles. How many wires are strung between 5 telephone poles?

Strategies and Skills Review

Solve. If there is not enough information, write what is needed. Use mental math or paper and pencil.

11. Helen roasted 7 marshmallows, and Hal roasted 9. Their father roasted more than either of them. How many marshmallows did they roast in all?

12. One evening after a rain, Helen counted 17 fireflies. Hal counted 8 fireflies. How many more fireflies did Helen count than Hal?

13. Hal counts 12 campsites along the road. There is a picnic table between every neighboring campsite. How many picnic tables are there?

14. There is a light pole at each end of the road. There is also a light pole at every third campsite. How many light poles are there for the 12 campsites?

15. Helen bought 3 postcards and 3 stamps. About how much would these items cost? $2? $12? $22?

16. **Write a problem** that can be solved with the help of a diagram. Ask others to solve it.

Act**i**V**i**ty **M**aking Bar Graphs

Karen kept track of the fruit her family ate in one week. She used these steps to show the data on a **bar graph**.

Step 1 Choose a scale.

Step 2 Draw and label the sides.

Step 3 Draw the bars on the graph.

Step 4 Write a title above the graph.

FRUIT MY FAMILY ATE	
Fruit	**Number Eaten**
Bananas	15
Plums	3
Apples	18
Oranges	16
Peaches	13

WORKING TOGETHER

1. Copy and complete Karen's bar graph.

2. Why did Karen count by 2s from 0 to 20 for the scale?

3. How tall did you make the bar for peaches? Why?

4. Which is the tallest bar? What does this tell you?

5. How did you title the graph?

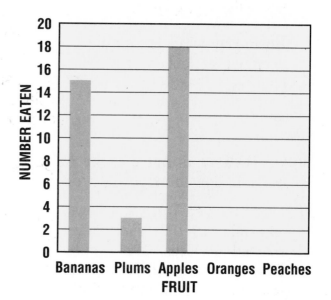

SHARING IDEAS

6. Compare your bar graph with those of others. How are they the same? How are they different?

7. **What if** Karen's family had eaten 40 oranges? How could you change the scale to keep the graph the same size?

8. Which fruit was eaten the least? Is it easier to read this from the graph than from the table? Why?

9. Why is a bar graph a useful way to record and display data?

PRACTICE

10. Paula's Pasta Palace sells special fruit flavors of pasta. Paula wants to compare the sales of four of her most popular types of pasta. Copy and complete the bar graph below.

11. Which type of pasta sold the least? Which type sold the most?

SALES OF PASTA	
Type	Boxes (to the Nearest Hundred)
Lemon	400
Berry	900
Orange	200
Cherry	700

12. Paula also sold 107 boxes of peach pasta. Show this data on the graph. What do you have to do before you can graph the data?

13. Paula did not sell any boxes of prune pasta. How would you show this on the graph?

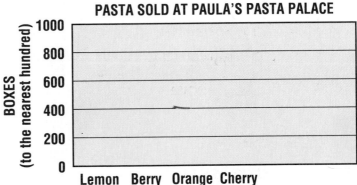

14. This table shows the different pasta sauces sold in Paula's store last week. Make a bar graph to show this data. Compare your graph with those of others.

15. What does your graph tell you about sales of different sauces?

16. How can Paula use this data to help her order more pasta sauces for her store?

SALES OF PASTA SAUCE	
Type	Number of Jars
Garlic	40
Tomato	65
Curry	10
Onion	30
Spinach	25

17. Collect data about the number of fruits eaten by other students during one week. Make a bar graph to show the results. Compare your graph with those of others.

Mixed Review

Write the number.

18. 2 thousands 5 tens   19. 10,000 + 800 + 5   20. one hundred fourteen

DECISION MAKING

Problem Solving: Planning a Vacation

SITUATION

Judy and Frank DeSanto are on vacation at Coyote Lake Campgrounds with their parents and grandparents. They want to spend one day seeing some of the sights near the lake.

PROBLEM

Which sights should they see?

DATA

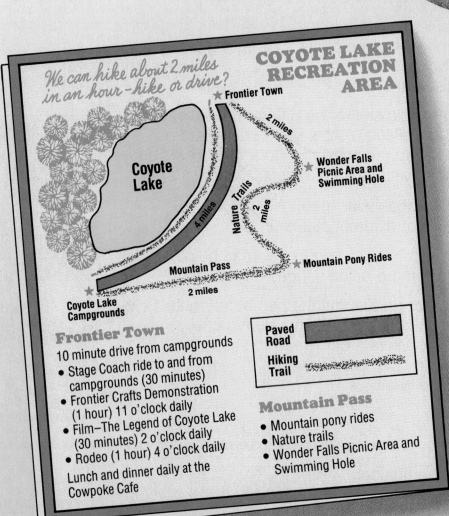

We can hike about 2 miles in an hour – hike or drive?

COYOTE LAKE RECREATION AREA

Coyote Lake

Frontier Town
2 miles

Wonder Falls Picnic Area and Swimming Hole

4 miles

Nature Trails
2 miles

Mountain Pony Rides

Mountain Pass
2 miles

Coyote Lake Campgrounds

Frontier Town
10 minute drive from campgrounds
- Stage Coach ride to and from campgrounds (30 minutes)
- Frontier Crafts Demonstration (1 hour) 11 o'clock daily
- Film—The Legend of Coyote Lake (30 minutes) 2 o'clock daily
- Rodeo (1 hour) 4 o'clock daily

Lunch and dinner daily at the Cowpoke Cafe

Paved Road

Hiking Trail

Mountain Pass
- Mountain pony rides
- Nature trails
- Wonder Falls Picnic Area and Swimming Hole

USING THE DATA

1. How many miles is it from the campgrounds to Frontier Town by Mountain Pass?

Tell how long it would take to hike to each site from the campgrounds. Include a 10-minute rest after each mile.

2. Pony Rides

3. Wonder Falls

4. Frontier Town by Mountain Pass

5. What are the different ways the DeSantos could get to Frontier Town?

MAKING DECISIONS

6. **Write a list** of the things the DeSantos should think about when planning their day trip.

7. **What if** the DeSantos want to see The Legend of Coyote Lake and take a pony ride? How should they travel to each place?

8. **What if** Frank wants to take a pony ride and Judy wants to see the rodeo? If they start at 9:00 A.M., do they have time for both? Why or why not?

9. **What if** the DeSantos want to take a pony ride and picnic at Wonder Falls? Do they still have time to see all the attractions at Frontier Town? Why or why not?

10. **Write a schedule** for a day at Coyote Lake. What would you see and do? How would you get to each attraction? Where would you eat?

Math and Health

In gym class you learn many different kinds of exercises. But what does exercising do for you?

One type of exercise makes your muscles flexible. The warm-up exercises in gym class are this type. A second type of exercise builds strong muscles. This type involves pushing, pulling, and lifting. A third type of exercise helps your heart and lungs work well. Most sports that include running do this. All exercises burn fat to help you stay at a healthy weight.

An hour of exercise three days a week is the least you need to do to be in good shape. An hour each day is even better. Some professional athletes work out as many as 50 hours a week!

What if Frank's goal is 15 hours of exercise each week? He plays frisbee and baseball and rides his bike, and by Thursday has exercised 8 hours. How many more hours must he exercise to meet his weekly goal?

Think: Subtract. 15 − 8 = 7

Frank must exercise 7 more hours.

ACTIVITY

1. Make a weekly exercise plan. Show your plan in a chart with these column heads: Day of the Week, Activity, and Number of Hours. At the bottom, write the Total Weekly Time. Try to include all three types of exercise.

Calculator: Challenge

Tom challenged Denise and Bruce to use their calculators to go from 15 to 100 in three steps, using only the number keys and the $\boxed{+}$, $\boxed{-}$, and $\boxed{=}$ keys. They had to use the $\boxed{-}$ key at least one time.

This is what Denise did:

She entered 15.

Calculator Display

$$\boxed{15.}$$

Then she pressed the keys below:

		Calculator Display
Step 1 $\boxed{+}$ 70 $\boxed{=}$		$\boxed{85.}$
Step 2 $\boxed{-}$ 5 $\boxed{=}$		$\boxed{80.}$
Step 3 $\boxed{+}$ 20 $\boxed{=}$		$\boxed{100.}$

This is what Bruce did:

He entered 15.

Calculator Display

$$\boxed{15.}$$

Then he pressed the keys below:

		Calculator Display
Step 1 $\boxed{+}$ 35 $\boxed{=}$		$\boxed{50.}$
Step 2 $\boxed{+}$ 75 $\boxed{=}$		$\boxed{125.}$
Step 3 $\boxed{-}$ 25 $\boxed{=}$		$\boxed{100.}$

Are there other ways to do it? Try it. Show two more ways to go from 15 to 100 in three steps.

USING THE CALCULATOR

Use number keys and only the $\boxed{+}$, $\boxed{-}$, and $\boxed{=}$ keys.

1. Enter 12. Go to 30 in three steps. Use the $\boxed{-}$ key at least once.

2. Enter 15. Go to 40 in four steps. Use the $\boxed{-}$ key at least twice.

3. Enter 25. Go to 50 in four steps. Use the $\boxed{-}$ key at least twice.

4. Enter 15. Go to 50 in five steps. Use the $\boxed{-}$ key at least twice.

5. Enter 20. Go to 60 in five steps. Use the $\boxed{-}$ key at least twice.

6. Enter 60. Go to 100 in six steps. Use the $\boxed{-}$ key at least 3 times.

EXTRA PRACTICE

Meaning of Addition and Subtraction, page 53 ....

Find the sum or difference.

1. 0	**2.** 8	**3.** 3	**4.** 10	**5.** 7	**6.** 1
+8	−0	+2	−6	−7	+6

7. 6 − ■ = 6 **8.** ■ + 7 = 7 **9.** 4 − ■ = 0 **10.** 3 + ■ = 4 + 3

11. ■ + 0 = 5 **12.** 1 − ■ = 1 **13.** ■ − 9 = 0 **14.** 8 + 2 = ■ + 8

Fact Families, page 55 ....

Find the sum or difference. Write the related
number sentences that make up the fact family.

1. 4 + 7 = ■   **2.** 12 − 6 = ■   **3.** 15 − 7 = ■   **4.** 18 − 9 = ■

5. 0 + 4 = ■   **6.** 10 − 7 = ■   **7.** 8 + 8 = ■   **8.** 1 + 8 = ■

Write the fact family for the set of numbers.

9. 3, 9, 12   **10.** 1, 6, 7   **11.** 0, 2, 2   **12.** 2, 7, 9

Complete the fact. Find the missing number.

13. 7 + ■ = 13   **14.** 8 − ■ = 5   **15.** ■ + 7 = 10   **16.** 8 + ■ = 16

17. 6 + ■ = 9   **18.** 16 − 7 = ■   **19.** 6 + ■ = 6   **20.** ■ + 4 = 11

Mental Math: Addition Facts, page 57 ....

Add. Use mental math.

1. 4	**2.** 6	**3.** 3	**4.** 5	**5.** 2	**6.** 9
+5	+2	+3	+7	+5	+0

7. 5	**8.** 1	**9.** 8	**10.** 7	**11.** 5	**12.** 3
+5	+4	+3	+7	+8	+7

13. 7 + 6   **14.** 8 + 4   **15.** 6 + 6   **16.** 5 + 9

17. 0 + 3   **18.** 2 + 2   **19.** 3 + 9   **20.** 4 + 7

Mental Math: Subtraction Facts, page 59 ....

Subtract. Use mental math.

1.	16 − 8	**2.**	14 − 5	**3.**	12 − 3	**4.**	11 − 6	**5.**	13 − 7	**6.**	15 − 9
7.	10 − 3	**8.**	12 − 7	**9.**	14 − 8	**10.**	14 − 7	**11.**	16 − 9	**12.**	18 − 9

13. 14 − 6   **14.** 17 − 9   **15.** 16 − 7   **16.** 11 − 7

17. 10 − 5   **18.** 11 − 5   **19.** 10 − 2   **20.** 17 − 8

Mental Math: Three or More Addends, page 61 ....

Find the sum. Use mental math.

1.	7 2 + 3	**2.**	8 5 + 3	**3.**	6 2 + 4	**4.**	5 7 + 2	**5.**	9 1 + 7	**6.**	2 3 + 9

7. 3 + 4 + 9   **8.** 8 + 3 + 2   **9.** 6 + 4 + 7   **10.** 2 + 1 + 4

11. 1 + 3 + 1 + 5   **12.** 2 + 3 + 5 + 6   **13.** 3 + 4 + 4 + 5

Find the missing addend.

14. $(3 + 2) + 5 = 2 + (\blacksquare + 5)$ **15.** $7 + (3 + 6) = 3 + (6 + \blacksquare)$

Problem Solving: Finding Needed Information, page 63 ....

Solve. If there is not enough information, write what is needed.

1. Heather saw 4 birds. Her father saw 9 birds. How many more birds did her father see?

2. Garrett bought three postcards. He gave the clerk $10.00. How much change should he get?

3. Valerie went rafting on the Colorado River. The raft traveled 5 miles each hour. How many miles was her trip?

4. Pete hiked 4 miles on Monday and 7 miles on Tuesday. How many miles did he hike in the two days?

EXTRA PRACTICE

Measuring Length: Metric Units, page 67 ....

Copy and complete this chart. Estimate. Then use your centimeter ruler to measure.

	Object	Estimate	Measurement
1.	height of a door	■	■
2.	width of your desk	■	■
3.	depth of a shelf	■	■
4.	width of your hand	■	■

Use your centimeter ruler. Draw lines with the following lengths.

5. 12 cm   **6.** 9 cm   **7.** 2 cm   **8.** 7 cm

Estimating Length: Metric Units, page 69 ....

Tell whether you would use cm, dm, m, or km to measure.

1. the distance across an ocean

2. the length of an airplane

3. the length of a ribbon

4. the distance from the floor to the ceiling

Write the letter of the best estimate.

5. the height of a spool of thread   **a.** 3 cm   **b.** 3 dm   **c.** 3 m

6. the width of a basket   **a.** 6 cm   **b.** 6 dm   **c.** 6 m

7. the height of a giraffe   **a.** 4 dm   **b.** 4 m   **c.** 4 km

Complete the chart. Use the units given.

Object	Estimate	Measurement
distance around your wrist (cm)	**8.** ■	**9.** ■
length of your leg (dm)	**10.** ■	**11.** ■
length of the chalkboard (m)	**12.** ■	**13.** ■

Problem Solving: Drawing a Diagram, page 71 ....

Draw a diagram to help you solve the problem.

1. Yvette is going to cut a piece of yarn to tie 5 presents. How many cuts will she need to make?

2. Five trucks are parked bumper to bumper. How many bumpers are touching?

3. Jason lives in an apartment building on the ground floor. Jenny lives 8 floors above him. How many floors are there between Jason's and Jenny's apartments?

4. Rob hangs his coat in the middle of a row of hooks. There are 7 hooks to the right of his coat. How many hooks are in the row?

Making Bar Graphs, page 73 ....

Solve. Use the table and graph.

1. Ben's Bread Bakery sells different kinds of bread. Ben wants to compare the sales of four of his most popular types of bread. Complete the bar graph.

BREAD SOLD AT BEN'S BREAD BAKERY

Type	Loaves (to the nearest hundred)
White	300
Wheat	800
Rye	700
Raisin	200

2. Which type of bread did Ben sell the least of? the most of?

3. Ben also sold 118 loaves of banana bread. Show this data on the graph. What do you have to do before you can graph the data?

4. Ben did not sell any bran bread. How would you show this on the graph?

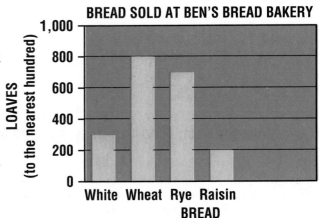

PRACTICE PLUS

KEY SKILL: MENTAL MATH: ADDITION FACTS (Use after page 57.)

Level A ....

Add. Use mental math.

1. 3 +2	**2.** 4 +3	**3.** 1 +5	**4.** 4 +4	**5.** 9 +1	**6.** 5 +2

Write the letter of the correct answer.

7. 8 + 2
  a. 10 **b.** 2 **c.** 82

8. 7 + 5
  a. 75 **b.** 11 **c.** 12

9. 9 + 4
  a. 14 **b.** 94 **c.** 13

10. Alfonso has 4 baseball caps from American League teams and 5 baseball caps from National League teams. How many baseball caps does he have?

Level B ....

Add. Use mental math.

11. 5 +3	**12.** 8 +1	**13.** 6 +5	**14.** 3 +8	**15.** 9 +5	**16.** 2 +9

17. 7 + 1   **18.** 6 + 3   **19.** 4 + 6   **20.** 9 + 6   **21.** 8 + 9

22. 8 plus 8 is what number?   **23.** What is the sum of 7 plus 9?

24. The school band purchased 8 new flutes and 5 new violins. How many instruments did the band buy?

Level C ....

Add. Use mental math.

25. 6 + 7   **26.** 9 + 3   **27.** 7 + 4   **28.** 2 + 8   **29.** 6 + 8

Complete the fact. Find the missing number.

30. 9 + ■ = 11   **31.** 7 + ■ = 13   **32.** 8 + ■ = 15   **33.** 5 + ■ = 14

34. Janice takes 9 books from the shelf. There are 7 books left. How many books were there to start with?

KEY SKILL: MENTAL MATH: SUBTRACTION FACTS (Use after page 59.)

Level A ....

Subtract. Use mental math.

1.	7	**2.**	4	**3.**	5	**4.**	9	**5.**	10	**6.**	8
	-6		-1		-4		-3		-9		-6

Write the letter of the correct answer.

7. $3 - 1$
   a. 4 **b.** 2 **c.** 1

8. $11 - 3$
   a. 14 **b.** 7 **c.** 8

9. $9 - 4$
   a. 5 **b.** 13 **c.** 6

10. Jessica found 9 starfish. She gave 5 of them to Mark. How many starfish does Jessica have left?

Level B ....

Subtract. Use mental math.

11.	12	**12.**	7	**13.**	15	**14.**	8	**15.**	10	**16.**	9
	$-\ 5$		-2		$-\ 6$		-5		$-\ 8$		-6

17. $6 - 1$ **18.** $10 - 4$ **19.** $13 - 8$ **20.** $8 - 4$ **21.** $12 - 3$

22. the difference between 10 and 1   **23.** 6 less than 13

24. Tracie has 9 dimes in her bank. Bo has 17 dimes in his. How many fewer coins does Tracie have than Bo?

Level C ....

Subtract. Use mental math.

25. $11 - 2$ **26.** $13 - 9$ **27.** $7 - 4$ **28.** $14 - 9$ **29.** $10 - 8$

Complete the fact. Find the missing number.

30. $13 - \blacksquare = 8$ **31.** $10 - \blacksquare = 4$ **32.** $9 - \blacksquare = 8$ **33.** $14 - \blacksquare = 8$

34. The Snake River is 8 miles longer than the Gekko River. The Snake River is 17 miles long. How long is the Gekko River?

CHAPTER REVIEW/TEST

LANGUAGE AND MATHEMATICS

Complete the sentences. Use the words in the chart.

1. The total of two addends is the ■.

2. The centimeter is a ■ unit of length.

3. The ■ is used to measure length and distance.

4. A bar graph is used to organize ■.

CONCEPTS AND SKILLS

Complete. Find the missing number.

5. $4 - ■ = 4$ 6. $7 + (3 + ■) = 3 + (6 + 7)$ 7. $4 + ■ = 2 + 4$

Add or subtract.

8. $8 + 8$ 9. $4 + 3$ 10. $15 - 9$ 11. $14 - 8$

12. $10 - 3$ 13. $8 + 1 + 7$ 14. $1 + 3 + 2 + 5$

Use your centimeter ruler. Draw a line.

15. 1 cm   16. 9 cm   17. 13 cm

Write the letter of the best estimate.

18. the height of a tree   a. 5 dm   b. 5 m   c. 5 km

19. the distance of a hiking trail   a. 6 dm   b. 6 m   c. 5 km

20. the length of a table   a. 2 dm   b. 2 m   c. 2 km

Use the graph for Questions 21–22.

21. How many more violets than tulips were sold in June?

22. Dan sold 35 lilacs in June. How would you show this?

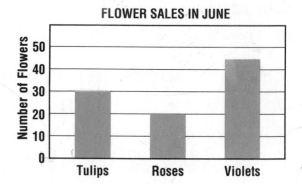

FLOWER SALES IN JUNE

Critical Thinking

23. Tara says that her book is 2 dm wide. Herb says the book is 19 cm wide. They are both right. How can this be?

Mixed Applications

Solve. If there is not enough information, write what is needed.

24. Gabrielle wants to invite 10 boys and 10 girls to her party. So far, she has invited 15 people. Has she invited enough girls?

25. Kara wants to cut a board into 6 pieces. How many cuts does she need to make?

PERFORMANCE ASSESSMENT

Work with your group to solve this problem.

Complete this table for each member of your group.

Object	Length to the Nearest Centimeter
Index finger	
Little finger	
Thumb	
Width of palm	

Make a bar graph to compare the lengths of your fingers to the fingers of each member of your group. Use addition and subtraction facts to help you write two conclusions that you can make from the data.

1. *Think about:*
- how to make a bar graph to display the data
- how to use addition and subtraction facts to compare the data

2. Write two word problems that use addition and subtraction facts and the information in your graph.

Portfolio

CUMULATIVE REVIEW

Choose the letter of the correct answer.

1. 8 + 3 + 6

  a. 9   **c.** 17

  b. 11   **d.** not given

2. Round $.26 to the nearest ten cents.

  a. $.10   **c.** $.25

  b. $.20   **d.** $.30

3. 16 − 9

  a. 5   **c.** 7

  b. 6   **d.** not given

4. Estimate the length of an eraser.

  a. 3 cm   **c.** 3 m

  b. 3 dm   **d.** 3 km

5. Compare: 350 ● 503

  a. <   **c.** =

  b. >   **d.** not given

6. Choose the number for fifty thousand.

  a. 5,000   **c.** 50,000

  b. 500,000   **d.** not given

7. 2 + 6

  a. 4   **c.** 8

  b. 5   **d.** not given

8. Round 5,426 to the nearest hundred.

  a. 5,000   **c.** 5,430

  b. 5,400   **d.** 5,500

9. How much more than 5 is 14?

  a. 7   **c.** 9

  b. 8   **d.** not given

10. Cost: 45¢   Given: 50¢
What is the change?

  a. 1 penny   **c.** 1 dime

  b. 1 nickel   **d.** not given

11. What is 8 more than 4?

  a. 11   **c.** 13

  b. 12   **d.** not given

12. Which would you use to measure the length of a room?

  a. cm   **c.** m

  b. dm   **d.** km

13. Compare: $41.95 ● $14.95

  a. <   **c.** =

  b. >   **d.** not given

14. 4 + 7 + 3 + 1

  a. 17   **c.** 16

  b. 18   **d.** not given

ROMAN NUMERALS

The ancient Romans used letters to write numbers. Today we still use Roman numerals to mark the building date on monuments and public buildings. Here are the letters used to write numbers from 1 to 1,000.

I	V	X	L	C	D	M
1	5	10	50	100	500	1000

You can write other numbers by combining letters. When a letter is repeated, add.

III	XX	CCC
1 + 1 + 1 = 3	10 + 10 = 20	100 + 100 + 100 = 300

A letter is never repeated more than 3 times.

When a letter of less value is to the *right* of a letter of greater value, add.

LX
50 + 10 = 60

When a letter of less value is to the *left* of a letter of greater value, subtract.

XL
50 − 10 = 40

1. Is the Roman numeral system a place-value system?

What does MCMLV equal?

Think: M = 1,000
CM = 1,000 − 100 = 900
LV = 50 + 5 = 55
1,000 + 900 + 55 = 1,955

Match the building with the year it was built.

2. White House (1817)

3. Empire State Building (1931)

4. Roman Colosseum (70 A.D.)

a. MCMXXXI

b. LXX

c. MDCCCXVII

PYRAMIDS
AROUND THE WORLD

Pyramids have been built by both ancient and modern people. Near the Egyptian city of Cairo stands the Great Pyramid of Giza. This tomb for Pharaoh Khufu was built during his 23-year reign which ended with his death in 2556 B.C. Thousands of workers laid over two million stones. Each weighed about two and a half tons. The Great Pyramid is still the largest pyramid ever built.

Here are some of the dimensions of these pyramids.

PYRAMID	LENGTH OF EACH SIDE OF SQUARE BASE	HEIGHT
Great Pyramid of Giza	about 755 feet	about 480 feet
Pyramid of the Sun	about 700 feet	about 210 feet
Transamerica Building	about 145 feet	about 850 feet

Near Mexico City, a large city known as Teotihuacán [tay-o-tee-hua-KHAN] developed in the fourth century A.D. Little is known about the people who built this city. It is believed, however, they left behind the Pyramid of the Sun. A temple once stood at the top of this step pyramid, which was the center of many religious ceremonies.

Today, modern pyramids take the form of office buildings. A tall, thin pyramid rises high above downtown San Francisco, California. This building is called the Transamerica building.

1 How are the shapes of the three structures alike? How are they different?

2 Which pyramid would take the longest for you to walk around? Why?

Mental Math: Adding 10s; 100s; 1,000s

A. The Corner Deli kept this record of the number of sandwiches it sold. How many sandwiches did it sell in the two weeks?

Week	Number of Sandwiches Sold
1	300
2	400

Add: 300 + 400

You can use basic facts to find the sum mentally.

$$\begin{array}{r} 300 \\ + 400 \\ \hline \end{array}$$
Think:
$$\begin{array}{r} 3 \\ + 4 \\ \hline 7 \end{array}$$
3 hundreds
+ 4 hundreds
7 hundreds = 700

300 + 400 = 700
The Corner Deli sold 700 sandwiches.

1. Use basic facts to find 3,000 + 9,000.

2. How can you use this method to find 20 + 60 + 50?

B. You can adjust some numbers so you can add mentally.

Add: 43 + 29

Look to make one of the addends end in zero.

$$\begin{array}{r} 43 \longrightarrow 42 \\ + 29 \longrightarrow + 30 \\ \hline 72 \end{array}$$
Think: Take 1 away from 43 to make 42.
Add 1 to 29 to make 30.

So 43 + 29 = 42 + 30 = 72.

3. Use this method to find 337 + 198.

TRY OUT Write the letter of the correct answer. Add mentally.

4. 4,000 + 7,000   **a.** 1,100   **b.** 11   **c.** 11,000   **d.** 110

5. 600 + 30 + 40   **a.** 1,030   **b.** 730   **c.** 130   **d.** 670

6. 57 + 89   **a.** 146   **b.** 147   **c.** 148   **d.** 137

7. 98 + 125   **a.** 225   **b.** 223   **c.** 126   **d.** 209

PRACTICE

Add. Use mental math.

8. 20
    + 70

9. 100
    + 500

10. 2,000
    + 4,000

11. 4,000
    + 300

12. 600
    + 900

13. 20
    40
    + 20

14. 30
    40
    + 70

15. 900
    60
    + 20

16. 200
    100
    + 500

17. 600
    400
    + 700

18. 19
    + 31

19. 23
    + 59

20. 65
    + 69

21. 322
    + 499

22. 799
    + 626

23. 101
    + 89

24. 299
    + 52

25. 151
    + 799

26. 999
    + 507

27. 561
    + 429

28. 10 + 40 + 20 **29.** 5,000 + 5,000 **30.** 71 + 29 **31.** 49 + 36

32. 400 + 800 **33.** 199 + 714 **34.** 74 + 68 **35.** 800 + 30 + 70

36. 99 + 123 **37.** 50 + 30 + 60 **38.** 98 + 142 **39.** 498 + 213

Mixed Applications

40. The Corner Deli sold 400 cans of juice last month and 200 cans this month. How many cans of juice did it sell in the two months?

41. A group of customers orders 15 bowls of soup. The Corner Deli can fill all but 6 bowls. How many bowls of soup can the group get?

42. On Monday Ben made 30 sandwiches. Ray made 20 more sandwiches than Ben. Rachel made 30 more than Ray. How many sandwiches did Rachel make?

43. The Corner Deli used 59 paper bags on Saturday and 44 paper bags on Sunday. How many paper bags did it use on the weekend?

Estimating Sums by Rounding

A. Martin uses the number of cartons of milk sold this month to order for next month. About how many cartons were sold?

Sometimes you do not need to know the exact answer. You can round to find an estimate.

Estimate: 489 + 378 + 265

MILK MART

Flavor	Number of Cartons
Vanilla	489
Chocolate	378
Strawberry	265

Step 1

Round each number to the greatest place of the greatest number.

$$489 \longrightarrow 500$$
$$378 \longrightarrow 400$$
$$+\ 265 \longrightarrow +\ 300$$

Think: Round to the nearest hundred.

Step 2

Add the rounded numbers.

$$\begin{array}{r} 500 \\ 400 \\ +\ 300 \\ \hline 1,200 \end{array}$$

About 1,200 cartons of milk were sold.

1. How does this estimate compare with the exact answer? Why?

B. You can also estimate sums when adding money.

Estimate: $5.47 + $.24 + $8.35

Step 1

Round each number to the greatest place of the greatest number.

$$\$5.47 \longrightarrow \$5.00$$
$$.24 \longrightarrow 0.00$$
$$+\ 8.35 \longrightarrow +\ 8.00$$

Think: Round to the nearest dollar.

Step 2

$$\begin{array}{r} \$5.00 \\ 0.00 \\ +\ 8.00 \\ \hline \$13.00 \end{array}$$

Think: Remember to put in the dollar sign and decimal point.

2. How does this estimate compare with the exact answer? Why?

TRY OUT Estimate by rounding.

3. 1,898 + 7,701   **4.** $3.45 + $6.19 + $.82   **5.** 43 + 108 + 279

PRACTICE

Estimate by rounding.

6.   532
       + 290

7.   905
       + 185

8.   5,775
       + 2,680

9. $5.75
       + 3.25

10. $63.80
        + 22.15

11.   160
        308
      + 150

12.   4,050
        2,030
      + 3,200

13. $5.60
        6.25
      + 2.20

14.   2,050
        3,500
      + 350

15. $23.96
        8.14
      + 54.05

16.   788
        350
      + 90

17. $65.00
        15.00
      + 30.00

18.   3,608
        650
      + 4,025

19.   7,604
        1,925
        830
      + 342

20. $30.86
        24.99
        51.09
      + 6.30

21. 329 + 25 + 620

22. 199 + 399 + 299

23. 6,300 + 1,360 + 720

24. $62.20 + $14.80 + $3.10

25. $22.70 + $37.90 + $11.80 + $5.00

Critical Thinking

26. How can you easily tell that this sum is incorrect?

856 + 742 + 699 = 3,297

Mixed Applications

27. Denise bought a quart of fudge ice cream for $2.69. Lee bought a quart of vanilla ice cream for $1.98. Did Lee and Denise spend more than $5.00?

28. Milk Mart gets the milk it sells from 700 cows. When sales go up, it buys 400 more cows. How many cows does Milk Mart use now?

29. The clerk at Milk Mart drops a box of 144 eggs and breaks them. In the next two days, he breaks 276 eggs and 192 eggs. About how many eggs does he break in three days?

30. Dudley's Dairy produces 3,964 gallons of milk in a week. Fern's Cow Farm produces 3,694 gallons of milk in a week. Which place produces more milk in a week?

Front-End Estimation

A. Nancy has $5.28, Tom has $4.98, and Kathy has $7.75. Do they have enough money to buy a large deluxe pizza?

PIZZA PALACE		
Pizza	Small	Large
Plain	$9.50	$11.75
Deluxe	$12.55	$15.00
Extra Toppings $2.50 each		

Nancy uses **front-end estimation**.

Estimate: $5.28 + $4.98 + $7.75

Add the front digits.
Write zeros for the other digits.

$$\begin{array}{r} \$5.28 \\ 4.98 \\ + 7.75 \\ \hline \$16.00 \end{array}$$

She thinks:
$5 + $4 + $7 = $16

We have enough to buy a large deluxe pizza.

1. Is Nancy's estimate greater than or less than the exact sum? How do you know?

B. You can adjust a front-end estimate to get closer to the exact answer.

Estimate: 343 + 62 + 409

Step 1

Add the front digits.
Write zeros for the other digits.

$$\begin{array}{r} 343 \\ 62 \\ + 409 \\ \hline 700 \end{array}$$

Step 2

Adjust the estimate.

$$\left.\begin{array}{r} 343 \\ 62 \end{array}\right\} \quad \textit{Think: } 43 \text{ and } 62 \text{ is about } 100.$$
$$\begin{array}{r} + 409 \\ \hline 700 + 100 = 800 \end{array}$$

TRY OUT Write the letter of the correct answer.
Estimate. Use the front digits and adjust.

2. 618 + 284   **a.** 400   **b.** 800   **c.** 900   **d.** 1,000

3. $8.65 + $6.55   **a.** $2.00   **b.** $14.00   **c.** $15.00   **d.** $16.00

PRACTICE

Estimate. Use only the front digits.

4. 369
+ 936

5. 4,986
+ 6,559

6. 54
2
+ 81

7. $2.85
6.81
+ .35

8. 7,559
1,750
+ 2,735

9. $49.74 + $99.37   **10.** 6,873 + 220   **11.** $2.64 + $20.66 + $15.99

Estimate. Use the front digits and adjust.

12. 392
+ 317

13. $2.39
+ 7.75

14. $.42
.48
+ .70

15. 4,330
4,489
+ 301

16. 4,923
104
+ 9,015

17. $41.88 + $28.93   **18.** 74 + 99 + 17   **19.** $1.45 + $34.23 + $55.50

Write the letter of the best estimate.

20. $4.48   **a.** less than $12.00
5.29   **b.** greater than $12.00
+ 3.43

21.   8,374   **a.** less than 15,000
820   **b.** greater than 16,000
+ 7,011

Critical Thinking   Write *always, sometimes,* or *never* to complete the sentence.

22. A front-end estimate that is not adjusted is _____ less than the exact sum.

23. A front-end estimate that is adjusted is _____ greater than the exact sum.

Mixed Applications   You may need to use the table on page 94.

24. Pizza Palace sold 1,200 pizzas in May, 889 in June, and 2,076 in July. It had 3,000 pizza boxes. Did it have enough boxes for all the pizzas it sold?

25. Kathy and her brother Joe buy a small deluxe pizza. They have a ten-dollar bill and a five-dollar bill. How much change should they get?

26. *Write a problem* about buying a pizza. Solve it. Trade problems with other students and solve them.

PROBLEM SOLVING

✓ UNDERSTAND
✓ PLAN
✓ TRY
✓ CHECK
✓ EXTEND

Checking for a Reasonable Answer

Lena Sanchez belongs to a theater group called *Teatro Chicano* (tay-AH-tro chi-CAH-no). She also teaches a one-day theater class. On Saturday, 99 students took her class. On Sunday, Lena had 84 students. How many students took the class?

Lena estimates by rounding.

$$
\begin{array}{rcr}
99 & \to & 100 \\
+\,84 & \to & +\,80 \\
\hline
 & & 180
\end{array}
$$

Then she uses a calculator to find the sum.

Lena compares her answer of 111 with the estimated answer of 180. She sees that they are not close. She realizes that she must have hit a wrong key because her answer is not reasonable.

She again uses the calculator to find the sum.

$$9 \quad 9 \quad + \quad 8 \quad 4 \quad = \quad \boxed{183.}$$

1. Is her new answer reasonable? Why?

2. How can you use estimation to tell if an answer is reasonable?

3. Can an estimate check that the answer is correct? Why or why not?

4. How can you check that your answer is correct?

5. How many students took Lena's course?

PRACTICE

Use estimation to decide which answer is reasonable.
Write the letter of the correct answer.

6. Luis buys a mask for $1.21 and a cap for $1.53 to use as a costume. What is the total cost of the costume?
a. $.32 **b.** $1.73 **c.** $2.74

7. During lunch break Latroy buys orange juice for $.73 and a burrito for $1.29. How much does she spend?
a. $2.02 **b.** $1.41 **c.** $1.14

8. Lena looks for used books to use as props in a play. She finds one book for $.92 and another book for $.76. How much would she spend for both books?
a. $1.04 **b.** $1.68 **c.** $2.39

9. In February *Teatro Chicano* performed for a total of 794 people. In March the group performed for a total of 425 people. For how many people did the group perform?
a. 819 **b.** 1,048 **c.** 1,219

Strategies and Skills Review

Solve. Use mental math or paper and pencil.

10. During one school year, Lena used over 200 songs in her course. She used 107 folk songs and 85 songs by Mexican American composers. Are these the only songs she used? How do you know?

11. At the theater, green paint is on a shelf above red paint. Yellow paint is on a shelf below white paint. Red paint is on a shelf between yellow paint and white paint. Yellow paint is between blue paint and red paint. Which is on the lowest shelf?

12. Anna has $6.25. She wants to buy 3 tickets to a play. What else does Anna need to know to decide whether she has enough money?

13. *Write a problem* that uses addition. Ask others to solve it. Then check that the answer is reasonable.

Adding Whole Numbers

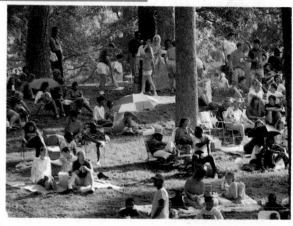

Last year 267 people went to the Wesley Picnic. This year there were 155 more people. How many people went to the picnic this year?

Add: 267 + 155

Estimate first.

Step 1	Step 2	Step 3
Add the ones. Regroup if necessary.	**Add the tens. Regroup if necessary.**	**Add the hundreds. Regroup if necessary.**
$\begin{array}{r} {\scriptstyle 1} \\ 267 \\ +\ 155 \\ \hline 2 \end{array}$	$\begin{array}{r} {\scriptstyle 1\ 1} \\ 267 \\ +\ 155 \\ \hline 22 \end{array}$	$\begin{array}{r} {\scriptstyle 1\ 1} \\ 267 \\ +\ 155 \\ \hline 422 \end{array}$

Think: 12 ones = 1 ten 2 ones   ***Think:*** 12 tens = 1 hundred 2 tens

Check: 155 + 267 = 422

This year 422 people went to the Wesley Picnic.

1. Is this sum reasonable? How do you know?
2. Why can you check addition by changing the order of the addends?

You add money amounts the same way you add whole numbers.

$\begin{array}{r} {\scriptstyle 1\ 1} \\ \$25.73 \\ +\quad 9.75 \\ \hline \$35.48 \end{array}$ ***Think:*** Write the dollar sign and the decimal point in the answer.

3. 456 + 385   **a.** 731   **b.** 741   **c.** 841   **d.** 851

4. 3,079 + 960   **a.** 4,049   **b.** 4,039   **c.** 3,939   **d.** 3,039

5. $5.64 + $.29   **a.** $7.54   **b.** $5.83   **c.** $8.54   **d.** $5.93

6. $4.56 + $9.25   **a.** $137.11   **b.** $13.71   **c.** $14.71   **d.** $13.81

PRACTICE

Add. Solve only for sums that are greater than 900 or $9.00.

7.	492	8.	439	9.	968	10.	5,268	11.	653
	+ 465		+ 346		+ 42		+ 85		+ 234

12.	772	13.	1,058	14.	7,586	15.	9,931	16.	5,486
	+ 644		+ 934		+ 851		+ 68		+ 2,497

17.	$4.79	18.	$8.28	19.	$5.00	20.	$72.96	21.	$89.55
	+ 4.42		+ 3.14		+ 3.50		+ 20.22		+ 40.05

22. 4,656 + 315   23. $6.84 + $.97   24. $40.89 + $40.07

25. $8.55 + $48.25   26. 389 + 951   27. $19.25 + $84.75

Critical Thinking

This is how Ruth added 423 and 214 mentally.

423	4 hundreds		423	2 tens		423	3 ones
+ 214	+ 2 hundreds		+ 214	+ 1 ten		+ 214	+ 4 ones
6	6 hundreds		63	3 tens		637	7 ones

28. How did Ruth add? Why was it easy to add this way mentally?

Mixed Applications

29. At the picnic, 123 tacos and 68 tamales are made. How many tacos and tamales are made?

30. Rudy spends $4.05 on food and $1.25 on drink. Does he spend more than $5.00?

Column Addition

Day	Pies Sold
Monday	35
Wednesday	29
Friday	45
Saturday	78

A. Sarah kept a record of the number of pies she sold in four days. How many pies did she sell in the four days?

Add: 35 + 29 + 45 + 78

Step 1

Add the ones.
Regroup if necessary.

```
  2
  35   Think: 27 ones =
  29          2 tens 7 ones
  45
+ 78
   7
```

Step 2

Add the tens.
Regroup if necessary.

```
  2
  35   Think: 18 tens =
  29          1 hundred 8 tens
  45
+ 78
 187
```

Sarah sold 187 apple pies in the four days.

1. How can you be sure this answer is reasonable?

2. How can you check the addition?

3. What is the sum of $16.75, $23.86, and $6.52?

B. You can use mental math to help you find sums quickly.

```
 1
 26
 32  10
+ 14
 72
```
Think: Make a ten.

```
 1
 24
 35   8
 14
+ 25  10
 98
```
Think: Use doubles.

TRY OUT   Write the letter of the correct answer.

4. 35 + 12 + 8 + 72   **a.** 117   **b.** 127   **c.** 137   **d.** 199

5. 309 + 90 + 454   **a.** 754   **b.** 843   **c.** 853   **d.** 1,744

6. $5.00 + $.98 + $6.79   **a.** $11.78   **b.** $12.77   **c.** $12.78   **d.** $109.70

7. $129 + $76 + $32 + $46   **a.** $273   **b.** $283   **c.** $284   **d.** $1,669

PRACTICE

Add.

8. 59 26 + 15	9. 88 75 + 16	10. 110 65 + 15	11. $2.08 6.24 + .89	12. $2.25 1.35 + 6.62

13. 89 58 17 + 52	14. 68 41 16 + 23	15. $.25 .36 .75 + .57	16. $2.03 6.95 1.55 + .93	17. 658 247 103 + 32

18. 62 + 99 + 127   **19.** $1.55 + $4.38 + $.80   **20.** 55 + 83 + 227

21. 98 + 140 + 663 + 99   **22.** $5.27 + $2.06 + $1.16 + $.21

Critical Thinking
23. What is the greatest sum you can get when you add three 2-digit numbers?

Mixed Applications
24. Juan buys two rolls for $.62, two cupcakes for $.70, and a loaf of bread for $1.35. How much does he spend?

25. David buys 16 cherry tarts and 7 peach tarts. How many fewer peach tarts than cherry tarts does David buy?

26. Last month Sarah made 462 apple pies, 325 cherry pies, 135 peach pies, and 415 banana cream pies. How many pies did she make in all?

27. Sarah used 4,788 bags of flour last year to bake pies. To the nearest hundred, how many bags did she use?

Mixed Review

Add or subtract.

28. 6 + 5	29. 9 + 3	30. 7 − 5	31. 8 + 2	32. 16 − 9	33. 9 + 5

34. 12 − 9   **35.** 7 + 8   **36.** 12 − 5   **37.** 11 − 7   **38.** 8 + 8

RINGS AROUND THINGS

Logical Reasoning

A. You can use circle pictures to sort different groups.

1. The outside rectangle is labeled with the name of the largest group. What is its name? What other groups are included in the largest group?

Things That Write

Pencils

Pens

Felt-Tip Pens

2. A circle within a circle means that a group is entirely a part of another group. Which group includes one other group?

3. If two circles overlap like the circles to the right, it means they share some members. Why don't the Pencils and Pens circles overlap?

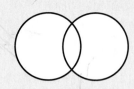

Copy the circle pictures. Write each label where you think it belongs.

4. Living Things
Flowers
Tulips
Trees

5. Zebras
Black and
White Animals
Pandas
Animals

6. Foods
Vegetables
Dairy Products
Desserts

7. Television
Programs
Comedies
News
Programs
Half-hour Shows

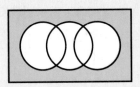

B. Now try to draw some circle pictures of your own. Here are some group lists to use.

8. Books
Mysteries
Biographies

9. Musical
Instruments
Violins
Stringed
Instruments
Drums

10. Money
Dimes
Coins
Dollar Bills

11. Vehicles
Automobiles
Station
Wagons
Red Vehicles

12. Create some group lists of your own. Ask a partner to draw the circle pictures.

Mental Math: Subtract 10s; 100s; 1,000s

A. The Golden Dragon Chinese Restaurant usually keeps a stock of 50 boxes of chopsticks. The owner, Mr. Wong, notices that they have only 20 boxes of chopsticks. How many boxes of chopsticks should he order?

Subtract: 50 − 20
You can use basic facts to find the difference mentally.

$$\begin{array}{r} 50 \\ -\ 20 \\ \hline \end{array}$$ ***Think:*** $\begin{array}{r} 5 \\ -\ 2 \\ \hline 3 \end{array}$ $\begin{array}{r} 5 \text{ tens} \\ -\ 2 \text{ tens} \\ \hline 3 \text{ tens} = 30 \end{array}$

50 − 20 = 30

Mr. Wong should order 30 boxes of chopsticks.

1. Use basic facts to find 1,200 − 700.

B. You can adjust some numbers so you can subtract mentally.

Subtract: 48 − 19
Look to make the number that is subtracted end in zero.

$$\begin{array}{r} 48 \\ -\ 19 \\ \hline \end{array} \longrightarrow \begin{array}{r} 49 \\ -\ 20 \\ \hline 29 \end{array}$$ ***Think:*** I can add 1 to both numbers without changing the difference.

So 48 − 19 = 49 − 20 = 29.

2. Use this method to find 356 − 299.

3. How can you find 71 − 38 using this method? What is the difference?

TRY OUT   Subtract. Use mental math.

4. 8,000 − 5,000   **5.** 1,500 − 600   **6.** 388 − 129   **7.** 67 − 38

PRACTICE

Subtract. Use mental math.

8.	80 − 30	9.	900 − 700	10.	1,100 − 600	11.	1,600 − 800	12.	7,000 − 2,000

13.	60 − 10	14.	800 − 300	15.	140 − 70	16.	1,700 − 800	17.	1,300 − 900

18.	68 − 29	19.	45 − 19	20.	82 − 38	21.	60 − 48	22.	100 − 79

23.	566 − 299	24.	652 − 439	25.	781 − 198	26.	494 − 128	27.	83 − 37

28. 90 − 40   29. 57 − 39   30. 150 − 60   31. 555 − 298

32. 6,000 − 3,000   33. 1,800 − 900   34. 900 − 199   35. 7,435 − 3,998

Mixed Applications

36. Mrs. Wong bought 1,300 containers to pack take-out orders. Last week she used 500 of the containers. How many containers are left?

37. The restaurant gives out 199 fortune cookies at lunch. They are left with 635 fortune cookies. How many fortune cookies did they have to start with?

38. Mr. Wong has 57 bottles of soy sauce and 38 bottles of duck sauce. How many more bottles of soy sauce than duck sauce does he have?

39. *Write a problem* about the Golden Dragon Chinese Restaurant. Solve it. Then ask others to solve your problem.

Mixed Review

Compare. Write >, <, or =.

40. 0 + 8 ● 8 − 0   **41.** $345.54 ● $345.45   **42.** $13.27 ● $6 + $3 + $4

43. 55 − 19 ● 46   **44.** 12 − 6 ● 3 + 4   **45.** 616 ● 589 + 27

46. 30 + 40 ● 10 + 20 + 30   **47.** 289 rounded to the nearest ten ● 300

Estimating Differences

A. The school lunchroom served 6,382 people last month. If 845 of them were teachers, about how many were students?

You can round to estimate the answer.

Estimate: 6,382 − 845

Step 1

Round to the greatest place of the greater number.

$$6,382 \longrightarrow 6,000$$
$$-\ \ \ 845 \longrightarrow -1,000$$

Think: Round to the nearest thousand.

Step 2

Subtract the rounded numbers.

$$6,000$$
$$-1,000$$
$$\overline{5,000}$$

About 5,000 students were served at the school lunchroom.

B. You can also use front-end estimation to estimate differences.

Estimate: 7,439 − 3,705

Step 1

Subtract the front digits. Write zeros for the other digits.

$$7,439$$
$$-3,705$$
$$\overline{4,000}$$

Step 2

Adjust the estimate.

$$7,439$$
$$-3,705$$
less than 4,000

Think: 4 < 7
The exact answer is less than 4,000.

1. Estimate 8,796 − 459. Will the exact answer be greater than or less than 8,000? How do you know?

TRY OUT

2. Estimate 5,894 − 3,226 by rounding.

3. Estimate 604 − 97 by using the front digits and adjusting.

PRACTICE

Estimate by rounding.

4. 874
    − 396

5. 2,397
    − 1,049

6. $3.50
    − 1.26

7. 8,100
    − 5,724

8. $39.75
    − 23.99

9. 509
    − 81

10. 8,622
    − 755

11. $4.28
    − .49

12. 3,027
    − 804

13. $14.14
    − 3.93

14. 9,630 − 3,389

15. $81.93 − $1.99

16. 7,500 − 629

Estimate. Use the front digits and adjust.

17. 863
    − 425

18. $8.37
    − 3.62

19. 3,906
    − 1,057

20. $91.35
    − 19.88

21. 9,655
    − 7,726

22. $7.35
    − .75

23. 989
    − 44

24. 1,370
    − 785

25. $93.75
    − 9.06

26. 6,508
    − 3,585

27. 478 − 83

28. $6.61 − $2.54

29. 828 − 423

Choose the letter of the best estimate.

30. 5,468
    − 307
  a. greater than 7,000
  b. greater than 5,000
  c. less than 5,000
  d. less than 3,000

31. $7.86
    − 2.55
  a. greater than $5.00
  b. greater than $6.00
  c. less than $4.00
  d. less than $5.00

Mixed Applications Solve. Which method did you use?

| ESTIMATION |
| MENTAL MATH |
| PAPER/PENCIL |

32. In one week the lunchroom served 436 boxes of raisins with lunch. They had 194 boxes left. How many boxes of raisins did they have to start with?

33. Tony has $4.47 to spend on lunch. He spends $3.65 on a hot turkey sandwich and some juice. He needs at least $1.19 to buy a piece of pie as well. Does he have enough money?

34. About 800 students ate in the lunchroom last week. About 500 students brought their lunch. About how many more students ate in the lunchroom than brought their lunch?

Subtracting Whole Numbers

The Yorktown Fair is becoming more popular each year. How many more tickets did the fair sell in 1991 than in 1989?

Estimate. Then subtract to find the answer.

Subtract: 324 − 145

TICKETS SOLD FOR THE YORKTOWN FAIR	
Year	Number Sold
1989	145
1990	263
1991	324

Step 1	Step 2	Step 3
Regroup if necessary. Subtract the ones.	**Regroup if necessary. Subtract the tens.**	**Subtract the hundreds.**
$\begin{array}{r} \overset{\scriptscriptstyle 1\ 14}{3\,2\,4} \\ -\,1\,4\,5 \\ \hline 9 \end{array}$	$\begin{array}{r} \overset{\scriptscriptstyle 2\ 1\ 14}{3\,2\,4} \\ -\,1\,4\,5 \\ \hline 7\,9 \end{array}$	$\begin{array}{r} \overset{\scriptscriptstyle 2\ 1\ 14}{3\,2\,4} \\ -\,1\,4\,5 \\ \hline 1\,7\,9 \end{array}$

Think: 2 tens 4 ones = 1 ten 14 ones   **Think:** 3 hundreds 1 ten = 2 hundreds 11 tens

Check: 179 + 145 = 324

In 1991 the fair sold 179 more tickets than it sold in 1989.

1. Is 179 a reasonable answer? How do you know?
2. Why can you check subtraction by adding?
3. How would you subtract $29.36 from $75.43?

TRY OUT   Write the letter of the correct answer.

4. 23 − 17   **a.** 6   **b.** 16   **c.** 30   **d.** 50

5. 567 − 278   **a.** 389   **b.** 299   **c.** 289   **d.** 399

6. $5.15 − $3.25   **a.** $2.30   **b.** $1.90   **c.** $2.90   **d.** $8.90

7. $71.36 − $6.87   **a.** $75.49   **b.** $65.59   **c.** $75.23   **d.** $64.49

PRACTICE

Subtract.

8.   68
     − 22

9.   81
     − 55

10.   216
      − 94

11.   367
      − 108

12. $9.25
      − 6.50

13. $10.95
      − 7.88

14.   760
      − 92

15.   1,185
      − 815

16.   614
      − 195

17.   2,274
      − 875

18. $25.35
      − 9.98

19. $35.50
      − 14.68

20.   3,374
      − 2,998

21. $7.81
      − 6.98

22.   4,522
      − 3,867

23. $.74 − $.25

24. 109 − 86

25. $8.65 − $.70

26. 1,048 − 930

27. $3.25 − $1.85

28. 3,746 − 707

29. 217 − 48

30. 734 − 559

31. $23.44 − $19.37

Mixed Applications

Solve. You may need to use the Databank on page 518.

32. The Plum Tree Café has a food stand at the fair. How much would it cost to buy a broiled fish dinner and some milk?

33. Bobby has $8.50. He buys a chicken salad sandwich from the Plum Tree Café. How much money does he have left?

34. Tina goes on the roller coaster 4 times, the Hurricane 3 times, the Ferris wheel 5 times, and the Whip 4 times. How many times does she ride in all?

35. Letitia brought 473 balloons to the fair. At the end of the fair, she had 196 balloons left. How many balloons did Letitia sell?

Mixed Review

Add or subtract. Which method did you choose?

MENTAL MATH PAPER/PENCIL

36. $3.65
      + 2.96

37.   220
      + 330

38.   364
      − 198

39. $47.58
      + 49.62

40. 850 − 300

41. $7.34 − $3.75

42. 79 + 62

Subtracting Across Zeros

There are 300 restaurants in Newton. Don Figg, the food critic, has eaten in 158 of them. In how many restaurants has he not eaten?

Subtract: 300 − 158

Step 1	Step 2	Step 3
Subtract the ones. **No tens.** **Regroup the hundreds.** $\overset{2\ 10}{\cancel{3}0\ 0}$ $-1\ 5\ 8$	**Regroup the tens.** $\overset{\ \ \ 9}{\overset{2\ 10\ 10}{\cancel{3}\cancel{0}\ 0}}$ $-1\ 5\ 8$	**Subtract.** $\overset{\ \ \ 9}{\overset{2\ 10\ 10}{\cancel{3}\cancel{0}\ \cancel{0}}}$ $-1\ 5\ 8$ $\overline{\ \ 1\ 4\ 2}$

Think: 3 hundreds 0 tens = 2 hundreds 10 tens   *Think:* 10 tens 0 ones = 9 tens 10 ones

So Don Figg has not eaten in 142 of the restaurants in Newton.

1. Is 142 a reasonable answer? How do you know?

2. How can you check your subtraction?

3. Subtract $9.00 − $3.47. What is the difference?

TRY OUT   Write the letter of the correct answer.

4. 306 − 129   **a.** 177   **b.** 187   **c.** 277   **d.** 435

5. 5,000 − 138   **a.** 4,862   **b.** 4,972   **c.** 3,862   **d.** 4,762

6. $7.00 − $.73   **a.** $5.36   **b.** $5.37   **c.** $6.37   **d.** $6.27

7. $9.00 − $6.04   **a.** $2.94   **b.** $2.95   **c.** $2.96   **d.** $3.06

PRACTICE

Subtract.

8. 400 $-\ 109$	**9.** 605 $-\ 586$	**10.** 200 $-\ 68$	**11.** 3,008 $-\ 2,779$	**12.** 8,000 $-\ 673$	

13. 6,200 $-\ 435$	**14.** $5.00 $-\ 2.89$	**15.** $1.00 $-\ .71$	**16.** $9.06 $-\ 7.38$	**17.** $60.05 $-\ 4.08$

18. 2,000 − 84   **19.** $10.00 − $.42   **20.** $90.00 − $71.06

21. $7.05 − $6.09   **22.** $25.05 − $17.99   **23.** 1,040 − 992

Mixed Applications

Solve. You may need to use the Databank on page 518.

24. Don Figg catches 263 clams for the Newton clambake. His friend Megan catches 400 clams. How many more clams does Megan catch than Don?

25. Stan has $7.00. He wants to buy a tuna salad sandwich, a lettuce and tomato salad, french fries, and a lemonade. Does he have enough money?

26. Carla has $6.00. If she buys a shrimp salad sandwich, how much money will she have left?

27. *Write a problem* about subtraction that uses the menu in the Databank.

MENTAL MATH

You can mentally subtract 600 − 438.

$$\begin{array}{ll} \mathbf{600} & \xrightarrow{-1} & \mathbf{599} \\ \mathbf{-438} & \xrightarrow{-1} & \mathbf{-437} \\ \hline & & \mathbf{162} \end{array}$$

Think:
If I subtract 1 from both numbers, the difference remains the same.

So 600 − 438 = 162.

Subtract mentally.

1. 700 $-\ 295$	**2.** 400 $-\ 260$	**3.** 80 $-\ 57$	**4.** 1,000 $-\ 496$	**5.** 3,000 $-\ 1,083$

Add and Subtract Larger Numbers

The table lists how many meals the Food Court in the mall sold each month. How many meals did the Food Court sell all together?

Month	Number of Meals
April	34,569
May	22,316
June	27,482

WORKING TOGETHER

You can use mental math, paper and pencil, or a calculator to find the answer. Work in a group. Have each person use a different method to solve the problem.

1. Can you easily find the total using mental math? Why or why not?

2. Tell how you can use paper and pencil to find the sum. What is the sum?

3. How can you be sure your sum is reasonable?

4. Which method was fastest in finding the sum?

5. **What if** the numbers had been rounded to 30,000; 20,000; and 30,000? Which method would be fastest?

How many more meals did the Food Court sell in April than in May? Solve the problem using all three methods.

6. Can you find the difference mentally? Why or why not?

7. Tell how you can use paper and pencil to find the difference. What is the difference?

8. Which method was fastest? Why?

Add or subtract. Which method did you use?

9. 40,000
  + 20,000

10. 4,037
  − 3,859

11. $53.41
  + 78.69

12. 75,000
  − 4,935

13. 3,226
  4,504
  + 321

14. 34 + 46 + 58 + 79   15. 27,689 − 16,327   16. $79.70 − $59.99

SHARING IDEAS

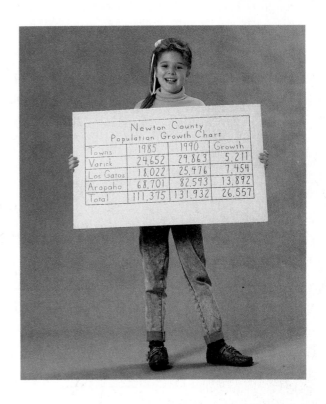

17. How is adding or subtracting 5-digit numbers like adding or subtracting smaller numbers? How is it different?

18. How did you decide which method to use to find the answers for Exercises 9–16?

19. When do you think it is easier to use mental math? paper and pencil? a calculator? Why?

20. Can you always be sure your answer is correct when you use a calculator? Why or why not?

ON YOUR OWN

Solve. Which method did you use?

MENTAL/MATH
CALCULATOR
PAPER/PENCIL

21. Last month the Food Court sold 36,765 soft drinks and 13,689 milk shakes. To the nearest ten thousand, how many drinks did the Food Court sell?

22. The Art Club spends $437.27 on lunch. The Music Club spends $673.13. How much more does the Music Club spend?

23. **Write a problem** that involves addition or subtraction of large numbers. Choose which method you think should be used to solve it. Trade your problem with other students and compare methods.

PROBLEM SOLVING

Strategy: Choosing the Operation

A. Hiko has 1 serving of cereal and 1 serving of orange juice for breakfast. How many calories are in his breakfast?

CALORIES PER SERVING				
Boiled egg 75	Oatmeal 65	Slice of toast 80	Cereal 140	Orange juice 100

1. What information does Hiko need?

To solve the problem he needs to decide which *operation* to use.

2. Hiko is *combining* groups of calories. Which operation should he use?

$$140 + 100 = \blacksquare$$

3. How many calories are in his breakfast?

B. Hiko wants to burn 400 calories by exercising. After riding his bicycle for 1 hour, how many more calories does he need to burn?

CALORIES BURNED PER HOUR (for a 75-pound person)			
Tennis 200	Bicycle riding 255	Bowling 150	Swimming 335

To solve the problem, he needs to *separate* the 400 calories into two parts.

4. Which operation should he use?

$$400 - 255 = \blacksquare$$

5. How many more calories does he need to burn?

6. How many calories would he burn if he rode his bicycle for 1 hour and swam for 1 hour?

7. Which operation should you use when you combine two groups?

8. Which operation should you use when you separate two groups?

PRACTICE

Decide which operation to use. Then solve the problem.

9. Mrs. Ho weighed 147 pounds before she went on a diet. She lost 19 pounds in six months. How much did she weigh then?

10. Paul took in 695 calories for breakfast and 585 calories for lunch. How many calories was that for both meals?

11. A medium-size peach has 35 calories. A medium-size pear has 100 calories. How many more calories does the pear have than the peach?

12. A serving of raisin cereal has 50 more calories than the 140 calories in a serving of regular cereal. How many calories are in a serving of raisin cereal?

Strategies and Skills Review

Solve. You may need to use the Databank on page 518.

13. The normal heart rate for a fourth grader is about 85 heartbeats a minute. For adults, it is about 72 heartbeats a minute. How many more times does the heart of a fourth grader beat in a minute than the heart of an adult?

14. The recommended daily intake of vitamin A for a fourth grader is 700 units. Phil has a fried egg and a glass of milk. He says he has met the vitamin A requirement for the day. Is he right? How do you know?

15. Lynn had a hamburger and a glass of milk for lunch. Then she exercised for an hour and burned 300 calories. Did she burn all the calories she took in for lunch? How do you know?

16. The average weight of a 9-year-old girl is 62 pounds. At age 14 her average weight is 107 pounds. How much greater is her average weight at age 14 than at age 9?

17. Maya notices that there is a scale between every two rowing machines at the gym. There are 4 rowing machines. How many scales are there?

18. **Write a problem** that can be solved by addition or by subtraction. Solve the problem. Then ask others to solve it.

ACTIVITY
Finding Perimeter

You can use what you know about measuring length to find the distance around objects.

The distance around an object is its **perimeter**.

WORKING TOGETHER

1. Estimate the perimeter of your desk.

2. Use a centimeter ruler to measure the distance around your desk to the nearest centimeter.

3. Record your estimate and actual measure in a chart like this.

Object	Estimate	Perimeter
desk		

4. Estimate and then measure the perimeter of other objects in your classroom. Record your findings in your chart.

5. Compare your chart with those of others.

6. What other metric units of measure could you use to measure the perimeter of objects?

You can use addition to find the perimeter of objects.

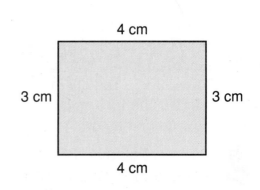

The perimeter of this rectangle is 3 cm + 3 cm + 4 cm + 4 cm, or 14 cm.

7. What is the perimeter of a triangle with sides 5 m, 8 m, and 10 m?

8. What is the perimeter of a square with sides 4 cm?

9. How would you measure the perimeter of your home? Compare your methods with those of others.

10. What is the least number of sides you can measure to find the perimeter of a rectangle? of a square? How do you know?

11. What must you do before you can find the perimeter of this triangle? Why?

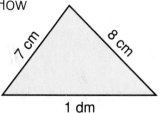

PRACTICE

Find the perimeter.

12.

6 m

6 m · 6 m

6 m

13.

5 cm

4 cm

6 cm

14.

5 m

1 m · 1 m

5 m

15.

15 cm

8 cm · 8 cm

15 cm

16.

4 m

4 m · 4 m

4 m · 4 m

4 m

17.

12 m

12 m · 12 m

12 m

18.

3 m · 3 m

3 m

19.

8 m

2 m · 4 m

8 m

20.

2 cm
2 cm

4 cm

2 cm

3 cm

Critical Thinking

21. The perimeter of this rectangle is 20 m. What is the length of the rectangle? How do you know?

?

4 m · 4 m

?

Mixed Applications

22. A rectangle has a width of 22 m and a length of 7 m. What is the difference between its width and length?

23. Tanya runs around a square field that is 100 m on each side. How far does Tanya run?

Problem Solving: Planning a Lunch

SITUATION

Emmanuel, Monica, Vincent, and Michele are planning to have lunch in the park on Saturday. They are going to meet at Jim's Deli and buy their lunch to take to the park.

PROBLEM

Should they buy sandwiches or buy the things they need to make their own sandwiches?

DATA

1 loaf of bread – 12 sandwiches
1 pound of cold cuts – 8-10 sandwiches
1 pound of cheese – 12 sandwich-size slices
half pint – 1 drink
half gallon – 8 drinks

JIM'S DELI

Cold Cuts
Sold in half and whole pounds only

	Half Pound	One Pound
Turkey	$2.50	$5.00
Roast Beef	4.00	8.00
Cheddar Cheese	2.00	4.00

Sandwiches

Turkey	$3.00
Roast Beef	3.50
Cheddar Cheese	2.00
Lettuce + Tomato	50¢ EXTRA
On a roll	50¢ EXTRA

...ped ...heese
...9¢

Lettuce
75¢
a head

Tomatoes
35¢
each

Sandwich Roll
40¢ each

Whole Wheat Bread
$1.40 a loaf

Milk:
half-gallon **$1.50**
half-pint **$ .50**

Juice:
half-gallon **$1.40**
half-pint **$ .40**

USING THE DATA

How much will 4 of the following sandwiches cost?

1. roast beef

2. roast beef on a roll

3. roast beef on a roll, lettuce and tomato

4. cheddar cheese

5. cheddar cheese on a roll

6. turkey with lettuce and tomato

How much of each must they buy to make 4 sandwiches?

7. rolls

8. lettuce

9. roast beef

10. tomatoes

11. whole wheat bread

12. cheddar cheese

Find the total cost to make these sandwiches.

13. 4 cheddar cheese on whole wheat with lettuce and tomato

14. 4 roast beef on a roll

MAKING DECISIONS

15. The children all want the same sandwich. Will it cost more to make or to buy the 4 sandwiches? Tell how you made your choice.

16. *What if* only one child wants lettuce and tomato and three want sandwich rolls? Is it cheaper to make or buy 4 cheese sandwiches?

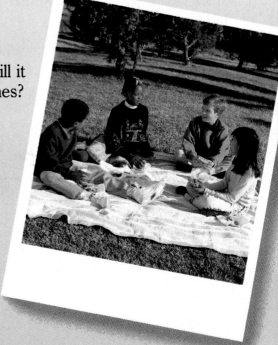

17. What other things will the children need to bring if they want to make sandwiches in the park?

18. Would you buy or make sandwiches for a lunch in the park? Tell how you made your choice.

19. The children must also decide what to drink with their lunches. Should they buy a half gallon or half-pint containers? Why might they not want to buy a half-gallon container?

20. *Write a list* of the things you would buy for a picnic if you had $15.00 to spend.

Math and Social Studies

People from many different cultures have built pyramids as monuments or temples. One of the most famous pyramids still standing is the Great Pyramid of Khufu in Giza, Egypt. This monument to the pharaoh, or ruler, Khufu, was built from 2,300,000 blocks of stone. When it was built, it was 146 meters tall. Each of its four sides is 230 meters long.

What is the perimeter of the Great Pyramid?

Think: Perimeter is the distance around an object. Each of the four sides of the pyramid is 230 meters long.

$$230 + 230 + 230 + 230 = 920$$

The perimeter of the Great Pyramid is 920 meters.

ACTIVITIES

1. The Pyramid of Quetzalcoatl in Cholula, Mexico, stands 64 meters tall, and each of its four sides is 350 meters long. What is its perimeter? How does its perimeter compare to the Great Pyramid's perimeter? Find out why it was built.

2. Find out about other pyramids. Who built them and why? What were they built of? When and where were they built? Have any pyramids been built recently?

Computer: Perimeter

In the figure at the right, the lengths of sides A through F are shown. Notice that the length of side E is 60 units. This is equal to the sum of the lengths of sides A and C. The length of side F is 80 units. This is equal to the sum of the lengths of sides B and D.

A = 30 units B = 40 units
C = 30 units D = 40 units
E = 60 units F = 80 units

You can use this relationship to explore perimeter.

AT THE COMPUTER

The program to the right draws six-sided figures like the one above and gives their perimeter. The letters in the program match the labels on the figure. Enter the program.

```
TO PERIMETER :A :B :C :D :E :F
RT 90 FD :A RT 90 FD :B LT 90
FD :C RT 90 FD :D RT 90
FD :E RT 90 FD :F
PR [DISTANCE TRAVELED = ]
PR :A + :B + :C + :D + :E + :F
END
```

Clear the screen after completing each problem below.

1. To draw the figure above, enter the name of the program and the length of each side: PERIMETER 30 40 30 40 60 80. Which side of the figure is drawn first? Which side of the figure is drawn last? What is the perimeter of the figure?

2. Now enter PERIMETER 20 40 20 20 40 0. To close the figure, use a forward (FD) command to draw side F. What is the length of side F?

3. How can you complete this command to draw a closed figure: PERIMETER 40 10 20 30 __ __? How do you know? Check by entering the completed command.

4. Draw a closed figure with a perimeter of 260. Then draw a different figure with the same perimeter. What did you enter?

5. Work with a partner. Challenge each other to draw figures with different perimeters.

EXTRA PRACTICE

Mental Math: Adding 10s; 100s; 1,000s, page 91...................................

Add. Use mental math.

1.	30 + 50	2.	100 + 400	3.	40 30 + 60	4.	900 10 + 70	5.	500 500 + 300
6.	79 + 201	7.	399 + 43	8.	162 + 699	9.	888 + 309	10.	452 + 507

11. 20 + 10 + 50   12. 300 + 600   13. 39 + 17   14. 398 + 143

Estimating Sums by Rounding, page 93.......................................

Estimate by rounding.

1.	335 + 480	2.	809 + 175	3.	4,375 + 2,870	4.	$4.55 + 2.17	5.	$52.65 + 21.17
6.	130 209 + 150	7.	3,090 2,010 + 2,200	8.	$3.52 5.10 + 1.17	9.	2,070 4,500 + 125	10.	$24.89 9.12 + 49.87

11. 319 + 10 + 410   12. 299 + 499 + 399   13. 2,400 + 1,470 + 620

Front-End Estimation, page 95.......................................

Estimate. Use only the front digits.

1.	478 + 218	2.	3,987 + 7,109	3.	34 3 + 79	4.	$2.39 7.71 + .25	5.	6,452 1,817 + 2,809

6. $52.73 + $89.15   7. 4,372 + 5,872   8. $1.89 + $20.05 + $16.89

Estimate. Use the front digits and adjust.

9.	293 + 117	10.	$2.17 + 8.95	11.	$.35 .27 + .80	12.	3,880 2,189 + 207	13.	3,817 204 + 8,019

Problem Solving: Checking for a Reasonable Answer, page 97 ....

Use estimation to decide which answer is reasonable.

1. Josie spent $3.52 on lunch. Her brother Terry spent $4.65 on lunch. How much did the two spend?

   a. $5.87   **b.** $6.42   **c.** $8.17

2. David buys 156 mL of tomato juice and 245 mL of grape juice. How much juice does David buy?

   a. 401 mL   **b.** 621 mL   **c.** 261 mL

3. The Bagel Bonanza store has sold 653 bagels so far this month. If they sell 761 more bagels this month, how many bagels will they have sold all together?

   a. 714 bagels   **b.** 1,414 bagels   **c.** 13,114 bagels

Adding Whole Numbers, page 99 ....

Add.

1. 387 + 292	**2.** 420 + 204	**3.** $8.58 + .32	**4.** 3,159 + 88	**5.** $4.57 + 2.10
6. 2,069 + 835	**7.** $66.88 + 7.21	**8.** 9,871 + 58	**9.** 3,673 + 2,417	**10.** $95.52 + 46.68

11. $89.52 + $38.50   12. 4,476 + 2,389   13. $129.85 + $74.50

Column Addition, page 101 ....

Add.

1. 63 24 + 39	**2.** $3.12 2.19 + 4.07	**3.** 53 29 18 + 37	**4.** $3.07 2.12 4.10 + .93	**5.** 353 217 104 + 22

6. 39 + 89 + 143   7. $1.57 + $4.19 + $.70   8. 44 + 87 + 212

9. 87 + 130 + 554 + 89   10. $5.19 + $2.17 + $1.14 + $.22

EXTRA PRACTICE

Mental Math: Subtract 10s; 100s; 1,000s, page 105 ....

Subtract. Use mental math.

1. 90
    − 20

2. 800
    − 600

3. 1,200
    − 600

4. 1,300
    − 700

5. 6,000
    − 1,000

6. 57
    − 28

7. 47
    − 19

8. 455
    − 319

9. 387
    − 128

10. 681
     − 227

11. 80 − 30

12. 78 − 19

13. 120 − 40

14. 700 − 299

Estimating Differences, page 107 ....

Estimate by rounding.

1. 763
    − 274

2. 2,175
    − 1,050

3. $4.50
    − 1.12

4. 7,575
    − 895

5. $3.27
    − .39

6. $6.17 − $2.89

7. 8,962 − 4,129

8. 8,500 − 529

Estimate. Use the front digits and adjust.

9. 755
    − 109

10. $7.43
     − 2.65

11. 2,809
     − 1,072

12. $94.12
     − 8.07

13. 6,907
     − 2,873

14. 389 − 25

15. $7.69 − $2.12

16. 812 − 324

Subtracting Whole Numbers, page 109 ....

Subtract.

1. 77
    − 12

2. 89
    − 27

3. $7.12
    − .81

4. 458
    − 109

5. $8.15
    − 4.50

6. $24.09
    − 8.98

7. 3,173
    − 1,899

8. 780
    − 479

9. $38.12
    − 27.85

10. 4,808
     − 725

11. 209 − 89

12. 892 − 375

13. $7.95 − $5.40

Subtracting Across Zeros, page 111 ....

Subtract.

1.	2.	3.	4.	5.
300 − 107	704 − 365	100 − 57	408 − 399	900 − 553

6.	7.	8.	9.	10.
600 − 345	$5.00 − 3.89	$1.00 − .62	$8.07 − 3.28	$4.03 − 2.07

11. 600 − 214   **12.** $8.00 − $6.09   **13.** $2.03 − $.55

Problem Solving: Choosing the Operation, page 115 ....

Decide which operation to use. Then solve the problem.

1. Miles wants to burn 350 calories. He burns 220 calories playing basketball. How many more calories does he have to burn?

2. Daphne had 765 calories at lunch and 809 calories at dinner. How many calories did she have at both meals?

3. A serving of raisin bran has 170 calories. A serving of cornflakes has 140 calories. How many more calories does a serving of raisin bran have?

Finding Perimeter, page 117 ....

Find the perimeter.

1.

7 m, 7 m, 7 m, 7 m

2.
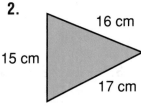
16 cm, 15 cm, 17 cm

3.

7 cm, 3 cm, 3 cm, 7 cm

4.

35 km, 35 km, 35 km

5.

12 m, 9 m, 9 m, 12 m

6.

7 m, 7 m, 7 m, 7 m, 7 m, 7 m

PRACTICE *PLUS*

KEY SKILL: COLUMN ADDITION (Use after page 101.)

Level A

Add.

1.	2.	3.	4.	5.
12	31	$.56	$.16	31
23	28	.22	.62	48
+ 14	+ 10	+ .10	+ .02	+ 11

6. $.43 + $.22 + $.65   7. 29 + 31 + 20   8. 83 + 13 + 87

9. Kasha buys three pastel pencils for $.49, two paintbrushes for $.89, and four tubes of oil paint for $1.51. How much does she spend in all?

Level B

Add.

10.	11.	12.	13.	14.
123	$3.08	198	$3.67	454
49	2.78	12	1.43	577
+ 22	+ .32	+ 310	+ .34	+ 40

15. 88 + 34 + 115   16. 76 + 117 + 483   17. 583 + 297 + 86 + 19

18. Professor Yampa found 179 brontosaurus bones on a dig in Utah last summer. He also found 651 tyrannosaurus bones and 39 stegosaurus bones. How many bones did he find?

Level C

Add.

19.	20.	21.	22.	23.
72	$6.86	529	$13.43	1,625
87	2.38	237	.89	2,209
+ 54	+ 1.77	188	24.63	342
		+ 650	+ 5.06	+ 3,848

24. 435 + 78 + 22 + 169   25. 1,167 + 529 + 4,298 + 331

26. Mary Jo scores 651 points on a video game. Li scores 418 points more than Mary Jo. Alix scores 163 more points than Li. How many points does Alix score?

Practice PLUS

KEY SKILL: SUBTRACTING ACROSS ZEROS (Use after page 111.)

Level A
Subtract.

1. 306
− 89

2. $4.01
− .66

3. 904
− 35

4. 702
− 17

5. $1.02
− .24

6. $8.07
− .49

7. 505
− 326

8. 803
− 565

9. $2.06
− 1.48

10. 603
− 567

11. Terry has 427 calories. Gary has 603 calories. How many more calories does Gary have than Terry?

Level B
Subtract.

12. 600
− 211

13. 700
− 418

14. 302
− 109

15. 908
− 779

16. 407
− 289

17. 3,705 − 289

18. $11.04 − $8.95

19. $24.03 − $5.47

20. Lacrosse sticks are on sale for $45.77. They usually cost $51.01. How much can you save by buying one now?

Level C
Subtract.

21. 2,600
− 1,731

22. $70.02
− 46.38

23. 4,005
− 1,159

24. 8,003
− 6,926

25. $93.08
− 74.49

26. $95.07
− 76.78

27. 7,005
− 4,369

28. 4,702
− 3,884

29. $90.01
− 87.34

30. 7,803
− 3,919

31. One year the Boston Celtics scored 9,004 points and the L.A. Clippers scored 5,906 points. What was the difference in point totals between the two teams?

CHAPTER REVIEW/TEST

LANGUAGE AND MATHEMATICS

Complete the sentences. Use the words in the chart.

1. The distance around an object is its ■.

2. You can ■ numbers to find an estimate.

3. Use ■ to check for reasonableness.

4. ■ is the opposite of subtraction.

CONCEPTS AND SKILLS

Estimate by rounding.

5.	6.	7.	8.
368 + 812	5,298 − 3,712	$7.95 .92 + 2.26	2,675 − 619

Estimate. Use the front digits and adjust.

9.	10.	11.	12.
293 + 314	285 − 107	3,411 3,322 + 201	$8.95 − 4.25

Add or subtract.

13.	14.	15.	16.
800 + 40	700 − 40	$9.03 − 4.09	5,623 − 89

17. 3,599 + 625

18. $3.11 + $5.60 + $.72 + $1.24

Find the perimeter.

19.

9 cm

6 cm / 6 cm

9 cm

20.

12 cm 13 cm

5 cm

21.

3 m

3 m

2 m

7 m

5 m

Critical Thinking

Write *always*, *sometimes*, or *never* to complete the sentence.

22. The sum of two 2-digit numbers is ■ a 4-digit number.

23. A front-end estimate is ■ less than the exact difference.

Mixed Applications

24. Delia bought a pen for $1.24 and a pencil for $.69. What is her total bill? Choose the letter of the most reasonable answer.
a. $4.09 **b.** $1.93 **c.** $19.23

25. Mr. Watt baked 412 muffins in the morning and 228 in the afternoon. How many more muffins did he bake in the morning?

PERFORMANCE ASSESSMENT

Work with your group to solve this problem.

Imagine that your group is going to order a chain-link fence to enclose a rectangular playground. The playground is 87 yards long and 43 yards wide. There will be three openings in the fence. Each opening will be between 2 yards and 9 yards wide. Choose the length of each opening. You will not need to order fencing for these openings. Find the total length of the fence you should order for the playground. Include a sketch or diagram of the playground to illustrate your answer.

1. *Think about:*
- the distance around the outside of the playground
- the length of each opening in the fence

2. Write two statements explaining how you decided on the length of the openings in the fence and how you found the total length of fencing needed.

CUMULATIVE REVIEW

Choose the letter of the correct answer.

1. $5.89 − $3.99

    a. $1.90   **c.** $2.09
    b. $1.99   **d.** not given

2. Estimate by rounding:
892 + 435

    a. 1,100   **c.** 1,300
    b. 1,230   **d.** 1,400

3. What is 17 take away 8?

    a. 7   **c.** 9
    b. 8   **d.** not given

4. $72.91 + $.85

    a. $73.76   **c.** $72.06
    b. $72.76   **d.** not given

5. Choose the number for ten million.

    a. 1,000,000   **c.** 10,000
    b. 10,000,000   **d.** not given

6. 5,300 + 900

    a. 5,200   **c.** 6,200
    b. 5,900   **d.** not given

7. Estimate by rounding:
$7.85 − $2.31

    a. $9.00   **c.** $5.00
    b. $6.00   **d.** $4.00

8. What is 6 and 5 more?

    a. 1   **c.** 16
    b. 11   **d.** not given

9. Estimate the width of a pillow.

    a. 4 cm   **c.** 4 m
    b. 4 dm   **d.** 4 km

10. 72 + 263 + 56

    a. 154   **c.** 381
    b. 291   **d.** not given

11. Compare: 598 ● 589

    a. <   **c.** =
    b. >   **d.** not given

12. 600 − 132

    a. 468   **c.** 532
    b. 458   **d.** not given

13. Round 287 to the nearest ten.

    a. 200   **c.** 290
    b. 280   **d.** 300

14. Find the perimeter of a square with 7-cm sides.

    a. 14 cm   **c.** 28 cm
    b. 21 cm   **d.** not given

PALINDROMES

Reverse the order of the letters in the words in the box.

What do you notice about each word?

Reverse the order of the digits in the numbers in the box.

What do you notice about each number?

Words and numbers that can be read the same in either direction are called **palindromes.**

Is the number 42 a palindrome? Why or why not?

You can use the number 42 to find a palindrome.

```
   42
 + 24  ◄─── Reverse the digits and add.
   66  ◄─── Palindrome
```

1. How would you use the number 36 to find a palindrome?

Tell if the number is a palindrome.
Write *yes* or *no*.

2. 26   **3.** 88   **4.** 414   **5.** 123   **6.** 707

Use the number to find a palindrome.

7. 15   **8.** 63   **9.** 71   **10.** 53   **11.** 13

Use these numbers to find palindromes. You may need to reverse the digits and add more than once.

12. 82   **13.** 76   **14.** 84   **15.** 59   **16.** 164

17. Can you think of more words that are palindromes?

EAST AFRICAN TIME

AFRICA
Kenya
Equator Uganda

You may be surprised to learn that many people in parts of East Africa begin their day at 1:00 each morning. Because the East African countries of Kenya (KEN-yuh) and Uganda (you-GAN-duh) lie directly on the equator, the sun rises and sets at the same time every day of the year. This makes the sun a very dependable time-keeper! In fact, it's so dependable that many East Africans start counting the hours of the day at sunrise, which is 1:00 in East African or "Swahili" time. This is the same as 7:00 A.M. standard time. Standard time is a system that divides the world into 24 different time zones.

To change from Swahili time to standard time, mentally turn the hour hand on the clock forward six hours. The chart can help you understand the

	Breakfast	Lunch	Dinner
Standard Time			
Swahili Time			

People in remote parts of East Africa often associate times of the day with activities. For the Ankole (an-KOH-luh) cattle herders of Uganda, each hour of the day is associated with cattle. The time when cattle drink is 8:00 East African time. The time to herd cattle home is 11:00 East African time. The second milking time occurs as the sun sets at 1:00 East African time.

1. If you lived in East Africa and used East African time, at what hours would you eat breakfast, lunch and dinner?

2. Why do you think people in Kenya and Uganda use East African time as well as standard time?

3. Why do you think the Ankole associate the hours of their day with activities related to cattle?

Estimating Time

Brian studies the exhibit on the history of travel.

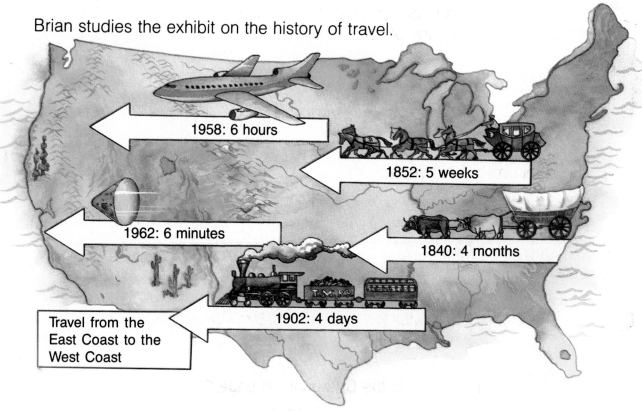

1958: 6 hours

1852: 5 weeks

1962: 6 minutes

1840: 4 months

1902: 4 days

Travel from the East Coast to the West Coast

1. What happened to the amount of time it takes to travel from coast to coast? Why do you think this happened?

This table shows different units used to measure time.

2. Which units measure long periods of time?

3. Which units measure short periods of time?

UNITS OF TIME

60 seconds (s)	= 1 minute (min)
60 minutes	= 1 hour (h)
24 hours	= 1 day (d)
7 days	= 1 week (wk)
12 months (mo)	= 1 year (y)
about 52 weeks	= 1 year
365 days	= 1 year
366 days	= 1 leap year

Choose the best unit of time to measure the activity.

4. sleep at night

5. take a shower

6. count by fives to 100

7. become a doctor

8. go to summer camp

9. run 100 yards

10. drive from Los Angeles, California to Washington, D.C.

SHARING IDEAS

11. Name three activities that take about one minute to complete; about one hour to complete.

12. Name three activities that take about one day to complete; about one month to complete.

PRACTICE

Which is the more reasonable estimate for the activity?

13. see a movie
120 seconds, 120 minutes

14. go from home to school
30 minutes, 130 minutes

15. make a sand castle
60 minutes, 600 minutes

16. learn to play a guitar
24 weeks, 240 weeks

17. build a tree house
2 hours, 2 days

18. grow an inch
230 days, 230 weeks

19. take a test
45 minutes, 245 minutes

20. walk a mile
25 minutes, 125 minutes

Mixed Applications

Solve. You may need to use the Databank on page 519.

21. Shara spent 2 hours at the science museum and 100 minutes at the art museum. Where did she spend more time?

22. One museum display showed inventions made in the last 100 years. Would the telephone be in the display?

23. How many years apart were the invention of television and the invention of radio?

24. *Write a story* about an adventure at a museum. Be sure it involves time.

CALCULATOR

A fourth-grader's heart beats about 84 times each minute. Complete the table to find out how many times your heart beats in 1 hour, 1 day, or longer. (*Hint:* Multiply to find the answer.)

Time	1 minute	1 hour	1 day	1 week	1 year	your lifetime
Total	84	■	■	■	■	■

Measuring Time, Capacity, and Mass **135**

Telling Time

A. Lauren and her friend Shara are going to the museum at 9:00.

They see a movie.

$\frac{1}{4}$ hour

9:15

Read: nine-fifteen, fifteen minutes after nine, or a quarter after nine

The movie ends.

$\frac{1}{2}$ hour

9:30

Read: nine-thirty, thirty minutes after nine, or half past nine

They go on a tour.

$\frac{3}{4}$ hour

9:45

Read: nine forty-five, forty-five minutes after nine, or a quarter to ten

1. As the clock goes from 9:00 to 10:00, how far does the hour hand go? how far does the minute hand go?

2. What number is the hour hand closest to at 9:15? at 9:30? at 9:45?

B. The hour hand goes around the clock two times each day. It goes around once for A.M. hours and once for P.M. hours. A.M. means the time between midnight and noon. P.M. means the time between noon and midnight.

3. List three things that you might do during A.M. hours.

4. List three things that you might do during P.M. hours.

TRY OUT Write the letter of the correct time.

5.

 a. 2:25
 b. 5:10
 c. 6:10
 d. 5:12

6.

 a. two-fifteen
 b. two-thirty
 c. three forty-five
 d. three-fifteen

PRACTICE

Write the time using numbers and A.M. or P.M. Then write the time in words.

7. Jeff eats lunch at:

8. The sun rose at:

9. Lois makes her bed at:

7:45

10. The birthday party begins at:

1:35

Mixed Applications

11. Morrie went to the museum cafeteria at 4:35 P.M. Tara went to the cafeteria at 4:15 P.M. Who went to the cafeteria first?

12. Nancy arrives for the noon movie about dinosaurs at 11:50 A.M. Is she early or late? By how much?

13. Mrs. Katz does volunteer work at the museum 5 hours a day on Sunday, Tuesday, and Friday. How many hours does she volunteer each week?

14. Museum tickets are $1.50 for adults and $.85 for children. How much more does an adult's ticket cost than a child's ticket?

Mixed Review

Find the answer. Which method did you use?

15. 60 + 70   **16.** 3,917 + 9,496   **17.** 74 − 38

18. 1,000 − 305   **19.** 172 − 61   **20.** 218 + 35 + 9

MENTAL MATH
CALCULATOR
PAPER/PENCIL

Elapsed Time

A. A class spends 2 hours and 15 minutes at the nature preserve. The class arrives at 1:45 P.M. What time will it leave?

Here is a way you can find the time after 2 hours and 15 minutes have **elapsed.**

Step 1

Count the hours.

Begin at: 1:45 P.M. ⎱ *Think:*
           2:45 P.M. ⎰ 1 hour
Stop at: 3:45 P.M. ⎰ 2 hours

Step 2

Count the minutes.

Begin at: 3:45 P.M. ⎱ *Think:*
Stop at: 4:00 P.M. ⎰ 15 minutes

The class will leave at 4:00 P.M.

1. How could you find the starting time of the trip if you were given the end time?

B. A guided tour of the Wildlife Trail begins at 2:30 P.M. and ends at 3:42 P.M. How long is the tour?

Step 1

Count the hours.

Begin at: 2:30 P.M.
Stop at: 3:30 P.M.
        Think: 1 hour

Step 2

Count the minutes.

Begin at: 3:30 P.M.
Stop at: 3:42 P.M.
        Think: 12 minutes

Step 3

Write the hours and minutes.

1 hour and 12 minutes

The tour is 1 hour and 12 minutes long.

TRY OUT Find the start time, end time, or elapsed time.

2. Start time: 6:53 P.M.   End time: ■   Elapsed time: 3 h 35 min

3. Start time: ■   End time: 3:40 P.M.   Elapsed time: 1 h 18 min

4. Start time: 9:45 A.M.   End time: 11:30 A.M.   Elapsed time: ■

PRACTICE

What time will it be:

5. in 15 minutes?

6. in 2 hours 35 minutes?

7. in 1 hour 56 minutes?

What time was it:

8. a half hour ago?

9. 1 hour and 15 minutes ago?

10. 50 minutes ago?

What time will it be:

11. 20 minutes after 10:40 A.M.?

12. 30 minutes before 3:15 P.M.?

13. 1 hour and 12 minutes before 5:00 P.M.?

14. 50 minutes after 6:15 A.M.?

How much time passes between:

15. two-thirty and two-fifty?

16. half past twelve and 1:08?

17. 3:35 and a quarter to four?

18. midnight and noon?

Critical Thinking   Solve. Tell how you answered each question.

19. How much time elapses between 11:30 A.M. and 3:40 P.M.?

20. What time will it be 40 minutes before 12:20 P.M.?

Mixed Applications

21. Ramón and Lucia went to the park at 1:14 P.M. They stayed for 3 hours and 20 minutes. At what time did they leave?

22. It takes two days to walk through the nature preserve. What metric unit would best measure its length?

PROBLEM SOLVING

Identifying Extra Information

The Sanchez family is looking forward to Thanksgiving weekend. Today is Election Day. Carmen sees on the calendar that Veterans Day is November 11th and Thanksgiving Day is November 23rd. How many days is it until Thanksgiving?

NOVEMBER

S	M	T	W	T	F	S
			1	2	3	4
5	6	7 Election Day	8	9	10	11 Veteran's Day
12	13	14	15	16	17	18
19	20	21	22	23 Thanksgiving Day	24	25
26	27	28	29	30		

1. What information does Carmen know?

2. What does she need to find out?

The calendar has more information than Carmen needs to solve the problem.

3. List the information Carmen needs to solve the problem.

4. What information is not needed?

5. How many days is it until Thanksgiving?

6. Why is it important to know what information you need to solve a problem?

PRACTICE

**List the extra information. Then solve the problem.
Use mental math, a calculator, or paper and pencil.**

7. There were 27 boys and 19 girls in the Columbus Day pageant. Another 48 students watched the pageant. How many students were in the pageant?

8. There are 198 school days and 9 holidays this year. If there are 365 days this year, how many days are there with no school?

9. There are 7 people running for mayor. Another 4 people are running for sheriff. There are 24 people running for some office this election. How many are not running for mayor?

10. The class members used 46 sheets of green construction paper and 61 sheets of red paper to make 158 holiday decorations. How many sheets did they use?

11. The Veterans Day parade has 8 floats with a total of 24 people on them. There are 3 people on each float. There are 21 people in the marching band. How many more people ride on the floats than march in the band?

Strategies and Skills Review

12. A string of lights is made of red and green bulbs. A red bulb always follows a green bulb, and a green bulb always follows a red bulb. The first bulb is green. What color is the seventh bulb? the tenth bulb?

13. It is 29 days from Columbus Day to Election Day, 16 days from Election Day to Thanksgiving, and 39 days from Thanksgiving to New Year's Eve. How many days is it from Columbus Day to New Year's Eve?

14. Mindy made macaroons for a party. She ate 6. Then she had 21 left. How many macaroons did Mindy make?

15. **Write a problem** that has extra information. Solve your problem. Ask others to solve it.

Informal Algebra: Ordered Pairs

A. Beth and Mike use a map to find their way to the Art Museum. Where is the Art Museum on the map?

An **ordered pair** of numbers can be used to describe the location of a point.

Beth and Mike start at 0. On the map they move 4 spaces to the right and 3 spaces up. So the ordered pair (4, 3) gives the location of the Art Museum.

1. Write the ordered pair that tells where the Science Hall is on the map.
   Think: First move to the right; then move up.

2. Compare these two ordered pairs. Why is the order of the numbers important when you name a point?

B. You can find a point given an ordered pair.

What is at the point named by the ordered pair (2, 5)?

Start at 0. Move 2 spaces to the right. Move 5 spaces up. City Hall is at (2, 5).

3. What is at the point named by (5, 2)? Tell how you found the point.

TRY OUT   Write the letter of the correct answer.

4. Give the ordered pair that names the location of the Fountain.

   a. (2, 2)   **b.** (3, 2)   **c.** (3, 3)   **d.** (2, 3)

5. Tell what is at the point named by (6, 1).

   a. Aquarium   **b.** Subway   **c.** Library   **d.** Park

PRACTICE

Write the ordered pair that gives the location.

6. C   **7.** F   **8.** K   **9.** N

10. A   **11.** G   **12.** D   **13.** E

Tell what letter is at the point named by the ordered pair.

14. (5, 6)   **15.** (2, 3)   **16.** (3, 2)

17. (4, 5)   **18.** (0, 1)   **19.** (6, 5)

20. Make a grid map of your classroom. List some ordered pairs for your map. Challenge another student to name what is at each location.

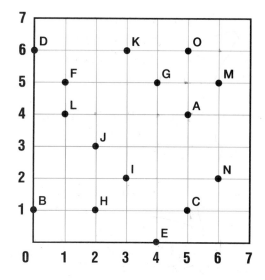

Mixed Applications   Use the map on page 142.

21. A parking lot is being built between the Science Hall and the Aquarium. What ordered pair names this location?

22. The museum had 134 visitors on Saturday. This was 16 more than on Sunday. How many visitors came on Sunday?

23. Beth and Mike met at the point named by (1, 6). Where in the city did they meet?

24. Janine walks from the Park to the Library. How many spaces on the map does she walk?

CHALLENGE

Hidden Treasure

Make a treasure map on a grid that is 5 squares long and 5 squares wide. Draw treasures such as gold coins, silver coins, and diamonds. Let your partner try to find each treasure by naming ordered pairs. You can answer "hot," "cold," or "warm," while your partner marks your answers on a blank grid.

ActiVity **M**aking Line Graphs

The rangers at Grandee State Park keep track of how many people visit the park each week. They want to see how the numbers change during the summer.

A **line graph** shows changes over time.

VISITORS DURING THE SUMMER

Week in July	Number of People (rounded to the nearest ten)	Week in August	Number of People (rounded to the nearest ten)
1	150	1	190
2	170	2	210
3	180	3	210
4	200	4	170

A ranger used these steps to show the data on a line graph.

Step 1 Choose a scale for the vertical side.

Step 2 Draw and label the horizontal and vertical sides.

Step 3 Place the points on the graph.

Step 4 Connect the dots in order.

Step 5 Write a title above the graph.

WORKING TOGETHER

1. Copy and complete the graph.

2. Why do you think 150 to 210 was used for the scale?

3. Why do you think there is a broken line below 150?

4. **What if** 154 people visited the park in Week 1 of September? How would you show this on the graph? What do you need to do to the data first?

SHARING IDEAS

5. Compare your graph with those of other students. How are they similar? How are they different?

6. Where do you see the greatest changes? Are they increases or decreases?

7. Why is a line graph useful for showing how things change over time?

PRACTICE

8. Complete the line graph, using the data in the table. Then answer the questions below.

9. In which hour did the most cars pass? the fewest cars pass?

10. How would you describe the changes as the day went on?

11. Between 3:00 and 4:00 41 cars passed and between 4:00 and 5:00, 76 cars passed. Show this data on your graph.

CARS PASSING SCHOOL EACH HOUR

Time	8–9	9–10	10–11	11–12	12–1	1–2	2–3
Cars (to the nearest ten)	60	40	20	50	80	70	30

12. On Saturday Kevin and Andrea counted people going into Kerry's Korner Market. The table below shows their data. Make a line graph of their data. Tell what the graph shows.

From To	10:00 10:15	10:15 10:30	10:30 10:45	10:45 11:00	11:00 11:15	11:15 11:30	11:30 11:45	11:45 12:00
People	10	12	9	15	18	20	25	28

13. Record the outdoor temperature at the same time each day for one week. Make a line graph of the data.

GO WITH THE PUNCHES

Visual Reasoning

A. You can use a hole puncher to conduct an experiment. Take a sheet of paper. Fold it in half like this:

Then punch two holes in this pattern:

What will the paper look like when you open it up? How many holes will there be? How do you know?

This is what the opened paper will look like:

Were you correct?

1. Now fold and punch another square sheet this way:

What will it look like unfolded?

2. Fold a square sheet of paper in half. Then fold it in half again. Now punch it in the middle. What will the unfolded square look like? How many holes will there be?

3. Fold another square in half twice. Punch it like this:

4. What will the unfolded square look like? How do you know?

B. Work on these puzzles. Try to guess what the unfolded square will look like before opening the paper.

5.

6.

7.

Now try to guess how each paper was folded and punched to get the design. Experiment with your own paper. Try to make the fewest punches possible.

8.

9.

10.

11. Design three hole-punching puzzles of your own. Have another student try to solve your puzzles.

Capacity

The **capacity** of a container is the amount of liquid it can hold.

WORKING TOGETHER

1. Collect three cups of different sizes. About how many of each size cup will it take to fill a large juice carton? Make a table to record your findings.

2. Compare the sizes and the numbers of cups needed to fill the juice carton. What do you notice?

The **milliliter (mL)** is a metric unit for measuring small amounts of liquid. A teacup holds about 100 mL. The **liter (L)** is a metric unit for measuring larger amounts of liquid.

3. Collect large containers. Use a liter container. Estimate and measure the capacities of your large containers.

CAPACITY TABLE

Size of juice carton:	
Size of cup	Number of cups
small	■
medium	■
large	■

1 milliliter

1 liter

CAPACITY IN LITERS

Container	Estimate	Measure
juice carton	■	■
milk carton	■	■
pail	■	■

1,000 mL = 1 L

SHARING IDEAS

4. What other kinds of containers have large capacities? small capacities? Which units would you use to measure their capacities?

5. What would happen if people used different-size containers to measure the same capacity?

6. What would be a better way to measure the same capacity?

PRACTICE

Choose the best estimate of capacity. Write the letter of the answer.

7. a vase	**a.** 1 mL	**b.** 1 L	**c.** 10 mL
8. a teaspoon	**a.** 5 mL	**b.** 500 mL	**c.** 5 L
9. a water pitcher	**a.** 10 mL	**b.** 1 L	**c.** 10 L
10. a sink	**a.** 7 mL	**b.** 70 mL	**c.** 7 L
11. a soup bowl	**a.** 25 mL	**b.** 250 mL	**c.** 25 L
12. a tablespoon	**a.** 25 mL	**b.** 250 mL	**c.** 25 L

Tell why the sentence does not make sense.

13. Jack drank 250 L of orange juice for breakfast.

14. The Murphys bought 20 mL of paint to paint their whole house.

Critical Thinking

15. Look for some 1 liter containers. Are they all the same shape? Why or why not? How can you show that they have the same capacity?

Mixed Applications

16. A rare plant needs to be fed every 3 hours. The last feeding was at 1:15 P.M. When is the next feeding?

17. Roy puts a few tablespoons of liquid plant food in each can of water. Would he put in about 30 mL or 30 L?

18. Roy is a Botanical Gardens gardener. Would his watering can hold about 4 mL or 4 L?

19. Lisa buys a plant for $4.50 and a book for $7.79. How much does she spend all together?

Mixed Review

Find the answer. Which method did you use?

20. 803 + 288	**21.** 97,216 + 38,965	**22.** 2,002 − 795	**23.** 575 − 200

MENTAL MATH
CALCULATOR
PAPER/PENCIL

Mass

The **mass** of an object tells how much of it there is.

WORKING TOGETHER

1. Hold a calculator in one hand and a book in the other. Which has the greater mass?

2. Compare a calculator and a pencil. Which has the greater mass?

3. Find two different books that have the same mass. See if others agree.

The **gram (g)** is a metric unit for measuring the mass of light objects.

A shoelace has a mass of about 1 gram.
A nickel has a mass of about 5 grams.
An apple has a mass of about 200 grams

4. Name other things that could be measured using grams.

The **kilogram (kg)** is a metric unit for measuring heavier things.

$$1,000 \text{ g} = 1 \text{ kg}$$

A baseball bat has a mass of about 1 kilogram.

A bowling ball has a mass of about 7 kilograms.

A television set has a mass of about 20 kilograms.

5. Name some other things that could be measured using kilograms.

1 gram

1 kilogram

SHARING IDEAS

6. Why do you use small units to measure light things and large units to measure heavy things?

PRACTICE

Choose the best estimate of mass. Write the letter
of the answer.

7. calculator	**a.** 2 g	**b.** 130 g	**c.** 20 kg
8. can of tomatoes	**a.** 370 g	**b.** 37 kg	**c.** 370 kg
9. bicycle	**a.** 25 g	**b.** 510 g	**c.** 15 kg
10. dictionary	**a.** 3 g	**b.** 3 kg	**c.** 30 kg
11. dog	**a.** 18 kg	**b.** 18 g	**c.** 180 kg
12. ice skates	**a.** 2 g	**b.** 2 kg	**c.** 20 kg

Mixed Applications Solve. Which method did you use?

ESTIMATION
MENTAL MATH
CALCULATOR
PAPER/PENCIL

13. The Gold Rush Museum has 3 gold nuggets on
display. They have masses of 350 g, 29 g, and
128 g. What is the total mass of these nuggets?

14. A gold miner's pack has a pan for sifting gold. The
pan has a mass of 682 g. The pack has a mass of
399 g. Does the gold miner carry more than 1 kg?

15. Suppose a miner found
750 g of gold. How much
more gold does he need
to have 1 kg of gold?

16. Nelle's class arrived at
the museum at 1:30 P.M.
The museum closes at
5:00 P.M. How much
time can the class
spend there?

LOGICAL REASONING

Apples in the Bag
You need to fill a bag with 14 kg of apples. You
have a balance scale and these weights: 1 kg, 5 kg,
and 10 kg. How can you measure out 14 kg of apples?

PROBLEM SOLVING

Strategy: Solving a Two-Step Problem

A. The Ellis Island Immigration Museum charges $3.50 admission for adults and $1.25 for children. Jackie McCann takes her nieces Katy and Chris to the museum. She gives the cashier a $10 bill. How much change should Jackie get?

1. What information do you know?

2. What do you need to find out?

When it takes more than one step to solve a problem, it is a good idea to make a *plan*.

3. What do you need to find out *before* you can decide how much change Jackie should get? What do you need to do next?

Try your plan.

4. How much change should she get?

PLAN	
Step 1	Step 2
$3.50	$10.00
1.25	− ■
+ 1.25	■
■	

B. A display case holds 12 pieces of silverware that a family who came from Russia donated to the museum. On Monday 4 pieces were removed. On Tuesday 6 pieces were added. How many pieces of silverware were on display then?

5. Make a plan.

What do you need to do first?

What do you need to do next?

6. How many pieces of silverware were on display at the end of Tuesday?

7. Why is it important to make a plan when solving a two-step problem?

PLAN	
Step 1	Step 2
12	■
− 4	+6
■	■

PRACTICE

Make a two-step plan. Then solve the problem.
Use mental math, a calculator, or paper and pencil.

8. The Costas donated 147 old photos of family members to the museum. They donated 12 more photos. The Slezaks gave the museum 203 photos of family members. How many more photos did the Slezaks give the museum than the Costas did?

9. Jackie gives $2.50 to each niece to spend on lunch in the cafeteria. Katy buys a grilled cheese sandwich for $1.95, a drink for $.85, and an apple for $.60. How much of her own money does Katy spend on lunch?

10. A group of 78 students and 3 teachers are going to the museum on two buses. One bus leaves with 45 people. How many people are on the second bus?

11. In the museum shop Chris chooses 15 postcards. She puts back 7 postcards and chooses another 6 postcards. How many postcards does Chris buy?

Strategies and Skills Review

Solve. Make a two-step plan if you need one.

12. A total of 4,783 people saw a special exhibit on Irish immigrants last summer. There were 1,364 visitors in June and 1,807 in July. The rest came in August. How many people saw the exhibit in August?

13. A display contained a collection of 168 drawings of Ellis Island and 84 photos of the construction of the museum. Jackie McCann saw 37 of the drawings of Ellis Island. How many drawings did she not see?

14. Chris walked through the entire museum. Did she walk about 2 miles? 20 miles? 200 miles?

EXTRA PRACTICE, page 167

ACTIVITY

Renaming Metric Measures

You can find and use patterns among the metric units of measurement.

WORKING TOGETHER

1. Look at a meter stick. How many decimeters are equal to 1 meter? How many centimeters are equal to 1 meter?

2. Use the meter stick to measure. Cut off a piece of string 2 m long. Use your meter stick to find its length in decimeters and centimeters.

3. Suppose you had a piece of string 3 m long. What would be its length in decimeters? in centimeters?

4. Complete the table.

m	1	2	3	4
dm	■	■	■	■
cm	■	■	■	■

5. You know that 1,000 meters is equal to 1 kilometer. How many meters are equal to 2 kilometers? How do you know?

6. Complete the table.

km	1	2	3	4
m	■	■	■	■

SHARING IDEAS

7. As the size of the unit decreases, what happens to the number of units in the measure of the same length?

8. If you know a length in meters, how can you find the length in decimeters? in centimeters?

ON YOUR OWN

9. You know that 1,000 milliliters is equal to 1 liter. If you know a capacity in liters, how can you find the capacity in milliliters?

10. If you know a mass in kilograms, how can you find the mass in grams?

Complete.

11. 6 m = ■ cm

12. 900 cm = ■ m

13. 7 dm = ■ cm

14. 80 dm = ■ m

15. 5 m = ■ dm

16. 5 L = ■ mL

17. 3,000 mL = ■ L

18. 4 kg = ■ g

19. 2,000 g = ■ kg

Solve.

20. Lucy's class walked 3 km to the aquarium. How far did the class walk in meters?

21. Sam saw an eel that was 90 cm long. What was its length in decimeters?

22. At home or at a grocery store, find three bottles that show their capacities in liters or milliliters.
Write a problem about the capacity of the three bottles. Have another student solve your problem.

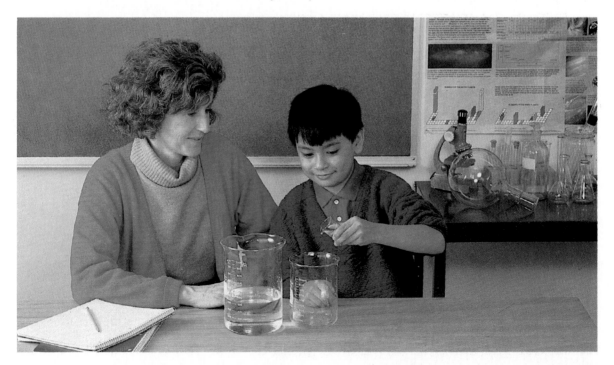

Temperature

To measure temperature in metric units, use a **Celsius thermometer.**

To read the temperature on a thermometer, look at the mark or number next to the top of the red column. Each mark on the thermometer at the right shows one **degree Celsius (°C).**

A warm bath is about 50°C.

A glass of iced tea is about 3°C.

Water boils — 100

Room temperature — 20

Water freezes — 0

Cold day — ⁻10

°C

1. What is room temperature?

2. At what temperature does water boil?

3. At what temperature does water freeze?

On the thermometer, the temperature mark for a cold day is at ⁻10°. Read this as "minus 10 degrees Celsius" or "10 degrees below 0, Celsius."

4. Write the temperature for 15 degrees below 0, Celsius.

TRY OUT
Write the letter of the correct answer.
Choose the most reasonable temperature.

5. hot oatmeal	**a.** 0°C	**b.** 23°C	**c.** 40°C	**d.** 72°C
6. snowball	**a.** 0°C	**b.** 35°C	**c.** 55°C	**d.** 72°C
7. winter day	**a.** 22°C	**b.** 56°C	**c.** ⁻13°C	**d.** 90°C
8. hot desert	**a.** 12°C	**b.** 40°C	**c.** 100°C	**d.** 200°C

PRACTICE

Write the temperature in degrees Celsius.

9.

10.

11.

Choose the most reasonable temperature.

12. swimming at the beach   **a.** ⁻3°C   **b.** 10°C   **c.** 35°C   **d.** 115°C

13. building a snow sculpture   **a.** ⁻10°C   **b.** 5°C   **c.** 30°C   **d.** 100°C

14. raking leaves on a cool day   **a.** 0°C   **b.** 12°C   **c.** 50°C   **d.** 90°C

Choose the object closest to the given temperature.

15. 50°C   **a.** glass of cold water   **b.** pan of warm water   **c.** ice cube

16. 85°C   **a.** cup of hot tea   **b.** campfire   **c.** warm bath

17. ⁻20°C   **a.** glass of lemonade   **b.** frozen yogurt   **c.** food freezer

Mixed Applications

18. Carl wants to wear shorts today. The temperature outside is 10°C. Should Carl wear shorts? Why or why not?

19. Gail left the house at 7:30 A.M. She arrived at school at 8:10 A.M. How long did it take Gail to get to school?

20. *Write a problem* about temperature. Solve it. Then trade your problem with others.

Mixed Review

Compare. Use >, <, or =.

21. 1,046 − 368 ● 728   **22.** 4 + 8 + 6 ● 23 − 5   **23.** 389 ● 97 + 281

24. 650 + 250 ● 850   **25.** $42.88 − $36.52 ● $9.37

26. 3 dm ● 30 cm   **27.** the perimeter of a square with 5 m sides ● 25 m

ACTiViTY
What Do You Measure?

How you measure an object depends on
what you need to know about the object.

WORKING TOGETHER

1. Suppose you have a large watering can. What would
   you measure to find out if it fits on a shelf?

2. What would you measure to find out how much water
   the can will hold?

3. What would you measure to see if someone can lift the
   can if it is filled with water?

4. Most fish cannot take very cold water. What should
   you measure before putting fish in an aquarium?

5. Fill a container with water. Estimate all of its measures.
   Find every measure that you can.

SHARING IDEAS

6. Name some situations at school or at home when you might
   need to measure length, capacity, mass, or temperature.

ON YOUR OWN

Write *capacity, length, mass,* or *temperature* to tell what should be measured in each of the following situations. Then tell what tool should be used to measure it.

7. You need to know if a table will fit in your room.

8. You want to know if you should wear a sweater outside today.

9. You need to know how much punch to make to fill a punch bowl.

10. A mail clerk wants to know how much postage to put on a large package.

Match the descriptions to the objects at the right.

11. Height: 3 cm
Width: 4 cm
Length: 12 cm
Mass: 90 g

12. Temperature: 0°C
Length: 23 cm
Width: 15 cm
Mass: 500 g

13. Temperature: 75°C
Mass: 850 g
Capacity: 250 mL

14. Find some common object in your classroom or at home. Describe it with different measurements. Then ask another student to guess the object.

DECISION MAKING

COOPERATIVE LEARNING

Problem Solving: Planning a Trip to the Museum

SITUATION

The fourth-grade students in Mr. Levinsky's class are going to the Natural History Museum. The travel time between school and the museum is 30 minutes. The class will leave at 9:30 A.M. and must be back in school by 3:00 P.M.

PROBLEM

Which tours, exhibits, and films should the students see? How should they arrange their day's schedule?

DATA

Natural History Museum

Exhibits open from 10:00 A.M. until 5:30 P.M.

Museum Tours (No charge)

Tours	Time	Length	Comments
Touch a Dinosaur (Hands-On Tour)	10:30 A.M.	$1\frac{1}{2}$ hours	Tour of the Dinosaur exhibit: Includes a classroom program during which students can touch fossils of dinosaur bones.
Dinosaurs	1:00 P.M.	1 hour	Tour of the Dinosaur exhibit.
Birds and Reptiles	12 noon	1 hour	Tour of the Bird and Reptile exhibits.
Marvelous Sea Mammals (Hands-On Tour)	12:30 P.M.	$1\frac{1}{2}$ hours	Tour of the Ocean Animal exhibit: Includes a classroom program during which students can touch a whale's skeleton.
Ocean Animals	2:00 P.M.	1 hour	Tour of the Ocean Animal exhibit.
Gems and Minerals	1:00 P.M.	20 minutes	Tour of the Gems and Minerals exhibit.
Ancient Peoples	10:30 A.M.	45 minutes	Tour of the exhibits of ancient cultures.

	Museum Theater Schedule	
Films	Times	Length
Meet Mother Nature	10:00 A.M. and 1:30 P.M.	20 minutes
Animals of the Ocean	11:00 A.M. and 2:15 P.M.	60 minutes
Life in Space	12:45 P.M. and 4:30 P.M.	30 minutes

The museum has a lunchroom on the ground floor. It is open from 11:00 A.M. until 2:00

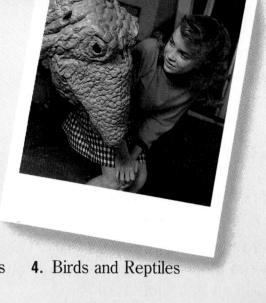

USING THE DATA

1. When will the students arrive at the museum? When must they leave? How many hours will they be at the museum?

What time will the following end?

Tours:

2. Ocean Animals   3. Ancient Peoples   4. Birds and Reptiles

Films:

5. 12:45 P.M. *Life in Space*   6. 2:15 P.M. *Animals of the Ocean*

The students need 25 minutes to eat lunch. Should they eat lunch before or after they take these tours?

7. Touch a Dinosaur

8. Marvelous Sea Mammals

9. Dinosaurs and Birds and Reptiles

MAKING DECISIONS

10. **Write a list** of the things that the students should consider when deciding which museum tours to see.

11. The students want to take both Hands-On tours. Will they have time to take any other tours? To see any film?

12. **What if** the students are studying about ocean animals? Will they have time for both the film and the tour on the subject?

13. **What if** the students want to take the Dinosaur Tour and also want to learn more about ocean animals? Decide how you would arrange a schedule.

14. **Write a schedule** for the subjects that interest you. Be sure to include a break for lunch. Give reasons for your choices.

STEGOSAURUS

Math and Social Studies

There are 24 hours in a day, but we use a 12-hour clock. We show that a time is before or after noon by writing A.M. or P.M.

A **24-hour clock** is used in space travel and for other science projects, when it is important to be very precise.

On a 24-hour clock, the first two digits tell the hour. For example, 1100 is 11:00 A.M. Add 100 to find each hour that follows. So 1200 is 12:00 noon, 1300 is 1:00 P.M., and so on to 2400, or 12:00 midnight.

The second two digits on a 24-hour clock tell the minutes after the hour. So 0130 is 1:30 A.M. and 1745 is 5:45 P.M.

What if you flew to the moon? Lift-off is at 1530. What time would you tell your friends to watch you take off if they have a 12-hour clock only?

Think: Subtract. 1530 − 1200 = 330 1530 is after noon, so it is P.M.

Lift-off time is at 3:30 P.M.

ACTIVITIES

1. Make a set of flash cards. Show a time in the 12-hour system on one side and the same time in the 24-hour system on the other. Work with a partner to practice reading the time both ways.

2. Write a schedule of your day using the 24-hour system. List everything you do from the time you get up until the time you go to bed.

Computer Graphing: Line Graph

A new restaurant, Megabite Café, opened in the mall. The owners keep track of how many customers come into the restaurant and at what times of day they come. They want to know how many workers to hire and how much food to order. They use a computer to draw a line graph to keep track of the information.

AT THE COMPUTER

Run the computer graphing program called RESTAURANT. The owners have already entered the number of customers that came in from 8:00 A.M. to 4:00 P.M.

1. The restaurant has 56 customers from 4:00 P.M. to 6:00 P.M. and 83 customers from 6:00 P.M. to 8:00 P.M. Enter this data and draw the line graph. Does the computer plot the points exactly? What happens to the data?

2. During which two-hour time period did the most customers come in? Why do you think this was so?

3. Write a summary of the information the graph provides for the owners of Megabite Café. Based on the data, for what period should the owners hire the most workers?

4. On Saturdays the movie theater next to the Megabite Café shows a popular movie from 12:00 noon to 2:00 P.M. How do you think this affects the number of customers? Change the data to show this effect and draw a new line graph.

5. **What if** another restaurant in the mall decides to offer breakfast and lunch specials at very low prices. Change any data in the graph to show how Megabite Café's business might be affected. Then draw a new line graph.

6. Why is a computer useful in drawing line graphs to display information?

EXTRA PRACTICE

Estimating Time, page 135..

Choose the most reasonable unit.

1. see a play (hours or days)

2. learn to play the piano (minutes or months)

3. read a book (minutes or days)

4. graduate from college (months or years)

Telling Time, page 137...

Write the time using numbers and A.M. or P.M. Then write the time in words.

1. Jim does his homework at:

2. Zoe eats breakfast at:

Elapsed Time, page 139..

What time will it be:

1. in 15 minutes?

2. in 1 hour and 25 minutes?

3. in 2 hours and 46 minutes?

4. 15 minutes after 11:35 A.M.?

5. 1 hour and 6 minutes before 3:00 P.M.?

How much time passes between:

6. half past six and 7:08?

7. noon and midnight?

Problem Solving: Identifying Extra Information, page 141 ....

Solve. Then list the extra information.

1. The fourth and fifth grades made floats for the parade. The fourth grade has 48 students and the fifth grade has 54. There were 86 students at the parade. How many students worked on floats?

2. Lia needs 8 yards of fabric for her costume. Andy needs 12 yards and Mia needs 3 yards. How many yards of fabric will Andy and Mia need?

3. The Adams County Courthouse has 4 flags flying. The LaPlata County Courthouse has 16 flags and the Fremont County Courthouse has 3 banners. How many flags are flying?

4. Nan and Pete are having a cookout. They have 20 hamburgers and 68 hot dogs. They bought 40 plates. How many hamburgers and hot dogs do they have?

Ordered Pairs, page 143 ....

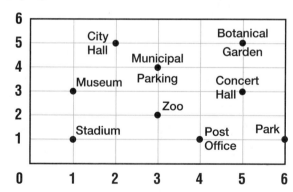

Name the ordered pair for each location.

1. City Hall   **2.** Park   **3.** Zoo   **4.** Museum

What is located at each ordered pair?

5. (1, 1)   **6.** (3, 4)   **7.** (4, 1)   **8.** (5, 3)

EXTRA PRACTICE

Making Line Graphs, page 145 ....

1. Complete the line graph using the data in the table.
   Then answer Questions 2–4.

People Getting on the City Bus							
Time	8–9	9–10	10–11	11–12	12–1	1–2	2–3
People	50	80	70	20	20	30	60

2. Which hours had the most people getting on the bus?

3. Which had the fewest?

4. How would you describe the changes as the day went on?

Capacity, page 149 ....

Choose the best estimate of the capacity of the containers.

1. thermos   1 mL or 1 L

2. coffee cup   150 mL or 150 L

3. tablespoon   15 mL or 15 L

4. baby's bottle   250 mL or 250 L

5. watering can   2 mL or 2 L

Mass, page 151 ....

Choose the best estimate of the mass of the object.

1. kitten   **a.** 35 g   **b.** 3 g   **c.** 3 kg

2. box of cereal **a.** 380 g   **b.** 10 g   **c.** 630 kg

3. man   **a.** 8 kg   **b.** 100 g   **c.** 80 kg

4. moving van   **a.** 100 kg   **b.** 3,000 kg   **c.** 300 g

EXTRA PRACTICE

Problem Solving Strategy: Solving a Two-Step Problem, page 153............
Use a two-step plan to solve the problem.

1. There are 89 students and 4 teachers going to the museum. One bus leaves school with 48 passengers. How many passengers are on the other bus?

2. In the museum shop, Ginger buys 12 Old West keychains. She returns 6 Old West keychains and buys 5 leather keychains instead. How many keychains did she buy?

3. The Adams Museum has a collection of 18 statues. Another 11 statues are donated to the museum. The Potz Museum has 35 statues. How many more statues does the Potz Museum have?

4. Mr. Gilmore has 14 paintings. He buys 11 more. He donates 15 of them to the museum. How many paintings does he have left?

Temperature, page 157...
Choose the most reasonable temperature.

1. cross-country skiing   **a.** ⁻5°C   **b.** 10°C   **c.** 45°C   **d.** 100°C

2. sunbathing   **a.** ⁻15°C   **b.** 10°C   **c.** 40°C   **d.** 80°C

3. mowing the lawn   **a.** 30°C   **b.** 3°C   **c.** ⁻3°C   **d.** 80°C

4. sled riding   **a.** ⁻8°C   **b.** 8°C   **c.** 18°C   **d.** 80°C

Choose the object closest to the given temperature.

5. 1°C   **a.** hot tea   **b.** icicles   **c.** glass of milk

6. 10°C   **a.** cold water   **b.** room temperature   **c.** hot soup

7. 100°C   **a.** lemonade   **b.** room temperature   **c.** hot tea

PRACTICE PLUS

KEY SKILL: Elapsed Time (Use after page 139.)

Level A

Give the time:

1. in 5 minutes.
2. in 10 minutes.
3. in 15 minutes.
4. 5 minutes ago.
5. 1 hour ago.
6. 30 minutes ago.

Level B

Give the time:

7. in 20 minutes.
8. in 1 hour 45 minutes.
9. in 1 hour 38 minutes.
10. 11 minutes ago.
11. 1 hour 45 minutes ago.
12. 33 minutes ago.

What time will it be:

13. 15 minutes after 9:50 A.M.?
14. 1 hour 14 minutes before 6:00 P.M.?

Level C

What time will it be:

15. 36 minutes after 8:50?
16. 42 minutes before 12:20 P.M.?

How much time passes between:

17. seven thirty-one and 8:09?
18. 12:09 and half past one?

KEY SKILL: Mass (Use after page 151.)

Level A

Choose the best estimate of the mass of the object.

1. robin   **a.** 3 g   **b.** 4 kg   **c.** 50 g

2. girl   **a.** 300 g   **b.** 30 kg   **c.** 10 g

Choose the correct unit.

3. Janice's book has a mass of 650 (g or kg).

4. Matthew's basketball has a mass of 2 (g or kg).

Level B

Choose the best estimate of the mass of the object.

5. truck   **a.** 1,800 g   **b.** 180 kg   **c.** 1,800 kg

6. watermelon   **a.** 2 g   **b.** 2 kg   **c.** 20 kg

Match the object with a possible mass.

7. man   **a.** 11 kg

8. 50 nickels   **b.** 75 kg

9. bicycle   **c.** 1 kg

Level C

Choose the best estimate of the mass of the object.

10. airplane   **a.** 6,000 kg   **b.** 40 kg   **c.** 4,000 g

11. computer   **a.** 25 kg   **b.** 15 g   **c.** 1 kg

12. medicine bottle   **a.** 79 kg   **b.** 7 g   **c.** 150 g

Match the unit with a possible mass.

13. motorcycle   **a.** 15 kg

14. toolbox   **b.** 190 kg

15. skateboard   **c.** 2 kg

CHAPTER REVIEW/TEST

LANGUAGE AND MATHEMATICS

Complete the sentences. Use the words in the chart.

1. There are 12 ■ in the year.

2. ■ is the time between noon and midnight.

3. (3, 5) is called an ordered ■.

4. The ■ of a container tells how much it holds.

VOCABULARY
pair
A.M.
capacity
week
P.M.
months

CONCEPTS AND SKILLS

Choose the more reasonable unit.

5. swim 5 laps: minutes or hours

What time will it be:

6. ten after six at night?

Find the start time, end time, or elapsed time.

7. Start time: 7:21 A.M.   End time: 8:36 A.M.   Elapsed time: ■

8. Start time: 5:47 A.M.   End time: ■   Elapsed time: 5 h, 15 min

Choose the better estimate.

9. pitcher of cream: 1 L or 1 mL

10. jar of jam: 120 g or 12 kg

11. temperature inside a refrigerator:
   a. 5°C   **b.** 25°C

12. hiking on a hot day:
   a. 3°C   **b.** 32°C

Use this grid to name or locate the ordered pair.

13. A   **14.** (2, 1)

15. (3, 3)   **16.** D

17. Use the data in the table to make a line graph.

NUMBER OF BIRDS SEEN DURING MIGRATION FOR A WEEK

Sunday	Monday	Tuesday	Wednesday	Thursday	Friday	Saturday
12	20	38	41	59	51	40

Critical Thinking

18. Which has more mass: a kilogram of feathers or a kilogram of lead? How do you know?

Mixed Applications

Solve. If there is extra information, list it.

19. Mr. Hou bought a cup of cocoa for $.85 and a bagel for $1.29. How much change does he get from $5.00?

20. Four teachers and 25 students are going on a field trip. If 13 of the students are girls, how many people are going on the field trip?

PERFORMANCE ASSESSMENT

Work with your group to solve this problem.

Some students conducted an experiment to see how long it would take for a block of ice to melt under a heat lamp. The students placed the 650-gram block of ice under the lamp at 8:00 A.M. They measured the mass of the block at different times during the morning. The results are in the table on the right.

Time	Mass
8:00 A.M.	650 g
9:00 A.M.	490 g
10:00 A.M.	330 g
11:00 A.M.	170 g
12 noon	0 g

Make a line graph that shows the results of the experiment and determine the amount of time it took for the block of ice to melt completely.

1. *Think about:*
   - how to make a line graph to show the results of the experiment
   - how to find the amount of time it took for the ice to melt

2. Write one statement to explain how the mass of the ice changed from one time to another. Then, write another statement to explain how you figured the total amount of time it took for the ice to melt.

CUMULATIVE REVIEW

Choose the letter of the correct answer.

1. Estimate the amount of water in a small spoon.

   a. 1 L   **c.** 10 L
   b. 10 mL   **d.** 100 mL

2. A cold winter's day is about:

   a. -100°C.   **c.** 16°C.
   b. -6°C.   **d.** 30°C.

3. To plot an ordered pair, start

   a. at (0, 0).   **c.** at (1, 1).
   b. at (0, 1).   **d.** at (1, 0).

4. $4.98 + $12.42 + $.29

   a. $16.69   **c.** $17.69
   b. $17.59   **d.** not given

5. What is 16 minus 7?

   a. 6   **c.** 8
   b. 7   **d.** not given

6. A bowl of hot cereal is about:

   a. 10°C.   **c.** 80°C.
   b. 40°C.   **d.** 200°C.

7. Round 542 to the nearest hundred.

   a. 500   **c.** 550
   b. 540   **d.** 600

8. How much time passes between 7:55 and 8:23?

   a. 18 minutes   **c.** 33 minutes
   b. 28 minutes   **d.** not given

9. What is 7 plus 5?

   a. 2   **c.** 12
   b. 11   **d.** not given

10. Estimate the mass of a dog.

    a. 10 g   **c.** 10 kg
    b. 100 g   **d.** 100 kg

11. Compare: 99,999 ● 91,999

    a. <   **c.** =
    b. >   **d.** not given

12. 3,974 − 1,999

    a. 5,973   **c.** 1,075
    b. 1,975   **d.** not given

13. The capacity of a bathtub is:

    a. 15 L.   **c.** 150 L.
    b. 15 mL.   **d.** 150 mL.

14. What time is 8 minutes before 1 P.M.?

    a. 12:52 A.M.   **c.** 1:08 A.M.
    b. 12:52 P.M.   **d.** not given

TIME ZONES

The world is divided into different time zones.
This map shows the six time zones in the United States.
The clocks show you what time it is in each time zone
when it is 12 noon in the Pacific Time Zone.

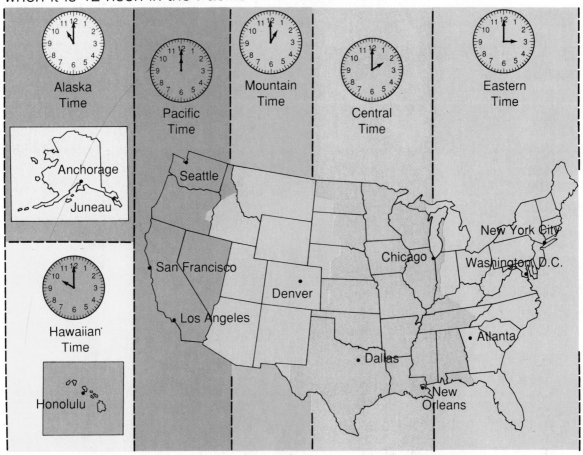

1. You are on the East Coast and telephone the West Coast.
   What is the time difference?

2. How much earlier or later is the time in these cities than in Seattle?
   a. Denver   **b.** Dallas   **c.** Anchorage   **d.** Atlanta

3. When it is 7:00 A.M. in the Eastern Time Zone, what time
   is it in these time zones?
   a. Central   **b.** Mountain   **c.** Pacific   **d.** Hawaiian

4. It is 10:30 P.M. in Denver. What time is it in these cities?
   a. San Francisco   **b.** Chicago   **c.** New York   **d.** Honolulu

NORTH AMERICA

Aztec
Empire

SOUTH AMERICA

WAYS of MEASURING

MEASURING

AREA

The ancient Aztecs who lived in most of Mexico and parts of Central America grew crops such as corn, tomatoes, and squash. Many Aztec farms were built on mountainsides. Because of the rough terrain, it was difficult to figure out how much land made up each farm. In order to measure the area of their farms, the Aztecs used a special unit of measure called a *quahuitl* [kwah-WEE-tl].

A *quahuitl* was about $2\frac{1}{2}$ meters, or 8 feet, in length. Aztec farmers used measuring ropes that were divided into *quahuitls* and fractions of *quahuitls*. The ropes were stretched along the boundaries of the farm and the measurements recorded.

1. What kinds of things might be easier to measure with a rope than with something that does not bend?

2. What other ways can you think of to measure the distance around irregular shapes?

The Meaning of Multiplication

There are 5 groups of dogs at the pet show. There are 3 dogs in each group. How many dogs are there?

WORKING TOGETHER

Use counters to model the problem.

1. Write an addition sentence to show what you have modeled.

2. How many counters are there in all? How many dogs are there?

You can write a **multiplication sentence** to show what you have modeled.

5	×	**3**	=	**15**		3 ← factor
↑	↑	↑	↑	↑		×5 ← factor
factor	times	**factor**	equals	**product**		15 ← product

Compare your two number sentences to your model.

3. Which factor tells the number of addends? Which factor tells the number of groups?

4. Which factor names the addend? Which factor tells how many in each group?

5. What does the sum or the product tell you?

When a multiplication fact contains two factors that are the same, it is called a **square.**

6. ***What if*** there are 3 groups of 3 dogs? How many dogs are there? Use counters to model the problem. Why do you think 3 × 3 is called a square?

7. ***What if*** one group has 7 dogs, another has 3 dogs, and another has 4 dogs? How many dogs will there be? Can you write a multiplication sentence? Why or why not?

SHARING IDEAS

8. When can you multiply to find how many in all? When must you add?

PRACTICE

Complete the multiplication sentence.

9. **10.** **11.**

$4 \times 3 = \blacksquare$ $3 \times \blacksquare = \blacksquare$ $\blacksquare \times \blacksquare = \blacksquare$

Write a multiplication sentence.

12. $5 + 5 + 5 + 5$ **13.** $9 + 9$ **14.** $8 + 8 + 8 + 8 + 8$

Multiply. Use counters if needed.

15. 3×6 **16.** 8×3 **17.** 2×5 **18.** 3×9

19. 4×3 **20.** 6×8 **21.** 8×6 **22.** 3×4

23. 9×4 **24.** 5×8 **25.** 5×6 **26.** 5×1

27. $\begin{array}{r} 7 \\ \times 6 \\ \hline \end{array}$ **28.** $\begin{array}{r} 9 \\ \times 9 \\ \hline \end{array}$ **29.** $\begin{array}{r} 4 \\ \times 2 \\ \hline \end{array}$ **30.** $\begin{array}{r} 5 \\ \times 9 \\ \hline \end{array}$ **31.** $\begin{array}{r} 2 \\ \times 7 \\ \hline \end{array}$ **32.** $\begin{array}{r} 2 \\ \times 6 \\ \hline \end{array}$

33. How many are in 2 groups of 8?   **34.** Multiply 3 by 2.

35. What is 4 times 6?   **36.** Find the product of 1×8.

Mixed Applications

37. The pet show winners get 7 blue, 7 red, and 7 gold ribbons. How many ribbons is this?

38. There are 80 pets in the show. Only 21 will win a prize. How many pets will not win a prize?

39. A group picture is taken of the top 2 winners in each of the 7 showings. How many winners are in the picture?

40. *Write a problem* that can be solved using multiplication. Solve your problem. Ask others to solve it.

The Meaning of Division

There are 24 horses grazing on the range. The horses are standing in groups of 3. How many groups of horses are there?

WORKING TOGETHER

Use counters to model the problem. Start with 24 counters. Take away groups of 3 counters until no counters remain.

1. How many groups of 3 did you make? How many groups of horses are there?

You can write a division sentence to show what you have modeled.

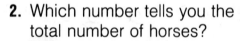

24	÷	3	=	8
↑	↑	↑	↑	↑
dividend	divided by	**divisor**	equals	**quotient**

$$3)\overline{24}$$

8 ← quotient
dividend
divisor

2. Which number tells you the total number of horses?

3. Which number tells you the number in each group?

4. Which number tells you the number of equal groups?

The 24 horses regrouped into 3 equal groups. How many horses were in each group?

Use counters to model this problem. Start with 24 counters. Put them in 3 groups, one by one, until you run out of counters.

5. How many counters are in each group? How many horses are in each group?

6. Write a division sentence to show what you modeled.

7. Find other groups you can make with 24 counters. Record your results in a table like this.

Number in All	÷	Number in Each Group	=	Number of Equal Groups
24	÷	3	=	8
24	÷	8	=	■

8. Find other ways to separate 24 counters into equal groups. Record them in a table like this.

Number in All	÷	Number of Equal Groups	=	Number in Each Group
24	÷	3	=	■
24	÷	8	=	■

SHARING IDEAS

9. Compare the division sentences in each table. What do you notice?

10. What two questions does a division sentence answer?

PRACTICE

Complete the division sentence.

11.

$10 \div ■ = 2$

12.

$■ \div ■ = 4$

13.

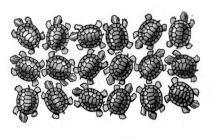

$■ \div ■ = ■$

Divide. Use counters if needed.

14. $16 \div 8$

15. $8 \div 2$

16. $18 \div 6$

17. $15 \div 5$

18. $9\overline{)27}$

19. $6\overline{)36}$

20. $5\overline{)30}$

21. $4\overline{)32}$

22. $3\overline{)18}$

23. How many groups of 5 are in 20?

24. What is 27 divided by 3?

Mixed Applications

25. Alexis has 16 horses lined up in groups of 4. How many groups do the horses make?

26. A magician made 2 groups of 6 pigeons disappear. How many pigeons disappeared?

27. There are 21 monkeys living in equal groups in 7 trees. How many monkeys live in each tree?

28. *Write a problem* that can be solved using division. Have others solve it.

ACTIVITY

Informal Algebra: Multiplication and Division Properties

A. You can use counters and diagrams to explore the properties of multiplication.

Here are two ways to show a group of 6 counters.

← 3 groups of 2   ← 2 groups of 3

$3 \times 2 \qquad = \qquad 2 \times 3 \qquad = \qquad 6$

1. What do you notice about the products?

2. What if one of the factors is 1? What do you notice about the product?

$3 \times 1 = 3 \qquad\qquad 1 \times 3 = 3$

3. What if one of the factors is 0? What do you notice about the product?

$3 \times 0 = 0 \qquad$ You cannot show 0 groups of 3.

$0 \times 3 = 0$

4. What if you multiply 3 numbers? What happens to their product if you group them in different ways?

$(3 \times 2) \times 4 = 6 \times 4 = 24$
$3 \times (2 \times 4) = 3 \times 8 = 24$

B. You can also explore the properties of division.

5. What is the quotient when you divide a number by 1?

← 1 group of 4
$4 \div 1 = 4 \quad$ ***Think:*** $1 \times 4 = 4$

6. What is the quotient when you divide a number by itself?

← 4 groups of 1
$4 \div 4 = 1 \quad$ ***Think:*** $4 \times 1 = 4$

7. What if you divide zero by a number? What is the quotient?

← 4 groups of 0
$0 \div 4 = 0 \quad$ ***Think:*** $4 \times 0 = 0$

8. What if you divide a number by 0? What do you notice?

You cannot show 0 groups of 4.
$4 \div 0 = \blacksquare \quad$ ***Think:*** $0 \times \blacksquare = 4$
No number works.

9. Use counters or diagrams to model each of the multiplication and division properties using different numbers. What do you notice?

SHARING IDEAS

With which statements do you agree? disagree? If you disagree, tell why.

10. If you multiply a number by 1, the product is 1.

11. When you divide a number by itself, the quotient is 1.

12. Changing the way factors are grouped changes the product.

13. Any number divided by 0 equals 0.

14. When you divide a number by 1, the quotient is 1.

15. When 0 is divided by a number, the quotient is the number.

16. If you change the order of the factors, the product remains the same.

PRACTICE

Find the missing number.

17. $2 \times 0 = \blacksquare$ **18.** $1 \times 4 = \blacksquare$ **19.** $0 \div 8 = \blacksquare$ **20.** $1 \div 1 = \blacksquare$

21. $8 \times 1 = \blacksquare$ **22.** $5 \div 1 = \blacksquare$ **23.** $\blacksquare \times 2 = 0$ **24.** $6 \div 0 = \blacksquare$

25. $7 \div \blacksquare = 1$ **26.** $\blacksquare \times 2 = 2$ **27.** $3 \times 5 = \blacksquare \times 3$

28. $(2 \times 3) \times 6 = \blacksquare \times (3 \times 6)$ **29.** $(4 \times \blacksquare) \times 2 = 4 \times (2 \times 2)$

Find the rule.

30. Multiply by $\blacksquare$.

0	1	2	3	4	5	6	7	8	9
0	1	2	3	4	5	6	7	8	9

31. Divide by $\blacksquare$.

1	2	3	4	5	6	7	8	9
1	1	1	1	1	1	1	1	1

Mixed Applications

32. Len takes 10 pictures of deer and 2 pictures of elk. How many more pictures of deer than elk does he take?

33. There are 3 tigers. Each tiger has 3 cubs. How many tiger cubs are there?

ACTIVITY

Informal Algebra: Fact Families

You can use number cubes to explore fact families. Suppose that you roll two number cubes and get a 3 and a 5.

You can write related multiplication sentences.

Factor	×	Factor	=	Product
3	×	5	=	15
5	×	3	=	15

You can then write related division sentences.

Dividend	÷	Divisor	=	Quotient
15	÷	3	=	5
15	÷	5	=	3

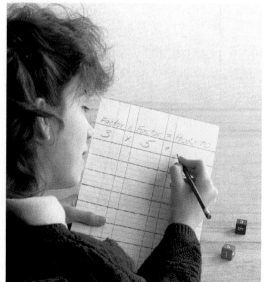

WORKING TOGETHER

Copy the charts above.

1. The number sentences in both charts belong to the same **fact family.** Tell how they are related.

2. Use two number cubes and repeat this activity four more times. See how many related sentences you can write. Record them on your charts.

SHARING IDEAS

3. Did you write the same number of related sentences for every fact family? Why or why not?

4. Compare your sentences with those of other students. How are they alike? How are they different?

5. How do the multiplication and division properties help you write fact families?

6. How does the relationship between multiplication and division help you write fact families?

PRACTICE

Find the product or quotient. Write the related
number sentences that make up the fact family.

7. 3)$\overline{21}$ **8.** 1)$\overline{6}$ **9.** 4 × 5   **10.** 2)$\overline{4}$ **11.** 2 × 8

12. 9 ÷ 3   **13.** 5 × 5   **14.** 5 × 3   **15.** 18 ÷ 9   **16.** 3 ÷ 3

Write the fact family for the set of numbers.

17. 3, 4, 12   **18.** 4, 1, 4   **19.** 2, 4, 8   **20.** 8, 8, 64   **21.** 2, 5, 10

Complete the fact. Find the missing number.

22. 7 × ■ = 28   **23.** 27 ÷ ■ = 9   **24.** ■ × 4 = 16   **25.** 5 ÷ ■ = 1

26. ■ × 8 = 40   **27.** ■ ÷ 3 = 6   **28.** 6 × ■ = 48   **29.** ■ ÷ 6 = 0

Mixed Applications

30. Lisa walks dogs in groups of 4.
She walks 5 groups a day. How
many dogs does she walk a day?

31. Mark has 15 tropical fish. He
puts 5 in each fishbowl. How
many fishbowls does he use?

32. Nona bought a book about the
care of gerbils. It cost $4.79.
She paid with a $10 bill.
What was her change?

33. Harry started riding his horse at
3:30 P.M. He rode for 1 hour 30
minutes. At what time did he
finish riding?

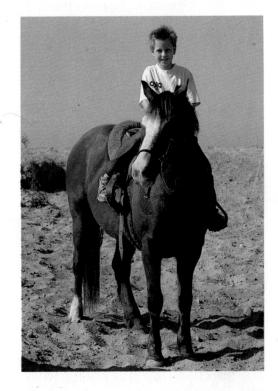

Mixed Review

Find the answer. Which method did you use?

34. 1   **35.**   247   **36.** 4)$\overline{32}$ **37.**   126   **38.** $768.32
  × 2   − 168   − 10   + 205.19

MENTAL MATH
CALCULATOR
PAPER/PENCIL

EXTRA PRACTICE, page 208

2 Through 9 as Factors

Mario and Jill are making a table so that they will be sure not to skip any multiplication facts. When the table is complete, they will use it for a fact race.

1. Make a table like this for yourself.

Mario says that it is easy to fill in the first two rows and columns.

2. What does Mario know about multiplying by 0 and 1 that makes this easy?

COLUMNS

×	0	1	2	3	4	5	6	7	8	9
0	0	0	0	0	0	0	0			
1	0	1	2	3	4	5				
2	0	2	4			10				
3	0	3	6			15				
4			8			20				
5										
6										
7										
8										
9										

ROWS

Jill uses skip-counting to fill in column 2 and column 5.

3. Why can Jill fill in row 2 and row 5 the same way?

Jill uses a table to remember the squares.

4. Use the rule to complete Jill's table.

Rule: Multiply the Number by Itself.

1	2	3	4	5	6	7	8	9
1	4	9	■	■	■	■	■	■

Think: 2 × 2

Mario says that he can use squares to help him multiply mentally.

3 × 3 = 9, so 4 × 3 = 9 + 3 = 12 and 2 × 3 = 9 − 3 = 6.

5. What other facts can you find from 4 × 4 = 16?

6. Complete the multiplication table. You can use counters to check your work.

TRY OUT   Multiply.

7. 8 × 4   **8.** 3 × 9   **9.** 0 × 6   **10.** 9 × 1

11. 6 × 2   **12.** 5 × 5   **13.** 2 × 8   **14.** 7 × 7

PRACTICE

Multiply.

15. $\begin{array}{r} 2 \\ \times 5 \\ \hline \end{array}$	**16.** $\begin{array}{r} 1 \\ \times 1 \\ \hline \end{array}$	**17.** $\begin{array}{r} 5 \\ \times 0 \\ \hline \end{array}$	**18.** $\begin{array}{r} 4 \\ \times 3 \\ \hline \end{array}$	**19.** $\begin{array}{r} 4 \\ \times 7 \\ \hline \end{array}$	**20.** $\begin{array}{r} 3 \\ \times 9 \\ \hline \end{array}$
21. $\begin{array}{r} 9 \\ \times 5 \\ \hline \end{array}$	**22.** $\begin{array}{r} 2 \\ \times 4 \\ \hline \end{array}$	**23.** $\begin{array}{r} 3 \\ \times 5 \\ \hline \end{array}$	**24.** $\begin{array}{r} 6 \\ \times 2 \\ \hline \end{array}$	**25.** $\begin{array}{r} 8 \\ \times 7 \\ \hline \end{array}$	**26.** $\begin{array}{r} 3 \\ \times 6 \\ \hline \end{array}$
27. $\begin{array}{r} 7 \\ \times 8 \\ \hline \end{array}$	**28.** $\begin{array}{r} 1 \\ \times 7 \\ \hline \end{array}$	**29.** $\begin{array}{r} 6 \\ \times 6 \\ \hline \end{array}$	**30.** $\begin{array}{r} 7 \\ \times 3 \\ \hline \end{array}$	**31.** $\begin{array}{r} 0 \\ \times 9 \\ \hline \end{array}$	**32.** $\begin{array}{r} 7 \\ \times 9 \\ \hline \end{array}$

33. 0×4 **34.** 9×2 **35.** 4×8 **36.** 8×5 **37.** 7×0

38. 8×2 **39.** 8×8 **40.** 1×9 **41.** 9×5 **42.** 9×8

43. 7×5 **44.** 6×9 **45.** 8×3 **46.** 9×9 **47.** 6×7

48. Multiply 5 by 7.

49. What is 6 times 4?

50. Find the product of 0×3.

51. How many are in 9 groups of 3?

Give the rule. Complete the table.

52.

0	1	2	3	4	5	6	7	8	9
0	4	8	▣	▣	▣	▣	▣	▣	▣

53.

0	1	2	3	4	5	6	7	8	9
0	7	14	▣	▣	▣	▣	▣	▣	▣

Mixed Applications

54. There are 48 swans living on the lake. If there are 6 swans in each family, how many families of swans live on the lake?

55. Ramon has 4 sets of books about animals. There are 2 books in each set. How many books are there in all?

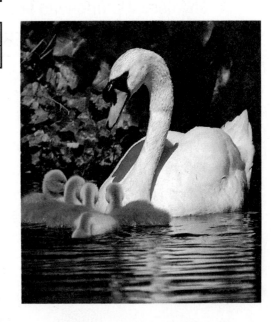

Dividing by 2 through 9

Joy and Rick are helping each other learn division facts. They use all the models, properties, and relationships they have learned.

A. To find the quotient of 24 ÷ 8, Joy draws a picture. She makes rows of 8 until she has 24 items.

1. What is the quotient?

2. What is the related division fact?

To find the quotient of 20 ÷ 4, Rick draws circles. He makes groups of 4 until he has 20 items.

3. What is the quotient?

4. What is the related division fact?

B. Joy uses a property to find the quotient of 9 ÷ 9.

5. Which property does Joy use? What is the quotient?

6. Write the related division fact.

To find the quotient of 45 ÷ 5, Rick thinks of the related multiplication sentence.

7. What is the related multiplication sentence? What is the quotient?

8. What is the related division fact?

TRY **OUT**   Divide.

9. $3\overline{)24}$ 10. $5\overline{)35}$ 11. 6 ÷ 3   12. 36 ÷ 9

PRACTICE

Divide.

13. $2\overline{)16}$ **14.** $7\overline{)14}$ **15.** $9\overline{)27}$ **16.** $5\overline{)25}$ **17.** $8\overline{)0}$ **18.** $8\overline{)24}$

19. $5\overline{)30}$ **20.** $8\overline{)40}$ **21.** $6\overline{)42}$ **22.** $9\overline{)45}$ **23.** $4\overline{)20}$ **24.** $7\overline{)28}$

25. $7\overline{)49}$ **26.** $8\overline{)72}$ **27.** $2\overline{)18}$ **28.** $1\overline{)9}$ **29.** $6\overline{)30}$ **30.** $4\overline{)36}$

31. $4\overline{)28}$ **32.** $9\overline{)81}$ **33.** $6\overline{)24}$ **34.** $8\overline{)8}$ **35.** $6\overline{)54}$ **36.** $7\overline{)56}$

37. $0 \div 5$ **38.** $6 \div 2$ **39.** $32 \div 8$ **40.** $12 \div 6$ **41.** $42 \div 7$

42. $36 \div 6$ **43.** $21 \div 3$ **44.** $72 \div 9$ **45.** $40 \div 5$ **46.** $0 \div 1$

47. $32 \div 4$ **48.** $7 \div 1$ **49.** $24 \div 4$ **50.** $2 \div 2$ **51.** $64 \div 8$

52. $14 \div 2$ **53.** $35 \div 7$ **54.** $63 \div 7$ **55.** $54 \div 9$ **56.** $48 \div 8$

57. Divide 8 by 1.

58. How many 6s are in 42?

59. Find the quotient of $56 \div 7$.

60. What is 0 divided by 9?

Use the rule to complete.

61. Rule: Divide by 5.

0	5	10	15	20	25	30	35	40	45
0	1	2	■	■	■	■	■	■	■

62. Rule: Divide by 8.

0	8	16	24	32	40	48	56	64	72
0	1	2	■	■	■	■	■	■	■

Mixed Applications

63. Joy keeps her 36 glass animals on 4 shelves. She puts the same number of animals on each shelf. How many animals are on each shelf?

64. Rick is going to buy 5 sets of animal posters. There are 6 posters in each set. How many posters will Rick buy?

65. *Write a problem* involving multiplication or division. Solve it. Then ask others to solve it.

✓ UNDERSTAND
✓ PLAN
✓ TRY
CHECK
✓ EXTEND

PROBLEM SOLVING

Strategy: Choosing the Operation

Kai's grandparents are celebrating their fiftieth wedding
anniversary with a banquet at the Yong Sing Restaurant.
Guests will sit at 7 tables. Each table has 8 seats. How many
guests can attend?

UNDERSTAND	
What do I know?	I know there are 7 tables. There are 8 seats at each table.
What do I need to find out?	I need to find out how many seats there are in all.
PLAN	
What can I do?	Since each table has the same number of seats, I can multiply the number of seats at each table by the number of tables.
TRY	
Let me try my plan.	Number of seats at each table $$7 \times 8 = 56$$ ↑ Number of tables So 56 guests can attend.
CHECK	
Have I answered the question?	Yes. There are 56 seats so 56 guests can attend.
Does my answer make sense?	Yes. I get the same answer if I add. $8 + 8 + 8 + 8 + 8 + 8 + 8 = 56$
EXTEND	
What have I learned?	I have learned that I can use multiplication to solve problems that combine groups of the same size. I can check my answer by adding.

PRACTICE

Decide which operation to use. Then solve the problem.
Use mental math, a calculator, or paper and pencil.

1. Kai has made 19 placecards for the banquet and his sister has made 23. How many have they made in all?

2. The restaurant has 30 tables. Each table seats 8 people. How many people can sit at the tables?

3. There are 7 tables. Each table drank 3 pots of tea during the banquet. How many pots of tea were drunk by the whole party?

4. The guests include 17 children and 39 adults. How many more adults than children are at the banquet?

Strategies and Skills Review

5. Corylin lives 36 miles from the restaurant. This is 4 times the distance that her cousin Wayne lives from the restaurant. How far is Wayne's house from the restaurant?

6. There are 2 fish tanks at the restaurant. One tank has 349 fish swimming in it, and the other has 307 fish in it. Do the tanks have at least 600 fish? How can you tell?

7. All 56 guests said they would come. There are still 12 more to arrive. How many are already at the banquet?

8. **Write a problem** using one of the four operations. Solve your problem. Ask others to solve your problem.

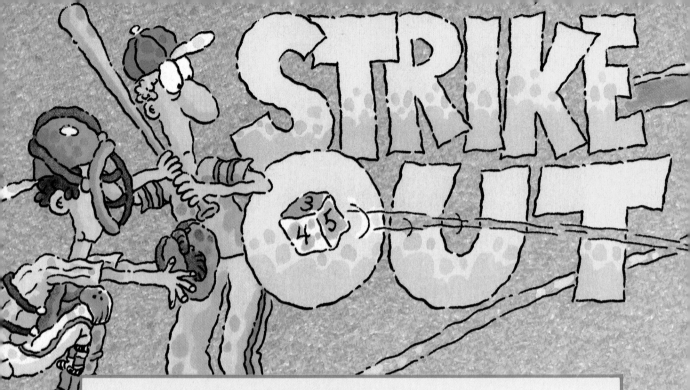

Experimenting and Predicting

A. Here's a game you can play to test your luck and skill. It's called STRIKE. You will need two number cubes. Each cube should be numbered 1–6. You will also need a sheet of paper to keep track of your score.

Take turns. On your turn, roll the cubes and add the numbers shown on the cubes to your score. Then decide if you want to roll again. You can keep rolling but watch out for STRIKE and STRIKE OUT!

If **one** of the cubes shows a 1, you have rolled STRIKE. You lose all of the points you scored that turn. Your turn is over as well.

If **both** of the cubes show a 1, you have rolled STRIKE OUT. You lose all of the points you have so far. It is also the end of your turn.

Roll		Score
6	3	9
5	2	16
3	1	0

↑
STRIKE

The first player to get 100 points wins the game!

Play several games of STRIKE with another student. Think about the best way to play.

B. How do you decide when to stop rolling the cubes?

1. Suppose you have already rolled the cubes 5 times and have not rolled STRIKE or STRIKE OUT. Will you roll again?

You can change the game by adding new rules. Try some of these:

2. BIG STRIKE: All points are doubled. How does this change the way you play?

3. DOUBLE-TROUBLE STRIKE: If you roll double sixes, you lose 20 points. You do not lose your turn.

4. Invent your own STRIKE variations and try them out. Discuss how the new rules change your method of play.

Informal Algebra: Missing Factors

Martin and Peggy are buying dog food. The cans are packed into 6-packs, and there are 48 cans in a large case. How many 6-packs are there in a large case?

You need to find the missing factor: ■ × 6 = 48.

Martin and Peggy use related facts.

Martin thinks:
I know that 48 ÷ 6 = 8, so
8 × 6 = 48.

Peggy thinks:
I know that 6 × 8 = 48, so
8 × 6 = 48.

There are eight 6-packs of cans in a large case.

1. Use a related fact to find the missing factor in ■ × 7 = 63.

2. Find each missing factor. Tell how you know.

   a. 3 × ■ = 3   **b.** 6 × ■ = 0   **c.** 1 × ■ = 7

TRY OUT
Write the letter of the correct answer.
Find the missing factor.

3. ■ × 6 = 54   **a.** 6   **b.** 9   **c.** 48   **d.** 60

4. 7 × ■ = 35   **a.** 5   **b.** 7   **c.** 28   **d.** 42

5. ■ × 9 = 0   **a.** 10   **b.** 9   **c.** 1   **d.** 0

6. 8 × ■ = 64   **a.** 72   **b.** 9   **c.** 8   **d.** 7

PRACTICE

Find the missing factor.

7. ■ × 9 = 27   **8.** 8 × ■ = 32   **9.** 6 × ■ = 30   **10.** ■ × 6 = 42

11. ■ × 7 = 28   **12.** 1 × ■ = 5   **13.** 4 × ■ = 36   **14.** ■ × 5 = 40

15. 8 × ■ = 0   **16.** ■ × 6 = 24   **17.** 8 × ■ = 56   **18.** ■ × 6 = 54

19. 3 times what number is 15?   **20.** What number times 4 is 16?

Critical Thinking

Find the missing number. Tell how you found it.

21. 49 ÷ ■ = 7   **22.** 24 ÷ ■ = 3   **23.** 35 ÷ ■ = 7   **24.** 72 ÷ ■ = 8

Mixed Applications Solve. Which method did you use?

ESTIMATION
MENTAL MATH
CALCULATOR
PAPER/PENCIL

25. Emmy Lou buys a bag containing 652 g of bird food and a box containing 391 g of fish food. Does she buy more than 1 kg of pet food?

26. There are 36 bags of cat food on sale. There are 9 bags on each shelf. How many shelves have bags of cat food?

27. During a sale the pet store gets 2,142 customers. For the rest of the month, it gets 978 customers. How many more customers came during the sale?

28. The pet store gets a shipment of 6 boxes of cat toys. Each box contains 9 cat toys. The store sells 50 of the toys in a week. How many toys are left?

CHALLENGE

1. Pick two even numbers. Multiply them.

2. Pick two odd numbers. Multiply them.

3. Pick an even number and an odd number. Multiply them.

4. Repeat Steps 1–3 five times.

5. Compare your products. What does this tell you about multiplying even and odd numbers?

Other Fact Strategies

A. During summer vacation Vida and Vera take care of pets and plants for people who are away from home. They charge $7 a week. This week they have 8 customers. How much will they earn?

Vida and Vera use **squares** to find 7×8.

Vida thinks: $7 \times 7 = 49$.   Vera thinks: $8 \times 8 = 64$.
I can count up from 7×7.   I can count down from 8×8.
$7 \times 8 = (7 \times 7) + 7$, or 56 $7 \times 8 = (8 \times 8) - 8$, or 56

Vida and Vera will earn $56 this week.

1. Find 7×5. Use a square and count up. Then find 7×5 by using a square and counting down.

B. You can use multiplication facts you know to help you remember other facts.

Think of 4×7 as $(2 \times 7) + (2 \times 7)$.   Think of 7×6 as $(7 \times 3) + (7 \times 3)$.
Then add: $14 + 14 = 28$.   Then add: $21 + 21 = 42$.

2. Use this method to find 8×6.

C. One week Vida and Vera earned $42. How many customers did they have that week?

You need to find $42 \div 7$.

Think of finding the missing factor: $\blacksquare \times 7 = 42$.

$6 \times 7 = 42$, so $42 \div 7 = 6$.

They had 6 customers that week.

3. Use the missing factor to find $72 \div 9$.

TRY OUT   Multiply or divide.

4. 8×6 **5.** 9×8 **6.** $63 \div 9$ **7.** $40 \div 5$

PRACTICE

Multiply.

8. 7
     × 5

9. 6
     × 9

10. 8
      × 6

11. 6
      × 7

12. 7
      × 7

13. 9
      × 8

14. 6 × 7 **15.** 8 × 6 **16.** 6 × 9 **17.** 7 × 5 **18.** 9 × 9

Divide.

19. 7)63 **20.** 6)54 **21.** 9)72 **22.** 5)45 **23.** 9)81 **24.** 7)56

25. 48 ÷ 6 **26.** 35 ÷ 7 **27.** 72 ÷ 8 **28.** 56 ÷ 8 **29.** 54 ÷ 9

Complete the table. Use the rule.

30. Rule: Multiply by 8.

4	5	6	7	8	9
■	■	■	■	■	■

31. Rule: Multiply by 9.

4	5	6	7	8	9
■	■	■	■	■	■

32. Rule: Divide by 6.

24	30	36	42	48	54
■	■	■	■	■	■

33. Rule: Divide by 7.

28	35	42	49	56	63
■	■	■	■	■	■

Mixed Applications

34. The Millers paid $7 each week for pet and plant service. How much did it cost them for 6 weeks?

35. One week Vida and Vera earned $63. If each customer paid $7, how many customers did they have that week?

36. Mrs. Garcia has 42 African violets and 7 ferns. How many plants does she have?

Mixed Review

Find the answer. Which method did you use?

37. 6 + 8 + 4 + 3 **38.** $704.23 − $68.44 **39.** 45 + 786

40. 5 × 8 **41.** 504 − 167 **42.** 12 ÷ 2

| MENTAL MATH |
| CALCULATOR |
| PAPER/PENCIL |

Factors and Multiples

A. The **multiples** of a number are the products of that number and other numbers.

Complete the tables of multiples. Multiply or skip-count.

MULTIPLES OF 2

1.

×	0	1	2	3	4	5	6	7	8	9
	0	2	4	■	■	■	■	■	■	■

MULTIPLES OF 3

2.

×	0	1	2	3	4	5	6	7	8	9
	0	3	6	■	■	■	■	■	■	■

Multiples of 2 are called **even numbers.** All other counting numbers are called **odd numbers.**

If two or more numbers have the same number as a multiple, that number is called a **common multiple.** The number 6 is a common multiple of 2 and 3.

3. Name another common multiple of 2 and 3.

B. The **factors** of a number are the numbers that can be multiplied to produce that number.

The factors of 3 are 1 and 3. $3 \times 1 = 3$ and $1 \times 3 = 3$

The factors of 6 are 1, 2, 3, and 6. $6 \times 1 = 6$, $3 \times 2 = 6$,
                                          $2 \times 3 = 6$, and $1 \times 6 = 6$

Two or more numbers can have some of the same factors. These factors are called **common factors.**

The common factors of 3 and 6 are 1 and 3.

4. What are the factors of 8 and 16? What are their common factors?

C. If a number has only two factors, itself and 1, it is called a **prime number.** If a number has more than those two factors, it is called a **composite number.**

5. Show that 5 is a prime number.

6. Show that 10 is a composite number.

7. Which number is not a multiple of 8?
   a. 56   **b.** 18   **c.** 48   **d.** 8

8. The number 4 is a factor of both:
   a. 4 and 14.   **b.** 4 and 10.   **c.** 14 and 24.   **d.** 8 and 12.

PRACTICE

Copy and complete to find the multiples.

×	0	1	2	3	4	5	6	7	8	9
9. Multiples of 6	■	■	■	■	■	■	■	■	■	■
10. Multiples of 7	■	■	■	■	■	■	■	■	■	■
11. Multiples of 8	■	■	■	■	■	■	■	■	■	■
12. Multiples of 9	■	■	■	■	■	■	■	■	■	■

Write *even* or *odd.*

13. 4   **14.** 12   **15.** 7   **16.** 15   **17.** 24   **18.** 35

Name a common multiple of the pair of numbers.

19. 2 and 6   **20.** 4 and 5   **21.** 3 and 4   **22.** 3 and 9

Name the factors of each pair of numbers. What are the common factors?

23. 7, 14   **24.** 8, 24   **25.** 11, 15   **26.** 21, 35   **27.** 18, 27

28. Which numbers in Exercises 23–27 are prime? Which are composite?

Critical Thinking
29. What number is a multiple of all other numbers? a factor of all other numbers?

Mixed Applications
Solve. You may need to use the Databank on page 519.

30. How many times faster than a chicken can a human being run?

31. What is the difference between the speed of a cat and the speed of a cheetah?

PROBLEM SOLVING

Strategy: Finding a Pattern

A. During a sale at the Peppy Pet store, Bertha gives away 2 cat toys for every 6 cans of cat food sold, 4 toys for every 12 cans, and 6 toys for every 18 cans. She gives away 12 cat toys on Tuesday. How many cans of cat food did she sell?

Bertha plans to make a table to help her find a pattern to solve the problem.

She knows that for every 6 cans of cat food sold she gives away 2 cat toys.

1. What can she do to continue the pattern for the number of cans sold?

2. What can she do to find the number of cat toys sold for each group of 6 cans?

3. Complete the table. How many cans of cat food did she sell?

Cans	Toys
6	2
12	4
18	6
24	8

B. When a dog collar first goes on sale the price is $12.00. After a month the price is $10.00. After 2 months it costs $8.00. If the price keeps decreasing like this, how much will the collar cost after 4 months?

Sometimes you do not need a table to find a pattern.

4. By how much does the cost of the collar decrease each month?

5. What can you do to find what the cost of the collar will be the next month?

6. Continue the pattern. How much does the collar cost after 4 months?

7. How does finding a pattern help you solve problems like these?

PRACTICE

**Find a pattern to solve the problem. Use a table if needed.
Use mental math, a calculator, or paper and pencil.**

8. Bertha gives away 3 free cans of fish food for every 5 fish sold, 6 cans for every 10 fish, and 9 cans for every 15 fish. She gives Bert 15 cans of fish food. How many fish did Bert buy?

9. Gary is buying dog food for a kennel. He sees that 6 cans cost $3.00, 12 cans cost $6.00, and 18 cans cost $9.00. Gary spends $15.00 on dog food. How many cans does he buy?

10. Tom sells 8 guppies on Monday, 16 guppies on Tuesday, and 24 guppies on Wednesday. If this pattern continues, how many guppies will he sell on Friday?

11. Pat stacks 8 rows of dog dishes in a pattern. There are 16 dishes in the bottom row, 14 dishes in the row above that, and 12 dishes in the next row. How many dishes will be in the top row?

Strategies and Skills Review

12. Chang has a 34-minute video about horses. He watches it for 12 minutes. Then he takes an 8-minute break before watching the rest of the video. How much time is left on the video?

13. The pet store has a sale on the 1st, 8th, and 15th of the month. If this pattern continues, on what day will the fifth sale fall?

14. When Tamla walked her dog, she had to stop for a red light every other block. The first light was green. At the end of 5 blocks, was the light red or green?

15. *Write a problem* that can be solved by finding a pattern. Solve your problem. Ask others to solve it.

ACTIVITY
Area

The **area** of a figure is the number of square units it takes to cover the figure. A metric unit for measuring area is the **square centimeter.**

1 cm

1 cm

WORKING TOGETHER

Draw shapes like these on heavy paper. Cut them out and trace around them on centimeter graph paper.

1. Count squares inside each figure to find the area. Combine incomplete squares in any reasonable way.

2. Have another student find the area of each of your figures. Compare results. Are they the same? Why or why not?

3. Draw some rectangles and squares on the graph paper. Count to find the area. Make a table.

4. What pattern do you see in the table?

5. How could you find the area without counting each square?

Number of Rows	Number of Squares in Each Row	Total Number of Squares (Area)
8	2	■

6. Which method is easier for finding the area of a rectangle or a square?

SHARING IDEAS

7. When you measured your figures on graph paper, which areas were easier to measure? Why?

8. What metric unit would you use to measure the area of your classroom? Why?

PRACTICE

Find the area in square centimeters

9.   **10.**   **11.**   **12.**

Measure the figure to the nearest centimeter. Find the area.

13.   **14.**   **15.**

Find the area.

16. rectangle with length 7 cm and width 5 cm

17. rectangle with length 6 dm and width 4 dm

18. square with sides 8 cm

19. square with sides 5 m

Critical Thinking

20. The area of a rectangular rug is 18 square m. The length is 6 m. How can you find the width? What is the width?

Mixed Applications

21. The school library is 30 m long and 20 m wide. What is the perimeter of the room?

22. A rug in the library is 9 m long and 6 m wide. What is the area of the rug?

Mixed Review

Find the answer. Which method did you use?

MENTAL MATH
CALCULATOR
PAPER/PENCIL

23. $63 \div 9$

24. $22{,}003 - 1{,}679$

25. $3{,}400 + 200$

26. 4×8

27. $\$24.33 + \$19.99$

28. $75 - 20$

EXTRA PRACTICE, page 211

ACTIVITY

Making Pictographs

Alicia has found data about rare animals.

She uses these steps to show the data in a pictograph.

Step 1 List each kind of animal.

Step 2 Choose a picture to represent the number of living animals.

Step 3 Draw pictures for each animal.
Let 🌎 = 100 animals

Step 4 Write the title above the graph.

Step 5 Write the number of animals each picture represents at the bottom of the graph.

WORLD POPULATION OF SOME RARE ANIMALS

Kind of Animal	Number Living
Golden lion tamarin monkey	350
Père David's deer	350
Spurred tortoise	100
Whooping crane	150

Kind of Animal	Number Living
Golden lion tamarin monkey	🌎 🌎 🌎 (
Père David's deer	
Spurred tortoise	
Whooping crane	
Each 🌎 = 100 animals	

WORKING TOGETHER

1. What does one half of the picture (🌓) equal?

2. Complete the pictograph.

3. How do you find the number of pictures for each animal?

SHARING IDEAS

4. Why do pictographs use one picture to show many items?

5. Why is it easier to compare data using a pictograph than using a table?

6. **What if** each 🌎 = 50 animals instead of 100 animals? How would this change what you draw for each kind of animal?

PRACTICE

Use this pictograph.

7. How many years is each picture worth?

8. Which animal has the greatest life span? the least life span?

9. How much greater is the life span of the box turtle than that of the horse?

10. List the life spans from the greatest to the least.

11. **Write a problem** using the information in the pictograph. Solve the problem. Then ask others to solve it.

Use the data to make a pictograph.

AVERAGE LIFE SPAN OF ANIMALS

Animal	Life Span
Box turtle	⧗ ⧗ ⧗ ⧗
Goat	⧗
Horse	⧗ ⧗
Pig	⧗
Rabbit	⧗

Each ⧗ = 10 years

12. **CATS IN THE CAT SHOW**

Kind of Cat	Number
American shorthair	45
Manx	15
Persian	20
Siamese	25

13. **ANIMALS BOUGHT LAST YEAR AT ANN'S ANIMAL HOUSE**

Kind of Animal	Number Bought
Cat	70
Dog	60
Goldfish	90
Hamster	50
Parrot	40

14. Make a survey among classes in your school to find the students' favorite pet. Make a pictograph to show the results.

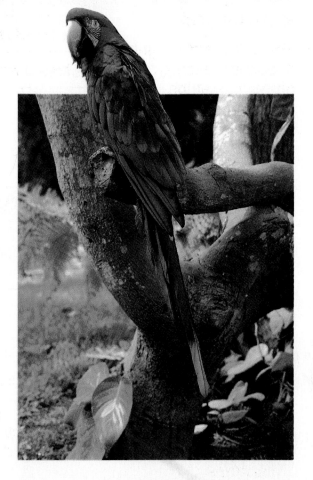

Problem Solving: Adopting a Pet

SITUATION

Kim and Dan and their parents are adopting a dog. At the Adopt-A-Pet center, they find two dogs they would like.

PROBLEM

Which dog should they adopt?

DATA

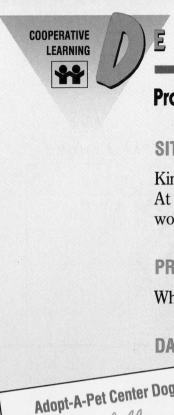

Adopt-A-Pet Center Dog Data Card

Name _Snowball_ Breed _Unknown_
Weight _70 lb_ Age _2 years_
Vaccinations Yes _X_ No ____
Date arrived _Nov. 10_ Date adopted ____
Health problems _None_
Daily feeding _5 packets and 2 bowls dry_
Lots of water!

Adopt-A-Pet Center Dog Data Card

Name _None_ Breed _Unknown_
Weight _10 lb (Adult-30 lb)_ Age _3 months_
Vaccinations Yes ____ No _X_
Date arrived _Nov. 15_ Date adopted ____
Health problems _None_
Daily feeding _2 packets and 1 bowl dry, till grown_
(Adult-2 packets and 2 bowls dry) Lots of water!

VACCINATIONS	
Puppy first year series	**$50**
Adult yearly booster	**$15**

Food	Puppy	Adult
Moist	20 packets for $10	25 packets for $5
Dry	$10 each 10-lb bag	$9 each 10-lb bag

DOG FOOD

USING THE DATA

How many packets of moist food will each dog eat in one week?

1. puppy   **2.** Snowball

Each bag holds 18 bowls of dry food. How long will it take each dog to finish a bag?

3. the puppy   **4.** the dog

5. How long will 25 packets feed Snowball? How much will it cost each day?

6. How long will 20 packets feed the puppy? How much will it cost each day?

7. Will the puppy cost more or less to feed as an adult than as a puppy? How much more or less?

MAKING DECISIONS

8. *Write a list* of the things Kim and Dan should think about before deciding which pet to adopt.

9. What will happen to Snowball's fluffy white coat in the summer? What extra care will Snowball need?

10. What are some reasons why Kim and Dan might prefer to adopt a dog that is already full-grown?

11. What are some reasons why Dan and Kim might prefer to adopt a puppy?

12. Would it make a difference in Kim's and Dan's decision whether they live in the country or in a city apartment? Why or why not?

13. *Write a list* of the things you would care about the most if you were adopting a dog.

Math and Literature

Tall tales are folk tales about heroes or heroines who do things no real person can do. These amazing deeds make us laugh. One popular tall-tale hero is Paul Bunyan.

The tales about Paul Bunyan say that he was the greatest lumberjack in history. He was so tall he towered over the trees. He crossed rivers in one step. His ax was as wide as a barn door, and the handle was made out of a whole oak tree.

When Paul was a baby, it took 14 cows to supply him with milk. Each day, Paul's parents found their baby son was 2 feet taller than he was the day before!

What if Paul grows 2 feet every day for a week? How much would Paul grow?

Think: Multiply. $7 \times 2 = 14$

Paul would grow 14 feet in a week.

ACTIVITIES

1. The pancakes Paul ate were so big that it took 5 ordinary men to eat one. Write a word problem about this that involves multiplication.

2. Write a tall tale about a hero or heroine you make up.

Calculator: Discover the Patterns

There are six different patterns on this page. You can use your calculator to discover them.

For each exercise, use your calculator to find the first few answers. When you discover a pattern, write the remaining answers without using a calculator. Then check your answers.

1. 4 × 9
   4 × 99
   4 × 999
   4 × 9,999
   4 × 99,999
   4 × 999,999

2. 1 × 999
   2 × 999
   3 × 999
   4 × 999
   5 × 999
   6 × 999

3. 9 × 9
   9 × 99
   9 × 999
   9 × 9,999
   9 × 99,999

4. 1 × 1
   11 × 11
   111 × 111
   1,111 × 1,111
   11,111 × 11,111

5. 1 × 2 × 101
   2 × 2 × 101
   3 × 2 × 101
   4 × 2 × 101
   5 × 2 × 101
   6 × 2 × 101

6. 1 × 12 × 101
   2 × 12 × 101
   3 × 12 × 101
   4 × 12 × 101
   5 × 12 × 101
   6 × 12 × 101

USING THE CALCULATOR

7. Make up two patterns of your own for others to find and complete.

EXTRA PRACTICE

The Meaning of Multiplication, page 177..

Write as a multiplication sentence and solve.

1. 3 + 3 + 3   **2.** 7 + 7 + 7 + 7 + 7   **3.** 6 + 6

Multiply.

4. 2 × 7   **5.** 4 × 6   **6.** 5 × 5   **7.** 3 × 9

8. How many in 4 groups of 9?   **9.** Find the product of 9 × 7.

10. 6 × 7	**11.** 8 × 8	**12.** 5 × 6	**13.** 2 × 9	**14.** 8 × 1	**15.** 9 × 6
16. 5 × 2	**17.** 3 × 6	**18.** 7 × 8	**19.** 6 × 6	**20.** 3 × 4	**21.** 4 × 5

The Meaning of Division, page 179..

Divide.

1. 16 ÷ 4   **2.** 28 ÷ 7   **3.** 14 ÷ 7   **4.** 10 ÷ 2

5. 3)18   **6.** 6)30   **7.** 8)32   **8.** 4)28   **9.** 7)49

10. 5)20   **11.** 7)21   **12.** 9)18   **13.** 2)16   **14.** 8)64

15. How many 4s are in 20?   **16.** What is 42 divided by 7?

Multiplication and Division Properties, page 181..

Find the missing number.

1. 3 × 0 = ■   **2.** 7 × 1 = ■   **3.** 6 × 2 × 3 = 2 × ■ × 6

4. 16 ÷ 4 = ■   **5.** 14 ÷ 2 = ■   **6.** 18 ÷ 6 = ■   **7.** 4 ÷ 4 = ■

Fact Families, page 183..

Write the fact family for the set of numbers.

1. 2, 6, 12   **2.** 5, 1, 5   **3.** 5, 4, 20   **4.** 5, 7, 35

2 Through 9 as Factors, page 185...

Multiply.

1. 7 × 1	**2.** 4 × 4	**3.** 6 × 7	**4.** 2 × 6	**5.** 4 × 7	**6.** 8 × 8

7. 6 × 3   **8.** 5 × 8   **9.** 9 × 3   **10.** 7 × 8   **11.** 4 × 6

12. 3 × 7   **13.** 6 × 5   **14.** 9 × 8   **15.** 6 × 8   **16.** 9 × 9

17. Multiply 7 × 7.   **18.** Find the product of 0 × 9.

Dividing by 2 Through 9, page 187...

Divide.

1. 2)$\overline{18}$ **2.** 4)$\overline{36}$ **3.** 5)$\overline{15}$ **4.** 8)$\overline{48}$ **5.** 9)$\overline{81}$ **6.** 6)$\overline{36}$

7. 4)$\overline{24}$ **8.** 8)$\overline{40}$ **9.** 5)$\overline{25}$ **10.** 7)$\overline{42}$ **11.** 9)$\overline{72}$ **12.** 3)$\overline{12}$

13. 5)$\overline{40}$ **14.** 8)$\overline{64}$ **15.** 6)$\overline{18}$ **16.** 3)$\overline{21}$ **17.** 7)$\overline{35}$ **18.** 8)$\overline{32}$

19. 14 ÷ 2   **20.** 54 ÷ 6   **21.** 8 ÷ 8   **22.** 30 ÷ 6   **23.** 45 ÷ 5

24. Find the quotient of 63 ÷ 7.   **25.** How many 4s are in 28?

Problem Solving Strategy: Choosing the Operation, page 189 ....

Decide which operation to use. Then solve the problem.

1. Brian changes his cat's water 3 times a day. How many times does he change the water in 1 week?

2. Chuck's turtle weighs 12 pounds. Tom's turtle weighs 7 pounds less. How many pounds does Tom's turtle weigh?

3. Cassie bought 63 dog treats for her dog. She put an equal number of treats into 9 bags. How many treats are in each bag?

4. The pet store owner has 45 gerbils. In one month, 8 more gerbils are born. How many gerbils are there in all?

EXTRA PRACTICE

Missing Factors, page 193 ....

Find the missing factor.

1. ■ × 3 = 27   2. 6 × ■ = 12   3. 4 × ■ = 12   4. ■ × 5 = 35

5. 6 × ■ = 48   6. ■ × 7 = 49   7. ■ × 9 = 45   8. 7 × ■ = 63

Find the missing number.

9. ■ ÷ 3 = 9   10. ■ ÷ 6 = 6   11. 36 ÷ ■ = 4   12. 18 ÷ ■ = 9

Other Fact Strategies, page 195 ....

Multiply or divide.

1. 8   2. 5   3. 9)54   4. 8)56   5. 3   6. 6)36
   × 9   × 8   × 8

Complete the table. Use the rule.

7. Rule: Multiply by 7.

3	4	5	6	7
■	■	■	■	■

8. Rule: Divide by 4.

16	20	24	28	32	36
■	■	■	■	■	■

Factors and Multiples, page 197 ....

Write *even* or *odd*.

1. 6   2. 14   3. 5   4. 17   5. 30   6. 45

Name a common multiple of the pair of numbers.

7. 3 and 6   8. 5 and 6   9. 4 and 8

Name the factors of the pair of numbers.
What are the common factors?

10. 5, 9   11. 6, 8   12. 13, 14   13. 10, 35   14. 7, 21

15. Which numbers in Questions 10–14 are prime? Which
    are composite?

Problem Solving Strategy: Finding a Pattern, page 199......................

Look for a pattern. Then solve the problem.

1. Tina is stacking cans of cat food in a pattern. She puts 4 cans in the first row, 9 cans in the second row, and 14 cans in the third row. How many cans will she put in the next 3 rows?

2. The pet store gives away 8 covers with 2 cases of food, 12 covers with 3 cases, and 16 covers with 4 cases. If this pattern continues, how many covers do they give away with 5 cases of food?

Area, page 201 ....

Find the area in square centimeters.

1.

2.

3.

2 cm

4 cm

4.

3 cm

Making Pictographs, page 203..............................

Use this pictograph.

1. How many votes is each picture worth?

2. Which kind of dog had the most votes? the least?

3. How many pictures do you need to show 54 dogs?

FAVORITE DOGS

Kind of Dog	Number of Votes
Poodle	🐕 🐕
German shepherd	🐕 🐕 🐕 🐕
Irish setter	🐕 🐕 🐕 🐕 🐕 🐕
Labrador	🐕 🐕 🐕 🐕 🐕 🐕 🐕
Each 🐕 = 6 votes	

Practice PLUS

KEY SKILL: Dividing by 2 Through 9 (Use after page 187.)

Level A

Divide.

1. $2\overline{)6}$ 2. $3\overline{)3}$ 3. $5\overline{)15}$ 4. $4\overline{)16}$ 5. $6\overline{)18}$

6. $7\overline{)14}$ 7. $9\overline{)18}$ 8. $3\overline{)9}$ 9. $2\overline{)14}$ 10. $5\overline{)30}$

11. $20 \div 4$ 12. $0 \div 3$ 13. $8 \div 2$ 14. $12 \div 6$ 15. $32 \div 4$

16. $7 \div 1$ 17. $12 \div 3$ 18. $8 \div 4$ 19. $10 \div 5$ 20. $30 \div 6$

21. Nan has 24 video games in 4 boxes. She has the same number in each box. How many games are in each box?

Level B

Divide.

22. $6\overline{)36}$ 23. $4\overline{)36}$ 24. $5\overline{)40}$ 25. $4\overline{)24}$ 26. $8\overline{)32}$

27. $3\overline{)27}$ 28. $2\overline{)18}$ 29. $4\overline{)0}$ 30. $6\overline{)30}$ 31. $8\overline{)24}$

32. $28 \div 4$ 33. $8 \div 8$ 34. $0 \div 5$ 35. $28 \div 7$ 36. $42 \div 7$

37. $18 \div 3$ 38. $25 \div 5$ 39. $16 \div 2$ 40. $54 \div 6$ 41. $40 \div 8$

42. Ned has 45 model planes. He puts 9 planes on each shelf. How many shelves does he use?

Level C

Divide.

43. $9\overline{)36}$ 44. $8\overline{)64}$ 45. $7\overline{)63}$ 46. $6\overline{)42}$ 47. $1\overline{)8}$

48. $7\overline{)49}$ 49. $8\overline{)48}$ 50. $9\overline{)45}$ 51. $5\overline{)35}$ 52. $8\overline{)56}$

53. $21 \div 7$ 54. $6 \div 1$ 55. $54 \div 9$ 56. $72 \div 8$ 57. $81 \div 9$

58. $48 \div 6$ 59. $56 \div 7$ 60. $45 \div 5$ 61. $0 \div 9$ 62. $72 \div 9$

63. Ann has 63 tickets to give away evenly to 9 friends. How many tickets does each friend get?

KEY SKILL: Factors and Multiples (Use after page 197.)

Level A ....

Write *even* or *odd*.

1. 6   **2.** 11   **3.** 13   **4.** 8   **5.** 16   **6.** 21

Name a common multiple of the pair of numbers.

7. 3 and 4   **8.** 2 and 5   **9.** 2 and 3   **10.** 4 and 5

Name the factors of the number.

11. 6   **12.** 9   **13.** 13   **14.** 15   **15.** 17

16. Name the common factors of 2 and 6.

Level B ....

Write *even* or *odd*.

17. 20   **18.** 25   **19.** 31   **20.** 49   **21.** 70   **22.** 104

Name a common multiple of the pair of numbers.

23. 5 and 6   **24.** 4 and 6   **25.** 7 and 8   **26.** 3 and 9

Name the factors of each pair of numbers. What are the common factors?

27. 8, 9   **28.** 15, 19   **29.** 10, 25   **30.** 12, 18   **31.** 14, 21

Level C ....

Name a common multiple of the pair of numbers.

32. 6 and 8   **33.** 5 and 7   **34.** 8 and 9   **35.** 6 and 9

Name the factors of each pair of numbers. What are the common factors?

36. 10, 13   **37.** 5, 35   **38.** 8, 12   **39.** 15, 21   **40.** 7, 49

41. Which numbers in Exercises 36–40 are prime numbers? Which are composite numbers?

CHAPTER REVIEW/TEST

LANGUAGE AND MATHEMATICS

Complete the sentences. Use the words in the chart.

1. The numbers being multiplied are called ■.

2. The ■ of a number are the products of that number and other numbers.

3. The ■ of a figure is the number of square units it takes to cover the figure.

4. In 56 ÷ 4, 4 is the ■.

CONCEPTS AND SKILLS

Find the missing factor.

5. $3 \times \blacksquare = 15$

6. $\blacksquare \times 4 = 0$

7. $4 \times (\blacksquare \times 2) = 40$

Write the fact family for the set of numbers.

8. 2, 2, 4

9. 3, 6, 18

10. 5, 4, 20

Name the factors of each pair. What are the common factors?

11. 5, 25

12. 9, 12

13. 4, 13

14. Which of the numbers in Exercises 11–13 are even? Which are odd? Which are prime? Which are composite?

Multiply or divide.

15. 5×8

16. 7×3

17. $8\overline{)56}$

18. $54 \div 6$

19. Find the area of a rectangle with length: 4 cm, width: 2 cm

Use the pictograph for Questions 20 and 21.

20. Which type of fish are there the most of?

21. How many more goldfish are there than catfish?

FISH AT THE AQUARIUM

Kind of Fish	Number
Goldfish	🐟🐟🐟🐟🐟
Angelfish	🐟🐟🐟
Swordfish	🐟🐟🐟🐟
Catfish	🐟
Each 🐟 = 5 fish	

Critical Thinking

Write *always,* *sometimes,* or *never* to complete the sentence.

22. The product of a number times 0 is ■ 0.

23. An odd number is ■ a multiple of 3.

Mixed Applications

24. A trivia contest has 3 competing teams. There are 9 people on each team. What is the total number of people in the contest? What operation did you use to find your answer?

25. Ada is painting dots on a box. There are 12 dots in the first row, 16 dots in the second, and 20 dots in the third row. If the pattern continues, how many dots will be in the fifth row?

PERFORMANCE ASSESSMENT

Work with your group to solve this problem.

Imagine that you work for a company that makes carpeting. Your job is to cut the carpet to the proper size to fit each order. On some orders only the area of a rectangular room is given. Pretend that you have just received 10 orders for carpets with areas ranging from 8 to 32 square meters. Decide the area of each of the ten carpets and give its length and width. Some of the carpets can have the same area, but should have different lengths and widths. Draw a sketch of each of the carpets.

1. ***Think about:***
    - the possible number of carpets with areas of 8 to 32 square meters
    - how to find the area of each carpet

2. Write a paragraph explaining how you and your group determined the shape of the carpets and found the areas of each.

CUMULATIVE REVIEW

Choose the letter of the correct answer.

1. Which is a factor of 21?

   a. 2   **c.** 7

   b. 4   **d.** not given

2. How much time passes between 2:39 and 3:01?

   a. 21 minutes   **c.** 40 minutes

   b. 22 minutes   **d.** not given

3. ■ × 8 = 40

   a. 4   **c.** 6

   b. 5   **d.** not given

4. The mass of a watermelon is:

   a. 5 g.   **c.** 5 kg.

   b. 50 g.   **d.** 50 kg.

5. Find the area of a square with 7-m sides.

   a. 14 sq m   **c.** 49 sq m

   b. 28 sq m   **d.** not given

6. Find the quotient of 36 ÷ 9.

   a. 4   **c.** 6

   b. 5   **d.** not given

7. What multiplied by 3 is 27?

   a. 6   **c.** 8

   b. 7   **d.** not given

8. Find the perimeter of a square with 3-cm sides.

   a. 6 cm   **c.** 12 cm

   b. 9 cm   **d.** not given

9. 15 is how many more than 9?

   a. 5   **c.** 7

   b. 6   **d.** not given

10. What is 0 divided by 4?

    a. 0   **c.** 4

    b. 1   **d.** not given

11. $24.38 − $.59

    a. $24.89   **c.** $23.79

    b. $23.89   **d.** not given

12. 6 + 2 + 3 + 5

    a. 8   **c.** 15

    b. 11   **d.** not given

13. Which number is prime?

    a. 2   **c.** 9

    b. 4   **d.** not given

14. What is 8 times 4?

    a. 2   **c.** 24

    b. 32   **d.** not given

ENRICHMENT FOR ALL

SIEVE OF ERATOSTHENES

Eratosthenes was a mathematician who lived in Africa and Greece about 2,000 years ago. He used these steps to separate prime numbers from composite numbers.

Think: A prime number has exactly two factors, itself and 1. A composite number has more than those two factors.

Follow Eratosthenes' steps to find the prime numbers less than 100.

1. Copy the list of numbers from 1 to 100.

2. Cross out the number 1. It is neither prime nor composite. Why?

3. Circle the number 2. It is the first prime number.

4. Cross out all the other multiples of 2. Why are these not prime numbers?

5. Circle the prime number 3. Cross out all the other multiples of 3.

6. What is the next prime number?

7. Circle it and cross out all its multiples.

1	2	3	4	5	6	7	8	9	10
11	12	13	14	15	16	17	18	19	20
21	22	23	24	25	26	27	28	29	30
31	32	33	34	35	36	37	38	39	40
41	42	43	44	45	46	47	48	49	50
51	52	53	54	55	56	57	58	59	60
61	62	63	64	65	66	67	68	69	70
71	72	73	74	75	76	77	78	79	80
81	82	83	84	85	86	87	88	89	90
91	92	93	94	95	96	97	98	99	100

8. Continue to circle the prime numbers and cross out their multiples until only prime numbers are left.

9. What is the last prime number that had multiples you had to cross out?

10. List all the prime numbers between 1 and 100.

11. How many prime numbers are there less than 100?

12. Why do you think this method is called the Sieve of Eratosthenes?

EGYPTIAN

DOUBLING

In ancient Egypt, few people had a chance to learn how to write. Those who were chosen to learn became honored scribes. Scribes had the responsibility of recording taxes paid to the ruling pharaoh. Some taxes were paid with grain or animals. In order to keep track of payments, the scribes used a number system based on ten. They used symbols for different numbers, such as a line for 1 (**/**), a heel bone for 10 (**∩**), and a snare (**℮**) for 100. The number 123 would be (**℮∩∩///**).

To multiply, the scribes doubled numbers. For example, suppose there are 5 meadows. In each meadow there are

6 goats. To figure out the total number of goats, make two columns. The column on the left is the number of meadows. Start with 1 and double it. Double each number until you see that the next number will be too large. Look at the numbers in the column. Are there two numbers that add up to 5? Put a check beside each number.

The column on the right is the number of goats. Start with 6, the number of goats in one meadow, and double each number until this column is even with the column on the left. Put a check beside the numbers in the right-hand column that add up to 30. The table below shows how this is done.

meadows	goats	meadows	goats
✓I	✓IIIIII	✓1	✓6
II	∩II	2	12
✓IIII	✓∩∩IIIII	✓4	✓24
sums IIIII	∩∩∩	5	30

1 What is another way to find the total number of goats in the 5 meadows?

2 Why does the Egyptian method of multiplying by doubling work?

3 Why were scribes important to the pharaoh?

Mental Math: Multiplying 10s and 100s

Bella, Carl, and Dora played a space game. Bella had to pay the fare to Mars 4 times. Carl had to pay the fare to Venus 5 times. Dora had to pay the fare to Mercury 6 times. The players used mental math to find the products.

Bella	Carl	Dora
$4 \times 1 = 4$	$5 \times 3 = 15$	$6 \times 5 = 30$
$4 \times 10 = 40$	$5 \times 30 = 150$	$6 \times 50 = 300$
$4 \times 100 = 400$	$5 \times 300 = 1,500$	$6 \times 500 = 3,000$
$4 \times 1,000 = 4,000$	$5 \times 3,000 = 15,000$	$6 \times 5,000 = 30,000$

The total fares were $4,000; $15,000; and $30,000.

1. Look at Bella's examples. Compare the number of zeros in each product with the number of zeros in each factor. What pattern do you see?

2. Does the pattern work in Carl's examples?

3. Does the pattern work in Dora's examples? Why or why not?

TRY OUT
Write the letter of the correct answer.
Multiply mentally.

4. 7×20 **a.** 14   **b.** 140   **c.** 1,400   **d.** 14,000

5. 5×800 **a.** 40   **b.** 400   **c.** 4,000   **d.** 40,000

6. 9×700 **a.** 63   **b.** 630   **c.** 6,300   **d.** 63,000

7. $2 \times 5,000$ **a.** 100   **b.** 1,000   **c.** 10,000   **d.** 100,000

PRACTICE

Multiply mentally.

8. 10
× 3

9. 10
× 7

10. 20
× 3

11. 30
× 4

12. 40
× 5

13. 100
× 2

14. 200
× 5

15. 1,000
× 6

16. 8,000
× 3

17. 7,000
× 7

18. 6 × 10

19. 9 × 10

20. 4 × 100

21. 5 × 100

22. 8 × 100

23. 7 × 1,000

24. 5 × 1,000

25. 3 × 1,000

26. 6 × 70

27. 9 × 50

28. 7 × 400

29. 8 × 600

30. 2 × 900

31. 6 × 9,000

32. 5 × 6,000

33. 8 × 8,000

Critical Thinking

34. How would you find the product of 8 × 50,000? What is the product?

Mixed Applications

35. The fare to the Moon was $800. Bella had to pay it 4 times. What was her total fare?

36. Dora bought a book about astronauts for $9.75 and one about astronomy for $11.59. How much did she spend for the two books?

CHALLENGE

You can write multiples of 10 using **exponents**.

There are 3 zeros after the 1.

$10 \times 10 \times 10 = 1,000 = 10^3$ Say: 10 to the 3rd power.

There are 3 factors.   The exponent is 3.

Write the power of 10 using an exponent.

1. 10 × 10

2. 10 × 10 × 10 × 10

3. 10 × 10 × 10 × 10 × 10

4. 100

5. 100,000

6. 1,000,000

Estimating Products

The State Astronomy Club has 476 members. The secretary sends about 6 books a year to each member. About how many books does the secretary send each year?

Estimate: 6 × 476

Here are two ways to estimate the product.

Rounding

Round the greater number to its greatest place.

$$\begin{array}{r} 476 \\ \times\ \ 6 \\ \hline \end{array}$$

Think:
$$\begin{array}{r} 500 \\ \times\ \ 6 \\ \hline 3,000 \end{array}$$

The estimate is 3,000 books.

Front-End Estimation

Use the front digits.

$$\begin{array}{r} 476 \\ \times\ \ 6 \\ \hline \end{array}$$

Think:
$$\begin{array}{r} 400 \\ \times\ \ 6 \\ \hline 2,400 \end{array}$$

The estimate is 2,400 books.

1. Which method results in an estimate that is greater than the exact answer? Why?

2. Which method results in an estimate that is less than the exact answer? Why?

3. Estimate 9 × 3,174 using both methods. How do the estimates compare? Why?

TRY OUT Write the letter of the correct answer.

Estimate by rounding.

4. 5 × 84   **a.** 40   **b.** 400   **c.** 4,000

5. 8 × $327   **a.** $2,400   **b.** $240   **c.** $24,000

6. 3 × 4,617   **a.** 150,000   **b.** 15,000   **c.** 1,500

Estimate by using the front digits.

7. 7 × $68   **a.** $4,200   **b.** $42   **c.** $420

8. 2 × 843   **a.** 160   **b.** 1,600   **c.** 16,000

9. 4 × 6,809   **a.** 24,000   **b.** 2,400   **c.** 240

PRACTICE

Estimate by rounding.

10. 29
    × 6

11. 83
    × 3

12. 18
    × 7

13. $47
    × 9

14. 621
    × 5

15. 869
    × 8

16. $535
    × 2

17. 3,095
    × 4

18. 7,730
    × 5

19. $1,927
    × 6

20. 4 × 53

21. 6 × 32

22. 3 × $95

23. 7 × 429

24. 5 × 417

25. 8 × $447

26. 9 × 3,350

27. 2 × 5,711

Estimate by using the front digits.

28. 14
    × 8

29. 39
    × 5

30. 72
    × 3

31. $68
    × 4

32. 226
    × 7

33. 555
    × 6

34. $829
    × 5

35. 4,706
    × 9

36. 2,275
    × 8

37. 3,579
    × 4

38. 6 × 16

39. 9 × 87

40. 4 × $93

41. 8 × 177

42. 7 × 342

43. 5 × $716

44. 3 × 4,882

45. 6 × 5,279

Write >, <, or = . Use estimation.

46. 4 × 284 ● 645

47. 6 × 329 ● 2,400

48. 4,511 ● 5 × 838

Mixed Applications

49. The Astronomy Club has $5,000. It wants to buy 3 telescopes that cost $1,397 each. Does the club have enough money?

50. The Planetarium has 786 new members this year. There are 1,427 members. How many people were members last year?

Mixed Review

Find the missing number.

51. 8 × ■ = 56

52. 632 − ■ = 114

53. ■ ÷ 9 = 4

54. 82 + ■ + 71 = 202

55. ■ × 5 = 5

56. 9 − ■ = 9

PROBLEM SOLVING

Strategy: Guess, Test, and Revise

There are 54 candidates at astronaut school. They are divided into 14 teams. Some teams have 3 members each, and the rest have 5 members each. How many teams have only 3 members? 5 members?

One way to solve the problem is to start with a guess; test your guess; and if it is wrong, revise it until you find the correct answer.

Barb first guesses that there are 7 teams with 3 members and 7 teams with 5 members. She tests her guess.

Guess
7 teams of 3
7 teams of 5

1. Is her guess correct? Why or why not?

2. Why should Barb lower her guess?

Test
$7 \times 3 = 21$
$7 \times 5 = + 35$
$\overline{ 56}$

Barb revises her guess. She tries 8 teams with 3 members and 6 teams with 5 members.

Revised Guess
8 teams of 3
6 teams of 5

3. Is her guess correct? Why or why not?

Test
$8 \times 3 = 24$
$6 \times 5 = + 30$
$\overline{ \blacksquare}$

4. **What if** some teams had 3 members each and the rest had 6 members each? How many of each would there be?

5. How did you make your guess? Did you have to revise it? Why or why not?

Use the Guess, Test, and Revise strategy to solve the problem.
Use mental math, a calculator, or paper and pencil.

6. There are twice as many men as women among the 54 candidates. How many men are there? How many women?

7. The weightless chamber is used 48 times a day by 10 astronauts. Only one astronaut may be in the chamber at a time. Senior astronauts use the chamber 6 times a day, and junior astronauts use it 4 times a day. How many senior astronauts are there? junior astronauts?

8. During training only 1 member of a team of 7 astronauts can be asleep at any time during a 24-hour period. Each astronaut may sleep for either 3 hours or 4 hours. How many may sleep for 3 hours? How many for 4 hours?

9. In a 24-hour day astronauts study 3 times as many hours as they exercise. They eat and sleep twice as many hours as they exercise. How many hours do they study? exercise? eat and sleep?

Strategies and Skills Review

10. Donna bought a model of a spaceship and a book on space travel for $22. She spent $4 more on the book than on the model. How much did she spend on each?

11. The space center sells booklets of 8 postcards of spaceships. Last month it sold 700 booklets. How many postcards of spaceships did it sell?

12. The Soviet spaceship *Soyuz 7* orbited earth 79 times. *Soyuz 11* orbited 360 times. How many fewer times did *Soyuz 7* orbit earth than *Soyuz 11*?

13. ***Write a problem*** that can be solved by the Guess, Test, and Revise strategy. Solve the problem. Ask others to solve your problem.

ACTIVITY

Multiplying by 1-Digit Factors

A spaceship can carry 48 people. How many people can it carry in 3 trips?

WORKING TOGETHER

Solve the problem by making a model.

1. How does your model show the number of people the ship can carry in 1 trip?

2. How does your model show the number of trips?

3. How many people can the ship carry in 3 trips?

Here is a way to solve the problem using place-value models.

Step 1 Make 3 groups of models with 4 tens and 8 ones in each group.

Step 2 Combine the ones. Regroup the ones.

4. How many ones are left? How many new tens are there?

Step 3 Combine the tens, including the new tens. Regroup the tens.

5. How many tens are left?

6. How many hundreds are there?

7. How does the model show the total number of people?

Use place-value models to find how many there are in all.

8. 3 groups of 32

9. 4 groups of 23

10. 5 groups of 34

11. 6 groups of 41

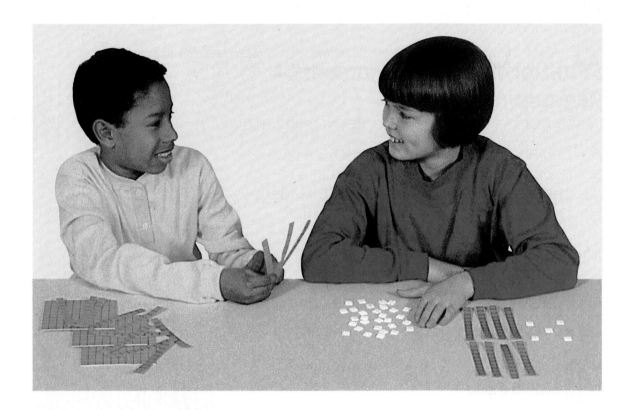

12. In which exercises above did you need to regroup ones? tens? Why?

13. Why is it better to combine the ones before the tens and the tens before the hundreds?

ON YOUR OWN

Solve using place-value models.
Tell how you solved the problem.

14. Each of 5 astronauts on a space flight has 21 experiments to work on. How many experiments will the astronauts perform?

15. On one mission 7 astronauts will spend 13 days in space. They each must write one report a day. How many reports will they write?

16. A space bus has 16 seats in each module. If there are 3 modules, how many seats are there?

17. *Write a problem* that you can solve by finding the total number of things in equal groups.

Multiplying 2-Digit Numbers— Regrouping Once

A. Erik and Kim are planning a school trip to the Space Museum. They know that 3 classes are going. Each class has 26 students. How many students are going on the trip?

Erik estimates: $3 \times 30 = 90$

He uses place-value models to find the exact answer.

Multiply: 3×26

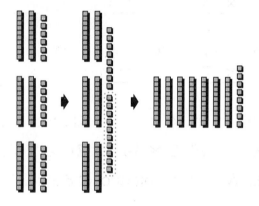

1. Did Erik regroup? Why or why not?

2. How many students are going on the trip?

B. Kim records the way that Erik multiplied. They both see that they can multiply without models.

Step 1	Step 2
Multiply the ones. **Regroup if necessary.**	**Multiply the tens.** **Add any new tens.**

Step 1:
$$\begin{array}{r} {}^{1} \\ 2\,6 \\ \times\ \ 3 \\ \hline 8 \end{array}$$

Think: 18 ones = 1 ten 8 ones

Step 2:
$$\begin{array}{r} {}^{1} \\ 2\,6 \\ \times\ \ 3 \\ \hline 7\,8 \end{array}$$

Think: 3×2 tens = 6 tens; 6 tens + 1 ten = 7 tens

SHARING IDEAS

3. Compare Kim's method with Erik's. How are they the same? How are they different?

4. What products do you see when using the models that you do not see when using the numbers?

5. Look at Step 2 of Kim's method. Why do you multiply the tens before you add the new tens?

PRACTICE

Multiply. Use place-value models if needed.

6. 49	**7.** 61	**8.** 23	**9.** 42	**10.** 14	**11.** 21
× 2	× 5	× 3	× 4	× 6	× 8

12. 32	**13.** 81	**14.** 36	**15.** 31	**16.** 29	**17.** 52
× 2	× 5	× 2	× 7	× 2	× 4

18. 8 × 31   **19.** 5 × 16   **20.** 2 × 35   **21.** 4 × 91   **22.** 6 × 15

23. 2 × 42   **24.** 3 × 53   **25.** 2 × 45   **26.** 5 × 19   **27.** 2 × 74

28. What is 4 times 16?   **29.** What is the product of 6 and 51?

Find the missing number. Tell how you found it.

30. 25 × ■ = 25   **31.** ■ × 37 = 0   **32.** 17 × 4 = ■ × 17

Mixed Applications

Solve. Which method did you use?

33. The students spent 4 weeks on a space travel project. They worked on it for 13 hours per week. How many hours did they spend on the project?

34. A rocket is traveling at a speed of 6,139 miles per hour. About how many miles does it travel in 5 hours?

35. Erik read a 179-page book on the history of space travel and a 101-page book on the training of astronauts. How many pages did he read in all?

> ESTIMATION
> MENTAL MATH
> PAPER/PENCIL
> CALCULATOR

Multiplying 2-Digit Numbers— Regrouping Twice

The students in 2 art classes are making space-station models. There are 57 students in each art class. How many students are making space-station models?

Estimate first. Then multiply: 2 × 57.

Step 1	Step 2
Multiply the ones. Regroup if necessary.	**Multiply the tens. Add any new tens. Regroup if necessary.**
$\begin{array}{r} \overset{1}{5}\,7 \\ \times\ \ 2 \\ \hline 4 \end{array}$	$\begin{array}{r} \overset{1}{5}\,7 \\ \times\ \ 2 \\ \hline 1\,1\,4 \end{array}$
Think: 14 ones = 1 ten 4 ones	***Think:*** 10 tens + 1 ten = 11 tens

There are 114 students making models.

1. Is the answer reasonable? How do you know?

2. What is the product of 57 × 2? How do you know?

TRY OUT Write the letter of the correct answer.

3. 4 × 39   **a.** 126   **b.** 156   **c.** 246   **d.** 1,236

4. 5 × 48   **a.** 200   **b.** 240   **c.** 400   **d.** 2,040

PRACTICE

Multiply.

5.	37	6.	65	7.	28	8.	22	9.	34	10.	39
	× 3		× 2		× 4		× 5		× 6		× 4

11.	73	12.	18	13.	16	14.	24	15.	26	16.	32
	× 5		× 7		× 8		× 9		× 7		× 8

17.	62	18.	49	19.	13	20.	54	21.	28	22.	47
	× 7		× 3		× 8		× 5		× 7		× 6

23. 9 × 44   **24.** 4 × 54   **25.** 8 × 76   **26.** 6 × 65   **27.** 7 × 89

28. 6 × 58   **29.** 4 × 44   **30.** 7 × 34   **31.** 3 × 96   **32.** 6 × 47

33. 8 × 35   **34.** 9 × 79   **35.** 3 × 87   **36.** 8 × 46   **37.** 5 × 65

Critical Thinking

38. If you multiply a 2-digit number by a 1-digit number (other than 0), what is the smallest product you can get? What is the largest product you can get?

Mixed Applications

39. Mia designs a space lab with 5 rooms. Each room holds 24 people. How many people could fit in Mia's space lab?

40. Maria designed a shuttle that has 18 seats. Teri's shuttle has 24 seats. How many more seats does Teri's shuttle have?

41. *Write a problem* that you solve by multiplying. Solve your problem. Ask others to solve your problem.

MENTAL MATH

Here is a way to multiply mentally. Find 6 × 23.

Think: 6 × 20 = 120 and 6 × 3 = 18;
so 6 × 23 = 120 + 18 = 138.

Multiply mentally.

1. 4 × 36   **2.** 2 × 75   **3.** 3 × 84   **4.** 7 × 56   **5.** 8 × 67

RIDDLE-O-RAMA

Experimenting and Predicting

A. Welcome to Riddle-O-Rama!
First you answer some tricky number riddles. Then you make up your own riddles. When you are done, you get to pick a prize.

Let's begin. Here is your first riddle:

> I'm a 2-digit number.
> My tens digit is 5 more than my ones digit.
> I'm greater than 65 and odd.
> What number am I?

1. Think about each clue. "A 2-digit number" tells you that it is a number between 10 and 99. The second clue tells you there are even fewer possibilities. There are only 5 numbers between 10 and 99 that fit this clue. What are they? The last clue removes four of these numbers as possible answers. How? What is the final answer?

Here are the rest of your number riddles:

2. I am a 2-digit number.
   The sum of my digits is 12.
   Both of my digits are the same.

3. I am a 2-digit number.
   My tens digit is 2 less than my ones digit.
   The sum of my digits is 10.

4. I am a 3-digit number.
   My hundreds digit is the same as my ones digit.
   My tens digit is 2 more than my ones digit.
   I'm less than 400 and even.

5. Create your own number riddles for other students to solve.

B. Congratulations! You have solved your number riddles. Now you get to pick your prize. Which one

About how much is each prize worth? You can experiment to find out.

6. Suppose you cannot get enough pennies to make a pound. Then how can you find how much a pound of pennies is worth? You could weigh one penny and then estimate how many are in a pound. But it would be easier to weigh 10 pennies or even a roll of 50 pennies.

Use one of the methods above. What is the approximate value of a pound of pennies?

How could you find the approximate value of the stack of quarters? Which prize would you choose? Why?

There are three more pairs of prizes to choose from. Experiment to find the approximate value of each. Then decide which one you would choose in each pair.

7.

8.

9.

Multiplying 3-Digit Numbers

The Franklin School students are going to the State Science Fair. It is 156 km from their town. How many km is the round-trip?

Multiply: 2 × 156

Step 1	Step 2	Step 3
Multiply the ones. **Regroup if necessary.**	**Multiply the tens.** **Add any new tens.** **Regroup if necessary.**	**Multiply the hundreds.** **Add any new hundreds.** **Regroup if necessary.**

Step 1:
```
    1
  1 5 6     Think:
×     2     12 ones =
─────────   1 ten 2 ones
      2
```

Step 2:
```
  1 1
  1 5 6     Think:
×     2     10 tens + 1 ten =
─────────   11 tens =
    1 2     1 hundred, 1 ten
```

Step 3:
```
  1 1
  1 5 6     Think:
×     2     2 hundreds +
─────────   1 hundred =
  3 1 2     3 hundreds
```

The round-trip is 312 km.

1. How do you know the answer is reasonable?

2. **What if** you multiplied 4 × 207? How many times do you need to regroup? What is the product?

3. **What if** you multiplied 3 × 479? How many times do you need to regroup? What is the product?

TRY OUT   Write the letter of the correct answer.

4. 4 × 413   **a.** 1,652   **b.** 1,661   **c.** 1,682   **d.** 16,412

5. 5 × 706   **a.** 3,503   **b.** 3,530   **c.** 4,050   **d.** 35,030

6. 3 × 589   **a.** 1,632   **b.** 1,767   **c.** 1,547   **d.** 4,007

PRACTICE

Multiply. Solve only for products that are greater than 900.

7.	216 × 4	**8.**	323 × 3	**9.**	611 × 5	**10.**	413 × 7	**11.**	609 × 8	**12.**	534 × 2
13.	409 × 3	**14.**	442 × 2	**15.**	624 × 6	**16.**	509 × 9	**17.**	480 × 4	**18.**	825 × 5
19.	763 × 3	**20.**	196 × 5	**21.**	794 × 7	**22.**	645 × 9	**23.**	842 × 8	**24.**	939 × 9

25. 6 × 340 **26.** 7 × 109 **27.** 6 × 725 **28.** 4 × 813

29. 8 × 423 **30.** 9 × 603 **31.** 3 × 908 **32.** 5 × 467

Mixed Applications

33. There are 5 rooms for showing the students' projects. Each room has 306 projects. How many projects are there?

34. Models of the solar system cost $126. The science teacher bought 2 of them. How much did she spend all together?

35. There are 205 projects on space science and 146 on biology. How many more projects on space science are there than projects on biology?

36. At the fair 355 students saw a show on planets, and 416 students saw a show on fossils. What was the total attendance at the two shows?

Mixed Review

Find the answer. Which method did you use?

37. 3,400 + 200

38. $405.37 − $287.89

39. 7 × 6,000

40. 72 ÷ 8

41. $3.75 + $5.98

42. 709 − 165

MENTAL MATH
CALCULATOR
PAPER/PENCIL

ACTIVITY

Multiplying Money

A. You can use a calculator to learn about multiplying money.

1. Use a calculator to multiply the following:
   a. 6 × 213
   6 × $2.13
   b. 9 × 1,851
   9 × $18.51
   c. 6 × 79
   6 × $.79

2. What pattern do you notice in each set of problems above?

3. Where is the decimal point in each of the factors in Question 1? Where is the decimal point in each of the products?

Multiply 7 × 624 on the calculator. [7][×][6][2][4][=]

4. What is the product?

5. Predict what the product of 7 × $6.24 will be. Check your prediction on the calculator.

B. You can multiply money without using a calculator.

Multiply: 4 × $8.59

First estimate. Round to the nearest dollar. 4 × $9 = $36

Step 1

Multiply as you would
multiply whole numbers.
```
  2 3
$8.5 9
×     4
3 4 3 6
```

Step 2

Write the dollar sign
and decimal point in the product.
```
  2 3
$8.5 9
×      4
$3 4.3 6
```

SHARING IDEAS

6. How is estimating products with money like estimating products with whole numbers?

7. How is multiplying money the same as multiplying whole numbers? How is it different?

8. **What if** you multiplied 5 × $7.92? What would be the product?

PRACTICE

Multiply. Use mental math, a calculator, or paper and pencil.

9. $.35
    × 2

10. $.18
    × 7

11. $.20
    × 5

12. $.58
    × 8

13. $.89
    × 6

14. $1.32
    × 4

15. $2.03
    × 3

16. $6.12
    × 8

17. $5.03
    × 6

18. $7.28
    × 3

19. $4.68
    × 5

20. $7.32
    × 9

21. $5.75
    × 6

22. $4.80
    × 7

23. $6.78
    × 4

24. 8 × $.37

25. 4 × $.70

26. 9 × $.35

27. 2 × $.98

28. 6 × $5.00

29. 3 × $8.75

30. 7 × $8.69

31. 9 × $6.08

Mixed Applications

Solve. You may need to use the Databank on page 519.

32. Lenny bought 3 packets of astronaut food. How much did they cost all together?

33. How much more do the kites cost than the flying disks?

34. **What if** you had $10 to spend in the souvenir shop? What would you buy? How much money would you have left?

35. **Write a problem** about buying things in the souvenir shop. Ask others to solve your problem.

Mixed Review

Find the answer. Which method did you use?

36. $3.75
    + 2.98

37. $6.80
    − 2.00

38. 80
    × 5

39. 506
    − 178

40. 200
    × 7

MENTAL MATH
CALCULATOR
PAPER/PENCIL

ACTIVITY

Multiplying Larger Numbers

The 4 new Discovery space satellites will be launched together. They will explore every planet in the solar system. Each satellite weighs 1,958 pounds. How much do they weigh all together?

WORKING TOGETHER

Work with a group. Have each one in the group use a different method to find the answer. You can use mental math, paper and pencil, or a calculator.

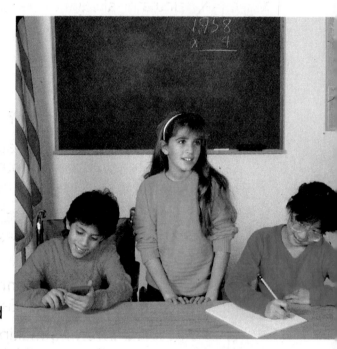

1. Is it easy to find the product mentally? Why or why not?

2. Show how to use paper and pencil to find the product.

3. Check to see if your answer is reasonable. How can you do this?

4. Which method was fastest?

5. **What if** the satellites weighed 2,000 pounds? Which method would be fastest?

Use all three methods to find 3 × 4,203.

6. What is the product? Can you find it mentally? Why or why not?

7. How long does it take you to find the product using paper and pencil?

8. Which method was fastest: mental math, a calculator, or paper and pencil?

Find the product. Which method did you use?

9.	10.	11.	12.	13.
2,415	6,001	$40.20	7,369	$56.89
× 7	× 5	× 3	× 8	× 2

SHARING IDEAS

14. How is multiplying 4-digit numbers like multiplying 3-digit or 2-digit numbers?

15. Tell how you decided which method to use in Exercises 9–13.

16. When do you think it is easier to use mental math? paper and pencil? a calculator? Tell why.

17. Is the calculator always easier to use with larger numbers? Why or why not?

ON YOUR OWN

MENTAL MATH
CALCULATOR
PAPER/PENCIL

Solve. Which method did you use?

18. Attendance at the Space Museum is about 4,500 on Saturdays in the summer. About what is the total attendance for 5 Saturdays in the summer?

19. One day 1,020 people each paid $8 to see a show about travel to Venus. What was the total amount paid to see the show?

20. A research satellite circles Earth 5,419 times a year. How many times will it circle Earth if it stays up 6 years?

21. *Write a problem* involving multiplication with a large factor. Choose which method you think should be used to solve it. Trade problems with other students and compare methods.

PROBLEM SOLVING

Strategy: Using Estimation

Sally manages the Space Museum gift shop. She wants to have at least 500 models of spaceships in stock. She has 243 models and expects a shipment of 125 next week. She plans to order another 230 models. Will she have enough models?

To make sure there will be enough models, Sally plans to **underestimate.**

Sally tries her plan. She rounds *down* to get an underestimate.

$$
\begin{array}{rcr}
243 & \rightarrow & 200 \\
125 & \rightarrow & 100 \\
230 & \rightarrow & +\ 200 \\
\hline
 & & 500
\end{array}
$$

1. Will she have enough models?

2. Why can Sally be sure she has enough if she underestimates?

Robert is in charge of selling tickets to the sky show. The auditorium seats 400 people. The museum sells 197 tickets through the mail, 72 over the phone, and 83 at the box office. Will there be enough seats for all ticket holders?

To make sure there are enough seats, Robert plans to **overestimate** the number of tickets sold. So he rounds *up*.

$$
\begin{array}{rcr}
197 & \rightarrow & 200 \\
72 & \rightarrow & 100 \\
83 & \rightarrow & +\ 100 \\
\hline
 & & 400
\end{array}
$$

3. Will there be enough seats?

4. Why can Robert be sure he has enough if he overestimates?

PRACTICE

Use estimation to solve the problem. Did you overestimate or underestimate?

5. Three astronauts who will travel together must not weigh more than 600 pounds. If two of the astronauts weigh 167 pounds and 153 pounds, can the third one weigh 198 pounds?

6. The record one-day attendance at the museum was 700. This morning 512 people came. If 245 people come this afternoon, will this break the attendance record?

7. The museum cafeteria plans to give away at least 500 samples of space food. It has 135 cookies, 163 pieces of fruit, and 348 nuts. Does it have enough samples?

8. Guido wants to buy a space set for $10.95, a planet book for $7.75, and a telescope for $109.50. Is $130.00 enough to pay for these items?

Strategies and Skills Review

Solve. Use mental math, a calculator, or paper and pencil.

9. Sally calculates that 180 people came into the store today. She knows that 22 people came in each hour and that the store is open for 6 hours. Is her answer reasonable? Why or why not?

10. Sally sells 45 posters of Jupiter. She also sells 69 buttons and 3 books on Jupiter. How many posters and buttons does she sell?

11. Robert is looking at the attendance figures for the sky show. Last month 357 people saw the show. This month 402 people saw the show. How many more people saw the show this month?

12. *Write a problem* that can be solved by estimation. Solve your problem. Ask others to solve it.

Multiplying by 1-Digit Factors **241**

DECISION MAKING

Problem Solving: Planning a Trip to Mars

SITUATION

The Sanger School Rocket Club wrote to NASA for data to plan a trip to Mars. They found that Earth and Mars pass near each other about every 780 days. For a long trip, the club could fly to Mars as the planets pass near each other. They could explore a long time, flying home as the planets get close again. For a short trip, the club could fly to Mars just before the planets pass near each other. They could stay a short time and fly back before the planets get too far apart.

PROBLEM

Should they take the long trip or the short trip?

DATA

DATA FOR MARS TRIP

	LONG TRIP	SHORT TRIP
Travel Time	6 months one way	7 months one way
Exploration Time	18 months	1 month
Total Time	30 months (912 days)	15 months (456 days)
Daily Food Supply	3 pounds per person	3 pounds per person
Daily Water Supply	5 pounds per person	5 pounds per person
Daily Oxygen Supply	2 pounds per person	2 pounds per person

COMPARISON OF TRIPS

LONG TRIP
o more back-up equipment needed
o less room for research equipment
o more time to research and explore
o more strain on equipment and people

SHORT TRIP
o less back-up equipment needed
o more room for research equipment
o less time to research and explore
o less strain on equipment and people

RESEARCH PROJECTS FOR TRIP

1) Collect and study soil samples
2) Look for signs of life, past or present
3) Draw map of entire planet
4) Study the effects of weightlessness and lower Martian gravity on the human body

USING THE DATA

1. How many pounds of food will each person need for the long trip? the short trip?

2. How many pounds of water will each person need for the long trip? the short trip?

3. How many pounds of oxygen will each person need for the long trip? the short trip?

4. How many pounds of supplies will each person need in all for the long trip? the short trip?

MAKING DECISIONS

5. On which trip would the members of the club be able to find out more about Mars?

6. Consider the research the club wants to complete and the supplies needed for each crew member. How many people should the club send to Mars?

7. What are some problems that might arise in 30 months away from Earth that might not arise in 15 months? What problems might not become as serious in a shorter time?

8. A lot of time, money, and effort are invested in a trip to another planet. Which trip will offer more in return for all that time, money, and effort?

9. **Write a list** of things that the Rocket Club should think about in deciding which trip to take.

10. Would you take a long trip or a short trip if you were going to Mars? How many people would you take? Why?

Math and Health

Have you ever had a sunburn? Then you know that the sun's rays can hurt your skin. The sun's rays can also cause wrinkles or more serious skin problems in the years to come.

Putting on sunscreen protects skin from sunburn. Sunscreens are labeled with **SPF** numbers. SPF stands for **Sun Protection Factor**. The higher the SPF number, the more protection the sunscreen gives. You may know how long you can stay in the sun before you start to burn. Sunscreen multiplies the amount of time you can stay in the sun by the SPF number.

Lynn can stay in the sun 2 hours without burning. She plans to play baseball for 4 hours. Using a sunscreen with an SPF of 2, Lynn can stay out 2 times as long, or 4 hours. To be safe, she should use a sunscreen with an even higher SPF.

What if Lynn chooses a sunscreen with an SPF of 8? How long can she stay in the sun without burning?

Think: $2 \times SPF = $ number of hours

$2 \times 8 = 16$

Lynn can stay in the sun for 16 hours without burning.

ACTIVITY

1. Plan a schedule of your outdoor activities for a weekend day. Include activities like sports, yard work, or watching a sporting event. After you have planned your schedule, decide what sunscreen you will need. How did you decide?

Computer Spreadsheet: Space Missions

The Space Center wants to launch six space missions in the next five years. The current budget has a limit of 7,000 food packs for all the missions. You are preparing a list of possible missions that will allow you to stay within the budget. Spaceships for these missions will hold from two to eight astronauts. You can use a **computer spreadsheet** to help you keep track of the data.

AT THE COMPUTER

Run the computer spreadsheet program call SPACE.

1. How are the data in columns 2, 3, and 4 related?

2. Which of the missions do you think are currently intended to be long trips? Which do you think are intended to be short trips? Why?

3. **What if** Mission 2 had one more astronaut? What parts of the spreadsheet would change?

4. Suppose you want Mission 6 to be a slightly longer trip than Mission 4. Enter a number of astronauts for Mission 6 and a reasonable number of food packs needed for each astronaut. See how close you can get to filling in the spreadsheet while staying within the food budget.

5. **What if** Mission 3 was a longer mission with fewer astronauts on it? Enter new data in columns 2 and 3. Try to stay within the food budget.

6. Suppose the food budget was increased to 10,000 food packs. Use the spreadsheet to make a list of six possible missions. Include three long missions that would require at least 450 food packs for each astronaut.

7. Describe what a computer spreadsheet does. Why is it a useful tool in working with budgets?

EXTRA PRACTICE

Mental Math: Multiplying 10s and 100s, page 221 ....
Multiply mentally.

1.	10	2.	100	3.	1,000	4.	30	5.	600
	× 3		× 9		× 5		× 2		× 5

6. 2 × 10   7. 8 × 10   8. 4 × 10   9. 7 × 10

10. 3 × 100   11. 1 × 100   12. 6 × 100   13. 5 × 100

14. 4 × 1,000   15. 2 × 1,000   16. 8 × 1,000   17. 7 × 1,000

18. 5 × 20   19. 8 × 50   20. 5 × 30   21. 8 × 60

22. 8 × 300   23. 3 × 400   24. 7 × 700   25. 4 × 800

Estimating Products, page 223 ....
Estimate. Use rounding.

1.	38	2.	72	3.	19	4.	$.38	5.	318
	× 7		× 4		× 5		× 8		× 3

6.	987	7.	$612	8.	4,012	9.	8,842	10.	$2,841
	× 4		× 3		× 5		× 7		× 6

11. 3 × 47   12. 6 × 53   13. 4 × $33   14. 8 × 317

15. 6 × 82   16. 5 × 466   17. 8 × $419   18. 3 × 8,728

Estimate. Use the front digits.

19.	23	20.	49	21.	62	22.	$57	23.	385
	× 9		× 6		× 5		× 8		× 7

24.	333	25.	$689	26.	4,307	27.	4,189	28.	6,487
	× 7		× 5		× 8		× 4		× 9

29. 5 × 14   30. 8 × 76   31. 3 × $85   32. 2 × 899

33. 7 × 91   34. 6 × 577   35. 9 × $529   36. 4 × 9,228

Problem Solving Strategy: Guess, Test, and Revise, page 225 ....

Use the guess, test and revise strategy to solve the problem.

1. Chris, Bret and Greg make 14 fliers to advertise the garage sale. Each boy makes a different number of fliers. Each boy makes fewer than 7 fliers. How many does each boy make?

2. Harry was sailing and fishing at the pond for 6 hours. He sailed for twice as long as he fished. How long did he sail?

3. Think of two numbers whose sum is 25 and whose difference is 3. What are the numbers?

4. Liza is two times as old as her brother. The sum of their ages is 21. How old is Liza?

Multiplying 2-Digit Numbers—Regrouping Once, page 229 ....

Multiply.

1. 12 × 2
2. 19 × 2
3. 11 × 3
4. 14 × 3
5. 11 × 7
6. 25 × 2

7. 13 × 3
8. 49 × 2
9. 31 × 3
10. 27 × 3
11. 33 × 3
12. 17 × 5

13. 32 × 4
14. 46 × 2
15. 17 × 2
16. 62 × 3
17. 13 × 7
18. 23 × 4

19. 17 × 3
20. 16 × 5
21. 81 × 5
22. 15 × 4
23. 36 × 2
24. 21 × 5

25. 8 × 71
26. 6 × 18
27. 9 × 21
28. 4 × 19
29. 5 × 18
30. 9 × 31
31. 2 × 22
32. 4 × 92
33. 3 × 93
34. 4 × 14
35. 8 × 12
36. 5 × 15

EXTRA PRACTICE

Multiplying 2-Digit Numbers—Regrouping Twice, page 231 ....

Multiply.

1. 22 × 7	**2.** 32 × 9	**3.** 43 × 5	**4.** 28 × 7	**5.** 42 × 8	**6.** 22 × 9
7. 43 × 7	**8.** 37 × 4	**9.** 58 × 5	**10.** 46 × 3	**11.** 55 × 7	**12.** 36 × 6
13. 32 × 5	**14.** 62 × 8	**15.** 26 × 7	**16.** 34 × 9	**17.** 44 × 3	**18.** 43 × 6
19. 73 × 9	**20.** 44 × 8	**21.** 75 × 3	**22.** 93 × 5	**23.** 97 × 8	**24.** 99 × 9

25. 3 × 66   **26.** 7 × 42   **27.** 9 × 53   **28.** 5 × 42

29. 6 × 69   **30.** 2 × 57   **31.** 4 × 63   **32.** 9 × 66

Multiplying 3-Digit Numbers, page 235 ....

Multiply.

1. 113 × 3	**2.** 206 × 8	**3.** 417 × 5	**4.** 522 × 7	**5.** 370 × 5
6. 302 × 5	**7.** 819 × 6	**8.** 638 × 3	**9.** 409 × 8	**10.** 537 × 4
11. 738 × 3	**12.** 603 × 9	**13.** 431 × 7	**14.** 240 × 5	**15.** 652 × 8

16. 4 × 313   **17.** 6 × 385   **18.** 7 × 517   **19.** 8 × 652

20. 2 × 783   **21.** 6 × 329   **22.** 5 × 438   **23.** 9 × 849

24. 7 × 413   **25.** 4 × 865   **26.** 9 × 989   **27.** 5 × 565

Multiplying Money, page 237 ....

Multiply.

1.	$.42 × 3	**2.**	$.16 × 8	**3.**	$.22 × 7	**4.**	$.38 × 5	**5.**	$.73 × 4
6.	$1.23 × 6	**7.**	$2.12 × 8	**8.**	$4.37 × 5	**9.**	$5.18 × 3	**10.**	$8.62 × 9
11.	$6.54 × 2	**12.**	$3.89 × 4	**13.**	$4.75 × 7	**14.**	$7.31 × 9	**15.**	$8.95 × 5

16. 3 × $.47   **17.** 8 × $.60   **18.** 7 × $.55   **19.** 2 × $.89

20. 5 × $6.00   **21.** 4 × $5.85   **22.** 3 × $7.09   **23.** 6 × $8.73

Problem Solving Strategy: Using Estimation, page 241 ....

Use estimation to solve. Did you overestimate or underestimate?

1. Michael has $65 to spend on books. He wants to buy a computer book for $16.95, a history book for $28.85, and a science fiction novel for $9.95. Does he have enough money to buy all three books?

2. The sponsors of the Book Fair projected that 187 students would attend the three-day fair. There were 67 students on Monday, 55 on Tuesday, and 83 on Wednesday. Did the Book Fair attract as many students as projected?

3. The author of a new fitness book hoped to speak to at least 70 students at the Book Fair. She talked to 26 students on Monday, 24 on Tuesday, and 39 on Wednesday. Did she meet her goal?

4. Kayla bought a book cover for $1.99 and a calendar for $7.69. Is $10 enough money to pay for these items?

Practice PLUS

KEY SKILL: Multiplying 2-Digit Numbers: Regrouping Twice
(Use after page 231.)

Level A ....

Multiply.

1. 23
    × 5

2. 19
    × 7

3. 39
    × 3

4. 55
    × 2

5. 66
    × 3

6. 54
    × 5

7. 22
    × 7

8. 38
    × 4

9. 25
    × 4

10. 76
     × 3

11. Robin has 7 bags of apples. Each bag has 16 apples. How many apples are there in all?

Level B ....

Multiply.

12. 83
     × 8

13. 26
     × 5

14. 27
     × 4

15. 23
     × 9

16. 86
     × 2

17. 8 × 42   18. 5 × 45   19. 3 × 37   20. 7 × 29

21. Terry has 6 packages of baseball cards. There are 24 cards in each package. How many baseball cards does Terry have?

Level C ....

Multiply.

22. 7 × 65   23. 8 × 47   24. 4 × 75   25. 6 × 87

26. 8 × 28   27. 7 × 98   28. 5 × 57   29. 9 × 74

30. 9 × 94   31. 8 × 35   32. 6 × 52   33. 7 × 49

34. Jake filled 69 pages in his photo album. Each page holds 9 photos. How many photos are there in all?

KEY SKILL: Multiplying Money (Use after page 237.)

Level A ....

Multiply.

1. $.20	2. $.16	3. $.24	4. $.62	5. $.35
× 2	× 3	× 4	× 3	× 6

6. $.39	7. $.42	8. $.55	9. $.80	10. $1.04
× 7	× 3	× 6	× 3	× 2

11. Cleo bought 4 softballs. Each ball cost $4.89. How much money did she spend in all?

Level B ....

Multiply.

12. $.85	13. $.93	14. $.59	15. $.45	16. $.63
× 4	× 2	× 7	× 8	× 7

17. $.89	18. $8.25	19. $4.12	20. $8.04	21. $9.33
× 5	× 6	× 7	× 6	× 4

22. 2 × $4.92   **23.** 4 × $5.19   **24.** 5 × $3.88   **25.** 3 × $9.75

26. Jeremy bought 6 tickets to the school play. Each ticket cost $5.95. How much money did he spend?

Level C ....

Multiply.

27. 3 × $7.98   **28.** 9 × $2.73   **29.** 7 × $6.08   **30.** 6 × $6.35

31. 5 × $8.13   **32.** 8 × $5.25   **33.** 9 × $4.24   **34.** 7 × $9.36

35. 6 × $3.15   **36.** 9 × $7.28   **37.** 7 × $4.52   **38.** 9 × $8.96

39. Linda bought 9 compact discs. Each disc cost $9.98. How much money did she spend in all?

CHAPTER REVIEW/TEST

LANGUAGE AND MATHEMATICS

Complete the sentences. Use the words in the chart.

1. The ■ is the answer in a multiplication problem.

2. Converting 20 ones to 2 tens is an example of ■.

3. ■ estimation results in an estimate that is less than the exact answer.

4. When multiplying money, the product must always have 2 places after the ■.

CONCEPTS AND SKILLS

Multiply mentally.

5.	10 × 4	6.	70 × 8	7. 7 × 600	8. 3 × 500	9. 7 × 2,000

Estimate. Use rounding.

10.	87 × 4	11.	$74 × 6	12. 5 × $78	13. 6 × 4,812

Estimate. Use the front digits.

14.	$58 × 7	15.	367 × 5	16. 9 × $811	17. 4 × 5,976

Multiply.

18.	399 × 9	19.	744 × 8	20.	279 × 8	21.	$8.52 × 7	22.	$961 × 6

23. 4 × 286   **24.** 9 × 327   **25.** 2 × $.39   **26.** 7 × $5.02

Critical Thinking

Find the missing number. Tell how you found it.

27. $35 \times \blacksquare = 35$ **28.** $19 \times 6 = \blacksquare \times 19$ **29.** $\blacksquare \times 84 = 0$

Mixed Applications

30. There are twice as many dogs as cats at the kennel. If there are 48 animals at the kennel, how many are dogs and how many are cats?

31. Julio wants to buy a bicycle pump for $59.95, a tire for $12.25, and a tube for $3.75. Is $80 enough to pay for these items?

32. Bill planted trees for the Forest Service for 5 days. Each day he planted 455 trees. How many trees did he plant?

33. Alva bought 3 shirts for $7.99. How much did she spend?

PERFORMANCE ASSESSMENT

Work with your group to solve this problem.

Imagine that your group is taking a trip to a local theater, museum, or amusement park. Write a budget to figure out how much the trip will cost. Include the prices for admission, food, and transportation. You may also include the cost of buying souvenirs, going on rides, or other expenses. Find the total cost for each of the students in your group. Then, estimate the amount of money needed for all the students taking the trip.

1. *Think about:*
   - the cost of admission, food, transportation, and other expenses for each student
   - how to estimate the total cost of the trip

2. Write a paragraph explaining how you estimated the total cost of the trip for the group.

CUMULATIVE REVIEW

Choose the letter of the correct answer.

1. Estimate by rounding: 6 × $324

   a. $18 c. $1,800
   b. $180 d. $8,000

2. How many are in 3 groups of 6?

   a. 2   c. 18
   b. 3   d. not given

3. How long does a movie last?

   a. seconds c. days
   b. hours d. years

4. $55.95 + $3.08 + $6.11

   a. $15.14 c. $147.85
   b. $65.86 d. not given

5. 4 × $6.28

   a. $25.82 c. $24.82
   b. $25.12 d. not given

6. Find the product of 8 and 72.

   a. 9   c. 567
   b. 566 d. not given

7. Subtract 312 from 5,000.

   a. 4,688 c. 4,968
   b. 4,798 d. not given

8. What is 3 times 34?

   a. 102 c. 72
   b. 92   d. not given

9. 6 × 900

   a. 5,600 c. 560
   b. 5,400 d. not given

10. Multiply 9 × 452.

    a. 3,658 c. 4,068
    b. 3,668 d. not given

11. What is 24 ÷ 6?

    a. 3   c. 144
    b. 4   d. not given

12. 5 × 308

    a. 1,540 c. 15,040
    b. 1,530 d. not given

13. What is 28 minutes after 4:53 P.M.?

    a. 4:25 P.M. c. 5:21 P.M.
    b. 5:20 P.M. d. not given

14. 7 × $.61

    a. $.42 c. $42.70
    b. $4.27 d. not given

NAPIER'S RODS

John Napier, a Scottish mathematician, created these rods to make using Hindu lattice multiplication easier.

Here is how Napier would have used the rods to find the product 3 × 698.

Step 1 Place the rods for 6, 9, and 8 next to the "times" rod.

Step 2 Use the numbers in row 3.

Step 3 Start at the right and add along the diagonals. Regroup when necessary.

3 × 698 = 2,094

Make your own set of Napier's Rods using strips of paper. Then use the rods to find the product.

1. 5 × 274   **2.** 8 × 175   **3.** 4 × 549   **4.** 3 × 637

5. Can you think of a way to use Napier's Rods to find the product of 40 × 387? Experiment with the rods to see if your idea works.

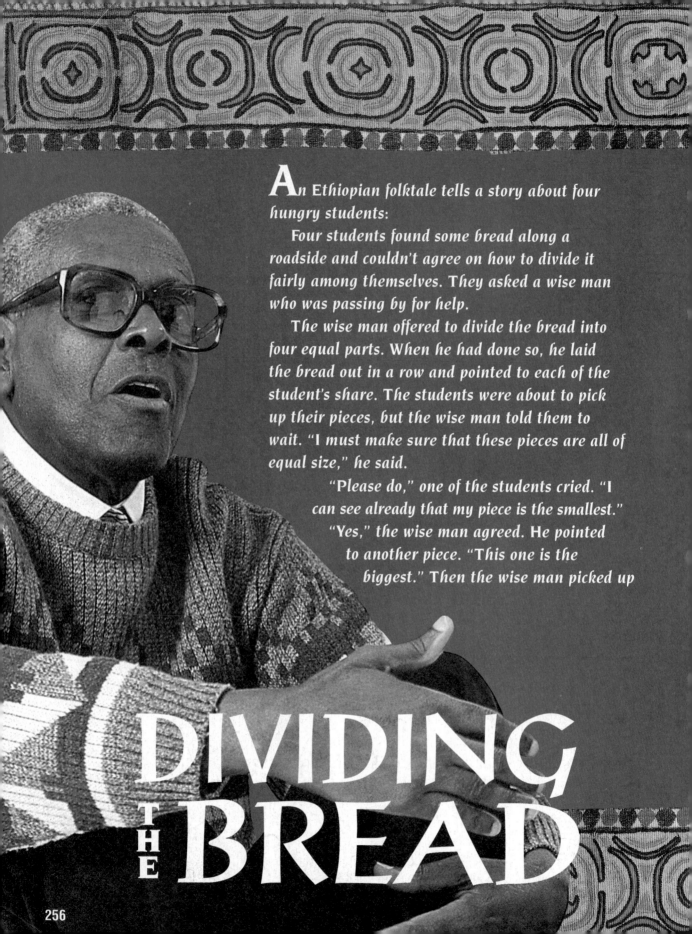

An Ethiopian folktale tells a story about four hungry students:

Four students found some bread along a roadside and couldn't agree on how to divide it fairly among themselves. They asked a wise man who was passing by for help.

The wise man offered to divide the bread into four equal parts. When he had done so, he laid the bread out in a row and pointed to each of the student's share. The students were about to pick up their pieces, but the wise man told them to wait. "I must make sure that these pieces are all of equal size," he said.

"Please do," one of the students cried. "I can see already that my piece is the smallest."

"Yes," the wise man agreed. He pointed to another piece. "This one is the biggest." Then the wise man picked up

DIVIDING THE BREAD

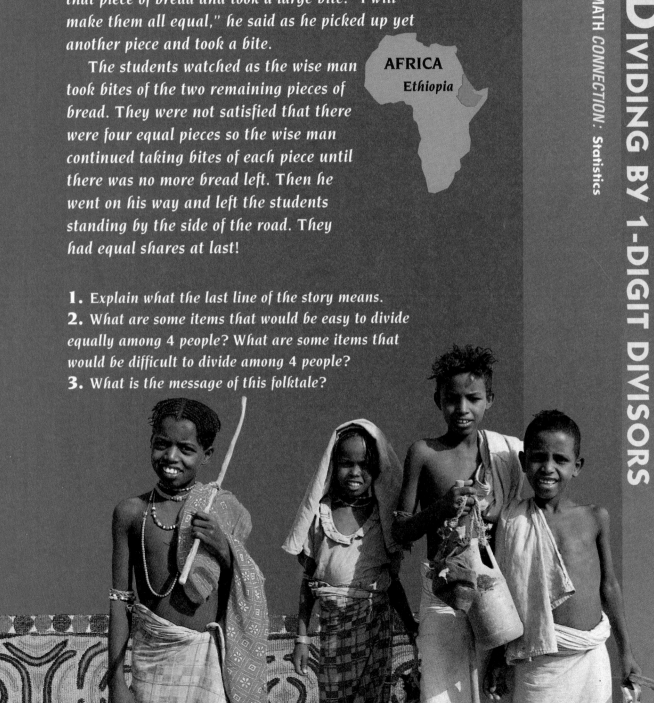

that piece of bread and took a large bite. "I will make them all equal," he said as he picked up yet another piece and took a bite.

AFRICA
Ethiopia

The students watched as the wise man took bites of the two remaining pieces of bread. They were not satisfied that there were four equal pieces so the wise man continued taking bites of each piece until there was no more bread left. Then he went on his way and left the students standing by the side of the road. They had equal shares at last!

1. Explain what the last line of the story means.
2. What are some items that would be easy to divide equally among 4 people? What are some items that would be difficult to divide among 4 people?
3. What is the message of this folktale?

ACTiViTY Dividing with Remainders

A. Earl has 13 pumpkins. He packs 4 pumpkins in each carton. He sees that he has 3 full cartons and 1 pumpkin left over.

Sometimes when you try to divide a number of objects into groups of equal size, you have some objects left over. The number of objects left over is called the **remainder**.

WORKING TOGETHER

You can do this activity to learn more about remainders.

Step 1 Copy the table at the right. Notice that the box for 13 shows a remainder of 1.

Step 2 Place 14 counters on your desk. Divide them into equal groups of 4. Record the remainder in the table.

Step 3 Make equal groups of 4 using 15, 16, and 17 counters. Record the remainders in the table.

EQUAL GROUPS OF 4

Total Number of Counters	13	14	15	16	17
Remainder	1				

1. What is the largest remainder you found? Is this the largest remainder you could get when making equal groups of 4? Why?

B. You can find a quotient and remainder without using counters.

Divide: 13 ÷ 4

Step 1

Think: How many fours are in 13?

$2 \times 4 = 8$	$8 < 13$
$3 \times 4 = 12$	$12 < 13$
$4 \times 4 = 16$	$16 > 13$

There are 3 fours in 13.

Step 2

Divide.

Write 3 in the quotient.
Multiply. $3 \times 4 = 12$
Subtract. $13 - 12 = 1$
Compare. $1 < 4$
Write the remainder.

$$\begin{array}{r} 3\ R1 \\ 4\overline{)13} \\ -12 \\ \hline 1 \end{array}$$

SHARING IDEAS

2. Can the remainder be greater than the divisor? Why or why not?

3. How can you use multiplication and subtraction to help you find the remainder in a division problem?

PRACTICE

Find the quotient and remainder.

4. $4\overline{)6}$ **5.** $8\overline{)9}$ **6.** $5\overline{)9}$ **7.** $2\overline{)9}$ **8.** $3\overline{)8}$ **9.** $6\overline{)8}$

10. $6\overline{)15}$ **11.** $9\overline{)20}$ **12.** $7\overline{)16}$ **13.** $2\overline{)17}$ **14.** $8\overline{)12}$ **15.** $5\overline{)11}$

16. $3\overline{)10}$ **17.** $5\overline{)27}$ **18.** $6\overline{)14}$ **19.** $4\overline{)19}$ **20.** $2\overline{)19}$ **21.** $4\overline{)18}$

22. $8\overline{)33}$ **23.** $6\overline{)35}$ **24.** $7\overline{)52}$ **25.** $9\overline{)80}$ **26.** $8\overline{)50}$ **27.** $5\overline{)47}$

28. $65 \div 8$ **29.** $41 \div 7$ **30.** $39 \div 5$ **31.** $16 \div 6$ **32.** $30 \div 4$

33. $26 \div 9$ **34.** $60 \div 8$ **35.** $42 \div 8$ **36.** $32 \div 5$ **37.** $52 \div 6$

38. What is 9 divided by 2?   **39.** What is 30 divided by 8?

Write the missing number.

40. $31 \div 4 = 7\ R\blacksquare$ **41.** $23 \div 3 = \blacksquare\ R2$ **42.** $35 \div \blacksquare = 5\ R5$

43. $25 \div \blacksquare = 6\ R1$ **44.** $36 \div 7 = 5\ R\blacksquare$ **45.** $19 \div 2 = \blacksquare\ R1$

Mixed Applications

46. There are 35 oranges in a box. If 8 children each get the same number of oranges, how many oranges will be left over?

47. Sam is putting 34 tomatoes in each carton. He fills 6 cartons. How many tomatoes does he pack all together?

48. There is room to park 5 cars in each row of the parking lot. How many rows are full if there are 32 cars?

49. Millie's Market opens at 12:30 P.M. each day. It closes at 6:00 P.M. For how much time is the market open?

Mental Math: Dividing 10s and 100s

Curtis, Fran, and Gary just finished playing a game. Each player scored an equal number of points in each move he or she made. Curtis scored 600 points in 3 moves, Fran scored 2,800 points in 4 moves, and Gary scored 3,000 points in 5 moves. Who scored the most points in each move?

Curtis	Fran	Gary
$6 \div 3 = 2$	$28 \div 4 = 7$	$30 \div 5 = 6$
$60 \div 3 = 20$	$280 \div 4 = 70$	$300 \div 5 = 60$
$600 \div 3 = 200$	$2,800 \div 4 = 700$	$3,000 \div 5 = 600$

Fran scored 700 points, the most points in each move.

1. Look at Curtis's examples. Compare the number of zeros in each dividend with the number of zeros in each quotient. What pattern do you see?

2. Does the pattern work in Fran's examples? in Gary's examples? Why or why not?

TRY OUT Write the letter of the correct answer.

3. $2\overline{)80}$ **a.** 4   **b.** 40   **c.** 400   **d.** 4,000

4. $5\overline{)1,000}$ **a.** 2   **b.** 20   **c.** 200   **d.** 2,000

5. $420 \div 7$ **a.** 6   **b.** 60   **c.** 600   **d.** 6,000

6. $3,000 \div 6$ **a.** 5   **b.** 50   **c.** 500   **d.** 5,000

PRACTICE

Divide. Use mental math.

7. 4⟌40 **8.** 2⟌60 **9.** 9⟌90 **10.** 3⟌90 **11.** 7⟌70

12. 4⟌80 **13.** 2⟌20 **14.** 5⟌50 **15.** 2⟌40 **16.** 3⟌30

17. 8⟌320 **18.** 4⟌160 **19.** 3⟌210 **20.** 7⟌560 **21.** 6⟌300

22. 5⟌200 **23.** 2⟌400 **24.** 4⟌800 **25.** 3⟌600 **26.** 8⟌400

27. 8⟌720 **28.** 6⟌480 **29.** 9⟌630 **30.** 7⟌490 **31.** 8⟌640

32. 4⟌2,000 **33.** 3⟌9,000 **34.** 6⟌4,200 **35.** 9⟌8,100 **36.** 7⟌4,200

37. 60 ÷ 6 **38.** 80 ÷ 2 **39.** 300 ÷ 5 **40.** 600 ÷ 2

41. 3,500 ÷ 7 **42.** 2,000 ÷ 5 **43.** 5,400 ÷ 9 **44.** 4,000 ÷ 8

CRITICAL THINKING

45. How would you find the quotient of 30,000 ÷ 5? What is the quotient?

Mixed Applications

46. Fran earned 800 points in 2 moves. She earned the same number of points in each move. What is that number?

47. The friends started playing the game at 3:15 P.M. They played for 3 hours and 15 minutes. When did they stop playing?

48. Gary made 1,400 points in each of the first 2 games. What was his total score for the 2 games?

49. There are 60 game cards. Each of the 3 players got the same number of cards. How many cards did each player get?

Mixed Review

Find the answer. Which method did you use?

50. 3 × $6.95 **51.** 8,400 − 200 **52.** $32.65 + $15.98

53. 64 ÷ 8 **54.** 420 + 600 **55.** $5.05 − $3.78

MENTAL MATH
CALCULATOR
PAPER/PENCIL

Estimating Quotients

Ed has 6 trucks and 255 crates of potatoes. He puts the same number of crates on each truck. About how many crates does he put on each truck?

Estimate: 255 ÷ 6
Here are two methods you can use.

Rounding	**Compatible Numbers**
Round the dividend to its greatest place.	Use a basic fact.
Think: 255 rounds to 300.	**Think:** 255 is close to 240.
300 ÷ 6 = 50	**240 ÷ 6 = 40**
He puts about 50 crates on each truck.	He puts about 40 crates on each truck.

1. Which estimate is greater than the exact answer? Which estimate is less? How do you know?

2. Estimate 2,315 ÷ 3 by using compatible numbers. Then estimate by rounding. Which method is more helpful in finding an estimate? Why? What is your estimate?

TRY OUT Write the letter of the correct answer.

Estimate by rounding.

3. 4)78   **a.** 2   **b.** 20   **c.** 80   **d.** 200

4. 6,318 ÷ 2   **a.** 3   **b.** 300   **c.** 3,000   **d.** 6,000

Estimate by using compatible numbers.

5. 3)716   **a.** 2   **b.** 20   **c.** 200   **d.** 700

6. 3,059 ÷ 7   **a.** 40   **b.** 400   **c.** 3,000   **d.** 4,000

PRACTICE

Estimate by rounding.

7. $2\overline{)38}$ **8.** $4\overline{)84}$ **9.** $3\overline{)87}$ **10.** $5\overline{)376}$ **11.** $2\overline{)635}$

12. $8\overline{)763}$ **13.** $6\overline{)295}$ **14.** $3\overline{)5,718}$ **15.** $4\overline{)2,206}$ **16.** $2\overline{)7,703}$

Estimate by using compatible numbers.

17. $4\overline{)71}$ **18.** $3\overline{)72}$ **19.** $5\overline{)61}$ **20.** $2\overline{)79}$ **21.** $6\overline{)75}$

22. $6\overline{)538}$ **23.** $8\overline{)495}$ **24.** $3\overline{)595}$ **25.** $7\overline{)320}$ **26.** $2\overline{)750}$

27. $4\overline{)1,575}$ **28.** $9\overline{)7,138}$ **29.** $6\overline{)2,068}$ **30.** $5\overline{)6,310}$ **31.** $8\overline{)3,844}$

Estimate the quotient.

32. $62 \div 3$ **33.** $82 \div 3$ **34.** $88 \div 4$ **35.** $73 \div 4$

36. $514 \div 5$ **37.** $758 \div 8$ **38.** $434 \div 6$ **39.** $392 \div 8$

40. $346 \div 5$ **41.** $906 \div 4$ **42.** $1,235 \div 2$ **43.** $4,106 \div 3$

44. $6,218 \div 3$ **45.** $4,475 \div 5$ **46.** $2,602 \div 5$ **47.** $4,376 \div 9$

Mixed Applications

Find the answer. Did you estimate or find an exact answer?

48. Carl had 70 crates of potatoes on his truck. He sold them for $9 per crate. How much money did he get?

49. One of Ed's drivers drove 596 km in 3 days. About how many kilometers did the driver travel each day?

50. Ed has $1,150 to give to the 6 drivers. He gives each driver the same amount. About how much money does he give each driver?

51. The workers picked 1,768 potatoes the first week. They picked 2,158 potatoes the second week. How many potatoes did they pick in the two weeks?

PROBLEM SOLVING

✓UNDERSTAND
✓PLAN
✓TRY
CHECK
✓EXTEND

Strategy: Making a Table

Nancy, Art, Mica, and Tyrone are picking apples, plums, pears, and grapes on Mr. Lyman's farm. Each picks a different kind of fruit. Nancy picks apples. Art does not pick plums or grapes. Tyrone picks plums. Who picks grapes?

You can solve the problem by making a table.

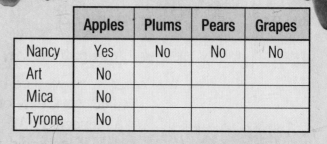

You know Nancy picks apples. Write *Yes* in the box for Nancy.

1. Why can you write *No* in the other boxes next to Nancy?

2. Why can you write *No* in the other boxes under Apples?

	Apples	Plums	Pears	Grapes
Nancy	Yes	No	No	No
Art	No			
Mica	No			
Tyrone	No			

You know Art does not pick plums or grapes.

3. Why can you write *Yes* in the box under Pears for Art?

You know Tyrone picks plums.

4. Complete the rest of the table. Who picks grapes?

5. How does making a table help you solve the problem?

	Apples	Plums	Pears	Grapes
Nancy	Yes	No	No	No
Art	No	No	Yes	No
Mica	No		No	
Tyrone	No		No	

PRACTICE

Make a table to solve.

6. Mr. Lundgren did a different chore each day. He did not clean his tools on Tuesday. He went to the market on Monday. He fixed the fence on Thursday. He did not paint the barn door on Wednesday. He took the rest of the week off. On what day did he paint the barn door?

7. Anna, Jo, and Sue each planted one kind of flower. Anna planted daisies. Jo will not touch roses. Who planted mums?

8. Bob, Lucy, Carl, and Rose each feed one kind of animal. Rose feeds the pigs. Bob does not feed the chickens. Lucy feeds the rabbits. Who feeds the chickens?

9. The farmer's children know what they want to be when they grow up. Bob wants to be a farmer. Lucy does not want to teach. Carl and Rose do not want to be movie stars. Carl does not want to be a truck driver. Who wants to be a teacher?

Strategies and Skills Review

Solve. Use mental math, a calculator, or paper and pencil.

10. Nancy, Art, and Tyrone each worked one day last week. They could work only on Monday, Tuesday, or Wednesday. Art did not work on Tuesday, and Tyrone did not work on Wednesday. Art worked before Tyrone. On what day did Nancy work?

11. Mrs. Gray plants 240 corn plants on her 16-acre farm. She plants them in rows of 8. How many rows does she plant?

12. Mrs. Gray buys 6 cows for $325 each and 1 horse for $275. How much does she pay for the animals?

13. **Write a problem** that can be solved by making a table. Solve your problem. Ask others to solve it.

ACTIVITY

Dividing by 1-Digit Divisors

Liane picked 56 apples. She packed them in 3 baskets. She put the same number in each basket. How many apples did she put in each basket? How many extra apples does she have?

You can divide to find the number of apples in each basket and the number of extra apples.

WORKING TOGETHER

Estimate. Then solve the problem by using place-value models.

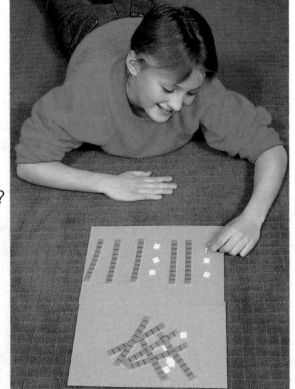

1. How did you model the 56 apples?

2. Which models did you separate first, tens or ones?

3. How many tens did you put in each group? How many were left?

4. What did you do with the tens that were left? Why?

5. How many ones did you put in each group? How many were left?

6. How many apples did she put in each basket? How many extra apples does she have?

7. **What if** Liane picked 57 apples? How many apples would she put in each basket? How many extra apples would she have?

8. How many extra apples would Liane have if she picked 54 apples? 55 apples?

Use models to find each quotient and remainder.

9. 84 ÷ 4   **10.** 98 ÷ 8   **11.** 100 ÷ 6   **12.** 319 ÷ 2

266 Lesson 7–5

SHARING IDEAS

13. How do your models compare with those of others?

14. Why should you start dividing with the models that have the greatest place value?

ON YOUR OWN

Solve. Use place-value models if needed.

15. Treat has 46 tomatoes to pack. He packs the same number of tomatoes in each of 4 bags. How many tomatoes does he pack in each bag? How many tomatoes are extra?

16. Kay has 60 melons. She puts them into 2 cartons. She puts the same number in each carton. How many melons does she put in each carton?

17. Last harvest, 3 helpers picked a total of 114 cucumbers. Each helper picked the same number of cucumbers. How many cucumbers did each helper pick?

18. *Write a problem* that can be solved by using division. Solve your problem. Then ask others to solve it.

Dividing 2-Digit Numbers

A. Juan and Holly have 41 plants to put in 3 boxes. They put the same number of plants in each box. To find how many plants will be in each box, Juan used models.

1. Did Juan regroup? How? Why?

2. How many plants will be in each box? How many plants will be left over?

B. Holly divided without using models. Here is what she did.

Divide: 41 ÷ 3

Step 1	Step 2	Step 3
Decide where to place the first digit of the quotient.	**Divide the tens.**	**Bring down the ones. Divide the ones.**

Step 1

$3\overline{)41}$

Think: 3 < 4
There are enough tens to divide.

Step 2

$\begin{array}{r} 1 \\ 3\overline{)41} \\ -3 \\ \hline 1 \end{array}$

Think: $3\overline{)4}^{1}$
Multiply. 1 × 3 = 3
Subtract. 4 − 3 = 1
Compare. 1 < 3

Step 3

$\begin{array}{r} 13 \text{ R2} \\ 3\overline{)41} \\ -3\downarrow \\ \hline 11 \\ -9 \\ \hline 2 \end{array}$

Think: $3\overline{)11}^{\,3}$
Multiply. 3 × 3 = 9
Subtract. 11 − 9 = 2
Compare. 2 < 3
Write the remainder.

divisor →   dividend →

Check. Multiply, then add: 3 × 13 = 39; 39 + 2 = 41

↑ quotient   ↑ remainder

SHARING IDEAS

3. Is the answer reasonable? How do you know?

4. Why can you multiply to check division?

5. How are Juan's and Holly's methods alike? How are they different?

6. How does each method show regrouping?

PRACTICE

Divide.

7. 4)23	**8.** 2)17	**9.** 6)49	**10.** 3)22	**11.** 7)30
12. 3)51	**13.** 6)79	**14.** 2)65	**15.** 3)36	**16.** 8)89
17. 5)75	**18.** 6)84	**19.** 4)29	**20.** 8)93	**21.** 9)50
22. 4)84	**23.** 5)71	**24.** 6)36	**25.** 2)76	**26.** 8)70

27. $58 \div 7$ **28.** $48 \div 4$ **29.** $78 \div 6$ **30.** $25 \div 3$ **31.** $47 \div 5$

32. $49 \div 5$ **33.** $63 \div 4$ **34.** $94 \div 6$ **35.** $25 \div 4$ **36.** $96 \div 8$

Mixed Applications

37. Holly has 70 new flowerpots to sell. She puts them in stacks of 5. How many stacks does she make?

38. Juan is making a new sign. He will use 6 different colors. Each can of paint costs $1.39. How much will Juan pay for paint?

39. Holly started the day with 65 rosebushes. By the end of the day, she had sold all but 7 of them. How many had she sold?

Mixed Review

Compare. Write $>$, $<$, or $=$.

40. $3 + 8 + 7 \bullet 20$ **41.** $210 \div 7 \bullet 90 \div 3$ **42.** $1 \times 8 \bullet 8 - 0$

43. $650 - 310 \bullet 400$ **44.** $6 \times 175 \bullet 4 \times 230$ **45.** $13 - 4 \bullet 72 \div 9$

Dividing 3-Digit Numbers

The owners of Fancy Plants are growing 458 marigold plants. They want to make equal-size groups to sell in 4 different markets. How many plants will they put in each group?

You can divide to find the answer.

First estimate. $400 \div 4 = 100$

Divide: $458 \div 4$

Step 1

Decide where to place the first digit of the quotient.

$4\overline{)458}$

Think: $4 = 4$
There are enough hundreds to divide.

Step 2

Divide the hundreds.

$$\begin{array}{r} 1 \\ 4\overline{)458} \\ -4 \\ \hline 0 \end{array}$$

Think: $4\overline{)4}^{\,1}$
Multiply. $1 \times 4 = 4$
Subtract. $4 - 4 = 0$
Compare. $0 < 4$

Step 3

Bring down the tens. Divide the tens.

$$\begin{array}{r} 11 \\ 4\overline{)458} \\ -4\downarrow \\ \hline 05 \\ -4 \\ \hline 1 \end{array}$$

Think: $4\overline{)5}^{\,1}$
Multiply. $1 \times 4 = 4$
Subtract. $5 - 4 = 1$
Compare. $1 < 4$

Step 4

Bring down the ones. Divide the ones.

$$\begin{array}{r} 114 \text{ R2} \\ 4\overline{)458} \\ -4 \\ \hline 05 \\ -4\downarrow \\ \hline 18 \\ -16 \\ \hline 2 \end{array}$$

Think: $4\overline{)18}^{\,4}$
Multiply. $4 \times 4 = 16$
Subtract. $18 - 16 = 2$
Compare. $2 < 4$

Check: $4 \times 114 = 456$; $456 + 2 = 458$

They will put 114 plants in each group.

1. Is the answer reasonable? How do you know?

2. **What if** they had 2 more plants? What would the quotient and remainder be?

TRY OUT Divide.

3. 3)532   **4.** 2)785   **5.** 906 ÷ 7   **6.** 891 ÷ 6

PRACTICE

Divide.

7. 5)626   **8.** 2)835   **9.** 3)663   **10.** 6)991   **11.** 2)376

12. 7)928   **13.** 5)575   **14.** 8)976   **15.** 4)910   **16.** 2)933

17. 3)956   **18.** 7)879   **19.** 4)898   **20.** 3)688   **21.** 2)709

22. 5)664   **23.** 6)953   **24.** 7)791   **25.** 8)929   **26.** 4)954

27. 689 ÷ 6   **28.** 896 ÷ 8   **29.** 919 ÷ 5   **30.** 999 ÷ 9

31. 870 ÷ 7   **32.** 956 ÷ 2   **33.** 907 ÷ 8   **34.** 888 ÷ 3

Mixed Applications Solve. Which method did you use?

35. Jon has 435 tulip bulbs to put in packages. He puts 3 bulbs in each package. How many packages does he fill?

36. There are 8 iris plants in each box. How many iris plants are in 40 boxes?

> **ESTIMATION**
> **MENTAL MATH**
> **CALCULATOR**
> **PAPER/PENCIL**

CALCULATOR

Rena used a calculator to divide 17 by 6 and got this: | 2.8333333 |
To find the remainder, Rena followed these steps.

Step 1 Multiply the divisor by the whole-number part of the answer. $2 \times 6 = 12$

Step 2 Subtract the product from the original dividend. The answer is the remainder. $17 - 12 = 5$

Step 3 Write the quotient and remainder. $17 \div 6 = 2 \text{ R}5$

Divide.

1. 4)30   **2.** 8)196   **3.** 6)201   **4.** 5)718

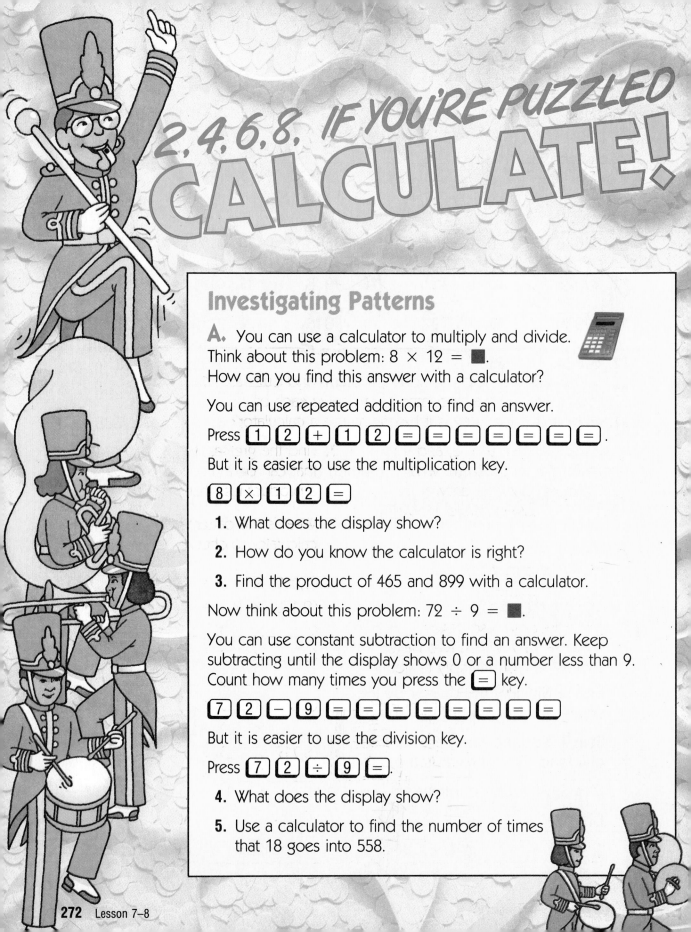

2, 4, 6, 8, IF YOU'RE PUZZLED CALCULATE!

Investigating Patterns

A. You can use a calculator to multiply and divide.
Think about this problem: 8 × 12 = ■.
How can you find this answer with a calculator?

You can use repeated addition to find an answer.

Press ⟨1⟩⟨2⟩⟨+⟩⟨1⟩⟨2⟩⟨=⟩⟨=⟩⟨=⟩⟨=⟩⟨=⟩⟨=⟩⟨=⟩.

But it is easier to use the multiplication key.

⟨8⟩⟨×⟩⟨1⟩⟨2⟩⟨=⟩

1. What does the display show?

2. How do you know the calculator is right?

3. Find the product of 465 and 899 with a calculator.

Now think about this problem: 72 ÷ 9 = ■.

You can use constant subtraction to find an answer. Keep subtracting until the display shows 0 or a number less than 9. Count how many times you press the ⟨=⟩ key.

⟨7⟩⟨2⟩⟨−⟩⟨9⟩⟨=⟩⟨=⟩⟨=⟩⟨=⟩⟨=⟩⟨=⟩⟨=⟩⟨=⟩

But it is easier to use the division key.

Press ⟨7⟩⟨2⟩⟨÷⟩⟨9⟩⟨=⟩.

4. What does the display show?

5. Use a calculator to find the number of times that 18 goes into 558.

B. A calculator can help you solve problems and puzzles. You can work quickly with a calculator. Try to solve each of the puzzles on this page. Why is it helpful to use a calculator?

6. Use the numbers 6, 7, 8, and 9 to complete each problem. What is the greatest possible answer for each? The least possible answer?

8. The product of these page numbers is 420. Which two page numbers can you multiply to get each of these products?

   a. 1,806

   b. 3,422

   c. 12,656

7. Find the greatest whole number that can be multiplied by 7 to get a product less than 25,000.

9. What is the pattern? Use a calculator to check your answer.

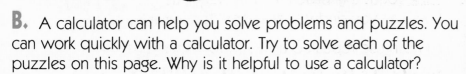

$(1{,}089 \times 9) \div 1 = 9{,}801$

$(2{,}178 \times 8) \div 2 = 8{,}712$

$(\underline{} \times \underline{}) \div \underline{} = 7{,}623$

$(\underline{} \times \underline{}) \div \underline{} = 6{,}534$

$(\underline{} \times \underline{}) \div \underline{} = 5{,}445$

$(\underline{} \times \underline{}) \div \underline{} = 4{,}356$

$(\underline{} \times \underline{}) \div \underline{} = 3{,}267$

$(8{,}712 \times \underline{}) \div \underline{} = \mathbf{2{,}178}$

$(\underline{} \times \underline{}) \div \underline{} = \mathbf{1{,}089}$

More Dividing 3-Digit Numbers

Ben and Tess are decorating the gym for the Future Farmers party. They have 215 gourds to put in bowls. They put 4 gourds in each bowl. How many bowls can they fill? How many gourds will they have left over?

Divide: 215 ÷ 4

Step 1	Step 2	Step 3
Decide where to place the first digit of the quotient.	Divide the tens.	Bring down the ones. Divide the ones. Write the remainder.

Step 1

$$4\overline{)215}$$ with ■

Think: 4 > 2   There are not enough hundreds.

4 < 21   There are enough tens to divide.

Step 2

$$4\overline{)215} \quad \begin{array}{r}5\\-20\\\hline 1\end{array}$$

Think: $4\overline{)21}$ with 5
Multiply. 5 × 4 = 20
Subtract. 21 − 20 = 1
Compare. 1 < 4

Step 3

$$\begin{array}{r}53\ R3\\4\overline{)215}\\-20\downarrow\\\hline 15\\-12\\\hline 3\end{array}$$

Think: $4\overline{)15}$ with 3
Multiply. 3 × 4 = 12
Subtract. 15 − 12 = 3
Compare. 3 < 4

Check: 4 × 53 = 212; 212 + 3 = 215

They can fill 53 bowls. They will have 3 gourds left over.

1. How can you tell when there will be only 2 digits in the quotient?

TRY OUT   Write the letter of the correct answer.

2. $5\overline{)347}$ **a.** 69   **b.** 69 R2   **c.** 72   **d.** 161 R2

3. $8\overline{)913}$ **a.** 11 R4   **b.** 114   **c.** 114 R1   **d.** 182 R2

4. $6\overline{)282}$ **a.** 47   **b.** 47 R5   **c.** 52   **d.** 313 R3

5. 827 ÷ 3   **a.** 27 R2   **b.** 212 R1   **c.** 275 R2   **d.** 311 R1

PRACTICE

Divide.

6. 3)149   **7.** 2)129   **8.** 7)397   **9.** 6)209   **10.** 4)284

11. 4)886   **12.** 6)933   **13.** 7)476   **14.** 3)937   **15.** 5)709

16. 6)496   **17.** 7)801   **18.** 4)593   **19.** 8)745   **20.** 4)372

21. 3)524   **22.** 6)385   **23.** 5)446   **24.** 8)995   **25.** 3)740

26. 655 ÷ 4   **27.** 299 ÷ 9   **28.** 818 ÷ 3   **29.** 325 ÷ 5

30. 758 ÷ 6   **31.** 200 ÷ 3   **32.** 896 ÷ 8   **33.** 894 ÷ 9

34. Divide 807 by 5.   **35.** Divide 472 by 8.

36. What is the quotient of 197 and 3? What is the remainder?

37. What is the quotient of 777 and 6? What is the remainder?

Critical Thinking

38. When you divide a 3-digit number by a 1-digit number, what is the greatest number of digits you can have in the quotient? What is the least number of digits?

Mixed Applications

39. The party committee collected $956 for tickets. The tickets cost $4 each. How many tickets did the committee sell?

40. Tess bought a new skirt for the party. It cost $23.89. She gave the clerk $30.00. What was her change?

Mixed Review

Find the answer. Which method did you use?

41. 7)52   **42.** 146 × 8   **43.** 9)3,600   **44.** 9)4,727

| MENTAL MATH |
| CALCULATOR |
| PAPER/PENCIL |

45. $59.77 + $86.95   **46.** 7,900 − 500   **47.** 1,000 − 721

Zeros in the Quotient

Greta is giving away apples at the Farmers Fair. She brought 325 apples. How many people could each get 3 free apples? How many apples would Greta have left?

Divide: 325 ÷ 3

Step 1

Decide where to place the first digit of the quotient.

3)325   **Think:** 3 = 3
There are enough hundreds to divide.

Step 2

Divide the hundreds.

$$\begin{array}{r} 1 \\ 3{\overline{)3}}25 \\ -3 \\ \hline 0 \end{array}$$

Think: 3)3
Multiply. 1 × 3 = 3
Subtract. 3 − 3 = 0
Compare. 0 < 3

Step 3

Bring down the tens. Divide the tens.

$$\begin{array}{r} 10 \\ 3{\overline{)3}}25 \\ -3\downarrow \\ \hline 02 \end{array}$$

Think: 2 < 3
There are not enough tens to divide. Write 0 in the quotient.

Step 4

Bring down the ones. Divide the ones. Write the remainder.

$$\begin{array}{r} 108 \text{ R1} \\ 3{\overline{)325}} \\ -3\downarrow\downarrow \\ \hline 025 \\ -24 \\ \hline 1 \end{array}$$

Think: 3)25
Multiply. 8 × 3 = 24
Subtract. 25 − 24 = 1
Compare. 1 < 3

So 108 people could each get 3 free apples. Greta would have 1 apple left.

1. Divide 62 by 3. Where do you put a 0 in the quotient? What does the 0 mean?

TRY OUT   Write the letter of the correct answer.

2. 4)363   **a.** 18 R1   **b.** 90   **c.** 90 R3   **d.** 900 R1

3. 541 ÷ 3   **a.** 10 R5   **b.** 113   **c.** 180   **d.** 180 R1

4. 861 ÷ 8   **a.** 107   **b.** 107 R5   **c.** 112   **d.** 118

PRACTICE

Divide.

5. $4\overline{)82}$ **6.** $9\overline{)90}$ **7.** $3\overline{)61}$ **8.** $5\overline{)53}$ **9.** $2\overline{)61}$

10. $2\overline{)816}$ **11.** $4\overline{)522}$ **12.** $8\overline{)324}$ **13.** $5\overline{)453}$ **14.** $7\overline{)910}$

15. $3\overline{)92}$ **16.** $5\overline{)540}$ **17.** $8\overline{)86}$ **18.** $3\overline{)662}$ **19.** $6\overline{)628}$

20. $2\overline{)60}$ **21.** $3\overline{)901}$ **22.** $4\overline{)83}$ **23.** $6\overline{)843}$ **24.** $2\overline{)619}$

25. $75 \div 7$ **26.** $802 \div 4$ **27.** $31 \div 3$ **28.** $813 \div 9$

29. $483 \div 4$ **30.** $92 \div 3$ **31.** $624 \div 6$ **32.** $83 \div 4$

33. What is 83 divided by 8?   **34.** What is 304 divided by 6?

35. Divide 76 by 7.   **36.** Divide 187 by 9.

Mixed Applications

37. There were 455 people sitting on benches at the hog show. If 9 people sat on each bench, how many benches did they fill?

38. Prizes were given for 5 different kinds of pie. There were 52 pies of each kind. How many pies were there?

MENTAL MATH

You can often divide mentally.

$$\overset{2}{3\overline{)7^{1}1\,5}} \qquad \overset{2\ 3}{3\overline{)7^{1}1^{2}5}} \qquad \overset{2\ 3\ 8\ R1}{3\overline{)7^{1}1^{2}5}}$$

Think: $2 \times 3 = 6$ *Think:* $3 \times 3 = 9$ *Think:* $8 \times 3 = 24$
        $7 - 6 = 1$ $11 - 9 = 2$ $25 - 24 = 1$

Use this method to divide.

1. $2\overline{)428}$ **2.** $3\overline{)693}$ **3.** $2\overline{)351}$ **4.** $4\overline{)257}$

ACTIVITY Dividing Money

A. You can use a calculator to learn about dividing money.

1. Use a calculator to divide the following:

   a. 395 ÷ 5   **b.** 92 ÷ 4   **c.** 1,463 ÷ 7
       $3.95 ÷ 5 $.92 ÷ 4 $14.63 ÷ 7

2. What pattern do you notice in each set of problems above?

3. Where is the decimal point in each of the dividends? in each of the quotients?

4. Divide 798 ÷ 6 on the calculator.   7 9 8 ÷ 6 =

5. Predict what the quotient of $7.98 ÷ 6 will be. Check your prediction on the calculator.

B. You can divide money without using a calculator.

Divide: $7.76 ÷ 8

First estimate. Use a compatible dollar amount. $8 ÷ 8 = $1

Step 1	Step 2
Divide as you would divide whole numbers.	**Write the dollar sign and the decimal point.**

Step 1:
```
      9 7
8)$7.7 6
 − 7 2 ↓
     5 6
   −5 6
       0
```

Step 2:
```
   $ .9 7
8)$7.7 6
 − 7 2 ↓
     5 6
   −5 6
       0
```

SHARING IDEAS

6. How is estimating quotients with money like estimating quotients with whole numbers?

7. How is dividing money amounts the same as dividing whole numbers? How is it different?

8. Use a calculator to divide $.49 ÷ 7. What do you notice about the quotient that is different from that of 49 ÷ 7? What would you have to do if you were dividing $.49 ÷ 7 using paper and pencil?

PRACTICE

Divide. Use mental math, a calculator, or paper and pencil.

9. 5)$.40 **10.** 4)$.36 **11.** 7)$.84 **12.** 6)$.78 **13.** 3)$.27

14. 8)$.96 **15.** 9)$.90 **16.** 5)$.65 **17.** 7)$.98 **18.** 8)$.64

19. 3)$2.79 **20.** 5)$8.50 **21.** 4)$8.56 **22.** 2)$2.08 **23.** 6)$5.22

24. 5)$6.75 **25.** 8)$6.32 **26.** 7)$8.05 **27.** 5)$6.00 **28.** 3)$9.27

29. $.84 ÷ 6 **30.** $.63 ÷ 9 **31.** $.36 ÷ 3 **32.** $.75 ÷ 5

33. $1.80 ÷ 3 **34.** $8.14 ÷ 2 **35.** $8.16 ÷ 4 **36.** $5.44 ÷ 8

Mixed Applications Solve. Which method did you use?

> **ESTIMATION**
> **MENTAL MATH**
> **CALCULATOR**
> **PAPER/PENCIL**

37. The price of hickory chips is 2 bags for $7.98. What is the cost of each bag?

38. Mark spent $16.89 for maple syrup and $21.65 for a snow shovel. How much did he spend all together?

39. Shirts cost $13.95. Zena wants to buy two of them. Is $30.00 enough money to buy the shirts?

CHALLENGE

Which is the **better buy:** 3 shirts for $9.78 or $3.35 for each shirt?

Divide to find the cost of each shirt: $9.78 ÷ 3 = $3.26
Compare: $3.26 < $3.35

So 3 for $9.78 is the better buy.

Find the better buy.

1. 7 patches for $3.01 or $.42 for each patch

2. 5 towels for $8.65 or $1.75 for each towel

ACTIVITY Dividing Larger Numbers

Prime Press prints 6,475 copies of a farm journal every week. The company's workers load the same number of journals on each of 5 trucks. How many journals do they load on each truck?

WORKING TOGETHER

Work with a group. Have each person in the group use a different method to find the answer. You can use mental math, a calculator, or paper and pencil.

1. Is it easy to find the quotient mentally? Why or why not?

2. Show how to use paper and pencil to find the quotient.

3. Check to see that your answer is reasonable. How can you do this?

4. Which method was fastest?

5. **What if** Prime Press printed 5,000 journals weekly? Which method would be fastest?

Use all the methods to divide 16,365 by 4.

6. Is it easy to divide mentally?

7. Show how to use paper and pencil to divide.

8. Which method was fastest—mental math, paper and pencil, or calculator?

Find the quotient. Which method did you use?

9. $3\overline{)6,025}$ 10. $7\overline{)1,894}$ 11. $2\overline{)84,066}$ 12. $8\overline{)39,507}$ 13. $9\overline{)\$650.88}$

SHARING IDEAS

14. How is dividing 4-digit and 5-digit numbers like dividing smaller numbers?

15. Tell how you decided which method to use in Exercises 9–13.

16. When do you think it is easier to use mental math? paper and pencil? a calculator? Tell why.

17. Is the calculator always easier to use with larger numbers? Why or why not?

ON YOUR OWN

Solve. Which method did you use?

MENTAL MATH
CALCULATOR
PAPER/PENCIL

18. Nat ordered 3 belts from an ad in the journal. Each belt cost the same amount. He paid $27.15 in all. How much did each belt cost?

19. Marty paid $51.75 to put an ad in the journal. The ad was 9 lines long. What was the cost per line?

20. Teri writes about 3,000 words each week for the journal. She writes 5 days a week and about the same number of words each day. About how many words does she write each day?

21. *Write a division problem* using a large dividend. Choose a method and solve it. Ask others to solve it and compare methods.

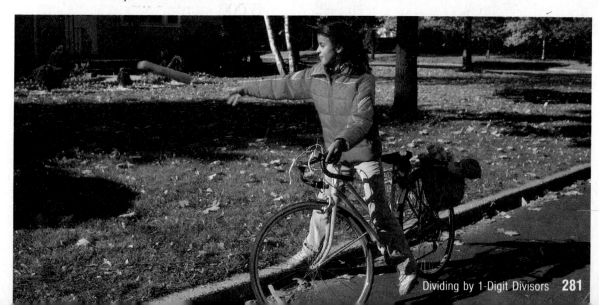

PROBLEM SOLVING

Interpreting the Quotient and Remainder

Farmer Jones has 43 chickens. He wants to put 8 chickens in each of his chicken coops. Into how many coops will he put 8 chickens?

You know that Farmer Jones has 43 chickens and that he will put 8 chickens in each coop. You can use division to find how many coops he needs.

1. Into how many coops will he put 8 chickens?

$$\begin{array}{r} 5 \\ 8\overline{)43} \\ -\ 40 \\ \hline 3 \end{array}$$

Farmer Jones decides to sell the chickens he did not put in a coop.

2. How many chickens will he sell?

3. **What if** he changed his mind and put the leftover chickens in a coop of their own? How many coops would have chickens then?

There are three ways to interpret the quotient and the remainder to answer division problems:

- The quotient answers questions like Problem 1.

- The remainder answers questions like Problem 2.

- The next greater number than the quotient answers questions like Problem 3.

4. How can you tell which type of answer is needed?

PRACTICE

Solve the problem. Tell how you
interpreted the remainder.
Use mental math, a calculator,
or paper and pencil.

5. Juanita is planting tomato plants. She
   wants to put exactly 8 plants in each
   row. She has 52 tomato plants. How
   many rows will she plant?

6. Whitney is laying down a white
   gravel garden path. She needs to
   cover 55 square feet. Each bag
   will cover 3 square feet. How
   many bags does she need?

7. Tomas has 36 pounds of apples to
   pack in boxes. Each box must
   have 5 pounds of apples. Any
   leftover apples are packed in
   bags. How many pounds of apples
   does Tomas pack in bags?

8. A dairy cow needs 3 acres of grazing land. Mr.
   Jones wants to buy as many cows as he can. If
   his farm has 160 acres of grazing land, how many
   cows should he buy?

Strategies and Skills Review

9. Horace wants to buy a bike that
   costs $119. He earns $9 a day
   working after school at Mrs.
   Blair's farm. How many days
   does he have to work to earn
   enough to pay for the bike?

10. Mr. McCall picked 273 pounds of
    peaches. He picked 65 more
    pounds of apples than peaches. He
    also picked 491 pounds of pears.
    How many more pounds of pears
    than peaches did he pick?

11. Mrs. Blair bought 24 ears of corn
    at the farmer's market. She paid
    $.75 for each bag of 6 ears. How
    much money did she pay?

12. *Write a problem* that can be
    solved by interpreting the quotient
    and remainder. Solve it. Ask
    others to solve your problem.

ACTIVITY

Median, Range, and Average

Maria sold handmade dolls during the two weeks of the
Green County Fair. She recorded the sales in a table.

You can describe a group of numbers in
several ways.

WORKING TOGETHER

Use graph paper to make a strip for the number
of dolls she sold each day during Week 1.

Arrange the strips in order from least to greatest.

The middle number is the **median**
of the group of numbers.

**NUMBER OF DOLLS SOLD AT
GREEN COUNTY FAIR**

Day	Week 1	Week 2
1	6	12
2	10	12
3	8	9
4	6	12
5	7	15
6	15	14
7	25	17

1. How many squares does the
   middle strip have? What is
   the median?

The difference between the least
number and the greatest number is
the **range**.

2. How many more squares are in
   the longest strip than in the
   shortest? What is the range?

3. Tape all of the strips together to
   form one long strip. Cut this
   strip into 7 equal strips. How
   many squares are in each strip?

You have just found the **average** of the group of numbers.

4. Use graph paper to find the median, range, and average
   for the number of dolls Maria sold during the second week.

5. Compare the medians, ranges, and averages of the two
   weeks. What do you notice?

6. Pick 5 numbers from 1 to 20. Use graph paper to find the
   median, range, and average of the numbers picked.

SHARING IDEAS

7. Tell how you find the median, range, and average of a group of numbers.

8. How does the median compare with the other numbers in a group if the range is small? if the range is large?

9. How does the average compare with the numbers in a group if the range is small? if the range is large?

ON YOUR OWN

10. Find the median, range, and average of the data in the graph below.

QUILTS SOLD DURING LAST FIVE DAYS OF THE FAIR

11. Measure the handspan in centimeters of 5 people in your class. Find the median, range, and average of the measures. Compare your results with those of others.

More Median, Range, and Average

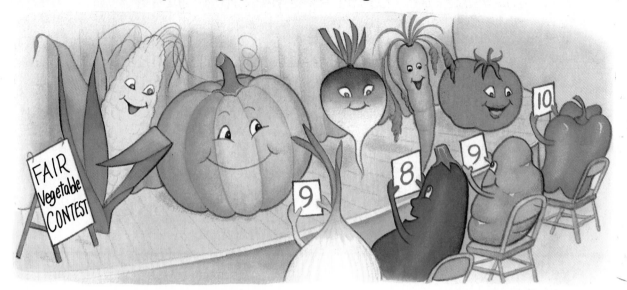

Steve keeps track of the number of vegetables entered in the competition at the fair. What is the median, range, and average of this group of numbers?

Recall that the median is the number in the middle when you order the numbers from least to greatest.

1. What is the median?

You can subtract the least number from the greatest number to find the range.

2. What is the range?

You can find the sum of the numbers. Then divide the sum by the number of addends to find the average.

3. What is the average?

4. Is the median one of the numbers in the group? Is the average?

5. *What if* 77 vegetables had been entered in 1986 and 78 vegetables in 1987? What would the median, range, and average be?

6. *What if* the group of numbers were 67, 75, 92, 88, and 103? What would their median, range, and average be?

VEGETABLES IN COMPETITION	
Year	Number
1986	68
1987	72
1988	93
1989	88
1990	104

SHARING IDEAS

Which statements below do you agree with? Which do you disagree with? Give examples to support your answers.

7. The average must equal one of the numbers in a group.

8. The median and the average can be the same number.

9. Different groups of numbers must have different medians, ranges, and averages.

PRACTICE

Find the median, range, and average.

10. 4, 11, 6, 9, 5

11. $5, $10, $6, $9, $10

12. 3, 5, 2, 8, 5, 3, 2

13. 30¢, 7¢, 40¢, 28¢, 35¢

14. 35, 26, 18, 25, 31

15. 25, 28, 20, 25, 21, 25, 24

16. 105, 100, 104

17. 112, 64, 67, 103, 79

18. $101, $100, $118, $95, $101

19. 96, 120, 102, 124, 95, 101, 125

Critical Thinking

20. To estimate the sum of $65 + 62 + 58 + 49 + 59$, Ann wrote: $5 \times 60 = 300$. So the sum is about 300. Why does Ann's method work?

Mixed Applications

Solve. You may need to use the Databank on page 520.

21. What is the average number of goats entered in the Green County Fair competition for the 5 years?

22. How many goats, hogs, and cows were entered in all in 1988?

23. What is the median number of hogs entered in the 5 years?

24. *Write a problem* about the number of animals entered in the fair competition. Have another student solve it.

DECISION MAKING

Problem Solving: Giving a Fruit Basket

SITUATION

Max's family wants to give their new neighbors a fruit basket as a welcome gift. They can buy a ready-made gift basket at the market. For an extra charge the market will deliver the basket. The market also sells all the things they need to make a fruit basket.

PROBLEM

Should Max's family buy a ready-made gift basket, or should they make a fruit basket themselves?

DATA

GIFT BASKETS
Skillfully arranged and decorated ■ ■ ■ ■ Delivery $5 extra

SMALL $12

1 **pound each:**
   apples, oranges, pears
½ **pound of nuts**

MEDIUM $20

2 **pounds each:**
   apples, oranges, pears
1 **pineapple**
½ **pound of nuts**

LARGE $30

3 **pounds each:**
   apples, oranges, pears
1 **pineapple**
1-**pound box of dates**
1 **pound of nuts**

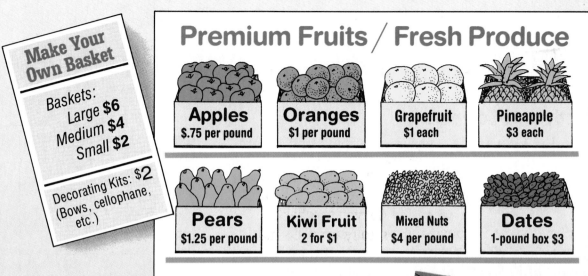

Premium Fruits / Fresh Produce

Apples $.75 per pound

Oranges $1 per pound

Grapefruit $1 each

Pineapple $3 each

Pears $1.25 per pound

Kiwi Fruit 2 for $1

Mixed Nuts $4 per pound

Dates 1-pound box $3

Make Your Own Basket

Baskets:
Large **$6**
Medium **$4**
Small **$2**

Decorating Kits: **$2**
(Bows, cellophane, etc.)

USING THE DATA

What will it cost to buy these baskets and decorate them?

1. large   **2.** medium   **3.** small

Find the cost of matching the contents of the ready-made baskets.

4. large   **5.** medium   **6.** small

What will it cost to buy each ready-made basket and have it delivered?

7. large   **8.** medium   **9.** small

MAKING DECISIONS

10. Is it cheaper for Max's family to make a medium fruit basket or to buy it ready-made?

11. *What if* the family knows one of their neighbors cannot eat pineapple? What should they do? Why?

12. *What if* they cannot deliver the basket? What could they do?

13. *What if* they can spend only $20? What choices do they have?

14. What advantages are there in buying a fruit basket? in making a fruit basket?

15. *Write a list* of things the family should think about before buying or making a fruit basket.

16. What would you do if you had $27.00 to spend on a fruit basket?

Math and Science

A **solar system** is a group of planets and other objects that move around a star, or sun. Our solar system is circular in shape and has nine planets, including the Earth.

A planet's path around the Sun is called its **orbit.** The time a planet takes to orbit the Sun is the length of its year. The Earth orbits the Sun in 365 days.

The chart to the right shows the planets arranged in order from the closest to the Sun to the farthest away. You can see that the farther a planet is from the Sun, the longer its year is.

Planets	Length of Year (in Earth days)
Mercury	88
Venus	225
Earth	365
Mars	687
Jupiter	4,333
Saturn	10,759
Uranus	30,685
Neptune	60,188
Pluto	90,700

What if a satellite sends pictures of Mars back to Earth every 7 Earth days for a full Mars year? About how many times will pictures be sent during the year?

Think: Divide. *687* ÷ *7* = *98.14285714*

Pictures will be sent about 98 times.

ACTIVITIES

1. How old would you be on Mercury, Venus, and Mars? First find your age in days by multiplying your age by 365. Then divide the number of days you have lived by the number of days in each planet's year.

2. How many Earth years equal one year on planets that are farther from the Sun? Divide the number of days in each planet's year by 365, the number of days in Earth's year.

Computer Graphing: Double-Bar Graph

Maureen is a travel agent. She usually has her customers fly on Eagle Air. But a new airline—Air Condor—may have lower fares. To help her customers save money, Maureen compares current round-trip fares of Eagle Air and Air Condor flights from New York to five cities.

Maureen uses a **double-bar graph** to display the fares. A double-bar graph compares related data. A computer makes it easy to draw double-bar graphs quickly and accurately. Maureen has already entered Eagle Air fares. The table gives Air Condor fares to the same cities.

AIR CONDOR FARES

Dallas	$300
Los Angeles	$350
Seattle	$400
Chicago	$300
Miami	$150

AT THE COMPUTER

Run the computer graphing program called AIR FARES.

1. Enter the Air Condor fares and make a **double-bar** graph. To which city are fares the same for both airlines? To which city are fares most expensive?

2. To which city is the difference in price the greatest between the two airlines?

3. Write a summary of how fares compare for the two airlines.

4. In May, Air Condor raises all ticket prices by $100. Change the data to show this and draw a new graph for May. How do the airline fares compare now?

5. In June, Eagle Air raises its fares to Seattle and Los Angeles by $50. Change the data to show this and draw a new graph for June. Now how do the airline fares compare?

EXTRA PRACTICE

Dividing with Remainders, page 259..

Find the quotient and remainder.

1. $4\overline{)5}$ 2. $7\overline{)8}$ 3. $5\overline{)8}$ 4. $2\overline{)7}$ 5. $3\overline{)10}$

6. $8\overline{)17}$ 7. $9\overline{)19}$ 8. $6\overline{)19}$ 9. $2\overline{)15}$ 10. $8\overline{)11}$

11. $5\overline{)23}$ 12. $3\overline{)7}$ 13. $6\overline{)13}$ 14. $8\overline{)34}$ 15. $4\overline{)18}$

16. $6\overline{)34}$ 17. $9\overline{)52}$ 18. $3\overline{)19}$ 19. $7\overline{)11}$ 20. $8\overline{)42}$

21. $26 \div 3$ 22. $33 \div 4$ 23. $65 \div 9$ 24. $48 \div 5$

25. $32 \div 5$ 26. $31 \div 6$ 27. $43 \div 7$ 28. $75 \div 9$

Mental Math: Dividing 10s and 100s, page 261..................................

Divide. Use mental math.

1. $2\overline{)10}$ 2. $5\overline{)100}$ 3. $7\overline{)700}$ 4. $9\overline{)3,600}$

5. $30 \div 3$ 6. $80 \div 2$ 7. $10 \div 5$ 8. $60 \div 3$

9. $60 \div 6$ 10. $40 \div 2$ 11. $800 \div 4$ 12. $240 \div 8$

13. $900 \div 3$ 14. $640 \div 8$ 15. $480 \div 6$ 16. $2,500 \div 5$

17. $8,100 \div 9$ 18. $6,000 \div 2$ 19. $3,200 \div 8$ 20. $1,800 \div 6$

Estimating Quotients, page 263...

Estimate by rounding.

1. $2\overline{)41}$ 2. $4\overline{)83}$ 3. $5\overline{)276}$ 4. $2\overline{)763}$

5. $59 \div 3$ 6. $61 \div 6$ 7. $896 \div 3$ 8. $8,322 \div 4$

Estimate by using compatible numbers.

9. $6\overline{)537}$ 10. $3\overline{)585}$ 11. $5\overline{)5,212}$ 12. $2\overline{)650}$

13. $523 \div 5$ 14. $637 \div 9$ 15. $4,073 \div 3$ 16. $4,417 \div 9$

Problem Solving Strategy: Making a Table, page 265..........................

Make a table to solve the problem.

1. Bill, Ron, and Cindy have different jobs after school. They deliver newspapers, babysit, or walk dogs. Ron is allergic to dogs. Cindy delivers newspapers. What after-school job does Bill have?

2. Paul, Carlos, Monica and her sister, Anna, are each buying different color sweatshirts. Monica's sister prefers red. Carlos does not like yellow. Paul buys a blue sweatshirt. Who buys the yellow one? the green one?

Dividing 2-Digit Numbers, page 269...

Divide.

1. $4\overline{)13}$ **2.** $2\overline{)15}$ **3.** $6\overline{)77}$ **4.** $3\overline{)53}$

5. $7\overline{)89}$ **6.** $3\overline{)54}$ **7.** $6\overline{)75}$ **8.** $2\overline{)87}$

9. $3\overline{)39}$ **10.** $7\overline{)79}$ **11.** $5\overline{)56}$ **12.** $6\overline{)72}$

13. $5\overline{)85}$ **14.** $8\overline{)92}$ **15.** $9\overline{)99}$ **16.** $4\overline{)86}$

17. $57 \div 8$ **18.** $72 \div 5$ **19.** $58 \div 5$ **20.** $85 \div 4$

Dividing 3-Digit Numbers, page 271...

Divide.

1. $2\overline{)435}$ **2.** $5\overline{)606}$ **3.** $6\overline{)990}$ **4.** $3\overline{)669}$

5. $7\overline{)876}$ **6.** $5\overline{)778}$ **7.** $4\overline{)952}$ **8.** $4\overline{)928}$

9. $4\overline{)573}$ **10.** $6\overline{)685}$ **11.** $2\overline{)673}$ **12.** $7\overline{)877}$

13. $6\overline{)795}$ **14.** $7\overline{)884}$ **15.** $2\overline{)825}$ **16.** $5\overline{)899}$

17. $500 \div 4$ **18.** $986 \div 3$ **19.** $935 \div 2$ **20.** $674 \div 5$

EXTRA PRACTICE

More Dividing 3-Digit Numbers, page 275..

Divide.

1. $2\overline{)131}$ **2.** $7\overline{)297}$ **3.** $6\overline{)111}$ **4.** $3\overline{)148}$

5. $8\overline{)624}$ **6.** $6\overline{)560}$ **7.** $9\overline{)623}$ **8.** $8\overline{)249}$

9. $5\overline{)437}$ **10.** $3\overline{)197}$ **11.** $5\overline{)906}$ **12.** $7\overline{)787}$

13. $347 \div 5$ **14.** $469 \div 3$ **15.** $379 \div 3$ **16.** $246 \div 9$

Zeros in the Quotient, page 277...

Divide.

1. $3\overline{)62}$ **2.** $2\overline{)41}$ **3.** $5\overline{)52}$ **4.** $4\overline{)82}$

5. $2\overline{)410}$ **6.** $5\overline{)603}$ **7.** $6\overline{)484}$ **8.** $9\overline{)993}$

9. $5\overline{)103}$ **10.** $4\overline{)883}$ **11.** $8\overline{)484}$ **12.** $2\overline{)81}$

13. $8\overline{)83}$ **14.** $6\overline{)602}$ **15.** $3\overline{)605}$ **16.** $4\overline{)202}$

17. $123 \div 6$ **18.** $516 \div 5$ **19.** $421 \div 7$ **20.** $313 \div 3$

Dividing Money, page 279...

Divide.

1. $6\overline{)\$3.60}$ **2.** $6\overline{)\$.78}$ **3.** $3\overline{)\$.39}$ **4.** $2\overline{)\$1.68}$

5. $3\overline{)\$6.18}$ **6.** $6\overline{)\$8.10}$ **7.** $8\overline{)\$4.96}$ **8.** $4\overline{)\$1.28}$

9. $9\overline{)\$7.02}$ **10.** $6\overline{)\$4.08}$ **11.** $6\overline{)\$.90}$ **12.** $7\overline{)\$9.80}$

13. $2\overline{)\$7.92}$ **14.** $4\overline{)\$6.24}$ **15.** $5\overline{)\$5.45}$ **16.** $7\overline{)\$7.98}$

17. $\$6.24 \div 6$ **18.** $\$9.12 \div 8$ **19.** $\$5.15 \div 5$ **20.** $\$8.32 \div 4$

Problem Solving: Interpreting the Quotient and Remainder, page 283 ....

Solve the problem. Tell how you interpreted the quotient and remainder.

1. Tania's dad is putting up bookshelves. He can fit only 8 books on each shelf. Tania has 36 books. How many shelves will be filled?

2. Harry has 327 stamps in his collection. He puts 8 stamps on each page in his album. How many of the pages in Harry's album are full?

3. Parent volunteers took 118 fourth graders on a trip to the science museum. Each parent was responsible for no more than 8 students. How many parents went on the trip?

4. Roy and Tomas have saved $31 to buy videotapes. The tapes they like are on sale at $9 each. How much money will they have left after they buy the videotapes?

More Median, Range, and Average, page 287 ....

Find the median, range, and average.

1. 3; 7; 12; 8; 5

2. $8; $12; $10; $4; $6

3. 2; 4; 1; 3; 8; 7; 3

4. 20¢; 30¢; 26¢; 14¢; 5¢

5. 42; 16; 35; 32; 25

6. 16; 18; 25; 37; 22; 23; 34

7. 108; 107; 103

8. 114; 63; 81; 107; 85

9. $118; $100; $107; $85; $75

10. 83; 118; 107; 139; 85; 101; 74

11. 33; 87; 52; 65; 83

12. 89; 107; 125; 47; 63; 49; 80

13. 80; 40; 60; 110; 75

14. 62; 72; 22; 35; 44

15. $214; $75; $138; $99; $159

16. 28; 42; 36; 48; 33; 41; 38

17. 109; 99; 108; 110; 89

18. 42; 37; 58; 29; 48; 32; 55

19. 111; 102; 125; 136; 121

20. $63; $78; $92; $104; $63

PRACTICE *PLUS*

KEY SKILL: Zeros in the Quotient (Use after page 277.)

Level A
Divide.

1. $3\overline{)31}$ **2.** $6\overline{)60}$ **3.** $4\overline{)80}$ **4.** $3\overline{)62}$ **5.** $4\overline{)42}$

6. $5\overline{)53}$ **7.** $2\overline{)41}$ **8.** $3\overline{)32}$ **9.** $8\overline{)85}$ **10.** $7\overline{)73}$

11. $4\overline{)804}$ **12.** $5\overline{)554}$ **13.** $3\overline{)962}$ **14.** $3\overline{)182}$ **15.** $7\overline{)213}$

16. Emma has 240 beads. She can fit 8 beads on a string to make a necklace. How many necklaces can she make?

Level B
Divide.

17. $9\overline{)96}$ **18.** $6\overline{)63}$ **19.** $2\overline{)815}$ **20.** $5\overline{)545}$ **21.** $6\overline{)424}$

22. $2\overline{)100}$ **23.** $6\overline{)305}$ **24.** $6\overline{)484}$ **25.** $5\overline{)540}$ **26.** $3\overline{)272}$

27. Divide 86 by 8.   **28.** What is 507 divided by 5?

29. Paul has 604 stickers. He fits 6 stickers on each page of a book. How many pages does he fill? How many stickers are left over?

Level C
Divide.

30. $52 \div 5$ **31.** $82 \div 4$ **32.** $122 \div 3$ **33.** $154 \div 5$

34. $723 \div 4$ **35.** $653 \div 5$ **36.** $646 \div 8$ **37.** $544 \div 6$

38. $304 \div 6$ **39.** $960 \div 9$ **40.** $740 \div 7$ **41.** $843 \div 6$

42. Divide 546 by 9.   **43.** What is 701 divided by 5?

44. Shane has 818 stamps in his collection. He puts 9 stamps in each envelope. How many envelopes does he fill? How many stamps are left over?

KEY SKILL: Dividing Money (Use after page 279.)

Level A

Divide.

1. 6)$.30 **2.** 8)$.40 **3.** 5)$.45 **4.** 6)$.72 **5.** 3)$.21

6. 8)$.80 **7.** 4)$.56 **8.** 2)$.34 **9.** 3)$.51 **10.** 7)$.84

11. 7)$.70 **12.** 3)$.24 **13.** 9)$.54 **14.** 7)$.42 **15.** 5)$.65

16. The cost of two grapefruits is $.88. How much does each grapefruit cost?

Level B

Divide.

17. 7)$.98 **18.** 6)$.78 **19.** 7)$.63 **20.** 3)$1.41 **21.** 2)$8.16

22. 4)$6.80 **23.** 3)$9.18 **24.** 5)$7.15 **25.** 4)$4.16 **26.** 7)$4.55

27. 5)$6.95 **28.** 7)$1.05 **29.** 5)$2.65 **30.** 6)$6.54 **31.** 3)$7.41

32. Charlie bought 5 pineapples for $7.25. What is the cost of each pineapple?

Level C

Divide.

33. $8.36 ÷ 4 **34.** $4.55 ÷ 7 **35.** $5.10 ÷ 6 **36.** $3.28 ÷ 8

37. $3.85 ÷ 7 **38.** $9.16 ÷ 4 **39.** $1.71 ÷ 9 **40.** $5.31 ÷ 9

41. $9.84 ÷ 8 **42.** $5.85 ÷ 5 **43.** $8.37 ÷ 9 **44.** $7.07 ÷ 7

45. $6.48 ÷ 9 **46.** $7.12 ÷ 8 **47.** $9.90 ÷ 6 **48.** $9.31 ÷ 7

49. Tina lives in Quebec, Canada. She makes a 9-minute phone call to Tampa Bay, Florida, that costs $8.91. What is the cost per minute for the phone call?

CHAPTER REVIEW/TEST

LANGUAGE AND MATHEMATICS

Complete the sentences. Use the words in the chart.

1. Use ■ to check division.

2. The answer in a division problem is the ■.

3. The middle number of a group of numbers is the ■.

4. The ■ of a group of numbers is the sum of the numbers divided by the number of addends.

CONCEPTS AND SKILLS

Divide. Use mental math.

5. $9\overline{)720}$ **6.** $8\overline{)480}$ **7.** $7\overline{)4,900}$ **8.** $6\overline{)5,400}$

9. $400 \div 5$ **10.** $600 \div 3$ **11.** $4,000 \div 2$ **12.** $3,600 \div 6$

Divide.

13. $8\overline{)49}$ **14.** $2\overline{)\$6.42}$ **15.** $6\overline{)836}$ **16.** $4\overline{)961}$

17. $759 \div 7$ **18.** $\$819 \div 9$ **19.** $368 \div 4$ **20.** $723 \div 8$

Estimate the quotients by rounding.

21. $3\overline{)92}$ **22.** $6\overline{)3,122}$ **23.** $515 \div 5$ **24.** $7,190 \div 7$

Estimate the quotients by using compatible numbers.

25. $4\overline{)374}$ **26.** $8\overline{)734}$ **27.** $437 \div 7$ **28.** $282 \div 3$

Find the median, range, and average.

29. 14, 27, 12, 33, 9   **30.** $104, $99, $101, $106, $100

Critical Thinking

31. Mia says that the average of a group of numbers can be greater than the greatest number in the group. Do you agree? Why?

Mixed Applications

Solve.

32. Kara, Bill, and Marc are each in a different school club. Bill is in the Track Club, Kara does not play chess. Who is in the Chess Club?

33. There are 148 jars of paint on the shelves in the closet. Each shelf holds 9 jars. How many full shelves of paint are there?

PERFORMANCE ASSESSMENT

Work with your group to solve this problem.

A group of four students competed in a "Mini-Olympics." The results are shown below.

RESULTS OF MINI-OLYMPICS

Student Name	Push-Ups	Sit-Ups	22-Yard Run (seconds)	Standing Broad Jump (in.)	Basketball Toss (feet)
Marcos	24	22	32	41	36
Ramon	30	36	44	38	49
Felita	12	28	29	27	27
Shawna	18	30	27	50	28

Estimate and compute the average (mean) result for each event in the Mini-Olympics. Then make a table showing the average result for each event.

1. ***Think about:***
   - how to estimate the average (mean) for each event
   - how to compute the averages (means)

2. Write a paragraph explaining how you determined the numbers in your table, and how the means compare to the actual results.

CUMULATIVE REVIEW

Choose the letter of the correct answer.

1. Find the range: 25, 11, 9

   a. 11   **c.** 16

   b. 15   **d.** not given

2. Estimate the capacity of a tablespoon

   a. 15 L   **c.** 15 mL

   b. 75 L   **d.** 75 mL

3. Find the remainder: $45 \div 7$

   a. 3   **c.** 5

   b. 4   **d.** not given

4. $\$2.64 \div 8$

   a. $.14   **c.** $.44

   b. $.33   **d.** not given

5. Estimate by rounding: $734 \div 7$

   a. 80   **c.** 100

   b. 90   **d.** 150

6. $4 \times \blacksquare \times 3 = 36$

   a. 1   **c.** 3

   b. 2   **d.** not given

7. What is 2 minutes before 3 A.M.?

   a. 2:52 A.M.   **c.** 3:02 A.M.

   b. 2:58 A.M.   **d.** not given

8. $478 \div 9$

   a. 43   **c.** 53 R1

   b. 43 R1   **d.** not given

9. 532×7

   a. 3,514   **c.** 3,714

   b. 3,524   **d.** not given

10. Find the common factor of 6 and 27.

   a. 2   **c.** 6

   b. 3   **d.** not given

11. $4,900 \div 7$

   a. 7   **c.** 700

   b. 70   **d.** not given

12. What is 8 times 26?

   a. 168   **c.** 228

   b. 208   **d.** not given

13. Find the median: 3, 9, 1, 2, 7

   a. 1   **c.** 3

   b. 2   **d.** not given

14. What is 625 divided by 3?

   a. 208 R1   **c.** 280 R1

   b. 208 R2   **d.** not given

DIVISIBILITY RULES FOR 2, 5, AND 10

You can tell when a number is divisible by
2, 5, or 10 without having to divide the number.

Think: A number is divisible by
another number when the
remainder is zero.

Use the numbers in the box with the questions
below to write some divisibility rules for 2, 5, and 10.

Divide each of the numbers in the box by 2.

1. Which numbers are divisible by 2? How do you know?

2. Look at the ones place of the numbers divisible by 2. What
digits do you find?

3. Try another number where the digit in the ones place is one
of the digits you found in Problem 2. Is it divisible by 2?

4. Write a rule that can help you decide, without dividing, if a
number is divisible by 2. Test your rule on other numbers.

21
22
23
24
25
26
27
28
29
30

Divide each of the numbers in the box by 5.

5. Which numbers are divisible by 5?

6. Write a rule that can help you decide, without dividing, if a
number is divisible by 5. Test your rule on other numbers.

Divide each of the numbers in the box by 10.

7. Write a rule that can help you decide, without dividing,
if a number is divisible by 10.

Copy the table. Complete by writing *yes* or *no*.

Number	59	84	175	210	415	3,102	4,000
Divisible by 2?	8. ■	9. ■	10. ■	11. ■	12. ■	13. ■	14. ■
Divisible by 5?	15. ■	16. ■	17. ■	18. ■	19. ■	20. ■	21. ■
Divisible by 10?	22. ■	23. ■	24. ■	25. ■	26. ■	27. ■	28. ■

29. Look at the table. What do you notice about the
numbers that are divisible by 10?

GEOMETRIC *Shapes* IN QUILTS

The art of quilting was practiced in ancient Africa. Using patchwork to decorate clothing and other items has continued in many parts of Africa. In America, patchwork quilting became a tradition as women created colorful bedcovers from scraps of clothing.

Some traditional American quilt patterns may have come from African cloth designs. Today's African American quiltmakers often change these traditional patterns slightly to make their own designs. Quilt artist Willia Ette Graham says, "I transfer patterns into different shapes and forms to make a different picture. I revise them just to see what a change will make."

1 What geometric shapes do you see in the quilts pictured? Describe any patterns you see.

2 Compare Emma Hall's quilt to the standard "Double Wedding Ring" pattern. How is her quilt the same? How is it different?

3 What kind of planning do you think goes into making a quilt?

4 What did the quilt maker in "Afro-American Women and Quilts" represent by her quilt patterns? What do you think she was remembering?

Traditional "Double Wedding Ring" pattern

Emma Hall's "Double Wedding Ring" pattern

Activity Geometry Around Us

Look around. Everywhere there are lines and shapes like circles, triangles, squares, and rectangles. Geometry is in the world around us, in the objects we use every day, in the rooms where we live, work, and play.

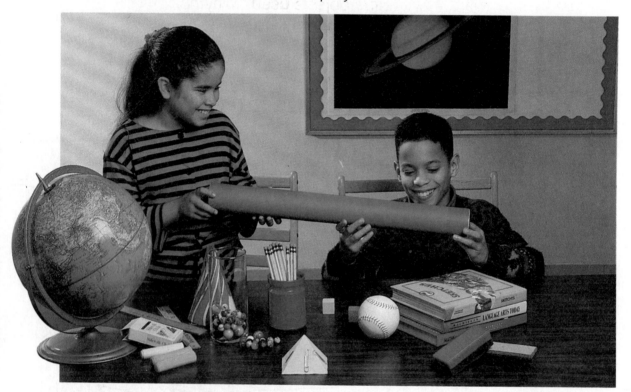

WORKING TOGETHER

Find some objects in your classroom to study.

1. List the objects that have geometric shapes you know. Sort these objects according to their shapes.

2. Which objects have only parts of geometric figures? Which combine two or more geometric figures?

3. Which objects are made of straight lines? of curves?

4. Where can you find lines that cross or meet?

5. Trace the edges of some of the objects on a piece of paper. What shapes do you see?

SHARING IDEAS

6. Which shapes did you see most often? Why do you think these shapes are used so much?

7. Look at your list of circular and curved objects. Why are they shaped that way?

8. Compare the objects that have straight lines with those that have curves. How are the objects used? Why do you think they are shaped the way they are?

ON YOUR OWN

9. Think about objects outside of your classroom. What shapes can you add to the list you made? How would you sort them? Compare your list with those of others.

10. Draw a picture of something you see every day. Identify the shapes in your picture. Compare your picture with those of others.

ACTIVITY
Lines, Line Segments, and Rays

To design houses, architects need to know about lines, line segments, and rays.

You can use paper and tape to learn about line segments.

Step 1   Place a strip of masking tape on a piece of paper. Trace along one edge of the tape. Then draw a point on each end of the tracing and label the points A and B. You have drawn a **line segment,** a straight figure with two endpoints.

Read: line segment AB or line segment BA
Write: $\overline{AB}$ or $\overline{BA}$

Step 2   Place two strips of masking tape on a piece of paper so that the strips cross each other. Trace a line segment along one edge of each strip of tape. Draw a point where the line segments meet. Line segments that meet at a point are **intersecting.**

$\overline{CD}$ intersects $\overline{EF}$ at point G.

Step 3   Trace along each edge of a strip of masking tape to draw two line segments that do not intersect. Notice that these line segments remain the same distance apart. They are **parallel.**

$\overline{LM}$ is parallel to $\overline{OP}$.
Write: $\overline{LM} \mid\mid \overline{OP}$.

A **line** is also a straight figure, but it has no endpoints. It goes on forever in both directions. To show a line, extend the ends of a line segment and draw arrowheads on each end.

Read: line AB or line BA
Write: $\overleftrightarrow{AB}$ or $\overleftrightarrow{BA}$

1. Draw and label two parallel lines.

A **ray** is another straight figure. It has one endpoint. It goes on forever in just one direction.

Read: ray ZY (Name the endpoint first.)
Write: $\overrightarrow{ZY}$ (Direct the arrow to the right.)

2. Draw and label two rays that intersect each other.

3. Name some things that suggest line segments, lines, and rays.

4. Name some things in your classroom that suggest intersecting lines and parallel lines.

PRACTICE

Write the name of the figure.

5.

6.

7.

8.

9.

10.

Tell if the figures are *intersecting* or *parallel*.

11.
12.
13.

Draw the figure.

14. $\overrightarrow{RT}$ **15.** $\overleftrightarrow{DF}$ **16.** $\overline{KL}$ **17.** $\overline{UZ} \mid \mid \overline{WY}$

18. line *AB* intersecting line *MR* at point *D*

19. ray *HN* parallel to ray *DE*

20. line segment *ET* intersecting line *SD* at point *A*

21. a capital letter made from only two intersecting line segments

Mixed Review

Find the answer. Which method did you use?

22. $3,005 - 978$ **23.** 6×20 **24.** $9 + 8$

25. $458 \div 6$ **26.** $5,789 + 6,857$ **27.** $32 \div 4$

MENTAL MATH
CALCULATOR
PAPER/PENCIL

ACTIVITY

Angles

A. Schools in the future may be covered by a dome like this. The dome would keep out bad weather. This type of dome is made of many angles.

An **angle** is formed by two rays with the same endpoint. The rays are the **sides** of the angle. The endpoint is its **vertex**.

Read: angle *ABC* or angle *CBA* or angle *B*
Write: ∠*ABC* or ∠*CBA* or ∠*B*

1. What do you notice about the vertex and the name of the angle?

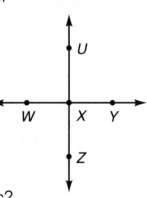

B. An angle that forms a square corner is a **right angle.** Intersecting lines that form right angles are called **perpendicular** lines.

∠*UXY* and ∠*WXZ* are right angles.
Read: Line *UZ* is perpendicular to line *WY*
Write: $\overleftrightarrow{UZ} \perp \overleftrightarrow{WY}$

2. Can you name things that suggest perpendicular lines?

3. Name another right angle in this figure.

C. You can make a model to help you learn about different types of angles.

Step 1 Take two strips of paper and fasten them together.

Step 2 Line up the sides of your model with the corner of a sheet of paper to form a right angle.

Step 3 Close the space between the sides of your model to form an angle less than a right angle. Then open the space between the sides of your model to form an angle greater than a right angle.

Step 4 Use your model to measure the angles of some objects in your classroom. Make a chart like the one to the right to sort the objects by angle size.

Object	Less Than Right Angle	Right Angle	Greater Than Right Angle

SHARING IDEAS

4. What does the size of an angle depend on?

5. Name some objects outside of your classroom that have right angles. Then name some objects that have angles greater than or less than a right angle.

PRACTICE

Use the figure to answer the problem.

6. Name a pair of perpendicular lines.

7. Name a pair of parallel lines.

8. How many right angles have point *D* as a vertex? Name one.

9. Name an angle with vertex *D* that is less than a right angle.

10. Name an angle with vertex *D* that is greater than a right angle.

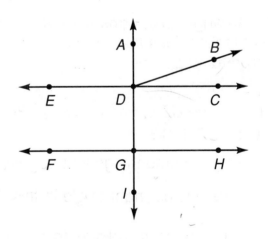

Draw the figure.

11. right angle *RST* **12.** $\overleftrightarrow{UZ} \perp \overleftrightarrow{WY}$ **13.** ∠LMN less than a right angle

Critical Thinking

Write *true* or *false*. Tell how you made your decision.

14. Longer rays make greater angles.

15. Two angles cannot share a vertex.

16. The corner of a book suggests a right angle.

17. The hands of a clock form angles.

Plane Figures

Peggy is learning to figure skate. The blades of her skates carve shapes into the flat surface of the ice.

— A flat surface that goes on in all directions is a **plane**.

Read: plane *DEF*

Shapes drawn on a plane are called **plane figures.**

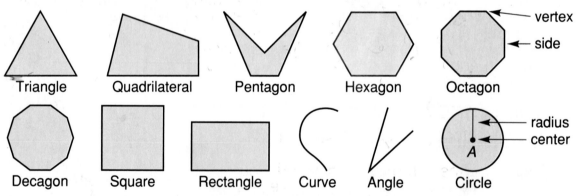

Triangle Quadrilateral Pentagon Hexagon Octagon vertex side

Decagon Square Rectangle Curve Angle Circle radius center

Plane figures can be **open** like an angle, or **closed** like a circle. **Polygons** are closed plane figures with sides that are line segments.

1. Which plane figures above are not polygons? Why?

2. Count the sides and vertices for each polygon. What do you notice?

3. How are rectangles and squares the same? How are they different?

TRY OUT Write *yes* or *no* to tell if the figure is a polygon.
Name the polygon.

4. 5. 6. 7.

PRACTICE

Name the figure.

8. 9. 10. 11.

12. a polygon with 4 sides

13. a polygon with 10 sides

14. a quadrilateral with 4 right angles and 4 equal sides

15. a polygon with 8 vertices

Draw the figure.

16. a pentagon with 1 right angle

17. a triangle with 3 equal sides

18. a quadrilateral with at least 2 right angles

19. a triangle with 1 angle greater than a right angle

20. **Describe a figure.** Have others draw and name your figure.

CHALLENGE

You can use a **compass** to draw a circle.

Step 1 Put the compass point where you want the center of the circle to be.

Step 2 Open the compass to the length you want the radius to be.

Step 3 Turn the pencil around the center point to draw the circle.

Use a compass to draw the circle.

1. radius = 3 cm   **2.** radius = 5 cm   **3.** radius = 7 cm

PROBLEM SOLVING

Strategy: Solving a Multistep Problem

Ryan is building a house that uses solar-heating window panels. He has 35 panels. He needs 4 panels for each of the 8 rooms in the house and 2 panels for the garage. How many panels will he have left?

1. What information do you know?

2. What do you need to find out?

Sometimes it takes several steps to solve a problem. When there is more than one step, it helps to make a plan.

3. What do you need to find out *before* you can decide how many panels will be left?

Try your plan.   **PLAN**

4. What can you do first?   **Step 1** $8 \times 4 = 32$

5. What do you do next?   **Step 2** $32 + 2 = 34$

6. What do you do last?   **Step 3** $35 - 34 = \blacksquare$

7. How many panels are left?

8. Could you have made a different plan to solve the problem? Try it.

PRACTICE

Make a plan. Then solve the problem. Use mental math, a calculator, or paper and pencil.

9. There are 87 homes in Spruceville and 16 homes in Greenleaf. Tandyville has 4 streets with 15 homes on each. How many more homes are there in Spruceville than in Tandyville and Greenleaf together?

10. In Carol's model castle there are 3 floors with 12 doors on each floor, 2 floors with 14 doors on each floor, and 1 floor with 11 doors. How many doors are there in all?

11. Jason is going to paint his model house. He buys 3 cans of paint for $6.00 each and 1 brush for $.95. How much change should he get from a $20 bill?

12. Mr. Roland is building a 6-room house with 2 large windows and 3 small windows in each room. He has already made 14 windows. How many windows does he have left to make?

Strategies and Skills-Review

13. All 137 light bulbs in the halls of an office building are being replaced. Light bulbs come in packages of 8. How many packages are needed?

14. Sir Christopher Wren was a famous English architect. He was born in 1632 and died in 1723. How long did he live?

15. In the Architectural Museum one room has 9 models of seaside homes and 14 blueprints. Another room has 3 times as many models and half as many blueprints. How many models and blueprints are there in the two rooms?

16. *Write a problem* that takes several steps to solve. Solve your problem. Ask others to solve it. Talk about whether there is more than one way to solve the problem.

COMING UNGLUED

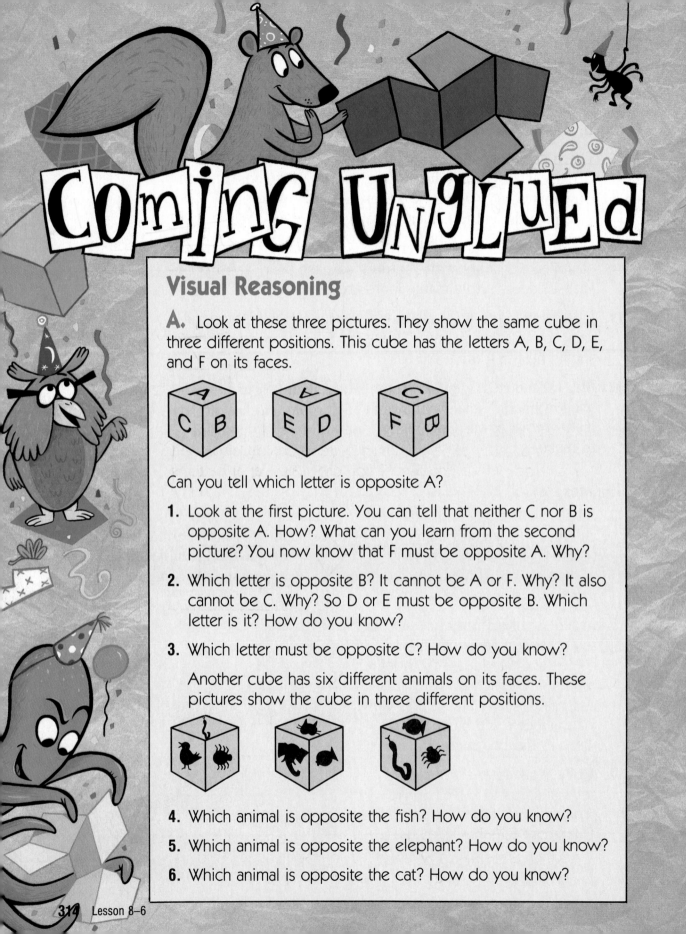

Visual Reasoning

A. Look at these three pictures. They show the same cube in three different positions. This cube has the letters A, B, C, D, E, and F on its faces.

Can you tell which letter is opposite A?

1. Look at the first picture. You can tell that neither C nor B is opposite A. How? What can you learn from the second picture? You now know that F must be opposite A. Why?

2. Which letter is opposite B? It cannot be A or F. Why? It also cannot be C. Why? So D or E must be opposite B. Which letter is it? How do you know?

3. Which letter must be opposite C? How do you know?

   Another cube has six different animals on its faces. These pictures show the cube in three different positions.

4. Which animal is opposite the fish? How do you know?

5. Which animal is opposite the elephant? How do you know?

6. Which animal is opposite the cat? How do you know?

B. Here is another type of cube puzzle. Think of a cube made of paper. It could be cut and unfolded to lie flat like this:

Can you see how to fold this shape back into a cube?

Now look at these patterns. Which patterns could be folded to form a cube? Which could not? You can make paper patterns to try yourself.

7.

8.

9.

10.

11. Now design 3 new patterns that could be folded into cubes. How many squares will you use for each pattern? Use paper models to help you make sure that your patterns work.

PROBLEM SOLVING

✓ UNDERSTAND
✓ PLAN
✓ TRY
✓ CHECK
✓ EXTEND

Strategies Review

Use these problem-solving strategies to solve the problems. Remember that some problems can be solved using more than one strategy.

- Using Number Sense
- Drawing a Diagram
- Choosing the Operation
- Solving a Two-Step Problem
- Finding a Pattern

- Guess, Test, and Revise
- Using Estimation
- Making a Table
- Solving a Multistep Problem

Solve. Tell which strategy you used. Use mental math, a calculator, or paper and pencil.

1. Chester is assembling his model house. He uses 3 hinges to attach 2 boards. How many hinges does he need to attach 4 boards in a row?

2. The stairs of the library have 18 steps between floors. How many steps must you walk to get to the sixth floor?

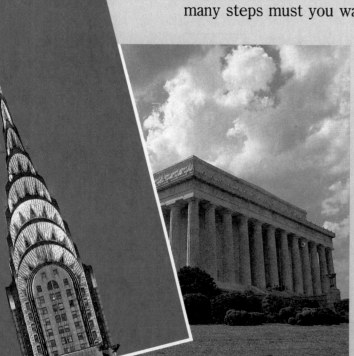

3. The Parker Hobby Shop wants to sell 150 model houses in three weeks. It sold 65 models the first week and 58 models the second week. Will it meet its goal if it sells 40 models the third week?

4. Brietta's apartment has 3 French windows and 5 regular windows. The French windows have 18 panes each, and the regular windows have 2 panes each. How many windowpanes does her apartment have in all?

5. A designer bought sheets of blueprint and transparent paper. The blueprint paper cost $3 a sheet, and the transparent paper cost $1 a sheet. He paid $58 for 30 sheets. How many sheets of each kind of paper did he buy?

6. Cheri is designing a pattern for a tile wall. She puts 2 red tiles in the first row, 4 red tiles in the second row, and 8 red tiles in the third row. How many tiles are in each of the next two rows?

7. Mike and Roberto are bricklayers. Mike finished 21 rows of bricks in one day, and Roberto finished 24 rows. Each row has 9 bricks. How many more bricks did Roberto lay than Mike?

8. The Scout troop needs to raise $300 for new equipment. They raised $148 from a card sale and $210 from a bake sale. Have they raised enough money?

9. The architect Henry Bacon, who built the Lincoln Memorial, lived from 1866 to 1924. The inventor of the geodesic dome, R. Buckminster Fuller, lived from 1895 to 1983. Who lived longer?

10. The Eiffel Tower in Paris weighs about 9,000 tons. The CN Tower in Toronto weighs about 160,000 tons. Does the CN Tower weigh more than 150,000 tons more than the Eiffel Tower?

11. Hal needs 30 round pegs to assemble his model house. If the pegs are packed 8 to a box, how many boxes of pegs should Hal buy?

12. *Write a problem* that can be solved by using one of the strategies. Ask others to solve your problem.

Slides, Flips, and Turns

Many artists make patterns by moving a geometric figure.

You can move a geometric figure in different ways.

You can **slide** a figure across a line.

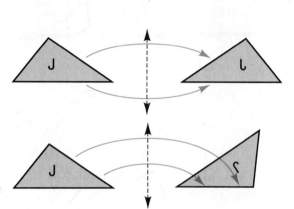

You can **flip** a figure over a line.

You can **turn** a figure around a point on a line.

WORKING TOGETHER

Step 1 Draw a geometric figure. Trace it and cut it out.

Step 2 Place the cutout over your drawing. Slide the cutout and trace its new position. Label this move on the back.

Step 3 Show a flip on another piece of paper. Show a turn on a third piece of paper.

Step 4 Share your figures with others. Tell how their figures have been moved.

SHARING IDEAS

1. Tell how each move changes the position of a figure.

2. Can you always tell how a figure was moved? Why or why not?

3. Does the shape of a figure change when you move it? Why or why not?

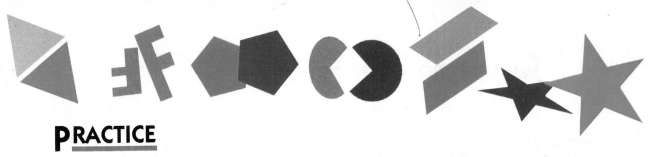

PRACTICE

Write *slide, flip,* or *turn* to tell how the figure was moved.

4. **5.** **6.**

7. **8.** **9.**

Critical Thinking

10. Tell how you can move the triangle to make the complete design.

Mixed Applications

11. Lotte uses 479 tiles to cover the wall. She uses 503 tiles to cover the floor. How many more tiles does she use on the floor than on the wall?

12. Ben uses 5 boxes of colored tiles to make a design on a wall. Each box holds 25 tiles. How many tiles does Ben use?

CHALLENGE

Look at the picture. A triangle has been slid, flipped, and turned to create a pattern. The triangles fit together with no space between them. A pattern that repeats one figure of the same size and shape in this way is called a **tessellation.**

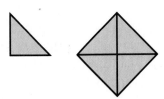

Which pattern blocks can be used to make a tessellation?

ACTIVITY

Congruence and Similarity

At the Lyndon B. Johnson Space Center in Houston, Jorge bought a poster of a planned space colony. He also bought two postcards of the same picture.

Figures that are the same shape and size are **congruent.** Figures that have the same shape but are different sizes are **similar.**

1. Which of Jorge's pictures are congruent?

2. Which of Jorge's pictures are similar?

WORKING TOGETHER

Step 1 Trace the figures on the page. Cut them out.

Step 2 Sort the figures by their shapes.

Step 3 Match the parts of the figures to see if they are similar.

Step 4 Show which figures are congruent by placing them on top of each other.

3. Which figures are similar?

4. Which figures are congruent?

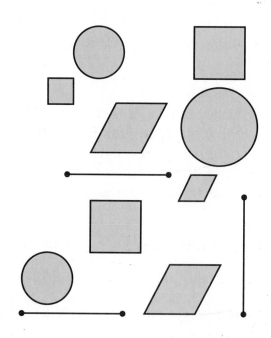

SHARING IDEAS

Tell if the statement is *true* or *false.* Tell how you made your decision.

5. All figures that are the same size are congruent.

6. Figures must be in the same position to be congruent.

7. All line segments are similar.

8. All circles are congruent.

PRACTICE

Tell which figure is congruent and which is similar.

9.

10.
 A B C D

11.
  A B C D

Write *congruent* or *similar*.

12. footprints in the sand

13. a photo and its enlargement

14. a newspaper ad and a billboard

15. covers of the same book

Mixed Applications

16. Miko has $15. She wants to buy a poster for $12.99 and a map for $1.98. Does she have enough money? How do you know?

17. **Make a list** of objects that have congruent shapes. Make another list of objects with similar shapes. Share your list with others.

Mixed Review

Find the answer. Which method did you use?

18. $630 \div 7$ 19. 6×352 20. $402 - 298$ 21. $642 + 968$

MENTAL MATH
CALCULATOR
PAPER/PENCIL

ACTIVITY

Line of Symmetry

Brad is making a model of a house. He knows a fast way to cut some of the pieces he needs. They have special shapes.

You can use Brad's method of cutting to explore the shape of figures.

WORKING TOGETHER

Step 1

Fold a piece of paper so that the two parts overlap exactly.

Step 2

From the fold, cut a triangle like the one in the picture.

Step 3

Unfold the paper.

1. Look at the two parts of the square. Are they congruent? How do you know?

A figure that can be folded so that its two parts match exactly is a **symmetric figure.** The fold line is a **line of symmetry.**

2. Fold the square in different ways. Can you find other lines of symmetry? How many?

3. Trace and cut out the figures on the right. Fold them to find how many lines of symmetry they have. Draw your own figures. Are they symmetrical?

SHARING IDEAS

4. Which figures have 1 line of symmetry? more than 1 line of symmetry?

5. Are all figures symmetrical? How can you show this?

6. Which figure has the most lines of symmetry?

PRACTICE

Tell whether the dotted line is a line of symmetry.

7.

8.

9.

10.

11.

12.

13.

14.

Tell how many lines of symmetry the figure has.

15.

16.

17.

18.

19.

20.

21.

22.

Critical Thinking

23. Would you slide, flip, or turn a copy of this figure to make a complete symmetric figure?

Mixed Applications

24. Which capital letters of the alphabet are symmetrical? Which have more than 1 line of symmetry?

25. Brad cuts out 24 pieces of paper for each house. How many pieces must he cut out for 7 houses?

Space Figures

Many buildings and objects in the world suggest **space figures**.

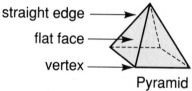

straight edge →
flat face →
vertex →
Pyramid

Cube

Sphere

Cone

Rectangular prism

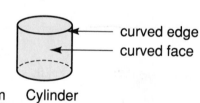

Cylinder

curved edge
curved face

1. Which figures have only flat faces? How many does each have?

2. Which figures have only curved faces? How many does each have?

3. Which figures have both flat and curved faces? How many of each type does each figure have?

4. How many edges does each figure have? How many vertices?

TRY OUT   Name the space figure suggested by each object.

5.

6.

7.

PRACTICE

Name the space figure suggested.

8.

9.

10.

11.

12.

13.

14.

15.

16. It has one vertex and a curved face.

17. Some of its faces are shaped like triangles.

18. Two of its faces are circles.

19. All of its faces are congruent.

Critical Thinking

Write *true* or *false*. Tell how you made your decision.

20. All cubes are congruent figures.

21. All spheres are similar.

22. All rectangular prisms are congruent.

Mixed Applications

Solve. You may need to use the Databank on page 520.

23. Which building is shaped like a pyramid? a rectangular prism? a sphere?

24. A square floor in Kiel's house is 5 m long. What is the area of the floor?

25. Marie's building has 5 floors. There are 75 apartments in it. Each floor has the same number of apartments. How many apartments are on each floor?

26. **Write a description** of a space figure. Have others identify the figure.

ACTIVITY

Volume

Colin is building a twenty-first century house with geometric blocks. First he builds the base with 3 rows of 4 cubes. What is the volume of the base?

Each block is one **cubic unit.** The number of cubic units in a figure is its **volume.**

WORKING TOGETHER

You can use centimeter cubes to find the volume of the base.

Use centimeter cubes to model Colin's blocks.

1. How many rows of cubes are there? How many cubes are in each row?

2. What is the total number of cubes?

3. How many cubic units does Colin use? What is the volume of the base?

4. **What if** Colin builds a figure 3 cubes long, 2 cubes wide, and 2 cubes high? What would the volume be?

5. See how many other figures you can make using this number of cubic units. What is the volume of each figure?

6. How many of the figures you made are shaped like rectangular prisms? Record the length, width, height, and volume of each in a table.

Length	Width	Height	Volume
3	4	1	■
3	2	2	■

7. Use different numbers of cubes to make other rectangular prisms. Record their measurements and volumes in the table.

SHARING IDEAS

8. Can different figures have the same volume? Why or why not?

9. Can you use the same number of cubes to make different figures that have different volumes? Why or why not?

10. What pattern do you see in the table? How can you use this pattern to find the volume of rectangular prisms without counting?

PRACTICE

Find the volume.

11.

12.

13.

14.

15.

16.

Find the volume of each of the following rectangular prisms. Use centimeter cubes if needed.

17. length: 2 cm; width: 4 cm; height: 1 cm

18. length: 5 cm; width: 3 cm; height: 2 cm

19. length: 3 cm; width: 5 cm; height: 3 cm

Mixed Applications Solve. Which method did you use?

20. Erin builds a large cube out of centimeter cubes. Each side is 3 cubes long. How many centimeter cubes did Erin use?

21. A box of blocks costs $14.37. Colin pays for it with a $20.00 bill. How much change will he get?

DECISION MAKING

COOPERATIVE LEARNING

Problem Solving: Arranging Your Room

SITUATION

Mrs. Esposito told Jackie to decide how she wants to arrange the furniture in her new room. The picture below shows the furniture Jackie has and a floor plan of her room.

PROBLEM

Where should Jackie put each piece of furniture? Will everything fit in her room?

DATA

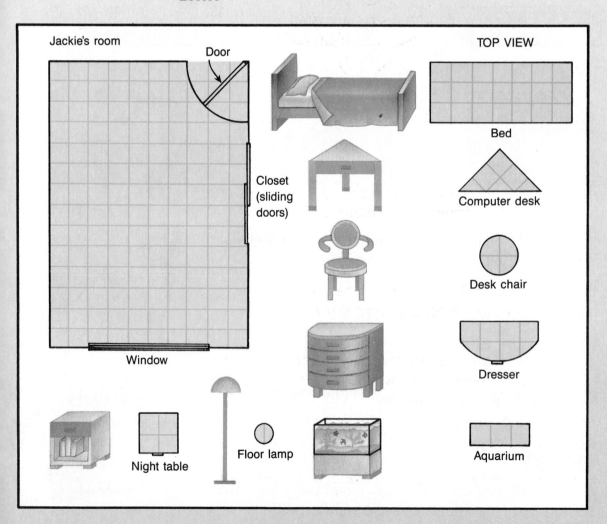

Jackie's room

Door

Closet (sliding doors)

Window

Night table

Floor lamp

TOP VIEW

Bed

Computer desk

Desk chair

Dresser

Aquarium

USING THE DATA

Trace and cut out each top view of furniture. Move the cutouts around the floor plan to answer the questions.

1. How many squares wide is Jackie's room? How many squares long is Jackie's room? What is the area of Jackie's room in square units?

2. What is the length and width of each of the following?

   a. bed   **b.** aquarium   **c.** dresser

3. Can all of these pieces of furniture fit against the wall opposite the closet?

   a. dresser, aquarium, night table
   b. bed, dresser, computer desk, floor lamp
   c. bed, computer desk, aquarium, night table

4. Which pieces of furniture will fit against the wall with the closet?

MAKING DECISIONS

5. **_Write a list_** of the things Jackie should think about when deciding how to arrange the furniture in her room.

6. Are there any parts of the room that Jackie should keep clear of furniture?

7. Can Jackie put all the furniture in the room and still have room to walk around comfortably? What pieces could Jackie leave out?

8. The floor lamp and the aquarium filter both need to be plugged into an outlet. How would this affect where you would place them in the room?

9. How would you arrange Jackie's room?

10. **_What if_** you could design a bedroom any way you chose. Use grid paper to show a picture of how it would look.

Math and Art

Some Navajo women in the American Southwest weave beautiful clothes, blankets, and rugs. Many of their weavings have geometric shapes that are repeated in a pattern.

Line of symmetry

Line of symmetry

Many patterns have a **line of symmetry.** This is an imaginary line on which you can pretend to fold an object so that its parts match exactly. The rug above has two lines of symmetry.

What if you saw this blanket? What line or lines of symmetry does it have?

Think: You can fold a vertical line through the middle of this blanket so that both parts match exactly.

The blanket has one line of symmetry.

ACTIVITIES

1. Use graph paper and crayons to draw a geometric pattern that has a line of symmetry. Draw the line of symmetry.

2. Find pictures of weavings or quilts that use geometric shapes. Do they have lines of symmetry? Discuss with your class how they are the same as the Navajo weavings and how they are different.

Computer: Parallel Lines

You can use Logo commands to explore parallel lines.

AT THE COMPUTER

You can write a program that will allow you to draw parallel lines on a computer. Enter the following program:

```
TO PARALLEL :L :D
FD :L BK :L
RT 90 PU FD :D
LT 90 PD
FD :L BK :L
END
```

To use the program to draw two parallel line segments each 30 units long and 40 units apart, enter PARALLEL 30 40.

Remember to clear the screen after completing each problem below.

1. Use the program to draw two parallel line segments 60 units long and 45 units apart. What did you enter?

2. Draw two parallel line segments 50 units long and 20 units apart. What did you enter?

3. Enter PARALLEL 40 20 LT 70. Then enter PARALLEL 20 40. What do you see on the screen?

4. Enter PARALLEL 40 20 LT 90. Then enter PARALLEL 20 40. What type of figure do you see on the screen?

5. What figure will you draw if you enter PARALLEL 40 40 LT 90 and then enter PARALLEL 40 40?

6. Use the PARALLEL program and other Logo commands to draw more figures like the ones in Exercises 2–5. Challenge a partner to draw figures that you name.

EXTRA PRACTICE

Lines, Line Segments, and Rays, page 307...................................

Name each figure.

1.

2. M ———————— N

3.

Tell if the figures are *intersecting* or *parallel.*

4.

5.

6.

Draw the figure.

7. ray *CB*

8. line *MD*

9. line segment *RN*

10. line *RS* intersects line *PQ* at point *B*

Angles, page 309...

Name the angle. Tell if it is a *right angle.*
If not, write *greater* or *less.*

1.

2.

3.

Draw the figure.

4. right angle *BCD*

5. $\overleftrightarrow{PQ} \perp \overleftrightarrow{XY}$

6. $\overleftrightarrow{RS} \parallel \overleftrightarrow{WY}$

Plane Figures, page 311...

Name the figure.

1.

2.

3.

4.

Problem Solving Strategy: Solving a Multistep Problem, page 313............

Make a plan. Then solve the problem.

1. On Jean's block there are 15 houses. There are 14 houses on Tim's block and 17 houses on Ray's block. How many more houses are there on Tim and Ray's blocks together than on Jean's block?

2. On Tim's block there are 3 families with 5 children, 4 families with 3 children, and 7 families with 2 children. How many children live on Tim's block?

3. Ray is washing the windows in his house. He lives in a 7-room house with 2 large windows and 2 small windows in each room. He has already washed 15 windows. How many windows does he have left to wash?

4. Jean is decorating her bedroom. She buys 2 pillows for $12 each and 1 curtain for $19.95. How much change should she get from a $50 bill?

Problem Solving: Strategies Review, page 317..............................

Solve. Tell which strategy you used.

1. Ray takes 3 minutes to wash each window. If there are 18 windows in his house, how many minutes does it take him to wash all of the windows?

2. Jean needs 50 paper cups to serve fruit punch at her garden party. The cups are packaged 12 to a pack. How many packages of cups does Jean need to buy?

3. The keys on a piano are each 1 inch in width. Serge's hand can span 6 inches. How many piano keys can Serge reach?

4. Lars, Daisy, and Fred each have a different pet. One has rabbits, one has a dog, and one has a cat. Lars raises rabbits. Fred does not own a dog. Who owns a dog?

EXTRA PRACTICE

Slides, Flips, and Turns, page 319.....................................

Tell whether each is a *slide, flip,* or *turn.*

1.

2.

3.

Congruence and Similarity, page 321...

Tell which figure is *congruent* and which is *similar.*

1.   **a.** A   **b.** B   **c.** C   **d.** D

2.   **a.** A   **b.** B   **c.** C   **d.** 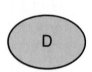 D

Line of Symmetry, page 323..

Tell whether the dotted line is a line of symmetry.

1.   **2.**   **3.**

Tell how many lines of symmetry each figure has.

4.   **5.**   **6.**   **7.**

Space Figures, page 325

Name the space figure suggested.

1.

2.

3.

4.

5.

6.

7.

8.

Volume, page 327

Find the volume.

1.

2.

3.

4.

5.

6.

Complete the table. Each figure is a rectangular prism. Use centimeter cubes if needed.

	Length (cm)	Width (cm)	Height (cm)	Volume (cubic cm)
7.	2	3	1	■
8.	3	4	4	■
9.	3	4	3	■
10.	4	6	2	■

PRACTICE PLUS

KEY SKILL: **Plane Figures** (Use after page 311.)

Level A ....

Name the figure.

1.   **2.**   **3.**   **4.**

5. a polygon with 5 sides   **6.** a polygon with 4 sides

Draw the figure.

7. a rectangle   **8.** a triangle with 3 equal sides

Level B ....

Name the figure.

9.   **10.**   **11.**   **12.**

13. a polygon with 10 sides   **14.** a quadrilateral with 4 right
angles and 4 equal sides

Draw the figure.

15. a pentagon   **16.** a triangle with one angle
smaller than a right angle

Level C ....

Name the figure.

17. a polygon with 5 sides and 5 angles

18. a figure with no sides and no angles

Draw the figure.

19. a decagon   **20.** a polygon with 4 sides
and 4 right angles

21. a circle with a
radius of 4 cm

KEY SKILL: **Space Figures** (Use after page 325.)

Level A
Name the space figure suggested.

1.

2.

3.

4.

5. Jenny uses a pastry bag to decorate a cake. The tip has 1 curved face and 1 edge. What shape is this?

Level B
Name the space figure suggested.

6.

7.

8.

9.

10. David makes a model of a skyscraper. It has 6 faces, 8 vertices, and 12 edges. What is the shape of the model?

Level C
Name the space figure suggested.

11.

12.

13.

14.

15. Priscilla makes a wind sock to hang outside. It has 2 flat faces and 2 curved edges. What is the shape of the wind sock?

CHAPTER REVIEW/TEST

LANGUAGE AND MATHEMATICS

Complete the sentences. Use the words in the chart.

VOCABULARY
vertex
plane
polygon
congruent
parallel

1. If the lines do not cross, they are ▪.

2. The rays of an angle meet at the ▪.

3. A flat surface that goes on in all directions is a ▪.

4. ▪ figures have the same shape and size.

CONCEPTS AND SKILLS

Tell whether the figure is a line, line segment, or ray.

Are the figures intersecting or parallel?

5.
   A   B

6.
   L   M

7.

8.

Name the figure.

9.

10.

11.

12.

Use the figure to answer.

13. Name an angle with vertex *O* that is greater than a right angle.

14. Name a right angle.

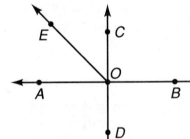

15. Is the figure the result of a *flip*, *slide*, or *turn*?

16. Tell how many lines of symmetry the figure has.

    a.   b.

17. Are the figures congruent or similar?

18. Find the volume.

Critical Thinking

19. Do congruent space figures have the same volume? Why?

Mixed Applications

20. Mo's house has 6 rooms with 2 windows each. Mo sews 2 curtains for each window. He finishes 10 curtains. How many more must he sew?

PERFORMANCE ASSESSMENT

Work with your group to create five pages for a class Geometry book. Choose five of the terms from the list below, and create one page for each term. Draw a picture or find a picture in a magazine to illustrate each term. Write a definition of the term, and give at least one example of where it is found in the real world.

Geometry Terms

line segment	line of symmetry	slide	sphere	similar
perpendicular	pentagon	angle	octagon	triangle
rectangular prism	cylinder	congruent	turn	flip
quadrilateral	hexagon	polygon	pyramid	parallel

1. *Think about:*
   - how to define each of the five terms
   - where they are found in the real world

2. Draw a picture of something from the real world that includes as many of the terms that you defined as possible. Label each term in the picture.

CUMULATIVE REVIEW

Choose the letter of the correct answer.

1. What is $\overline{AC}$?

   a. a line
   c. a line segment

   b. a ray
   d. not given

2. Name the angle.

   a. $\angle QRS$
   c. $\angle RSQ$

   b. $\angle RQS$
   d. not given

3.

A   B

E   F

The lines are:

   a. intersecting
   c. perpendicular

   b. parallel
   d. not given

4. 4×52

   a. 88
   c. 218

   b. 208
   d. not given

5.

What figure is shown?

   a. cone
   c. pyramid

   b. cylinder
   d. not given

6. Which figure is not a polygon?

   a. decagon
   c. triangle

   b. circle
   d. rectangle

7. $6\overline{)896}$

   a. 149
   c. 149 R2

   b. 149 R1
   d. not given

8. Divide 18 by 3.

   a. 6
   c. 15

   b. 54
   d. not given

9.

What is shown?

   a. slide
   c. flip

   b. turn
   d. circle

10. Find the median: 8, 7, 3, 6, 1.

   a. 5
   c. 7

   b. 6
   d. not given

11. 6×73

   a. 428
   c. 498

   b. 438
   d. not given

12. Estimate: $369 \div 4$

   a. 8
   c. 80

   b. 9
   d. 90

13. $\blacksquare \times 8 = 72$

   a. 8
   c. 576

   b. 80
   d. not given

14. $63 \div 7$

   a. 9
   c. 70

   b. 56
   d. not given

ENLARGING FIGURES ON A GRID

You can use coordinate grids to enlarge geometric figures.

Measure side *AB* of triangle *ABC* and line segment *DE*.

1. Compare their lengths.

2. What are the ordered pairs for points *A* and *B*?

3. What are the ordered pairs for points *D* and *E*?

4. Compare the ordered pairs.

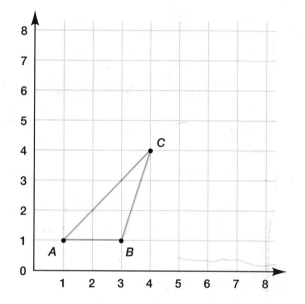

Suppose that you wanted to use line segment *DE* to draw a triangle *DEF* that is twice as large as triangle *ABC*.

5. What would be the ordered pair for point *F*?

6. Copy triangle *ABC*. Draw triangle *DEF* twice as large as triangle *ABC*.

7. How should the length of sides *AC* and *BC* compare with the length of sides *DF* and *EF*? Measure your drawing to check your answer.

8. Are the two triangles similar?

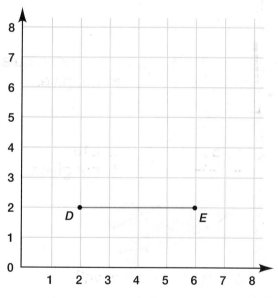

9. Draw and label this rectangle on grid paper: *W* (3, 1), *X* (3, 2), *Y* (5, 2), *Z* (5, 1). Draw a rectangle three times as large as rectangle *WXYZ*. Label the rectangle *RSTU*.

10. ***What if*** you wanted to reduce a figure? How would you find the ordered pairs of the reduced figure? Check your method by drawing a smaller triangle similar to triangle *FGH*: *F* (3, 3), *G* (6, 3), *H* (6, 6).

JAPANESE
TEMARI
BALLS

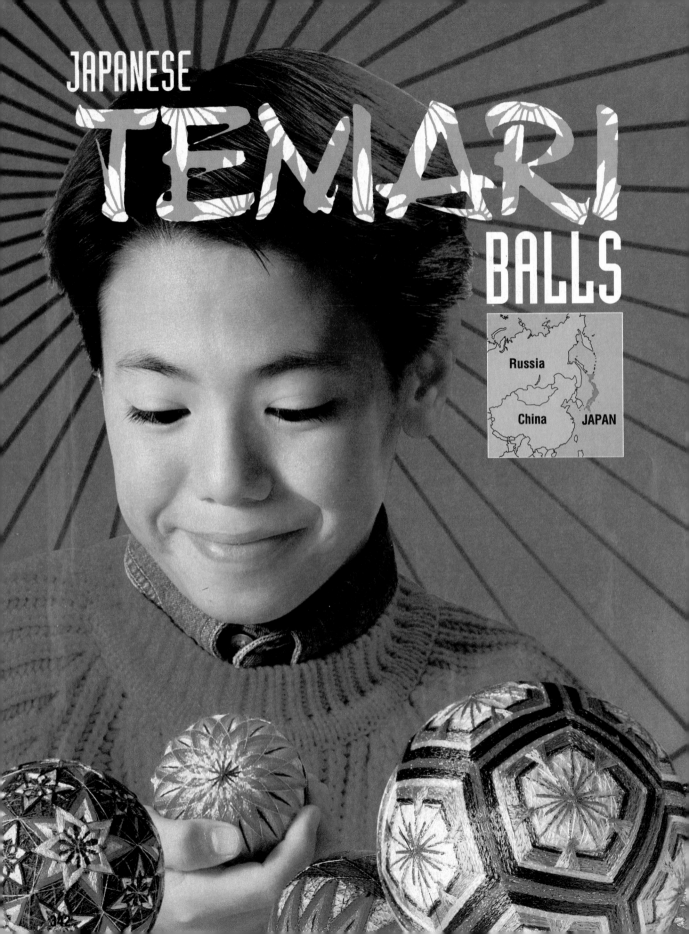

Russia

China   JAPAN

The word *temari* (teh-MAH-ree) comes from two Japanese words, *te* and *mari*, which mean "hand" and "ball." In the 1800s, the Japanese made *temari*. Scraps of cloth, leather, or bunches of dried grass or herbs were tied together to form the center. The outside was embroidered, or decorated with hand-sewn stitching.

The finished *temari* were used to play *mari* games. Japanese children sang songs and moved the balls in time with music. They learned how to make the *temari* balls, so the craft was passed from one generation to the next.

There is an organization today called the Temari Society of Japan that encourages people to learn more about *temari* balls and how they are made. Since *temari* balls are so beautiful, and so much time and care go into their making, the modern balls are used mostly for decoration.

1 Look at the photographs. How would you describe a *temari* ball to someone who has never seen one?

2 What types of balls do you play with that have geometric designs? Describe what they look like.

ACTIVITY The Meaning of Fractions

Uri is on the swim team. He uses the pool in the school gym to practice. Each of the lanes in the pool is the same size. Uri practices in one of the 4 lanes. How much of the pool does Uri use for practice?

You can use a geoboard to make a model of the pool.

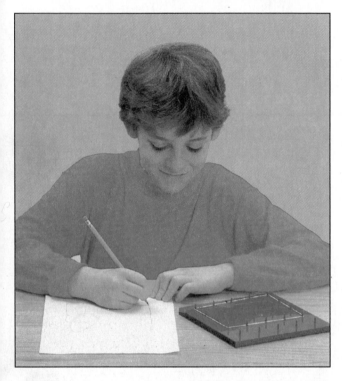

WORKING TOGETHER

Step 1 Use a rubber band to make a rectangle on the geoboard. Use other rubber bands to separate the rectangle into 4 equal parts.

Step 2 Record your geoboard design on dot paper. Shade one of the equal parts.

1. How do you know each part is equal?

Fractions name equal parts of a whole. Each equal part is **one-fourth** of the whole pool.

Uri uses one-fourth of the pool for practice.

2. Show one-fourth of the rectangle another way. Record your design on dot paper. Compare it with those of others.

3. Try making models of other fractions on the geoboard. Record your designs on dot paper.

Fractions can also name parts of a set.

Put out 4 cubes and 1 counter. One of the 5 objects is a counter.

One-fifth of the objects are counters.

4. What fraction of the objects are cubes?

5. Pick other sets of cubes and counters. Tell what fraction of the set are counters and what fraction are cubes.

SHARING IDEAS

6. How are finding parts of a whole and finding parts of a set the same? How are they different?

7. What information do you need to name a fraction?

8. As you separate a whole into more and more parts, what happens to the size of the parts?

PRACTICE

Tell which of these figures show sixths. Tell why or why not.

9.   **10.**   **11.**   **12.**

Match the fraction with a diagram.

13. one-sixth   **14.** two-thirds

15. two-fifths   **16.** one-fourth

a. ◯◯◯●●   b. ▦▦☐

c. ☐▦☐☐   d. ●◯◯
               ◯◯◯

Mixed Applications

17. There are 6 swimmers in the five-mile race. Only 2 swimmers finish the race. What fraction of the swimmers finish the race?

18. The bulletin board is separated into 8 equal sections. The results of the swim meet cover 5 of these sections. What fraction of the board do they cover?

19. Uri started to practice at 3:30 P.M. Practice lasted 2 hours. When did Uri finish practicing?

20. *Write a list* of things that are separated into fractions. Compare your list with those of others.

Parts of a Whole

Troy is planning the mural the Art Club will paint on a wall of the school. Troy separates the wall into 6 equal parts. He plans to paint one of the parts himself. What fraction of the wall will Troy paint?

You can draw a diagram to show the part of the wall Troy plans to paint.

He plans to paint one-sixth of the wall.

You can write the fraction.

part Troy paints → **1** ← numerator
total number of parts → **6** ← denominator

1. What fraction of the wall will other students paint?

2. What fraction of the wall has been painted so far?

3. What fraction of the wall will be painted when the mural is finished? What whole number is this equal to?

TRY **OUT** Write the letter of the correct answer.
What part of the figure is shaded?

4.

a. $\frac{3}{8}$ **b.** $\frac{1}{5}$ **c.** $\frac{5}{8}$ **d.** $\frac{8}{5}$

5.

a. $\frac{2}{3}$ **b.** $\frac{2}{5}$ **c.** $\frac{3}{5}$ **d.** $\frac{5}{2}$

PRACTICE

Write a fraction for the part that is shaded.

6. **7.** **8.** **9.**

Match the picture with a fraction.

10. **11.** **12.** **13.**

   a. $\frac{4}{6}$ **b.** $\frac{2}{3}$ **c.** $\frac{1}{2}$ **d.** $\frac{2}{6}$

Draw a shape. Then color in the fraction.

14. $\frac{3}{4}$ **15.** $\frac{4}{10}$ **16.** $\frac{7}{8}$ **17.** $\frac{1}{2}$ **18.** $\frac{6}{9}$

Write the fraction.

19. one-twelfth   **20.** six-eighths   **21.** nine-tenths   **22.** two-sevenths

Write the word name.

23. $\frac{1}{16}$ **24.** $\frac{4}{9}$ **25.** $\frac{3}{10}$ **26.** $\frac{3}{5}$ **27.** $\frac{11}{12}$

Critical Thinking

28. Kevin says he can show fourths like this: Is he correct? Why or why not?

Mixed Applications

29. Troy separates his part of the wall into 8 equal sections. He paints 3 of the sections. What fraction of his part has he painted?

30. There are 20 paintbrushes in a package. Nancy uses 3 of the brushes. How many brushes are left?

31. Li draws a shape that has 4 right angles and 4 sides that are the same length. What shape did Li draw?

32. *Write a problem* about separating something into equal parts. Solve your problem. Ask others to solve it.

Parts of a Set

Teresa asked 10 friends about their favorite way to exercise. She made this list of their answers. What fraction of Teresa's friends like swimming best?

You can use cubes to make a model of the set.

FAVORITE EXERCISE

Swimming 3

Biking 5

Running 2

You can write the fraction.

number who like to swim → **3** ← numerator
number in all → **10** ← denominator

Teresa knows that $\frac{3}{10}$ of her friends like swimming best.

1. What fraction of her friends like biking best?

2. What fraction like running best?

3. What fraction like push-ups best?

4. **What if** all 10 friends said biking was their favorite exercise? What fraction is this?

TRY OUT Write the letter of the correct answer. What fraction names the part?

5. red	a. $\frac{1}{6}$	b. $\frac{2}{4}$	c. $\frac{2}{6}$	d. $\frac{3}{6}$
6. blue	a. $\frac{1}{6}$	b. $\frac{1}{5}$	c. $\frac{3}{6}$	d. $\frac{6}{6}$
7. green	a. $\frac{1}{6}$	b. $\frac{2}{6}$	c. $\frac{3}{5}$	d. $\frac{3}{6}$
8. yellow	a. $\frac{0}{6}$	b. $\frac{1}{6}$	c. $\frac{3}{3}$	d. $\frac{6}{6}$

PRACTICE

Write a fraction that shows the part of the set that is shaded.

9.

10.

11.

12.

13.

14.

Write the fraction.

15. Seven out of ten answers are correct.

16. Three of the seven balls are soccer balls.

17. Eight of the twelve baskets are full.

18. All of the 4 tennis courts are full.

19. None of the 6 swimming lanes are being used.

Mixed Applications

20. Cindy went to the Bike Club meeting at 4:15 P.M. She stayed until 5:45 P.M. How long did she stay at the meeting?

21. Phil is playing basketball. He takes 8 shots and makes 5 of them. What fraction of his shots does he make?

22. Glen did 10 push-ups before breakfast and 12 more at bedtime. How many push-ups did he do?

23. Jesse is practicing golf. He makes 6 putts. Only 2 of them go in the hole. How many did not go in?

LOGICAL REASONING

Write a fraction for the part described.

1. red or square shapes

2. blue and circular

3. four sides and not blue

4. three sides and green

Understanding Fractions and Mixed Numbers **349**

Activity

Finding the Fraction of a Number

Eight scouts are going to the country for a hike. After the equipment is loaded, the first van has room for $\frac{1}{4}$ of the group. How many scouts ride in the first van?

WORKING TOGETHER

You can make a model to solve.

Step 1 Use counters to model the total number of scouts.

Step 2 Separate the counters into 4 groups of equal size.

1. How many counters do you need to show the total number of scouts?

2. How many counters are in one of the groups? What is $\frac{1}{4}$ of 8?

3. How many scouts ride in the first van?

4. How many counters are in two of the groups? What is $\frac{2}{4}$ of 8?

5. What is $\frac{3}{4}$ of 8? $\frac{4}{4}$ of 8?

Use counters to find the fraction of the number.

6. **a.** $\frac{1}{2}$ of 12   **b.** $\frac{2}{2}$ of 12

7. **a.** $\frac{1}{3}$ of 9   **b.** $\frac{2}{3}$ of 9   **c.** $\frac{3}{3}$ of 9

8. **a.** $\frac{1}{5}$ of 20   **b.** $\frac{2}{5}$ of 20   **c.** $\frac{3}{5}$ of 20   **d.** $\frac{4}{5}$ of 20   **e.** $\frac{5}{5}$ of 20

SHARING IDEAS

Look at your answers to exercises 2–8.

9. How can you use division to find the fraction of a number when the numerator is 1?

10. How can you use multiplication and division to find the fraction of a number when the numerator is greater than 1?

11. Can you use counters to find $\frac{1}{3}$ of 8? Why or why not?

PRACTICE

Find the part.

12. $\frac{1}{6}$ of 18   **13.** $\frac{3}{6}$ of 18   **14.** $\frac{1}{3}$ of 18

15. $\frac{2}{3}$ of 18   **16.** $\frac{1}{9}$ of 18   **17.** $\frac{1}{2}$ of 18

Find the fraction of the number. Use counters if needed.

18. $\frac{1}{3}$ of 6   **19.** $\frac{1}{4}$ of 24   **20.** $\frac{1}{6}$ of 24   **21.** $\frac{1}{3}$ of 15

22. $\frac{2}{3}$ of 3   **23.** $\frac{4}{5}$ of 10   **24.** $\frac{3}{8}$ of 32   **25.** $\frac{3}{4}$ of 16

26. $\frac{2}{3}$ of 6   **27.** $\frac{3}{5}$ of 25   **28.** $\frac{4}{4}$ of 16   **29.** $\frac{7}{8}$ of 24

Critical Thinking

30. Ten hikers arrived early. This is $\frac{2}{3}$ of the total number of hikers in a group. How many hikers are in the group? How did you find the answer?

Mixed Applications   Solve. Which method did you use?

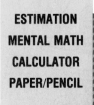

ESTIMATION
MENTAL MATH
CALCULATOR
PAPER/PENCIL

31. Mary saw 20 different types of trees in the forest. She knew the names of $\frac{2}{5}$ of them. How many different types of trees could Mary name?

32. One school bus can take 36 hikers on a trip. How many hikers can go on 5 buses?

33. There are 90 hikers in the camp today. They are in 5 equal groups. Are there more than 25 hikers in each group?

34. There are 10 girl scouts on a camping trip. If $\frac{1}{2}$ of them leave the campsite to gather firewood, how many scouts are left at the campsite?

Mixed Review

Compare. Write >, <, or =.

35. 4×3 ● $60 \div 5$ **36.** $14 + 2$ ● 3×4 **37.** $15 + 9$ ● $124 \div 4$

38. 5×15 ● $150 \div 5$ **39.** $1{,}305$ ● 2×598 **40.** 10 cm ● 1 m

Understanding Fractions and Mixed Numbers   **351**

PROBLEM SOLVING

Strategy: Working Backward

Heidi has 3 times as many baseball cards as Michael. Jimmy has 5 more cards than Michael. Josh has 3 fewer cards than Jimmy. Josh has 9 cards. How many cards does Heidi have?

You can work backward to solve the problem. Start with what you know at the end and work back to the beginning.

You know that Josh has 9 baseball cards and that he has 3 fewer cards than Jimmy.

1. What can you do to find how many cards Jimmy has?

2. How many cards does Jimmy have?   **9 + 3 = 12**

You also know that Jimmy has 5 more cards than Michael.

3. What can you do to find how many cards Michael has?

4. How many cards does Michael have?   **12 − 5 = 7**

Finally you know that Heidi has 3 times as many cards as Michael.

5. What can you do to find how many cards Heidi has?

6. How many cards does Heidi have?   **3 × 7 = ■**

7. How can you check your answer?

PRACTICE

Work backward to solve the problem. Use mental math, a calculator, or paper and pencil.

8. Three friends are rehearsing a play. Josephine has 5 times as many lines as Loren. Claire has 7 more lines than Josephine. Claire has 47 lines. How many lines does Loren have?

9. Sue, Jean, and Cindy exercise after school. Sue exercises 10 minutes less than Jean, and Cindy exercises half as long as Sue. Cindy exercises for 15 minutes. How long does Jean exercise?

10. Mark, Jim, and Chang are at soccer practice. Jim kicks the ball twice as far as Mark. Chang kicks the ball 8 meters farther than Jim. Chang kicks the ball 32 meters. How far does Mark kick the ball?

11. Peter, Mary, Quentin, and Tom sell tickets to the game. Peter sells $\frac{1}{2}$ as many tickets as Mary, and Quentin sells 5 fewer tickets than Peter. Tom sells 3 times as many as Quentin. If Tom sells 21 tickets, how many does Mary sell?

Strategies and Skills Review

12. Marcus practiced piano 2 hours every day of the year except on 6 days when he was sick. How many hours did he practice in the year?

13. Pam swims the breaststroke for 8 minutes and the backstroke for 6 minutes. She does this 3 times each day. How many minutes does Pam swim each day?

14. There are 6 more people in the first row of the stands than in the second row, and 5 fewer in the third row than in the second. There are twice as many people in the first row as in the fourth. There are 17 people in the fourth row. How many people are in each of the first three rows?

15. **Write a problem** that can be solved by working backward. Solve your problem. Ask others to solve it.

ACTIVITY

Finding Equivalent Fractions

One-half of Jakki's beach towel is orange. Eight-sixteenths of Carla's towel is orange. Is the same part of each towel orange?

WORKING TOGETHER

Step 1 Fold a piece of paper in half and color one part.

1. What fraction shows how much you colored?

Step 2 Fold the paper in half again.

2. How many equal parts did you make by folding? How many are colored? What fraction is colored?

Step 3 Fold the paper one more time.

3. How many equal parts did you make now? How many are colored? What fraction is this?

Step 4 Fold the paper again.

4. What fraction is colored?

$\frac{1}{2}$, $\frac{2}{4}$, $\frac{4}{8}$, and $\frac{8}{16}$ are **equivalent fractions.** Equivalent fractions name the same part of a whole or a set.

The same part of each towel is orange.

5. Fold another piece of paper to find fractions equivalent to $\frac{3}{4}$.

SHARING IDEAS

6. Look at the numerators and denominators in each set of equivalent fractions you found. What pattern do you see?

7. How can you use multiplication to find equivalent fractions? Why can you do this?

PRACTICE

Complete to name the equivalent fraction.

8.
$$\frac{1}{3} = \frac{\blacksquare}{6}$$

9.
$$\frac{1}{2} = \frac{\blacksquare}{8}$$

10.
$$\frac{1}{4} = \frac{\blacksquare}{12}$$

11.
$$\frac{3}{5} \neq \frac{\blacksquare}{10}$$

12.
$$\frac{3}{4} = \frac{\blacksquare}{12}$$

13.
$$\frac{2}{3} = \frac{\blacksquare}{6}$$

14. $\frac{1}{2} = \frac{\blacksquare}{4}$ **15.** $\frac{1}{3} = \frac{\blacksquare}{9}$ **16.** $\frac{3}{8} = \frac{\blacksquare}{16}$ **17.** $\frac{5}{6} = \frac{\blacksquare}{12}$

Complete the pattern of equivalent fractions.

18. $\frac{1}{5} = \frac{\blacksquare}{10} = \frac{\blacksquare}{15} = \frac{4}{\blacksquare} = \frac{5}{\blacksquare}$ **19.** $\frac{2}{3} = \frac{\blacksquare}{6} = \frac{6}{\blacksquare} = \frac{\blacksquare}{12} = \frac{10}{\blacksquare}$

Critical Thinking
20. Brenda says $\frac{3}{6}$ of the beach balls are blue. Carlos says $\frac{2}{4}$ of them are blue. Who is correct? Why?

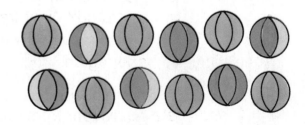

Mixed Applications
21. Bev and Sandra made 9 sand castles at the beach, but $\frac{2}{3}$ of them washed away. How many castles washed away?

22. Sol's beach towel is $\frac{8}{16}$ blue and $\frac{4}{8}$ green. Are the blue and green parts the same size? Why or why not?

Mixed Review
Find the answer. Which method did you use?

23. 24×7 **24.** $600 \div 6$ **25.** $\$36.59 + \$78.95$ **26.** $86 - 6$

MENTAL MATH
CALCULATOR
PAPER/PENCIL

MIND READING MADE EASY!

Investigating Patterns

A. Did you know that you can read minds? Here's a trick that will make your friends think you can. Tell a friend to follow these instructions carefully:

- Think of a number.
- Add 2 to your number.
- Double the amount you now have.
- Add 6.
- Divide by 2.
- Subtract your original number.

Now tell your friend to concentrate on the remaining number. Pretend you are reading your friend's mind. Then announce that the number is 5. You will be right!

Try the trick with a number of your own. Suppose you pick 10. Watch what happens.

10
$10 + 2 = 12$
$2 \times 12 = 24$
$24 + 6 = 30$
$30 \div 2 = 15$
$15 - 10 = 5$

Try it with another number. You will always get 5! Can you see how this trick works? Why don't you ever need to know your friend's starting number?

B. Let's draw pictures to see how this trick works. Let ??? stand for the mystery number. Use (○) to show how the number changes.

Think of a number.	???
Add 2 to your number.	??? ○ ○
Double the amount you now have.	??? ○ ○ ??? ○ ○
Add 6.	??? ○ ○ ○ ○ ○ ??? ○ ○ ○ ○ ○
Divide by 2.	??? ○ ○ ○ ○ ○
Subtract your original number.	○ ○ ○ ○ ○

No matter what ??? equals, the result is always 5.

1. Here is a chart for another trick. Copy the chart and fill in the second column.

Think of a number.	
Add 6 to your number.	
Triple the amount you now have.	
Add 9.	
Divide by 3.	
Subtract 2.	
Subtract your original number.	

2. What number is always the result?

3. Now invent your own trick. Draw pictures to check that your trick works.

357

Simplifying Fractions

Somati knows that 6 members of the band need new uniforms. There are 12 band members. What is the simplest fraction she can write to name the part of the band that needs new uniforms?

You can **simplify** a fraction by dividing the numerator and denominator by the same number. It is in **simplest form** when the numerator and denominator have no common factor greater than 1.

1. Complete: $\frac{6}{12} = \frac{6 \div 2}{12 \div 2} = \frac{\blacksquare}{\blacksquare}$

2. Is the fraction in simplest form? Can you divide again? Why or why not?

3. What is the simplest form of $\frac{6}{12}$?

Simplify the fraction if it is not in simplest form.

4. $\frac{4}{12}$ 5. $\frac{5}{12}$ 6. $\frac{2}{10}$ 7. $\frac{2}{4}$

SHARING IDEAS

8. Why can you divide the numerator and denominator by the same number without changing the value of the fraction?

9. Are $\frac{6}{12}$, $\frac{3}{6}$, and $\frac{1}{2}$ equivalent fractions? How can you tell?

PRACTICE

Complete.

10.

$$\frac{4}{8} = \frac{\blacksquare}{\blacksquare}$$

11.

$$\frac{8}{10} = \frac{\blacksquare}{\blacksquare}$$

12.

$$\frac{4}{6} = \frac{\blacksquare}{\blacksquare}$$

13. $\frac{6}{9} = \frac{6 \div 3}{9 \div 3} = \frac{\blacksquare}{\blacksquare}$

14. $\frac{8}{12} = \frac{8 \div 4}{12 \div 4} = \frac{\blacksquare}{\blacksquare}$

15. $\frac{12}{16} = \frac{12 \div 4}{16 \div 4} = \frac{\blacksquare}{\blacksquare}$

16. $\frac{6}{10} = \frac{\blacksquare}{5}$

17. $\frac{9}{12} = \frac{\blacksquare}{4}$

18. $\frac{6}{8} = \frac{\blacksquare}{4}$

19. $\frac{14}{16} = \frac{\blacksquare}{8}$

Is the fraction in simplest form? Write *yes* or *no*.

20. $\frac{1}{5}$

21. $\frac{5}{15}$

22. $\frac{5}{6}$

23. $\frac{4}{10}$

24. $\frac{8}{9}$

Write the fraction in simplest form.

25. $\frac{2}{8}$

26. $\frac{2}{6}$

27. $\frac{5}{10}$

28. $\frac{3}{9}$

29. $\frac{3}{12}$

30. $\frac{8}{16}$

31. $\frac{15}{18}$

32. $\frac{9}{15}$

33. $\frac{4}{16}$

34. $\frac{6}{15}$

Mixed Applications

35. The band spent 8 hours practicing in one week. Two of the hours were spent marching. Write this as a fraction in simplest form.

36. Kris has 18 tickets for the band concert. He wants to give them to 6 friends. How many tickets will each friend get?

37. Only 2 of the 12 band members carry a flag during a marching song. Write this as a fraction in simplest form.

38. Harry practiced 3 hours a day for 7 days. How many hours did he practice?

Mixed Review

Find the answer. Which method did you use?

39. $500 \div 5$

40. $153 - 92$

41. 4×34

42. $44 + 44$

43. $7,369 + 9,341 + 8,949$

44. 3×63

45. $651 \div 7$

MENTAL MATH
CALCULATOR
PAPER/PENCIL

ACTIVITY

Whole Numbers and Mixed Numbers

A. Jana is packing baseballs into boxes after gym class. Each box holds four baseballs. Jana has 10 baseballs. How many boxes will the 10 baseballs fill?

WORKING TOGETHER

You can make a model to solve the problem.

Step 1 Fold a sheet of paper to divide it into four equal parts. Shade one part to show one baseball.

1. What fraction of the whole sheet has been shaded?

Step 2 Shade the other parts of the sheet.

2. How many baseballs are shown now? What fraction of the whole sheet has been shaded?

Step 3 Continue to fold and shade sheets of paper until you have shown 10 baseballs.

3. What fraction has been shaded?

4. How many whole sheets of paper have you shaded?

5. What fraction of the partially filled sheet of paper has been shaded? Simplify this fraction if possible.

6. How many boxes will 10 baseballs fill?

B. You can rename a fraction greater than 1 as a mixed number.

Step 1	Step 2	Step 3
Divide the numerator by the denominator.	Write the quotient as the whole number. Write the remainder as a fraction.	Write the fraction in simplest form.

$$\frac{10}{4} \rightarrow 4\overline{)10} \quad \begin{array}{c} 2\ R2 \end{array}$$

quotient → $2\frac{2}{4}$ ← remainder
← divisor

$2\frac{2}{4} = 2\frac{1}{2}$

Read: two and one-half

7. *What if* Jana packed only 8 baseballs? How many boxes would this fill?

SHARING IDEAS

8. How can you identify fractions that can be renamed as mixed numbers?

9. Why do you divide by the denominator to rename such a fraction?

10. How can you tell if a fraction is another name for a whole number?

PRACTICE

Write the mixed number.

11. two and three-tenths   **12.** four and one-half   **13.** five and two-fifths

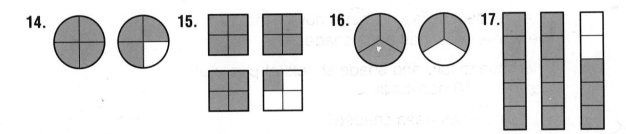

Write the fraction as a whole number or a mixed number in simplest form.

18. $\frac{4}{3}$ **19.** $\frac{8}{2}$ **20.** $\frac{6}{5}$ **21.** $\frac{12}{6}$ **22.** $\frac{9}{4}$ **23.** $\frac{7}{3}$

24. $\frac{15}{3}$ **25.** $\frac{18}{5}$ **26.** $\frac{24}{4}$ **27.** $\frac{2}{2}$ **28.** $\frac{9}{6}$ **29.** $\frac{34}{8}$

Complete.

30. $5 = \frac{15}{\blacksquare}$ **31.** $\frac{12}{3} = \blacksquare$ **32.** $\frac{\blacksquare}{8} = 2$ **33.** $\frac{30}{\blacksquare} = 5$ **34.** $9 = \frac{\blacksquare}{3}$

Mixed Applications

35. Paul did 53 push-ups in 1 min. How many push-ups will he do in 6 min. at this rate?

36. Lucia is packing 32 CDs into boxes. Each box holds·6 CDs. How many boxes can she fill?

37. The members of the skating team need $832 to go to the state contest. They can wash cars for $8 per car. How many cars will they need to wash to earn enough money?

Comparing Fractions and Mixed Numbers

A. The school choir gives a concert on Saturday that lasts $1\frac{3}{4}$ hours. It gives a concert that lasts $1\frac{1}{2}$ hours on Sunday. Which concert lasts longer?

You can compare fractions or mixed numbers on a number line.

Think: $1\frac{1}{2}$ comes **before** $1\frac{3}{4}$.

Read: $1\frac{1}{2}$ is **less than** $1\frac{3}{4}$.

Write: $1\frac{1}{2} < 1\frac{3}{4}$

Think: $1\frac{3}{4}$ comes **after** $1\frac{1}{2}$.

Read: $1\frac{3}{4}$ is **greater than** $1\frac{1}{2}$.

Write: $1\frac{3}{4} > 1\frac{1}{2}$

The Saturday concert lasts longer.

B. You can compare without a number line.

Compare: $1\frac{1}{2}$ and $1\frac{3}{4}$.

Step 1	Step 2	Step 3
Compare the whole numbers.	Compare the fractions. Write equivalent fractions with like denominators.	Compare the numerators.
$1\frac{1}{2}$ **Think:** $1 = 1$ $1\frac{3}{4}$	$\frac{1}{2} = \frac{1 \times 2}{2 \times 2} = \frac{2}{4}$ $\frac{3}{4}$ $\qquad$ $\frac{3}{4}$	$2 < 3$ $\frac{2}{4} < \frac{3}{4}$ $\quad$ $\frac{1}{2} < \frac{3}{4}$

So $1\frac{1}{2} < 1\frac{3}{4}$.

C. You can order $\frac{1}{3}$, $\frac{5}{6}$, and $\frac{7}{12}$ by comparing.

Step 1	Step 2	Step 3
Write equivalent fractions with like denominators.	Compare the fractions.	Order the fractions.
$\frac{1}{3} = \frac{1 \times 4}{3 \times 4} = \frac{4}{12}$	$\frac{4}{12} < \frac{7}{12}$	From least to greatest: $\frac{1}{3}, \frac{7}{12}, \frac{5}{6}$
$\frac{5}{6} = \frac{5 \times 2}{6 \times 2} = \frac{10}{12}$	$\frac{4}{12} < \frac{10}{12}$	
$\frac{7}{12} \qquad\qquad \frac{7}{12}$	$\frac{7}{12} < \frac{10}{12}$	From greatest to least: $\frac{5}{6}, \frac{7}{12}, \frac{1}{3}$

TRY OUT

Compare. Write $>$, $<$, or $=$.

1. $\frac{1}{4}$ ● $\frac{2}{4}$ 2. $\frac{2}{3}$ ● $\frac{4}{6}$ 3. $1\frac{3}{5}$ ● $1\frac{1}{10}$ 4. $2\frac{1}{8}$ ● $1\frac{1}{3}$

Write in order from least to greatest.

5. $\frac{3}{4}$, $\frac{3}{8}$, $\frac{5}{16}$ 6. $1\frac{2}{3}$, $2\frac{5}{9}$, $1\frac{5}{18}$ 7. $1\frac{3}{8}$, $1\frac{2}{3}$, $1\frac{7}{12}$

PRACTICE

Use the number line to compare. Write $>$, $<$, or $=$.

$0 \quad \frac{1}{6} \quad \frac{1}{3} \quad \frac{1}{2} \quad \frac{2}{3} \; \frac{3}{4} \quad 1 \quad 1\frac{1}{3} \quad 1\frac{1}{2} \quad 1\frac{2}{3} \quad 1\frac{5}{6} \quad 2$

8. $\frac{1}{2}$ ● $\frac{1}{6}$ 9. $\frac{1}{3}$ ● $\frac{1}{2}$ 10. $\frac{3}{4}$ ● $\frac{2}{3}$ 11. $1\frac{1}{2}$ ● $1\frac{2}{3}$

Compare. Write $>$, $<$, or $=$.

12. $\frac{3}{4}$ ● $\frac{1}{4}$ 13. $\frac{2}{5}$ ● $\frac{4}{5}$ 14. $\frac{5}{8}$ ● $\frac{3}{8}$ 15. $\frac{4}{7}$ ● $\frac{3}{7}$

16. $1\frac{5}{6}$ ● $2\frac{1}{6}$ 17. $1\frac{4}{9}$ ● $1\frac{7}{9}$ 18. $\frac{33}{10}$ ● $\frac{37}{10}$ 19. $6\frac{1}{3}$ ● $6\frac{2}{3}$

20. $7\frac{5}{8}$ ● $6\frac{3}{4}$ 21. $4\frac{7}{9}$ ● $4\frac{2}{3}$ 22. $\frac{27}{12}$ ● $2\frac{5}{6}$ 23. $1\frac{4}{16}$ ● $1\frac{1}{4}$

Write in order from least to greatest.

24. $\frac{1}{4}$, $\frac{1}{2}$, $\frac{1}{8}$ 25. $\frac{11}{18}$, $\frac{5}{9}$, $\frac{2}{3}$ 26. $4\frac{1}{2}$, $4\frac{5}{12}$, $4\frac{5}{6}$ 27. $1\frac{3}{8}$, 2, $1\frac{5}{6}$

Write in order from greatest to least.

28. $\frac{3}{4}$, $\frac{13}{16}$, $\frac{7}{8}$ 29. $\frac{2}{3}$, $\frac{5}{6}$, $\frac{11}{12}$ 30. $4\frac{7}{16}$, $5\frac{1}{4}$, $4\frac{5}{8}$ 31. $1\frac{1}{2}$, $1\frac{2}{3}$, $1\frac{4}{9}$

Mixed Applications

32. The Poetry Club meets for $1\frac{5}{8}$ hours. The French Club meets for $1\frac{3}{4}$ hours. Which club had the longer meeting?

33. **Write a problem** about comparing fractions or mixed numbers. Solve your problem. Ask others to solve it.

Activity

Measuring Length: Customary Units

An **inch (in.)** is a customary unit of length used to measure short lengths.

To measure something to the nearest inch:

Step 1 Line up the edge of the object with the left end of the scale.

Step 2 Look at the right end of the object. Find the closest inch mark.

1. Find the length of the paper clip to the nearest inch.

You can also measure length to the nearest **half inch** ($\frac{1}{2}$ **in.)** or **quarter inch** ($\frac{1}{4}$ **in.)**.

2. Find the length of the paper clip to the nearest $\frac{1}{2}$ inch, and $\frac{1}{4}$ inch.

3. Work with a partner. Estimate, then measure, the length of each other's foot to the nearest inch, the nearest $\frac{1}{2}$ in., and the nearest $\frac{1}{4}$ in. Record your measurements.

SHARING IDEAS

4. Compare your three groups of measurements. When are they the same?

5. When do you think you may need to measure something using a smaller unit?

PRACTICE

Measure to the nearest inch, $\frac{1}{2}$ in., and $\frac{1}{4}$ in.

6.

7.

Complete the chart. Estimate, then use your inch ruler to measure.

	Object	Estimate	Measurement
8.	length of a pencil	■	■
9.	width of a calculator	■	■
10.	length of your math book	■	■
11.	length of your arm	■	■

12. Choose other objects to measure. Record your work on your chart.

Use your inch ruler. Draw a line segment of the given length.

13. $3\frac{1}{4}$ in.   **14.** $2\frac{1}{2}$ in.   **15.** 4 in.

Mixed Applications

16. Ruth wants to buy a hat. Size $6\frac{5}{8}$ is too small. Which size should she try on next, $6\frac{3}{4}$ or $6\frac{3}{8}$?

17. Roger measured the length of his book to the nearest quarter inch as $13\frac{3}{4}$ in. What would it measure to the nearest inch?

18. Claire's clarinet is 25 in. long. She puts in a mouthpiece that is 3 in. long. How long is the clarinet with the mouthpiece?

19. Hank's electric guitar is 14 in. wide. This is 2 in. wider than June's acoustic guitar. How wide is June's guitar?

Estimating Length: Customary Units

The inch (in.), the **foot (ft),** and the **yard (yd)** are customary units used to measure length. The **mile (mi)** is the measure for a long distance.

The length of a football is about 1 foot.

The length of a guitar is about 1 yard.

A mile is about how far you can walk in 20 minutes.

This chart shows you how the units are related.

12 inches (in.)	=	1 foot (ft)
3 feet (ft)	=	1 yard (yd)
1,760 yards (yd)	=	1 mile (mi)

Tell whether you would use *inches, feet, yards,* **or** *miles* **to measure.**

1. the length of the playground

2. the width of a desk

3. the height of a cup

4. the height of a woman

TRY OUT Write the letter of the correct answer. Would you use inch, foot, yard, or mile to measure?

5. the width of a door **a.** in. **b.** ft **c.** yd **d.** mi

6. the length of a pencil **a.** in. **b.** ft **c.** yd **d.** mi

7. the distance across a state **a.** in. **b.** ft **c.** yd **d.** mi

8. the height of a telephone pole **a.** in. **b.** ft **c.** yd **d.** mi

PRACTICE

Tell whether you would use *inches, feet, yards,* or *miles* to measure.

9. the length of a baseball bat

10. the distance around a lake

11. the width of a piece of paper

12. the length of a crayon

Write the letter of the best estimate.

13. length of a car   **a.** 15 in.   **b.** 15 ft   **c.** 15 yd   **d.** 15 mi

14. distance a plane travels   **a.** 9 in.   **b.** 90 ft   **c.** 90 yd   **d.** 900 mi

15. height of a flagpole   **a.** 80 in.   **b.** 80 ft   **c.** 80 yd   **d.** 80 mi

16. width of a teacup   **a.** 3 in.   **b.** 3 ft   **c.** 3 yd   **d.** 3 mi

Complete the chart. Use the units given.

	Object	Estimate	Actual Measure
17.	height of your desk (ft)	■	■
18.	width of the door (in.)	■	■
19.	length of your classroom (yd)	■	■

Mixed Applications

Solve. You may need to use the Databank on page 521.

20. Peter throws the football 30 yd. John catches the ball and runs 35 yd before he is tackled. How many yards were gained on the play?

21. What is the tallest species of tree found in the United States? What is its height in yards?

22. How much taller is the Coast Douglas Fir than the Western Hemlock?

23. ***Write a problem*** using the information in the Databank. Solve it. Then trade your problem with others.

PROBLEM SOLVING

Strategy: Using Number Sense

Tom's goal is to run more than 9 miles on the weekend. He runs $4\frac{3}{4}$ miles on Saturday. If he runs $4\frac{3}{4}$ miles on Sunday, will he have run more than 9 miles on the two days?

Tom uses number sense to find out whether he will meet his goal.

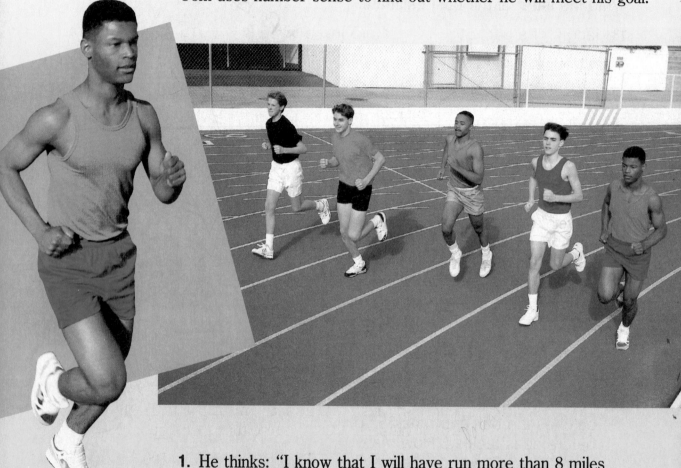

1. He thinks: "I know that I will have run more than 8 miles on the weekend." Do you agree? Why or why not?

2. Tom thinks: "Since $\frac{3}{4}$ is greater then $\frac{1}{2}$, I will run at least another mile." Do you agree? Why or why not?

3. Will Tom run more than 9 miles? How can you tell?

4. **What if** Tom runs $4\frac{1}{8}$ miles on Saturday and $4\frac{3}{8}$ miles on Sunday. Will he run more than 9 miles on the weekend?

5. Talk about how Tom used number sense to solve the problem.

PRACTICE

Use number sense to solve the problem.

6. Grace wants to exercise at least 4 hours this weekend. She exercises $1\frac{1}{4}$ hours on Saturday and $2\frac{1}{4}$ hours on Sunday. Has she met her goal?

7. Karen and Dave want to paint 3 walls of the kitchen by lunchtime. They each paint $1\frac{2}{3}$ walls. Have they met their goal?

8. Drew needs 6 pounds of fruit to make a fruit salad. He picks $2\frac{5}{16}$ pounds of apples and $3\frac{3}{16}$ pounds of pears. Does he have as much fruit as he needs?

9. Ruben wants to lose 4 pounds in 2 weeks. He loses $2\frac{3}{4}$ pounds the first week and $1\frac{3}{4}$ pounds the next week. Has he met his goal?

Strategies and Skills Review

Solve. Use mental math, a calculator, or paper and pencil.

10. Dave is packing 137 pounds of cans into boxes for recycling. Each box holds 4 pounds of cans. How many full boxes will he pack?

11. The Tigers won the football game by a score of 35 to 17. How many more points did the Tigers score than their opponent?

12. Sandy wants to buy a sketch pad for $3.73 and pastels for $6.57. She has $10.00. Does she have enough money?

13. A football field is 100 yards long. There is a line across the field every 10 yards. Including the end lines, how many lines are there?

14. In the skate-boarding competition, Ed receives scores of 46 points, 53 points and 61 points. The scorer records Ed's total as 150 points. Did the scorer record his total correctly?

15. *Write a problem* that you can solve using number sense. Ask others to solve your problem. Talk about how you used number sense.

DECISION MAKING

Problem Solving: Choosing a Musical Instrument to Play

SITUATION

For an after-school activity, Luis Allende wants to learn to play a musical instrument and join the school orchestra.

PROBLEM

Which instrument should Luis choose?

DATA

Whitman Elementary School Orchestra
Information Sheet for New Members

Learn to play one of these musical instruments:

	PIANO	TRUMPET	VIOLIN	DRUMS	FLUTE
Lessons	Monday 1 hour	Wednesday $\frac{3}{4}$ hour	Monday $\frac{3}{4}$ hour (Lessons start at 3:00 P.M.) 1 hour	Friday 40 min	Thursday 50 min $\frac{3}{4}$ hour
Daily Practice	1 hour	$\frac{3}{4}$ hour		$\frac{1}{2}$ hour	
	may use school piano	Rental available	Rental available	may use school drums	Rental available

School piano and drums available:

Monday-Friday
7:30 A.M.-8:30 A.M.
3:00 P.M.-4:30 P.M.

Saturday & Sunday
12:00 P.M.-3:00 P.M.

USING THE DATA

1. What fraction of an hour is a drum lesson? a flute lesson?

2. Which instrument has the longest lesson time? the shortest lesson time? the longest practice time? the shortest practice time?

3. Which instrument would Luis need to spend the most time on each week? the least time?

MAKING DECISIONS

4. What are the things Luis should think about when deciding which musical instrument to play?

5. **What if** Luis wants to play in the marching band? Which musical instrument should he choose?

6. **What if** Luis has Cub Scout troop meetings after school on Mondays? Are there instruments that he should not choose? Why?

7. How would choosing the piano or the drums affect Luis' after-school activities?

8. **What if** Luis' mom offers to buy the instrument he chooses to play? Luis lives in a small apartment. How will that affect his choice?

9. Which musical instrument would you choose? Why?

Math and Music

In music, musical notes are grouped in **measures.** Rhythm in each measure is counted in units called **beats.** Here are three measures of music. They each have the same number of beats.

Quarter notes   Half notes   Whole note

MEASURE   MEASURE   MEASURE

The numbers at the left are known as the **meter signature.** The top number of the meter signature tells how many beats are in each measure. In $\frac{4}{4}$ meter, there are four beats in a measure. The bottom number tells what kind of note sounds for one beat. The 4 means a quarter note (♩) sounds for one beat in $\frac{4}{4}$ meter. So each quarter note is $\frac{1}{4}$ of a measure. A half note (♩) sounds for 2 beats. A whole note (o) sounds for 4 beats.

In $\frac{4}{4}$ meter, what fraction of a measure is a half note?

Think: There are 4 beats in a measure. A half note gets 2 beats. 2 is $\frac{1}{2}$ of 4.

So a half note is $\frac{1}{2}$ of a measure in $\frac{4}{4}$ meter.

ACTIVITIES

1. Write as many different combinations of notes for one measure in $\frac{4}{4}$ meter as you can. Tap out the rhythm for each measure you write. Remember to tap only once for each note.

2. Suppose the meter signature is $\frac{3}{4}$. How many beats are in a measure? What kind of note sounds for 1 beat?

Computer Graphing: Circle Graph

José has invited 19 friends to a party. At the party he plans to show two videos. He asks his friends what their favorite kinds of vidoes are. He makes a tally of his friends' choices:

Comedy	ⅢⅡ II
Music	III
Adventure	II
Cartoons	III
Science Fiction	ⅢⅡ

José wants to display the results in a graph. He decides to use a **circle graph.** A circle graph will show what fraction of José's friends like each type of video. A computer makes it easy to draw circle graphs quickly and accurately.

AT THE COMPUTER

Run the computer graphing program called VIDEOS.

1. Use the results of José's tally. Enter the data in the correct columns and draw the circle graph.

2. What fraction of the circle graph is science fiction?

3. What fraction of the graph are music and comedy together?

4. Write a summary of what is shown in the circle graph. Based on the data, what two kinds of videos should José rent?

5. Take a survey of at least ten people. Find out which of the five categories of videos people would most want to see. Then enter the data to make a new circle graph. Write a brief summary of your results.

EXTRA PRACTICE

The Meaning of Fractions, page 345 ....
Write a fraction for the shaded part.

1.

2.

3.

4.

5.

6.

Parts of a Whole, page 347 ....
Write a fraction for the part of each figure that is shaded.

1.

2.

3.

Write the fraction.

4. two-thirds

5. two-sixths

6. five-eighths

7. nine-tenths

8. four-fifths

9. two-fifths

Parts of a Set, page 349 ....
Write a fraction that shows the part of each set
that is shaded.

1.

2.

3.

Write the fractions that are blue.

4. Seven of ten are blue.

5. Three of the five are blue.

6. Four of the nine are blue.

7. None of the six are blue.

8. All five are blue.

9. Six of the seven are blue.

EXTRA PRACTICE

Finding Parts of a Set, page 351 ....

Complete.

1. $\frac{1}{6}$ of 24 = ■   2. $\frac{1}{4}$ of 12 = ■   3. $\frac{1}{9}$ of 18 = ■

4. $\frac{1}{4}$ of 8 = ■   5. $\frac{1}{5}$ of 25 = ■   6. $\frac{1}{2}$ of 8 = ■

Use division and multiplication to find the part of the set.

7. $\frac{3}{4}$ of 24   8. $\frac{3}{4}$ of 12   9. $\frac{2}{6}$ of 12

10. $\frac{2}{5}$ of 10   11. $\frac{2}{4}$ of 8   12. $\frac{1}{4}$ of 24

Problem Solving Strategy: Working Backward, page 353 ....

Work backward to solve the problem.

1. Jay is 3 years older than Jeff. Jeff is 4 years younger than Pat. Pat is 12 years old. How old is Jay?

2. Meg is five times older than Evan. Evan is a year older than Emily. Emily is 3 years old. How old is Meg?

3. Sam is twice as old as Jeff. Jeff is 4 years older than Sadie. Rifka is 2 years younger than Sadie. Rifka is 8 years old. How old is Sam?

Finding Equivalent Fractions, page 355 ....

Complete to show the equivalent fraction.

1.

$\frac{4}{8} = \frac{1}{■}$

2.

$\frac{2}{8} = \frac{1}{■}$

3.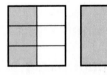

$\frac{3}{6} = \frac{1}{■}$

4. $\frac{3}{4} = \frac{■}{8}$ 5. $\frac{2}{4} = \frac{■}{8}$ 6. $\frac{1}{6} = \frac{■}{12}$ 7. $\frac{1}{2} = \frac{■}{10}$

8. $\frac{3}{4} = \frac{9}{■}$ 9. $\frac{2}{5} = \frac{10}{■}$ 10. $\frac{2}{3} = \frac{12}{■}$ 11. $\frac{2}{6} = \frac{6}{■}$

Understanding Fractions and Mixed Numbers **375**

EXTRA PRACTICE

Simplifying Fractions, page 359 ....

Simplify the fraction.

1. $\frac{6}{8} = \frac{\blacksquare}{4}$
2. $\frac{9}{12} = \frac{\blacksquare}{4}$
3. $\frac{10}{18} = \frac{\blacksquare}{9}$

4. $\frac{6}{10} = \frac{\blacksquare}{5}$
5. $\frac{10}{15} = \frac{\blacksquare}{3}$
6. $\frac{12}{14} = \frac{\blacksquare}{7}$

Write the fraction in simplest form.

7. $\frac{8}{12}$
8. $\frac{4}{10}$
9. $\frac{6}{9}$
10. $\frac{4}{8}$

11. $\frac{4}{6}$
12. $\frac{7}{14}$
13. $\frac{15}{40}$
14. $\frac{12}{15}$

Whole Numbers and Mixed Numbers, page 361 ....

Write the mixed number or whole number.

1.
2.
3.

Find the mixed number or whole number. Write fractions in simplest form.

4. $\frac{24}{4}$
5. $\frac{15}{3}$
6. $\frac{7}{3}$
7. $\frac{5}{2}$

8. $\frac{9}{4}$
9. $\frac{3}{2}$
10. $\frac{4}{4}$
11. $\frac{11}{10}$

Comparing Fractions and Mixed Numbers, page 363 ....

Compare. Write > or <.

1. $\frac{2}{3} \bullet \frac{3}{4}$
2. $4\frac{1}{2} \bullet \frac{4}{8}$
3. $1\frac{5}{6} \bullet 6\frac{1}{6}$

Write in order from least to greatest.

4. $\frac{1}{3}, \frac{5}{8}, \frac{1}{2}$
5. $\frac{9}{10}, 1\frac{1}{5}, 1$
6. $\frac{3}{4}, \frac{5}{6}, \frac{1}{8}$

Measuring Length: Customary Units, page 365.....................................

Complete the chart. Estimate. Then use your inch ruler to measure.

	Object	Estimate	Measurement
1.	height of a milk carton	■	■
2.	width of a window	■	■
3.	a piece of chalk	■	■
4.	width of your desk	■	■

Estimating Length: Customary Units, page 367...................................

Tell whether you would use in., ft, yd, or mi to measure.

1. the height of a house

2. the length of a pencil

3. the length of a field

4. the length of a shoe

5. the distance from New York to Chicago

Write the letter of the best estimate.

6.	the height of a refrigerator	**a.** 4 ft	**b.** 4 yd	**c.** 2 ft
7.	the length of a river	**a.** 10 ft	**b.** 10 yd	**c.** 10 mi
8.	the width of the classroom	**a.** 35 in.	**b.** 35 ft	**c.** 35 mi

Problem Solving Strategy: Using Number Sense, page 369.....................

Use number sense to solve the problem.

1. Lucy wants to videotape two movies that are on television. She can tape 3 hours of programs on one videocassette. Both movies are $1\frac{3}{4}$ hours long. Can Lucy tape both movies on one videocassette? Why or why not?

2. Lou walks $3\frac{3}{10}$ mi to the park and $6\frac{4}{10}$ mi to the library. Does Lou walk more than 10 miles? How do you know?

PRACTICE *PLUS*

KEY SKILL: Simplifying Fractions (Use after page 359.)

Level A

Is each fraction in simplest form? Write *yes* or *no.*

1. $\frac{4}{8}$ **2.** $\frac{1}{2}$ **3.** $\frac{2}{3}$ **4.** $\frac{6}{12}$ **5.** $\frac{9}{18}$ **6.** $\frac{9}{10}$

Write each fraction in simplest form.

7. $\frac{5}{10}$ **8.** $\frac{9}{12}$ **9.** $\frac{15}{18}$ **10.** $\frac{3}{9}$ **11.** $\frac{8}{16}$ **12.** $\frac{4}{12}$

13. Stephen had 12 concert tapes. He gave 6 away to his friends. Write this fraction in simplest form.

Level B

Is the fraction in simplest form? Write *yes* or *no.*

14. $\frac{11}{13}$ **15.** $\frac{9}{15}$ **16.** $\frac{1}{8}$ **17.** $\frac{8}{12}$ **18.** $\frac{4}{9}$ **19.** $\frac{3}{6}$

Write the fraction in simplest form.

20. $\frac{12}{15}$ **21.** $\frac{5}{20}$ **22.** $\frac{10}{25}$ **23.** $\frac{5}{15}$ **24.** $\frac{6}{9}$ **25.** $\frac{9}{18}$

26. $\frac{6}{12}$ **27.** $\frac{4}{8}$ **28.** $\frac{8}{12}$ **29.** $\frac{3}{27}$ **30.** $\frac{18}{21}$ **31.** $\frac{11}{22}$

32. Tom has 21 copies of the school song. He plans to give 7 of them away. Write this fraction in simplest form.

Level C

Write the fraction in simplest form.

33. $\frac{4}{18}$ **34.** $\frac{9}{15}$ **35.** $\frac{12}{24}$ **36.** $\frac{6}{18}$ **37.** $\frac{10}{12}$ **38.** $\frac{4}{16}$

39. $\frac{8}{40}$ **40.** $\frac{6}{18}$ **41.** $\frac{24}{48}$ **42.** $\frac{5}{25}$ **43.** $\frac{13}{26}$ **44.** $\frac{7}{35}$

45. There are 30 members of the school chorus. Ten of them are in the fourth grade. Write this fraction in simplest form.

KEY SKILL: Whole Numbers and Mixed Numbers (Use after page 361.)

Level A

Write the whole number or mixed number in simplest form.

1. $\frac{5}{3}$ **2.** $\frac{7}{4}$ **3.** $\frac{10}{4}$ **4.** $\frac{11}{10}$ **5.** $\frac{8}{4}$

Complete.

6. $\frac{\blacksquare}{2} = 2$ **7.** $\frac{\blacksquare}{7} = 2$ **8.** $\frac{\blacksquare}{2} = 1$ **9.** $\frac{\blacksquare}{3} = 3$

10. Taryn had 7 halves of apple. How many apples did she have?

Level B

Write the whole number or mixed number in simplest form.

11. $\frac{14}{10}$ **12.** $\frac{10}{3}$ **13.** $\frac{6}{2}$ **14.** $\frac{13}{3}$ **15.** $\frac{19}{6}$

Complete.

16. $\frac{\blacksquare}{3} = 2$ **17.** $\frac{\blacksquare}{6} = 3$ **18.** $\frac{\blacksquare}{5} = 5$ **19.** $\frac{\blacksquare}{4} = 1$

20. Robin had 9 orange quarters to share. How many oranges did she have?

Level C

Write the whole number and mixed number in simplest form.

21. $\frac{27}{3}$ **22.** $\frac{14}{5}$ **23.** $\frac{5}{2}$ **24.** $\frac{25}{4}$ **25.** $\frac{14}{3}$

Complete.

26. $\frac{\blacksquare}{4} = 1\frac{1}{4}$ **27.** $\frac{\blacksquare}{4} = 3$ **28.** $\frac{\blacksquare}{10} = 1\frac{1}{10}$ **29.** $\frac{7}{\blacksquare} = 2\frac{1}{3}$

30. It is equivalent to $\frac{6}{10}$. The denominator is 5.

31. Cathy practiced the piano for 17 fourths of an hour. How many hours did she practice?

CHAPTER REVIEW/TEST

LANGUAGE AND MATHEMATICS

Complete the sentences. Use the words in the chart.

VOCABULARY
denominator
numerator
mile
equivalent
fraction

1. A ■ names each of the equal parts of an object.

2. The top part of a fraction is called the ■.

3. A ■ is a measure for long distances.

4. ■ fractions name the same part of a whole.

CONCEPTS AND SKILLS

Write the fraction.

5. one-tenth   **6.** three-fifths

What fraction is shaded?

7.   **8.** △▲△▲△

Complete to show the equivalent fraction.

9. $\frac{1}{4} = \frac{2}{■}$ **10.** $\frac{3}{5} = \frac{9}{■}$ **11.** $\frac{1}{6} = \frac{■}{24}$ **12.** $\frac{2}{3} = \frac{■}{9}$

Write in simplest form.

13. $\frac{8}{20}$ **14.** $\frac{3}{9}$ **15.** $\frac{12}{4}$ **16.** $\frac{16}{5}$

Compare. Write $>$, $<$, or $=$.

17. $\frac{2}{5}$ ● $\frac{3}{4}$ **18.** $3\frac{1}{2}$ ● $3\frac{1}{3}$

Order from least to greatest.

19. $\frac{3}{4}, \frac{1}{3}, \frac{5}{6}$

Write the letter of the best estimate.

20. width of a driveway
   a. 15 inches
   b. 15 feet
   c. 15 yards

21. length of a caterpillar
   a. 2 inches
   b. 2 feet
   c. 2 yards

Critical Thinking

22. Zeke cuts a piece of paper into 8 equal parts. He colors half of them. He gives Clem half of the colored parts. How many parts does he give Clem?

23. Zeke says each part is two inches long. Clem says that each is $2\frac{1}{4}$ in. long. Can they both be right? Why or why not?

Mixed Application

24. Kim, Beth, and Eva are making ornaments. Kim has made 8 less than Eva. Eva has made twice as many as Beth. Beth has made 12. How many has Kim made?

25. Fay and Brian are asked to bring 5 pounds of hot dogs to a picnic. They each bring $2\frac{3}{4}$ pounds. Is this enough?

PERFORMANCE ASSESSMENT

Work with your group to make six fraction strips. Use strips of paper to make and label fraction strips for wholes, halves, thirds, fourths, sixths, and eighths. Then write five statements comparing the fractions on the different strips. For example, $\frac{1}{2}$ is greater than $\frac{1}{3}$.

Each statement should use "greater than," "less than," or "equal to."

1. *Think about:*
   - how to divide each strip into fractions
   - how to compare different fractions

2. Make a table listing six fractions and mixed numbers in order, from greatest to least. Then write a brief explanation of how you determined the numbers in your table.

CUMULATIVE REVIEW

Choose the letter of the correct answer.

1. Write $\frac{8}{32}$ in simplest form.

   a. $\frac{1}{3}$ c. $\frac{1}{4}$

   b. $\frac{2}{8}$ d. not given

2. Find $\frac{3}{4}$ of 12.

   a. 6   c. 12
   b. 9   d. not given

3. Rename $\frac{21}{18}$.

   a. $1\frac{1}{6}$ c. $1\frac{3}{8}$

   b. $1\frac{1}{5}$ d. not given

4. Name the shaded part.

   a. $\frac{3}{8}$ c. $\frac{5}{8}$

   b. $\frac{3}{5}$ d. $\frac{5}{3}$

5. $\frac{4}{9} = \frac{12}{\blacksquare}$

   a. 3   c. 17
   b. 7   d. not given

6. Which is a space figure?

   a. triangle   c. square
   b. cylinder   d. hexagon

7. Compare: $\frac{36}{12}$ ● 3

   a. <   c. =
   b. >   d. not given

8. What is 4 × 968?

   a. 3,622   c. 3,822
   b. 3,672   d. not given

9. Estimate the width of a mug.

   a. 3 in.   c. 3 yd
   b. 3 ft   d. 3 mi

10.

   The figures are:

   a. parallel   c. similar
   b. congruent   d. not given

11. Divide 189 by 5.

   a. 36 R1   c. 37 R4
   b. 36 R4   d. not given

12. Find the product of 8 × $.62.

   a. $.49   c. $4.96
   b. $.50   d. not given

13. Estimate: 5 × 887

   a. 400   c. 3,500
   b. 450   d. 4,500

14. 3,000 ÷ 6

   a. 50   c. 600
   b. 500   d. not given

RATIOS

Charlie and Jeannie helped make chili for a class supper. This is the basic recipe they used.

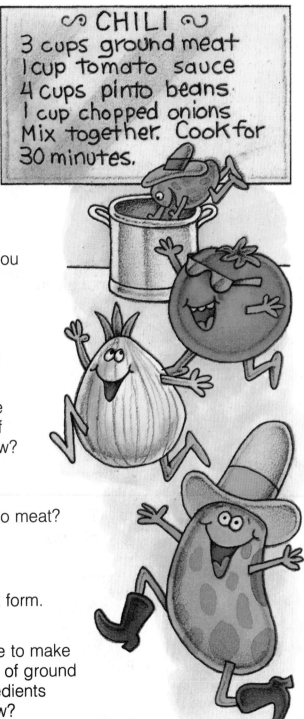

CHILI
3 cups ground meat
1 cup tomato sauce
4 cups pinto beans
1 cup chopped onions
Mix together. Cook for 30 minutes.

1. How many cups of meat did they use for the recipe?

2. How many cups of beans did they use for the recipe?

You can describe how these parts of the recipe compare to each other by writing a **ratio**. A ratio is a way to compare two numbers.

The ratio of meat to beans is 3 to 4. You can also write this ratio as 3:4 or 3/4.

3. What is the ratio of onions to meat in the recipe?

4. What is the ratio of sauce to beans in the recipe?

5. **What if** Charlie and Jeannie decide to double the recipe? How much of each ingredient would they use now?

6. What would be the ratio of meat to beans if the recipe were doubled? What would be the ratio of onions to meat? of sauce to beans?

7. You can simplify ratios the same way you simplify fractions. Give the ratios for Problem 6 in simplest form. What do you notice?

8. **What if** Charlie and Jeannie decide to make more of the chili? They use 9 cups of ground meat. How much of the other ingredients should they use? How do you know?

KPELLE

RICE MEASURES

The most common way of measuring rice in the markets of inland Liberia is by using a *sâmo-ko* (sah-moe-koe), or "salmon cup." A *sâmo-ko* holds about 2 cups of rice. The Kpelle (PEH-lay) people who live in this area buy and sell a lot of rice. Rice is their staple food, which means they eat it every day. Those who do not grow their own rice must buy it from a trader in the market.

The trader usually uses a *sâmo-ko* to measure the rice. Larger amounts of rice may be measured with a *bôke* (bah-key), or "bucket." A *bôke* is equal to about 12 *sâmo-ko* or $\frac{1}{2}$ of a *tin*. The largest Kpelle measure for rice is a *boro* (bah-roe), or "bag." A *bôke* is $\frac{1}{4}$ of a *boro*. A trader usually buys a *tin* or *boro* of rice. When a trader sells the rice, it is measured with either a *bôke* or a *sâmo-ko*.

When someone goes to the market and wants to buy 6 *sâmo-ko* of rice, the trader dips a "salmon cup" into a *bôke* 6 times. After buying the rice, the customer might take it home to serve with *palava* (pah-LAH-vah) sauce, a sauce made of spinach, okra, meat, and hot pepper.

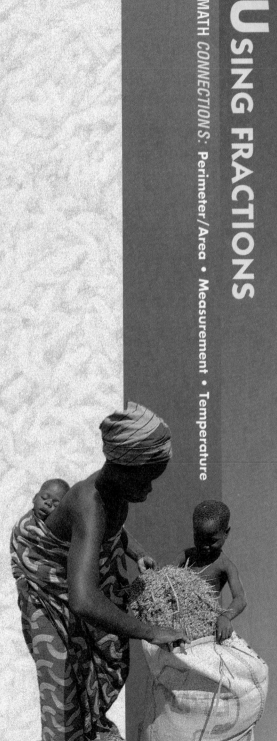

1. How are the units the Kpelle people use to measure rice related to each other?

2. Think of something you could measure using a *sâmo-ko*. What are some other ways of measuring the same thing?

ACTIVITY Adding Fractions

Cara walks $\frac{1}{8}$ mi from the park entrance to the information center. She then walks $\frac{5}{8}$ mi to the scenic view. How far does Cara walk?

WORKING TOGETHER

You can make a model with fraction strips to solve the problem.

Show $\frac{1}{8}$ with fraction strips. Then add $\frac{5}{8}$ next to it to make one long strip.

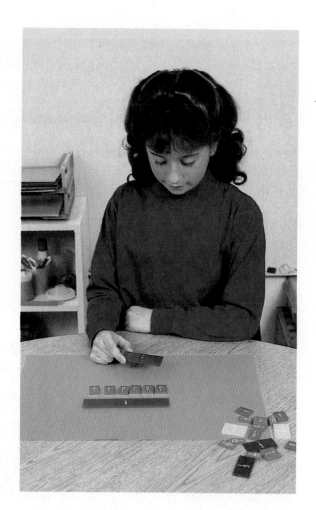

1. How many eighths are there in all? How far does Cara walk?

2. Write an addition sentence to show how you added the two fractions.

3. How does the sum compare to $\frac{1}{2}$? to 1? How can you tell?

4. What if Cara walks another $\frac{5}{8}$ mi? How far does she walk?

5. How can you write this fraction as a mixed number?

6. How does the sum compare to 1? How can you tell?

Use fraction strips to show each sum.
Tell how the sum compares to $\frac{1}{2}$ and to 1.

7. $\frac{1}{3} + \frac{1}{3}$

8. $\frac{1}{12} + \frac{4}{12}$

9. $\frac{1}{8} + \frac{7}{8}$

10. $\frac{5}{6} + \frac{5}{6}$

11. $\frac{3}{4} + \frac{2}{4}$

12. $\frac{7}{8} + \frac{3}{8}$

13. $\frac{1}{6} + \frac{2}{6}$

14. $\frac{2}{8} + \frac{1}{8}$

15. $\frac{2}{12} + \frac{6}{12}$

SHARING IDEAS

16. Look at the numerators of the addends and the sums. What do you notice?

17. Look at the denominators of the addends and the sums. What do you notice?

18. Tell how you can add two fractions with the same denominator.

ON YOUR OWN

Complete the table. Use fraction strips if needed.

19. Rule: Add $\frac{1}{8}$.

$\frac{0}{8}$	$\frac{1}{8}$	$\frac{2}{8}$	$\frac{3}{8}$	$\frac{4}{8}$	$\frac{5}{8}$	$\frac{6}{8}$	$\frac{7}{8}$
■	■	■	■	■	■	■	■

20. Rule: Add $\frac{1}{6}$.

$\frac{0}{6}$	$\frac{1}{6}$	$\frac{2}{6}$	$\frac{3}{6}$	$\frac{4}{6}$	$\frac{5}{6}$
■	■	■	■	■	■

Solve. Use fraction strips if needed.

21. Cara hikes $\frac{3}{8}$ mi from Rocky Ridge to the waterfall. Then she hikes $\frac{4}{8}$ mi back to her campsite. How far does Cara hike?

22. It takes Ben $\frac{3}{4}$ hour to walk to the park. It takes another $\frac{1}{4}$ hour to walk to the pond. How long does Ben walk?

23. *Write a problem* involving adding fractions with like denominators. Ask others to solve it.

ACTIVITY

Finding Sums

A. Joanna is testing how clean the lake water is. She fills $\frac{1}{8}$ of a jar with lake water. She fills another $\frac{1}{8}$ of the jar with test chemicals. What part of the jar has she filled? Has she filled over $\frac{1}{2}$ of the jar?

You can use fraction strips to answer these questions.

1. How many eighths are there in all?

2. How many fourths is this equal to?

3. What part of the jar has she filled?

4. How does this compare to $\frac{1}{2}$? to 1?

B. You can also use this method to add fractions with like denominators.

Step 1	Step 2	Step 3
Add the numerators.	Use the common denominator.	Write the sum in simplest form.
$\frac{1}{8} + \frac{1}{8} = {}^{2}$	$\frac{1}{8} + \frac{1}{8} = \frac{2}{8}$	$\frac{2}{8} = \frac{1}{4}$ *Think:* $\frac{2 \div 2}{8 \div 2} = \frac{1}{4}$

5. **What if** she had filled $\frac{4}{8}$ of the jar with water and $\frac{1}{8}$ of the jar with chemicals? What part of the jar would be filled?

SHARING IDEAS

6. Why does the denominator stay the same when you add fractions?

7. Do you always need to simplify the sum of two fractions? Why or why not?

PRACTICE

Add. Write the sum in simplest form.

8. $\frac{1}{5} + \frac{1}{5}$ **9.** $\frac{1}{3} + \frac{1}{3}$ **10.** $\frac{1}{6} + \frac{4}{6}$ **11.** $\frac{4}{9} + \frac{1}{9}$ **12.** $\frac{2}{8} + \frac{3}{8}$

13. $\frac{2}{4} + \frac{1}{4}$ **14.** $\frac{3}{7} + \frac{2}{7}$ **15.** $\frac{5}{12} + \frac{2}{12}$ **16.** $\frac{1}{6} + \frac{1}{6}$ **17.** $\frac{1}{4} + \frac{1}{4}$

18. $\frac{1}{10} + \frac{3}{10}$ **19.** $\frac{5}{8} + \frac{1}{8}$ **20.** $\frac{2}{9} + \frac{4}{9}$ **21.** $\frac{3}{16} + \frac{5}{16}$ **22.** $\frac{7}{12} + \frac{2}{12}$

23. $\begin{array}{r} \frac{1}{7} \\ + \frac{1}{7} \\ \hline \end{array}$ **24.** $\begin{array}{r} \frac{1}{8} \\ + \frac{2}{8} \\ \hline \end{array}$ **25.** $\begin{array}{r} \frac{3}{9} \\ + \frac{2}{9} \\ \hline \end{array}$ **26.** $\begin{array}{r} \frac{5}{16} \\ + \frac{6}{16} \\ \hline \end{array}$ **27.** $\begin{array}{r} \frac{3}{10} \\ + \frac{4}{10} \\ \hline \end{array}$ **28.** $\begin{array}{r} \frac{0}{4} \\ + \frac{3}{4} \\ \hline \end{array}$

29. $\begin{array}{r} \frac{1}{6} \\ + \frac{2}{6} \\ \hline \end{array}$ **30.** $\begin{array}{r} \frac{4}{10} \\ + \frac{2}{10} \\ \hline \end{array}$ **31.** $\begin{array}{r} \frac{1}{9} \\ + \frac{5}{9} \\ \hline \end{array}$ **32.** $\begin{array}{r} \frac{4}{8} \\ + \frac{0}{8} \\ \hline \end{array}$ **33.** $\begin{array}{r} \frac{11}{16} \\ + \frac{3}{16} \\ \hline \end{array}$ **34.** $\begin{array}{r} \frac{5}{12} \\ + \frac{3}{12} \\ \hline \end{array}$

Find the missing numerator.

35. $\frac{\blacksquare}{8} + \frac{3}{8} = \frac{3}{8}$ **36.** $\frac{5}{7} + \frac{1}{7} = \frac{\blacksquare}{7} + \frac{5}{7}$ **37.** $\frac{4}{12} + \frac{3}{12} + \frac{1}{12} = \frac{1}{12} + \frac{3}{12} + \frac{\blacksquare}{12}$

Mixed Applications

Solve. You may need to use the Databank on page 521.

38. Joanna walked $\frac{4}{8}$ mi on the park trails to the waterfall. Then she walked to the lake. How far did she walk?

39. There are 644 markers on 7 trails. Each trail has the same number of markers. How many markers are on each trail?

40. The trail markers come 25 to a box. If there are 4 boxes, how many trail markers are there?

41. How far is it from the picnic grounds to the lake and then to the waterfall?

Mixed Review

Find the answer. Which method did you use?

42. $7,007 - 889$ **43.** 8×40 **44.** $373 \div 4$

45. $\frac{3}{16} + \frac{5}{16}$ **46.** $400 \div 5$ **47.** 6×37

MENTAL/MATH
CALCULATOR
PAPER/PENCIL

Finding Greater Sums

Lars swam in the lake for $\frac{3}{4}$ hour.
He rowed a boat for another $\frac{3}{4}$ hour.
How much time did this take
in all?

You can add to find the answer.

Add: $\frac{3}{4} + \frac{3}{4}$

Step 1	Step 2	Step 3
Add the numerators.	**Use the common denominator.**	**Write the sum in simplest form.**
$\frac{3}{4} + \frac{3}{4} = 6$	$\frac{3}{4} + \frac{3}{4} = \frac{6}{4}$	$\frac{6}{4} = 1\frac{2}{4} = 1\frac{1}{2}$
		Think: $4\overline{)6}$ $\quad$ 1 R2

It took $1\frac{1}{2}$ hours in all.

1. ***What if*** Lars swam for $\frac{3}{4}$ hour, but rowed the boat for
   only $\frac{1}{4}$ hour? How much time would this have taken?

TRY OUT $\quad$ Write the letter of the correct answer.
Find the sum in simplest form.

2. $\frac{1}{2} + \frac{1}{2}$ $\qquad$ **a.** $\frac{2}{4}$ $\qquad$ **b.** $\frac{1}{2}$ $\qquad$ **c.** $\frac{2}{2}$ $\qquad$ **d.** 1

3. $\frac{3}{5} + \frac{4}{5}$ $\qquad$ **a.** $\frac{7}{10}$ $\qquad$ **b.** $\frac{1}{2}$ $\qquad$ **c.** $1\frac{2}{5}$ $\qquad$ **d.** $\frac{7}{5}$

4. $\frac{5}{8} + \frac{7}{8}$ $\qquad$ **a.** $1\frac{2}{8}$ $\qquad$ **b.** $1\frac{1}{2}$ $\qquad$ **c.** $\frac{12}{16}$ $\qquad$ **d.** $\frac{3}{4}$

PRACTICE

Add. Write the sum in simplest form.

5. $\frac{1}{8} + \frac{7}{8}$ **6.** $\frac{4}{5} + \frac{1}{5}$ **7.** $\frac{2}{6} + \frac{5}{6}$ **8.** $\frac{3}{4} + \frac{2}{4}$ **9.** $\frac{4}{7} + \frac{4}{7}$

10. $\frac{3}{5} + \frac{4}{5}$ **11.** $\frac{6}{9} + \frac{7}{9}$ **12.** $\frac{5}{16} + \frac{13}{16}$ **13.** $\frac{7}{10} + \frac{7}{10}$ **14.** $\frac{6}{8} + \frac{5}{8}$

15. $\frac{9}{10} + \frac{1}{10}$ **16.** $\frac{2}{3} + \frac{2}{3}$ **17.** $\frac{7}{12} + \frac{5}{12}$ **18.** $\frac{9}{16} + \frac{8}{16}$ **19.** $\frac{4}{10} + \frac{9}{10}$

20. $\frac{5}{6} + \frac{5}{6}$ **21.** $\frac{9}{10} + \frac{7}{10}$ **22.** $\frac{8}{9} + \frac{7}{9}$ **23.** $\frac{7}{8} + \frac{7}{8}$ **24.** $\frac{14}{16} + \frac{6}{16}$ **25.** $\frac{5}{12} + \frac{11}{12}$

Critical Thinking   Give examples. Write *not possible* if you cannot give an example.

26. Give two fractions that are both less than $\frac{1}{2}$ whose sum is:
     a. less than 1   **b.** equal to 1   **c.** greater than 1

27. Give two fractions that are both greater than $\frac{1}{2}$ whose sum is:
     a. less than 1   **b.** equal to 1   **c.** greater than 1

Mixed Applications   Solve. Which method did you use?

28. Last year 2,357 people rented boats on the lake. This year 3,004 people rented boats. How many more people rented boats this year?

29. Tamla sailed her boat $\frac{7}{8}$ mi to the buoy. Then she sailed $\frac{3}{8}$ mi to the dock. How far did she sail?

30. A swimming pass costs $2.10. Jo and Bo need 2 passes. They have $5.00. Do they have enough to buy the passes?

> **ESTIMATION**
> **MENTAL MATH**
> **CALCULATOR**
> **PAPER/PENCIL**

— LOGICAL REASONING —

Complete the statements. The first one is done for you.

1. If ## is 1, then ###### is 3.   **2.** If @@ is 4, then @ is ■.

3. If ∗ is 2, then ∗∗∗∗∗ is ■.   **4.** If §§§ is 9, then § is ■.

PROBLEM SOLVING

✓ UNDERSTAND
✓ PLAN
✓ TRY
✓ CHECK
✓ EXTEND

Strategy: Using Different Strategies

John has a collection of wildlife cards. He has 10 fewer reptile cards than insect cards. He has twice as many bird cards as reptile cards. He has 50 bird cards. How many insect cards does he have?

You can often use more than one strategy to solve a problem.

Maria is solving the problem by working backward.

She knows John has 50 bird cards and twice as many bird cards as reptile cards. So she divides to find how many reptile cards John has.

$$50 \div 2 = 25$$

She also knows that John has 10 fewer reptile cards than insect cards. She adds to find how many insect cards John has.

$$25 + 10 = \blacksquare$$

1. How many insect cards does John have?

Vincent is using the Guess, Test, and Revise strategy to check Maria's answer.

His first guess was too high. So he revised it lower.

First Guess
40 insect cards

Test
$$40 - 10 = 30$$
$$2 \times 30 = 60$$

2. Is his revised guess correct? Why or why not?

Revised Guess
35 insect cards

3. Does his answer match Maria's?

Test
$$35 - 10 = 25$$
$$2 \times 25 = \blacksquare$$

4. Which strategy do you prefer? Why?

392 Lesson 10–4

PRACTICE

Solve the problem. Then use a different strategy to check your answer. Tell which strategies you used. Use mental math, a calculator, or paper and pencil.

5. Animals drink at a water hole in the morning, at noon, in the afternoon, or in the evening. Lions drink in the afternoon. Giraffes do not drink at noon. Warthogs do not drink in the evening. Hyenas drink before warthogs. In what order do the animals drink?

6. The exhibits at the Nature Museum are in a row on one side of the building. The insects are between the mammals and the reptiles. The birds are to the right of the mammals, and the insects to the left of the mammals. In what order are the exhibits?

7. There are 4 times as many insects as mammals. There are 3 fewer birds than reptiles and half as many reptiles as insects. If there are 4 mammals, how many birds are there?

8. Mr. Lund is buying equipment for a hiking trip. He buys a pack for $69, a sweater for $32.75, boots for $97.50, and field glasses for $78. Will $300 be enough to pay for these items?

Strategies and Skills Review

9. Irene spent $18 for two ecology books. One book cost $4 more than the other. How much did the more expensive book cost?

10. If 7 girls and 6 boys each plant 8 trees, how many trees will they plant in all?

11. Oren wants to buy tomato seeds for $2.69 and lettuce seeds for $1.89. Will $5 be enough to pay for both items? How can you tell?

12. **Write a problem** that can be solved by more than one strategy. Solve the problem. Ask others to use a different strategy to check your answer.

POUR MORE

Measuring

A. Suppose you want to fill a pitcher with 4 ounces of water, but you have only these two glasses:

 3 ounces   5 ounces

How can you get exactly 4 ounces in the pitcher?

Think about the amounts you can measure with these glasses. You can measure 3 or 5 ounces easily.

1. How can you measure 8 ounces easily?

2. Here is a simple way to measure 2 ounces. Fill the 5-ounce glass. Then pour from that glass into the 3-ounce glass until it is full. How many ounces will be left in the 5-ounce glass? Will this help you measure 4 ounces? Tell how.

3. Some measuring problems will require many steps. You can use a table to keep track. This table shows how you measure 4 ounces. Tell what happens at each of the other steps.

3-Ounce Glass	5-Ounce Glass	Pitcher	
0	5	0	← Fill the 5-ounce glass.
3	2	0	← Fill the 3-ounce glass from the 5-ounce glass.
3	0	2	← Pour what remains in the 5-ounce glass into the pitcher.
0	0	2	← Empty the 3-ounce glass.
0	5	2	← ?
3	2	2	← ?
3	0	4	← ?

B. Can you tell how to fill the pitcher with 6, 7, 8, 9, or 10 ounces using a 3-ounce and a 5-ounce glass?

4. Use tables to show the steps for each amount.

5. Which amount takes the least number of steps?

6. Now imagine that you have three glasses:

 2 ounces   5 ounces   8 ounces

What is the easiest way you could fill a pitcher with each of these amounts of water?

a. 6 ounces   **b.** 9 ounces   **c.** 1 ounce

Remember, you can pour water back from the pitcher into any glass.

ACTIVITY
Subtracting Fractions

Jerry is trimming the bushes in his front yard. He cuts off $\frac{3}{8}$ yd from a bush that was $\frac{7}{8}$ yd tall. How tall is the bush after he trims it?

WORKING TOGETHER

You can make a model with fraction strips to solve the problem.

Show $\frac{7}{8}$ with fraction strips. Take away $\frac{3}{8}$ by taking away three of the strips.

1. How many eighths are left? How tall is the trimmed bush?

2. How does this compare to $\frac{1}{2}$? How can you tell?

3. Write a subtraction sentence to show how you subtracted the two fractions.

4. **What if** Jerry had cut $\frac{5}{8}$ yd from the bush? How tall would it be?

5. How does this difference compare to $\frac{1}{2}$? How can you tell?

Use fraction strips to find the difference.
Tell how it compares to $\frac{1}{2}$.

6. $\frac{2}{3} - \frac{1}{3}$

7. $\frac{5}{6} - \frac{1}{6}$

8. $\frac{5}{8} - \frac{3}{8}$

9. $\frac{9}{12} - \frac{3}{12}$

10. $\frac{3}{4} - \frac{3}{4}$

11. $\frac{10}{12} - \frac{3}{12}$

12. $\frac{3}{4} - \frac{2}{4}$

13. $\frac{5}{6} - \frac{2}{6}$

14. $\frac{8}{12} - \frac{1}{12}$

15. Look at the numerators of the fractions you subtracted. Then look at the numerators of the differences. What do you notice?

16. Look at the denominators of the numbers you subtracted. Then look at the denominators of the differences. What do you notice?

17. Tell how you can subtract two fractions with the same denominator.

ON YOUR OWN

Complete the table. Use fraction strips if needed.

18. Rule: Subtract $\frac{1}{8}$.

$\frac{8}{8}$	$\frac{7}{8}$	$\frac{6}{8}$	$\frac{5}{8}$	$\frac{4}{8}$	$\frac{3}{8}$	$\frac{2}{8}$	$\frac{1}{8}$
■	■	■	■	■	■	■	■

19. Rule: Subtract $\frac{1}{6}$.

$\frac{6}{6}$	$\frac{5}{6}$	$\frac{4}{6}$	$\frac{3}{6}$	$\frac{2}{6}$	$\frac{1}{6}$
■	■	■	■	■	■

Solve. Use fraction strips if needed.

20. Carlos has a piece of string $\frac{10}{12}$ ft long. He cuts off a piece $\frac{5}{12}$ ft long. How long is the string now?

21. Aisha has $\frac{3}{4}$ hour to wait before dinner. She reads a story for $\frac{1}{4}$ hour. How long is it until dinner?

22. *Write a problem* involving subtracting fractions with denominators. Ask others to solve it.

ACTIVITY Finding Differences

A. Martha bakes a loaf of oatmeal bread $\frac{5}{6}$ ft long. She cuts a piece $\frac{1}{6}$ ft long to give to Sara. How long is the loaf of bread now?

You can use fraction strips to answer these questions.

1. How many sixths are left?
2. How many thirds is this equal to?
3. How long is the loaf of bread now?
4. How does this difference compare to $\frac{1}{2}$?

B. You can also use this method to subtract fractions with like denominators.

Step 1	Step 2	Step 3
Subtract the numerators.	Use the common denominator.	Write the difference in simplest form.
$\frac{5}{6} - \frac{1}{6} = 4$	$\frac{5}{6} - \frac{1}{6} = \frac{4}{6}$	$\frac{4}{6} = \frac{2}{3}$ *Think:* $\frac{4 \div 2}{6 \div 2} = \frac{2}{3}$

5. **What if** Martha bakes another loaf $\frac{5}{8}$ ft long and cuts a piece $\frac{4}{8}$ ft long? How long would the loaf be then?

SHARING IDEAS

6. Why does the denominator stay the same when you subtract fractions?

7. Do you always need to simplify the difference of two fractions? Why or why not?

8. How can you check your answers?

PRACTICE

Subtract. Write the difference in simplest form.

9. $\frac{4}{5} - \frac{1}{5}$ **10.** $\frac{2}{3} - \frac{1}{3}$ **11.** $\frac{5}{6} - \frac{4}{6}$ **12.** $\frac{8}{9} - \frac{7}{9}$ **13.** $\frac{7}{8} - \frac{4}{8}$

14. $\frac{3}{4} - \frac{1}{4}$ **15.** $\frac{3}{7} - \frac{0}{7}$ **16.** $\frac{8}{12} - \frac{5}{12}$ **17.** $\frac{5}{6} - \frac{1}{6}$ **18.** $\frac{8}{16} - \frac{4}{16}$

19. $\frac{9}{10} - \frac{3}{10}$ **20.** $\frac{5}{8} - \frac{3}{8}$ **21.** $\frac{7}{9} - \frac{4}{9}$ **22.** $\frac{14}{16} - \frac{4}{16}$ **23.** $\frac{10}{12} - \frac{2}{12}$

24. $\begin{array}{r} \frac{5}{7} \\ -\frac{2}{7} \end{array}$ **25.** $\begin{array}{r} \frac{6}{8} \\ -\frac{3}{8} \end{array}$ **26.** $\begin{array}{r} \frac{8}{9} \\ -\frac{3}{9} \end{array}$ **27.** $\begin{array}{r} \frac{9}{16} \\ -\frac{6}{16} \end{array}$ **28.** $\begin{array}{r} \frac{8}{10} \\ -\frac{5}{10} \end{array}$ **29.** $\begin{array}{r} \frac{3}{4} \\ -\frac{0}{4} \end{array}$

30. $\begin{array}{r} \frac{5}{6} \\ -\frac{3}{6} \end{array}$ **31.** $\begin{array}{r} \frac{9}{10} \\ -\frac{4}{10} \end{array}$ **32.** $\begin{array}{r} \frac{5}{8} \\ -\frac{3}{8} \end{array}$ **33.** $\begin{array}{r} \frac{7}{9} \\ -\frac{1}{9} \end{array}$ **34.** $\begin{array}{r} \frac{15}{16} \\ -\frac{15}{16} \end{array}$ **35.** $\begin{array}{r} \frac{11}{12} \\ -\frac{7}{12} \end{array}$

Find the missing numerator.

36. $\frac{4}{12} - \frac{\blacksquare}{12} = \frac{4}{12}$ **37.** $\frac{8}{16} - \frac{\blacksquare}{16} = \frac{0}{16}$ **38.** $\frac{4}{7} + \frac{\blacksquare}{7} = 1$

Mixed Applications

Solve. You may need to use the Databank on page 521.

39. Which is farther from the parking lot, the picnic grounds or the waterfall? How much farther?

40. Geoff brings 8 muffins to the picnic. He gives $\frac{1}{4}$ of the muffins to Sam. How many muffins does he give Sam?

41. Khoury brings 4 bags of rolls to the picnic. Each bag holds 12 rolls. How many rolls did Khoury bring?

42. Sara mixes batter for $\frac{1}{4}$ hour. The cake bakes for $\frac{3}{4}$ hour. How long does it take Sara to make a cake?

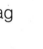

Mixed Review

Find the answer. Which method did you use?

MENTAL MATH
CALCULATOR
PAPER/PENCIL

43. $4,379 + 7,637$ **44.** $50 \div 5$ **45.** 48×6

46. $\frac{7}{12} - \frac{3}{12}$ **47.** $737 \div 4$ **48.** $5,999 - 4,999$

ACTIVITY

Add and Subtract Mixed Numbers

The Ecology Club is helping to plant trees on a bare hillside not far from their school. They plant $1\frac{7}{12}$ boxes of seedlings the first day and $2\frac{7}{12}$ boxes the next day. How many boxes did they plant?

WORKING TOGETHER

You can use fraction strips to make a model to solve the problem.

Step 1 Show $1\frac{7}{12}$ with fraction strips. Then show $2\frac{7}{12}$.

Step 2 Combine the twelfths.

1. How many twelfths are there in all? Can you regroup to form a whole?

Step 3 Combine the whole strips.

2. How many twelfths are there? How many whole strips? How many boxes did they plant?

3. How can you write the sum in simplest form?

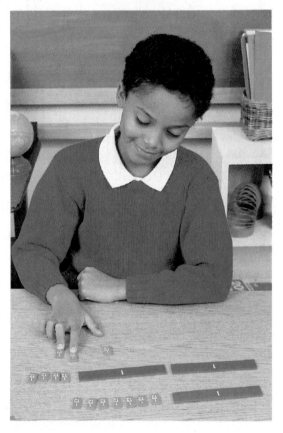

What if $2\frac{10}{12}$ boxes of the seedlings are pine trees? How many boxes are not pine tree seedlings?

Step 4 Take away $2\frac{10}{12}$ from your model of the total. Start with the twelfths.

4. Do you need to regroup a whole strip as twelfths before you can take away? Why?

5. How many twelfths are left? How many whole strips? How many boxes are not pine tree seedlings?

6. How can you write the difference in simplest form?

Use fraction strips to add or subtract. Write the answer in simplest form.

7. $3\frac{1}{8}$
$+ 2\frac{4}{8}$

8. $5\frac{11}{12}$
$- 3\frac{4}{12}$

9. $4\frac{2}{3}$
$+ 1\frac{2}{3}$

10. $6\frac{1}{4}$
$- 2\frac{2}{4}$

11. $2\frac{3}{6}$
$+ 1\frac{5}{6}$

12. $4\frac{1}{4}$
$- \frac{3}{4}$

13. $4\frac{1}{2} + 2\frac{1}{2}$

14. $2\frac{5}{12} - 1\frac{7}{12}$

15. $3\frac{5}{8} - 2\frac{5}{8}$

SHARING IDEAS

Compare your models with those of others.

16. When do you need to regroup the fraction part when you add mixed numbers?

17. When do you need to regroup the whole number part when you subtract mixed numbers?

18. Write a method to tell how to add mixed numbers.

19. Write a method to tell how to subtract mixed numbers.

ON YOUR OWN

20. In the morning Lyn uses $2\frac{3}{8}$ bags of fertilizer. She uses $1\frac{5}{8}$ bags that afternoon. How much fertilizer does Lyn use?

21. How much more fertilizer did Lyn use in the morning than in the afternoon?

22. *Write a problem* involving adding or subtracting mixed numbers. Ask others to solve it.

✓ UNDERSTAND
✓ PLAN
✓ TRY
CHECK
✓ EXTEND

PROBLEM SOLVING

Strategy: Solving a Simpler Problem

Dick went on a hike in the wildlife preserve. It took him $\frac{7}{8}$ hour to get to the wildflower meadow and $\frac{5}{8}$ hour to get back to his campsite. How long was he on his hike?

Dick cannot decide what he can do to solve the problem. He plans to solve a simpler problem by using whole numbers.

Dick thinks: If I took 3 hours to get to the meadow and 2 hours to get back to camp, I could add to find the amount of time I hiked.

3 + 2 = 5

Dick can solve the simpler problem by adding the hours.

1. What can he do to solve the original problem?

$$\frac{7}{8} + \frac{5}{8} = \blacksquare$$

2. How long was he on his hike?

3. **What if** Dick wants to know how much longer it took him to get to the meadow than to get back to his campsite? Write a simpler problem by using whole numbers. Then solve the original problem.

4. How can solving a simpler problem help you solve more difficult problems?

PRACTICE

Solve the problem. Solve a simpler problem first if you need to. Use mental math, a calculator, or paper and pencil.

5. Claudia buys $\frac{3}{4}$ pound of swiss cheese and $\frac{3}{4}$ pound of cheddar. How much cheese does she buy?

6. At the Smith Ridge campsite, 2,692 people are camped out. At the Condor site, 1,899 are camped out. How many more people are at Smith Ridge than at Condor?

7. A mountain stream is $\frac{1}{4}$ ft deep. It empties into a pool of water that is $\frac{3}{4}$ ft deep. How much deeper is the pool of water than the stream?

8. On Monday the park ranger patrolled 115 miles of park land. She patrolled 102 miles on Tuesday and 111 miles on Wednesday. How many miles did she patrol in all?

Strategies and Skills Review

9. The Kanes are conserving water. They used 380 gallons of water in June, 366 gallons in July, and 352 gallons in August. If they continue this pattern, how many gallons will they use in September?

10. The wildlife preserve has biking and hiking trails. There are 16 hiking trails. What else do you need to know to find how many trails there are in all?

11. Alexis bought 2 animal posters for $3.00 each and 1 postcard for $.50. How much change will she get from $10.00?

12. The wildlife preserve has 125 more acres of forest than of prairie. It has 385 acres of forest. How many acres of prairie does it have?

13. A baby chimp drinks $\frac{3}{4}$ bottle of milk and $\frac{3}{4}$ bottle of sugared water at a feeding. How much liquid does it drink at a feeding?

14. **Write a problem.** Solve it. Ask others to solve your problem by first writing a simpler problem.

Perimeter and Area

Felipe is helping to build a new corral for the burros used on the mountain trails. The corral is 20 feet long on 2 sides and 9 feet long on the other 2 sides. What is the perimeter of the corral? What is its area?

Think: *Perimeter* is the distance around an object.
Area is the number of square units it takes to cover the surface of the object.

WORKING TOGETHER

1. What is the perimeter of the corral? How did you find it?

2. What is the area of the corral? How did you find it?

3. Estimate, then measure the perimeter and area of objects around you. Make a table.

4. Use graph paper to draw different figures with an area of 12 square inches. Find the perimeter of each shape. What do you notice?

SHARING IDEAS

5. Why can you add the length and the width and multiply by 2 to find the perimeter of a rectangle?

6. Can you always multiply to find the area of a rectangle? Why or why not?

7. Do figures with the same area always have the same perimeter? Give examples to support your answer.

PRACTICE

Measure to the nearest inch. Find the perimeter and area.

8.

9.

Find the perimeter and area.

10.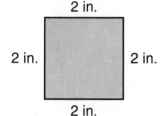

2 in.

2 in.　　　　2 in.

2 in.

11.

4 ft

2 ft　　　　2 ft

4 ft

12.

12 yd

8 yd　　　　8 yd

12 yd

13. length = 10 ft
width = 7 ft

14. length = 42 in.
width = 8 in.

15. length = 15 yd
width = 5 yd

Find the missing length.

16.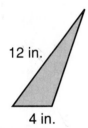

12 in.

4 in.
Perimeter: 24 in.

17.

9 ft

Perimeter: 32 ft

18.

Perimeter: 56 yd

Mixed Applications

19. The bottom of Hannah's fish tank is a square $\frac{1}{4}$ ft on each side. What is the perimeter of the fish tank?

20. The floor of Archie's storage shed is a rectangle 3 yd wide by 4 yd long. What is the area of the floor?

21. The area of a hog pen is 178 sq ft. The area of a sheep pen is 532 sq ft. How much larger is the area of the sheep pen?

22. *Draw a figure.* Find its perimeter and area. Ask·others to find them also.

ACTIVITY
Capacity

1 cup

1 pint

1 quart

1 gallon

Julie brings along a canteen of water on a hike. How much water does it hold?

The amount a container can hold is its **capacity.** The customary units of capacity are **cup (c), pint (pt), quart (qt),** and **gallon (gal).**

Cups and pints are customary units used for measuring small amounts of liquids.

There are 2 cups in 1 pint.

Quarts and gallons are customary units used to measure larger amounts.

There are 2 pints in a quart. There are 4 quarts in a gallon.

1. Do you think Julie's canteen holds a cup, a pint, a quart, or a gallon? Why?

2. Collect containers of different sizes. Choose the best unit. Estimate, then measure their capacities. Record your measures in a table. Compare them with those of others.

CAPACITY

Object	c	pt	qt	gal
Cereal bowl	■	■	■	■
Small glass	■	■	■	■
Large glass	■	■	■	■
Bucket	■	■	■	■

SHARING IDEAS

3. Why did you pick the units you chose to measure the different objects?

4. Why would you not want to tell someone the capacity of a container by the number of glasses it holds?

5. ***Write a list*** of the types of containers you use every day and how their capacities are labeled. Compare your list to those of others.

PRACTICE

Choose the best estimate of capacity.

6. glass of juice   **a.** 1 c   **b.** 1 pt   **c.** 1 qt   **d.** 1 gal

7. large jug of water   **a.** 1 c   **b.** 1 pt   **c.** 1 qt   **d.** 1 gal

8. container of cream   **a.** 1 c   **b.** 1 pt   **c.** 1 qt   **d.** 1 gal

9. large container of juice   **a.** 2 c   **b.** 2 pt   **c.** 2 qt   **d.** 2 gal

10. large bucket   **a.** 5 c   **b.** 5 pt   **c.** 5 qt   **d.** 5 gal

11. cocoa mug   **a.** 2 c   **b.** 2 pt   **c.** 2 qt   **d.** 2 gal

Choose the best unit to use to measure the capacity. Write *cup, pint, quart,* or *gallon.*

12. kitchen sink   **13.** bud vase   **14.** juice pitcher

15. large glass   **16.** bath tub   **17.** large can of paint

Critical Thinking

Do these sentences make sense? Why or why not?

18. Barry drank a gallon of milk with dinner.

19. Kevin used 3 cups of water in his bath.

Mixed Applications

20. Dale brings enough drinking water to last for 2 days. Does she bring 5 cups or 5 quarts?

21. Hank pours $\frac{1}{2}$ pint of apple juice and $\frac{1}{2}$ pint of grape juice into the same bottle. How much juice is in the bottle?

22. Yoko finds that each person drinks about 4 cups of juice each day. If there are 24 people on the camping trip, how much juice do they drink daily?

23. The pool at the camp usually holds 5,000 gallons of water. After a rain there are 6,243 gallons in it. How much rainwater went in the pool?

EXTRA PRACTICE, page 423

ACTIVITY **W**eight

Xavier's class is collecting aluminum cans as part of their recycling project. They can earn money based on the weight of the cans they collect.

The customary units of weight are **ounces (oz)** and **pounds (lb).**

Ounces are customary units used to measure light objects.

A slice of bread weighs about 1 oz. A small bowl of cereal weighs about 4 oz.

1. Name other things that could be measured using ounces.

Pounds are customary units used to measure heavier objects.

There are 16 ounces in 1 pound.

A loaf of bread weighs about 1 pound. A large box of cereal weighs about 1 pound.

2. Name other things that could be measured using pounds.

3. Collect objects in your classroom. Decide which units you would use to measure their weights. Record your decisions in a chart like this.

1 ounce

1 pound

WEIGHT

Object	oz	lb
■	■	■
■	■	■

SHARING IDEAS

4. How did you choose which units to use to measure the different objects?

5. Is the larger object always heavier than the smaller object? Why or why not?

PRACTICE

Choose the best estimate of weight.

6. tent   **a.** 1 oz   **b.** 10 oz   **c.** 1 lb   **d.** 10 lb

7. letter   **a.** 1 oz   **b.** 10 oz   **c.** 1 lb   **d.** 10 lb

8. textbook   **a.** 2 oz   **b.** 12 oz   **c.** 2 lb   **d.** 20 lb

9. sneaker   **a.** 3 oz   **b.** 13 oz   **c.** 3 lb   **d.** 13 lb

10. large cat   **a.** 4 oz   **b.** 14 oz   **c.** 4 lb   **d.** 14 lb

11. scissors   **a.** 5 oz   **b.** 15 oz   **c.** 5 lb   **d.** 15 lb

Choose the object closest to the given weight.

12. 2 oz   **a.** paper clip   **b.** eraser   **c.** desk

13. 8 lb   **a.** compass   **b.** blanket   **c.** hiking boots

14. 20 lb   **a.** record   **b.** television   **c.** car

Mixed Applications

15. Kathy wrote that her large bag of cans weighs 25. Does she mean ounces or pounds?

16. If there are 16 cans in 1 lb, how many cans are in 8 lb?

17. So far Dan has collected $\frac{7}{8}$ lb of cans. Stan has collected $\frac{5}{8}$ lb. How much more has Dan collected?

18. ***Write a problem*** that involves weight. Solve your problem. Ask others to solve it.

CHALLENGE

Gravity on the moon is $\frac{1}{6}$ the gravity on earth. So objects on the moon weigh $\frac{1}{6}$ what they would weigh on earth.

Tell how much the object would weigh on the moon.

1. a 24-oz book   **2.** a 168-lb astronaut   **3.** a 36-lb telescope

Ac**T**i**V**i**T**y **R**enaming **Customary Units**

Niko needs to buy special paper for a banner she is making. The banner is going to be 4 yards long. At the store Niko learns that the special paper is measured in feet. How many feet of paper will she need?

You can solve the problem by finding patterns and using them to rename the units.

WORKING TOGETHER

1. Look at a yardstick. How many feet are equal to 1 yard?

2. Use the yardstick to mark off 2 yards on the chalkboard. Then use the yardstick to find this length in feet.

3. What if you were to mark off 3 yd? What would be its length in feet?

4. Complete the table.

yd	1	2	3	4
ft	■	■	■	■

5. How many feet of special paper will Niko need?

6. You know that there are 12 inches in 1 foot. How many inches are in 2 feet?

7. Complete the table.

ft	1	2	3	4
in.	■	■	■	■

SHARING IDEAS

8. As the size of the unit decreases what happens to the number of units needed to measure the same length?

9. What patterns do you see in the two tables? How can they help you rename measures in yards as feet and measures in feet as inches?

ON YOUR OWN

10. You know that there are 4 quarts in a gallon. If you know the capacity of a container in gallons, how can you find the capacity in quarts?

11. You know there are 16 ounces in a pound. If you know the weight of an object in pounds, how can you find the weight in ounces?

Complete.

12. 5 yd = ■ ft

13. 7 ft = ■ in.

14. 3 gal = ■ qt

15. 8 qt = ■ gal

16. 10 lb = ■ oz

17. 64 oz = ■ lb

Complete the table.

18.

qt	1	2	3	4
pt	2	■	■	■

19.

pt	1	2	3	4
c	2	■	■	■

Solve.

20. How long is Niko's banner in inches?

21. Niko's printer weighs 6 lb. How many ounces does it weigh?

22. Carl's fish tank holds 10 gal of water. How many quarts does it hold?

23. *Write a problem* that involves renaming units of measure. Solve your problem. Then ask others to solve it.

Temperature

To measure temperature in customary units, use a **Fahrenheit thermometer.**

To read the temperature on a thermometer, look at the mark or number next to the top of the red column. You read the temperature in **degrees Fahrenheit (°F).**

A bowl of soup is about 120°F.

A glass of iced lemonade is about 3°F.

1. What is normal body temperature?

2. At what temperature does ice melt?

3. What is the temperature on a cold night?

The coldest day ever recorded in Florida so far was −2°F. Read this as "minus 2 degrees Fahrenheit" or "2 degrees below 0, Fahrenheit."

4. Write the temperature for minus 12 degrees Fahrenheit.

TRY OUT Write the letter of the correct answer. Choose the most reasonable temperature.

		a.	**b.**	**c.**	**d.**
5.	Arctic winter	−23°F	55°F	96°F	143°F
6.	summer day	−3°F	45°F	93°F	178°F
7.	bowl of oatmeal	16°F	32°F	76°F	98°F
8.	icicle	0°F	20°F	42°F	212°F

PRACTICE

Write the temperature in degrees Fahrenheit.

9.

10.

11.

Choose the most reasonable temperature.

12. ice-skating   **a.** ⁻42°F   **b.** 28°F   **c.** 43°F   **d.** 76°F

13. having a beach party   **a.** 13°F   **b.** 45°F   **c.** 85°F   **d.** 201°F

14. sleigh-riding   **a.** 24°F   **b.** 52°F   **c.** 73°F   **d.** 88°F

Choose the object closest to the given temperature.

15. 123°F   **a.** ice water   **b.** stew   **c.** yogurt

16. 30°F   **a.** ice cube   **b.** taco   **c.** shower

17. 75°F   **a.** igloo   **b.** oven   **c.** classroom

Mixed Applications

18. This morning the temperature was 45°F. By this afternoon the temperature was 68°F. What was the change in the temperature?

19. Paula is wearing a ski jacket. It is 83°F outside. Is Paula wearing the right clothes? Why or why not?

Mixed Review

Compare. Write >, <, or =.

20. 332 ÷ 7 ● 523

21. 3 × 60 ● 4 × 40

22. $\frac{5}{8} + \frac{3}{8}$ ● $\frac{3}{4}$

23. 650 − 250 ● 350

24. $73.23 + $22.52 ● $100.00

25. 26 in. ● 2 ft

26. perimeter of a square with 4-in. sides ● 16 in.

ACTiViTY

What Do You Measure?

The Jackson family plans to make a large bowl of lemonade to serve at the family reunion. What kinds of things do they need to know about the bowl?

What you need to know about an object determines what you should measure.

WORKING TOGETHER

1. Suppose you had a large bowl. What would you measure to find out how much lemonade it will hold?

2. **What if** you need to know if it will fit onto a small table? What would you measure?

3. **What if** you wanted to tell whether it was easier to carry the bowl or carry a stack of plates? What would you measure?

4. How could you check how cold the lemonade is?

5. Fill a large bowl with water. Estimate all of its measures. Find every measure you can.

SHARING IDEAS

6. Which of the measurements could the Jackson family estimate? Which should they actually measure? Why?

7. **Write a list** of situations where you need to measure the length, capacity, weight, or temperature of something. Tell if you can estimate or if you need to actually measure.

ON YOUR OWN

Write *capacity*, *length*, *weight*, or *temperature* to tell what should be measured in each of the following situations. Then tell what measuring tool should be used.

8. You need to know if a desk will fit through a door.

9. You want to know if the turkey is cooked enough.

10. You want to order some cheese from the deli counter.

11. You want to know how much water to add to a recipe.

Match the descriptions to the objects at the right.

12. Temperature: 32°F
Width: 6 in.
Length: 12 in.
Weight: 5 lb

13. Length: 12 in.
Width: 1 in.
Weight: 5 oz

14. Temperature: 145°F
Perimeter: 8 in.
Weight: $\frac{1}{4}$ lb

15. Temperature: 38°F
Weight: 3 lb
Capacity: 2 qt

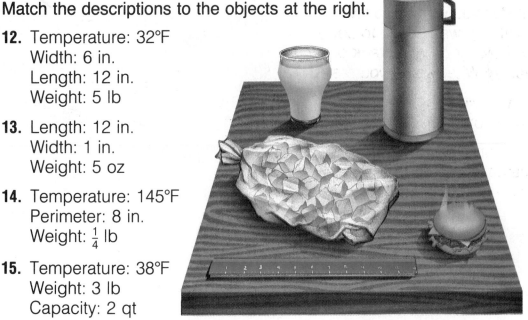

16. Find some common object in your classroom or at home. Describe it with different measurements. Then ask another student to guess the object.

DECISION MAKING

COOPERATIVE LEARNING

Problem Solving: Planning a Hiking Trip

SITUATION

Greg and Sara and their mom and dad are planning a three-day hiking trip. They will camp out for two nights.

PROBLEM

What should each hiker carry?

DATA

Campmate Family Camping Checklist

	Pounds	
sleeping bag	3	⎫
air mattress	1½	Each carry own personal gear
personal items (clothing, rain poncho, grooming kit, towel)	3½	
or { jr. back pack	3	
adult back pack	3½	⎭
cooking gear (utensils, dishes, pans, back pack stove, fuel) ..	5	⎫
trail meals for 4—		
2 dinner packs	5	
2 lunch packs	4	
2 breakfast packs	3	Who carries what?
first-aid kit	1	
survival kit (compass, map, flare, batteries, nylon cord) ...	2	Can we take all?
or { small canteen	1	
large canteen	1½	
or { high intensity lantern	2	
2 mini lights	1	⎭
tents—2-person (2)	15	⎫ Which should we take?
4-person	11½	⎭

Other gear:

field glasses	1½	⎫
bird guide book	½	
portable radio	1	can we take?
folding camp seat	1½	
camera	2	⎭

Weight we can each carry:
Dad 32 lb   Mom 25 lb   Greg 14 lb   Sara 14 lb

USING THE DATA

1. What is the weight of the personal gear that Greg and Sara will carry?

2. What is the weight of the personal gear that Mom and Dad will carry?

In addition to personal gear, how much more can each person carry?

3. Greg   4. Mom   5. Sara   6. Dad

7. How much do all the meals weigh?

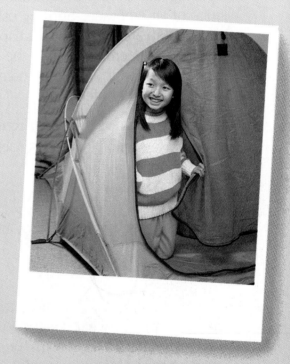

MAKING DECISIONS

8. What are the things the family should think about when planning their camping trip?

9. Who should carry the food and cooking equipment? Why? How much more can each person carry now?

10. Besides personal gear, Greg and Sara can each carry a little more. What should they choose? Who should carry each item?

11. Should the family use two 2-person tents or one 4-person tent? Why?

12. The five gallons of water that the family needs for three days weigh 40 lb. Should they carry their water or camp near the stream? Why?

13. Does the family have room to take anything else? If so, what should they take?

14. *Write a list* of things you would take on a two-day camping trip. Give reasons for your answers.

Math and Social Studies

Sailors need to know the depth of the water they are sailing in. Otherwise their boats might hit bottom.

Viking sailors used a rope with a lead weight on the end to measure depth. They let the weight hit bottom, then pulled it back up. As they pulled, they measured the length of the rope against their outstretched arms. The motion of opening and closing their arms reminded the Vikings of an embrace. So they called the length of their outstretched arms a **fathom,** the Viking word for embrace. For the Vikings, a fathom was about six feet. Today fathoms measure exactly six feet.

What if the distance to the bottom of a river is $\frac{1}{2}$ fathom? How many feet from the bottom is the boat?

Think: $\frac{1}{2}$ of 6 is 3.

The boat is 3 feet from the bottom.

ACTIVITY

1. Today we use sonar to measure depth. Find out what sonar is and how it works. How is sonar better than a rope? How is it worse?

Calculator: Finding Perimeter

A calculator can help you find the perimeter of many-sided figures.

Make a table like the one below. Examine each shape and fill in the table.

- Make an estimate of the perimeter of each shape.

- Use a calculator to find the exact perimeter of each shape.

- Check your estimated perimeter and your exact perimeter. Does your exact perimeter make sense?

Figure	Estimated Perimeter	Exact Perimeter
1		
2		
3		
4		

1.

2.

3.

4.
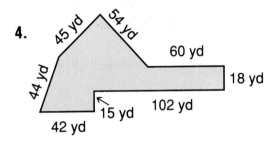

USING THE CALCULATOR

5. Did your estimates confirm your exact answers?

6. Draw and label your own many-sided figure. Have others calculate the perimeter.

EXTRA PRACTICE

Finding Sums, page 389...

Add. Write the sum in simplest form.

1. $\frac{2}{5} + \frac{2}{5}$
2. $\frac{2}{8} + \frac{3}{8}$
3. $\frac{3}{6} + \frac{1}{6}$
4. $\frac{4}{7} + \frac{1}{7}$
5. $\frac{1}{4} + \frac{2}{4}$

6. $\frac{4}{10} + \frac{2}{10}$
7. $\frac{4}{9} + \frac{3}{9}$
8. $\frac{7}{12} + \frac{2}{12}$
9. $\frac{4}{8} + \frac{2}{8}$
10. $\frac{5}{16} + \frac{5}{16}$

11. $\frac{1}{6}$
    $+ \frac{2}{6}$

12. $\frac{3}{10}$
    $+ \frac{5}{10}$

13. $\frac{3}{7}$
    $+ \frac{3}{7}$

14. $\frac{5}{12}$
    $+ \frac{3}{12}$

15. $\frac{1}{8}$
    $+ \frac{6}{8}$

16. $\frac{2}{10}$
    $+ \frac{3}{10}$

17. $\frac{5}{16}$
    $+ \frac{6}{16}$

18. $\frac{4}{8}$
    $+ \frac{3}{8}$

19. $\frac{2}{12}$
    $+ \frac{6}{12}$

20. $\frac{3}{9}$
    $+ \frac{3}{9}$

Find the missing numerator.

21. $\frac{2}{9} + \frac{\blacksquare}{9} = \frac{5}{9}$
22. $\frac{3}{8} + \frac{1}{8} = \frac{\blacksquare}{8} + \frac{3}{8}$
23. $\frac{5}{10} + \frac{2}{10} + \frac{1}{10} = \frac{2}{10} + \frac{1}{10} + \frac{\blacksquare}{10}$

Finding Greater Sums, page 391...

Add. Write the sum in simplest form.

1. $\frac{1}{7} + \frac{6}{7}$
2. $\frac{2}{4} + \frac{3}{4}$
3. $\frac{3}{5} + \frac{4}{5}$
4. $\frac{3}{6} + \frac{4}{6}$
5. $\frac{4}{5} + \frac{4}{5}$

6. $\frac{5}{8} + \frac{7}{8}$
7. $\frac{3}{9} + \frac{8}{9}$
8. $\frac{11}{12} + \frac{7}{12}$
9. $\frac{2}{3} + \frac{2}{3}$
10. $\frac{8}{10} + \frac{8}{10}$

11. $\frac{11}{12}$
    $+ \frac{1}{12}$

12. $\frac{5}{6}$
    $+ \frac{4}{6}$

13. $\frac{8}{9}$
    $+ \frac{8}{9}$

14. $\frac{6}{7}$
    $+ \frac{6}{7}$

15. $\frac{6}{8}$
    $+ \frac{7}{8}$

16. $\frac{4}{5}$
    $+ \frac{3}{5}$

17. $\frac{15}{16}$
    $+ \frac{15}{16}$

18. $\frac{6}{10}$
    $+ \frac{4}{10}$

19. $\frac{9}{12}$
    $+ \frac{9}{12}$

20. $\frac{7}{9}$
    $+ \frac{5}{9}$

Problem Solving Strategy: Using Different Strategies, page 393..............

Solve the problem. Then use a different strategy to check your answer. Tell which strategies you used.

1. Joyce is buying supplies for an art class. She buys pastels for $26.50, an easel for $57.50, oil paints for $45.85, and some charcoals for $17. Will $160 be enough to pay for these items?

2. Paco is less than 10 years old. He is half the age of his sister Sara. Sara is 3 times as old as Juan. Juan is 4 years old. How old is Paco?

Finding Differences, page 399 ....

Subtract. Write the difference in simplest form.

1. $\dfrac{3}{4} - \dfrac{1}{4}$ **2.** $\dfrac{5}{6} - \dfrac{1}{6}$ **3.** $\dfrac{6}{8} - \dfrac{5}{8}$ **4.** $\dfrac{7}{9} - \dfrac{3}{9}$ **5.** $\dfrac{4}{5} - \dfrac{3}{5}$

6. $\dfrac{8}{10} - \dfrac{6}{10}$ **7.** $\dfrac{6}{12} - \dfrac{3}{12}$ **8.** $\dfrac{4}{6} - \dfrac{1}{6}$ **9.** $\dfrac{15}{16} - \dfrac{5}{16}$ **10.** $\dfrac{3}{4} - \dfrac{3}{4}$

11. $\begin{array}{r} \frac{2}{8} \\ -\frac{1}{8} \\ \hline \end{array}$ **12.** $\begin{array}{r} \frac{5}{7} \\ -\frac{3}{7} \\ \hline \end{array}$ **13.** $\begin{array}{r} \frac{6}{10} \\ -\frac{4}{10} \\ \hline \end{array}$ **14.** $\begin{array}{r} \frac{8}{16} \\ -\frac{4}{16} \\ \hline \end{array}$ **15.** $\begin{array}{r} \frac{8}{9} \\ -\frac{6}{9} \\ \hline \end{array}$

16. $\begin{array}{r} \frac{6}{12} \\ -\frac{4}{12} \\ \hline \end{array}$ **17.** $\begin{array}{r} \frac{7}{8} \\ -\frac{3}{8} \\ \hline \end{array}$ **18.** $\begin{array}{r} \frac{9}{10} \\ -\frac{6}{10} \\ \hline \end{array}$ **19.** $\begin{array}{r} \frac{13}{16} \\ -\frac{4}{16} \\ \hline \end{array}$ **20.** $\begin{array}{r} \frac{6}{7} \\ -\frac{4}{7} \\ \hline \end{array}$

Find the missing numerator.

21. $\dfrac{4}{8} - \dfrac{\blacksquare}{8} = \dfrac{1}{8}$ **22.** $\dfrac{8}{10} - \dfrac{\blacksquare}{10} = \dfrac{3}{10}$ **23.** $\dfrac{\blacksquare}{7} - \dfrac{5}{7} = \dfrac{1}{7}$

24. $\dfrac{5}{9} - \dfrac{\blacksquare}{9} = \dfrac{2}{9}$ **25.** $\dfrac{7}{12} - \dfrac{\blacksquare}{12} = \dfrac{5}{12}$ **26.** $\dfrac{\blacksquare}{16} - \dfrac{5}{16} = \dfrac{3}{16}$

27. $\dfrac{6}{11} - \dfrac{\blacksquare}{11} = \dfrac{3}{11}$ **28.** $\dfrac{17}{19} - \dfrac{\blacksquare}{19} = \dfrac{6}{19}$ **29.** $\dfrac{3}{8} - \dfrac{\blacksquare}{8} = \dfrac{1}{8}$

EXTRA PRACTICE

Problem Solving Strategy: Solving a Simpler Problem, page 403 ....

Solve the problem. Solve a simpler problem if you need to.

1. The Day family drove 346 miles on Monday, 263 miles on Tuesday and 307 miles on Wednesday. How many miles did they drive in all?

2. Maya's little brother Ned was $35\frac{1}{4}$ inches tall last year. He is now $37\frac{3}{4}$ inches tall. How much did Ned grow?

Perimeter and Area, page 405 ....

Measure to the nearest inch. Then find the perimeter and area.

1.

2.

Find the perimeter and area.

3.

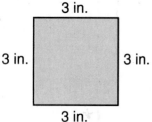

3 in. (top), 3 in. (left), 3 in. (right), 3 in. (bottom)

4.

5 ft (top), 3 ft (left), 3 ft (right), 5 ft (bottom)

5.

10 yd (top), 6 yd (left), 6 yd (right), 10 yd (bottom)

6. length = 30 ft
width = 6 ft

7. length = 18 in.
width = 7 in.

8. length = 29 yd
width = 7 yd

EXTRA PRACTICE

Capacity, page 407 ....

Choose the best estimate of capacity.

1. small bowl of soup   **a.** 1 c   **b.** 1 pt   **c.** 1 qt   **d.** 1 gal

2. can of gasoline   **a.** 1 c   **b.** 1 pt   **c.** 1 qt   **d.** 1 gal

3. large glass of milk   **a.** 1 c   **b.** 1 pt   **c.** 1 qt   **d.** 1 gal

Choose the best unit to use to measure the capacity. Write
cup, pint, quart, or *gallon.*

4. swimming pool   **5.** mixing bowl   **6.** watering can

Weight, page 409 ....

Choose the best estimate of weight.

1. dinner plate   **a.** 1 oz   **b.** 10 oz   **c.** 3 lb   **d.** 10 lb

2. stick of butter   **a.** 1 oz   **b.** 4 oz   **c.** 1 lb   **d.** 4 lb

3. muffin   **a.** 2 oz   **b.** 5 oz   **c.** 1 lb   **d.** 4 lb

Choose the object closest to the given weight.

4. 1 oz   **a.** eraser   **b.** book   **c.** blanket

5. 4 lb   **a.** bicycle   **b.** yardstick   **c.** coat

Temperature, page 413 ....

Write the temperature in degrees Fahrenheit.

1.   **2.**   **3.**

Choose the most reasonable temperature.

4. have a picnic   **a.** 25°F   **b.** 50°F   **c.** 75°F   **d.** ⁻68°F

5. build a snowman   **a.** 25°F   **b.** 50°F   **c.** 75°F   **d.** 110°F

PRACTICE PLUS

KEY SKILL: Finding Greater Sums (Use after page 391.)

Level A

Add. Write the sum in simplest form.

1. $\frac{3}{4} + \frac{1}{4}$ 2. $\frac{4}{8} + \frac{5}{8}$ 3. $\frac{6}{9} + \frac{3}{9}$ 4. $\frac{4}{6} + \frac{3}{6}$

5. $\frac{2}{3} + \frac{1}{3}$ 6. $\frac{1}{2} + \frac{1}{2}$ 7. $\frac{11}{16} + \frac{8}{16}$ 8. $\frac{6}{8} + \frac{4}{8}$

9. Gene floated $\frac{7}{8}$ mi to the dock. Then he floated $\frac{5}{8}$ mi to the island. How far did he float?

Level B

Add. Write the sum in simplest form.

10. $\frac{3}{8} + \frac{7}{8}$ 11. $\frac{4}{6} + \frac{2}{6}$ 12. $\frac{5}{7} + \frac{6}{7}$ 13. $\frac{7}{12} + \frac{11}{12}$

14. $\begin{array}{r} \frac{2}{5} \\ + \frac{4}{5} \\ \hline \end{array}$ 15. $\begin{array}{r} \frac{1}{4} \\ + \frac{3}{4} \\ \hline \end{array}$ 16. $\begin{array}{r} \frac{5}{6} \\ + \frac{3}{6} \\ \hline \end{array}$ 17. $\begin{array}{r} \frac{3}{4} \\ + \frac{3}{4} \\ \hline \end{array}$ 18. $\begin{array}{r} \frac{5}{9} \\ + \frac{5}{9} \\ \hline \end{array}$

19. Pat ran for $\frac{3}{4}$ hour. Then she walked for $\frac{3}{4}$ hour. How much time did this take in all?

Level C

Add. Write the sum in simplest form.

20. $\begin{array}{r} \frac{4}{6} \\ + \frac{5}{6} \\ \hline \end{array}$ 21. $\begin{array}{r} \frac{3}{7} \\ + \frac{6}{7} \\ \hline \end{array}$ 22. $\begin{array}{r} \frac{7}{12} \\ + \frac{7}{12} \\ \hline \end{array}$ 23. $\begin{array}{r} \frac{5}{9} \\ + \frac{4}{9} \\ \hline \end{array}$ 24. $\begin{array}{r} \frac{4}{6} \\ + \frac{3}{6} \\ \hline \end{array}$

25. $\begin{array}{r} \frac{4}{8} \\ + \frac{4}{8} \\ \hline \end{array}$ 26. $\begin{array}{r} \frac{8}{10} \\ + \frac{4}{10} \\ \hline \end{array}$ 27. $\begin{array}{r} \frac{7}{16} \\ + \frac{10}{16} \\ \hline \end{array}$ 28. $\begin{array}{r} \frac{9}{12} \\ + \frac{9}{12} \\ \hline \end{array}$ 29. $\begin{array}{r} \frac{6}{8} \\ + \frac{7}{8} \\ \hline \end{array}$

30. The handle of a small shovel is $\frac{15}{16}$ ft. long. Its blade is $\frac{7}{16}$ ft. long. How long is the entire shovel?

KEY SKILL: Finding Differences (Use after page 399.)

Level A

Subtract. Write the difference in simplest form.

1. $\frac{3}{4} - \frac{1}{4}$ **2.** $\frac{9}{10} - \frac{3}{10}$ **3.** $\frac{7}{8} - \frac{3}{8}$ **4.** $\frac{5}{6} - \frac{1}{6}$

5. $\frac{4}{5} - \frac{3}{5}$ **6.** $\frac{8}{12} - \frac{5}{12}$ **7.** $\frac{9}{10} - \frac{4}{10}$ **8.** $\frac{6}{16} - \frac{1}{16}$

9. Joan sold $\frac{3}{4}$ of a box of apples. Kate sold $\frac{1}{4}$ of a box. How much more did Joan sell?

Level B

Subtract. Write the difference in simplest form.

10. $\frac{3}{4} - \frac{2}{4}$ **11.** $\frac{6}{9} - \frac{4}{9}$ **12.** $\frac{14}{16} - \frac{8}{16}$ **13.** $\frac{11}{12} - \frac{7}{12}$

14. $\frac{9}{12} - \frac{1}{12}$ **15.** $\frac{4}{6} - \frac{2}{6}$ **16.** $\frac{5}{8} - \frac{1}{8}$ **17.** $\frac{7}{10} - \frac{3}{10}$

Find the missing numerator.

18. $\frac{4}{5} - \frac{\blacksquare}{5} = \frac{2}{5}$ **19.** $\frac{7}{12} - \frac{\blacksquare}{12} = \frac{7}{12}$ **20.** $\frac{9}{10} - \frac{\blacksquare}{10} = \frac{7}{10}$

21. Don mowed $\frac{4}{9}$ of the lawn. Tony mowed $\frac{5}{9}$ of the lawn. How much more did Tony mow?

Level C

Subtract. Write the difference in simplest form.

22. $\frac{9}{16} - \frac{1}{16}$ **23.** $\frac{6}{7} - \frac{4}{7}$ **24.** $\frac{5}{6} - \frac{2}{6}$ **25.** $\frac{7}{8} - \frac{1}{8}$ **26.** $\frac{8}{12} - \frac{4}{12}$

Find the missing numerator.

27. $\frac{6}{9} - \frac{\blacksquare}{9} = \frac{4}{9}$ **28.** $\frac{9}{12} - \frac{\blacksquare}{12} = \frac{9}{12}$ **29.** $\frac{15}{16} - \frac{\blacksquare}{16} = \frac{14}{16}$

30. Brenda spent $\frac{4}{10}$ of her time reading. She spent $\frac{2}{10}$ of her time writing. How much more of her time did she spend reading?

CHAPTER REVIEW/TEST

LANGUAGE AND MATHEMATICS

Complete the sentences. Use the words in the chart.

1. The ■ stays the same when you add fractions.

2. To measure temperature in customary units, use a ■ thermometer.

3. A ■ is a customary unit used to measure weight.

4. Four quarts equal one ■.

CONCEPTS AND SKILLS

Add or subtract. Write the answer in simplest form.

5. $\begin{array}{r} \frac{2}{3} \\ + \frac{1}{3} \\ \hline \end{array}$

6. $\frac{1}{9} + \frac{5}{9}$

7. $\begin{array}{r} \frac{3}{5} \\ + \frac{3}{5} \\ \hline \end{array}$

8. $\frac{5}{6} + \frac{5}{6}$

9. $\frac{7}{8} - \frac{3}{8}$

10. $\begin{array}{r} \frac{11}{12} \\ - \frac{5}{12} \\ \hline \end{array}$

11. $\frac{6}{7} - \frac{3}{7}$

12. $\begin{array}{r} \frac{3}{4} \\ - \frac{2}{4} \\ \hline \end{array}$

Find the perimeter and area.

13. 3 yd

14. 2 ft / 9 ft

15. 4 in. / 6 in.

Choose the best estimate of capacity or weight.

16. bottle of maple syrup   **a.** 1 c   **b.** 10 pt   **c.** 1 qt   **d.** 1 gal

17. glass of milk   **a.** 2 c   **b.** 2 pt   **c.** 2 qt   **d.** 2 gal

18. magazine   **a.** 1 oz   **b.** 10 oz   **c.** 10 lb   **d.** 100 lb

19. big dictionary   **a.** 1 oz   **b.** 3 oz   **c.** 3 lb   **d.** 30 lb

Choose the object closest to the given temperature.

20. 30°F   **a.** icicle   **b.** apple pie   **c.** cheese

21. 95°F   **a.** iced tea   **b.** hot day   **c.** hot oven

Critical Thinking

22. Give two fractions that are both less than $\frac{1}{4}$ whose sum is greater than 1.

23. Would Julie wash her car with 4 cups of water? Why?

Mixed Applications

24. A birthday cake is cut into 16 pieces. The boys eat $\frac{5}{16}$ of the cake. The girls eat $\frac{7}{16}$ of it. How much of the cake has been eaten?

25. Barb has 12 fewer plants than Judy. Judy has 8 more plants than Bob, who has twice as many as Chris. Chris has 14 plants. How many does Barb have?

PERFORMANCE ASSESSMENT

Work with your group to solve this problem.

Suppose your group orders a pizza for lunch, and it is delivered uncut. Draw a diagram that shows how your group will cut the pie into equal portions. Each person in your group should write down what fraction of the pie they eat. Write and solve an addition problem, and then a subtraction problem based on this information.

1. *Think about:*
   - what fraction of the pie each piece will be
   - how to add or subtract the fractions

2. Write a statement explaining how you determined the equal portions. Then write a paragraph explaining how you solved the problems written by your group.

CUMULATIVE REVIEW

Choose the letter of the correct answer.

1. Estimate the weight of a small frog.

   a. 8 oz   **c.** 8 lb
   b. 18 oz   **d.** 18 lb

2. Add $\frac{4}{5}$ plus $\frac{1}{5}$.

   a. 1   **c.** $1\frac{2}{5}$
   b. $1\frac{1}{5}$ **d.** not given

3. What is 52 divided by 6?

   a. 8 R3   **c.** 8 R5
   b. 8 R4   **d.** not given

4. Which polygon has 5 sides?

   a. pentagon   **c.** octagon
   b. hexagon   **d.** decagon

5. What is $\frac{7}{8} - \frac{5}{8}$ in simplest form?

   a. $\frac{2}{8}$ **c.** $\frac{1}{4}$
   b. $\frac{3}{8}$ **d.** not given

6. Name:

   M ●———————————● N

   a. $\overrightarrow{MN}$ **c.** $\overleftrightarrow{MN}$
   b. $\overline{MN}$ **d.** not given

7. Compare: $4\frac{3}{8}$ ● $\frac{35}{8}$

   a. <   **c.** =
   b. >   **d.** not given

8. What is $\frac{5}{12} + \frac{5}{12}$ in simplest form?

   a. $\frac{10}{12}$ **c.** $1\frac{5}{6}$
   b. $\frac{5}{6}$ **d.** not given

9. What is $\frac{5}{6}$ of 30?

   a. 5   **c.** 15
   b. 25   **d.** not given

10. Choose the temperature of a hot day.

    a. 32°F   **c.** 92°F
    b. 62°F   **d.** 150°F

11. What is $\frac{7}{9} + \frac{5}{9}$?

    a. $\frac{2}{9}$ **c.** $1\frac{2}{9}$
    b. $\frac{1}{3}$ **d.** not given

12. Find the area of a square with 8-ft sides.

    a. 64 sq ft   **c.** 32 sq ft
    b. 32 ft   **d.** not given

13. Find the average: 7, 8, 8, 5.

    a. 4   **c.** 28
    b. 7   **d.** not given

14. 58 ÷ 7

    a. 8   **c.** 10
    b. 8 R2   **d.** not given

TETROMINOES

Do you know what a tetromino is?
These are examples of tetrominoes.

A.

B.

These are not tetrominoes.

1. How could you describe a tetromino?

Turning a tetromino will not make a new one.
These two tetrominoes are the same.

  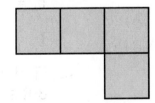

2. Is tetromino B the same as these two? Why or why not?

3. How many tetrominoes are there in all? Draw pictures to show your answer.

Suppose that each square has sides that measure 1 centimeter.

4. What is the perimeter of tetromino A? of tetromino B?

5. Find the perimeter of all the other tetrominoes. How are the squares arranged on the tetromino with the least perimeter?

THE HAWAIIAN

The Hawaiian game of chance called Lu-lu was played by young people on the beach. This was one way they relaxed after playing more active games. The name Lu-lu means to shake. The game pieces, which are shaken, are made out of volcanic stone.

Lu-lu can be played with any number of people. Each player has two throws. The four game pieces are shaken and then tossed on the ground. Only the stones that land blank side up get tossed again for a second throw. The number of dots showing on each toss are counted for the score. If all four game pieces land marked side up, the player tosses all four again and adds the scores of both the tosses together. The player with the highest score in a round wins. The game also may continue until a certain number of points is reached.

Kauai

Oahu   Molokai

Maui

PACIFIC
OCEAN

Hawaii

430

GAME LU-LU

1. Why do you think the game pieces for Lu-lu were made from volcanic stone?

2. Describe the best score you could make on a first throw. Describe the best score you could make on a second throw.

3. Describe all the different ways in which you could score 13 in two throws. Describe all the different ways in which you could score 5. Which are you more likely to score? Why?

ACTIVITY: Decimals

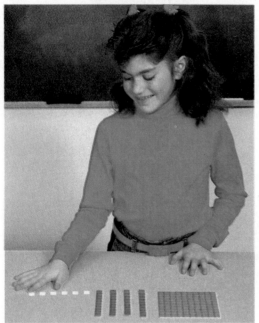

Alicia sells cartons of solar panels in her construction supply shop. Each carton has 10 panels, and each panel has 10 solar cells. Alicia records the sales in this chart.

Day	Cartons	Panels	Single Cells
Monday	0	3	0
Tuesday	0	2	5
Wednesday	1	4	6
Thursday	1	0	8
Friday	1	1	1

WORKING TOGETHER

1. Think of a carton as the number 1. What fraction of a carton is 1 panel? What fraction of a carton is 1 cell?

2. Use place-value models. Think of a hundreds square as the model for 1 carton. Model the part of a carton sold on Monday. What fraction names this part?

You can also show three tenths as a **decimal**.
3. Model the part of a carton sold on Tuesday. What fraction names the part?

Ones		Tenths
0	.	3

$\frac{3}{10}$

You can also show twenty-five hundredths as a decimal.

$\frac{25}{100}$

Ones		Tenths	Hundredths
0	.	2	5

4. Model the number of cartons sold on Wednesday. What mixed number names the amount? Complete the table to show the decimal for the amount.

Ones		Tenths	Hundredths
■	.	■	■

5. Model the number of cartons sold on Thursday. Write the mixed number for the amount. Write the decimal. Repeat for Friday.

6. How do decimal place values follow the same pattern as whole number place values?

7. What does a zero mean when it is written in a decimal?

ON YOUR OWN

8. You can use decimals with metric measures. Look at a meter stick. Think of the meter as the number 1. What part of a meter is 1 decimeter? What part of a meter is 1 centimeter?

9. Write the measure as a decimal. Show it as a number of meters.

a. 1 m 3 dm 5 cm   **b.** 3 m 2 cm   **c.** 6 m 8 dm
d. 4 dm   **e.** 7 cm   **f.** 15 dm

10. Money amounts are shown as decimals. What part of 1 dollar is 1 dime? What part of 1 dollar is 1 penny?

a. Put some dollar bills, dimes, and pennies in a bag. Take out some coins. Record the amount in a table like this. Repeat this 2 more times.
b. Take out some bills and coins. Record the amount. Repeat this 2 more times.

	Dollars	Dimes	Pennies
$	■ • ■		■
$	■ • ■		■
$	■ • ■		■
$	■ • ■		■
$	■ • ■		■
$	■ • ■		■

11. Look in almanacs for decimal numbers. Write about how the decimals are used.

ACTIVITY

Tenths and Hundredths

A. Devon used three tenths of his computer screen to draw a picture. How can you show and write the number three tenths?

WORKING TOGETHER

1. Use centimeter graph paper. Cut out a 10-cm by 10-cm square to model the whole screen. Draw lines to make 10 equal parts. What fraction of the whole is each part?

2. Color to show three tenths.

You can write three tenths as a fraction or as a decimal.

$$\text{fraction} \rightarrow \frac{3}{10} \qquad 0.3 \leftarrow \text{decimal}$$

Ones		Tenths
0	.	3

Read: three tenths

3. **What if** Devon used 35 hundredths of his screen? Make a model to show this.

You can write 35 hundredths as a fraction or as a decimal.

$$\text{fraction} \rightarrow \frac{35}{100} \qquad 0.35 \leftarrow \text{decimal}$$

Ones		Tenths	Hundredths
0	.	3	5

Read: thirty-five hundredths

B. You can write fractions greater than 1 as a mixed number or as a decimal.

Make a model of each of these numbers.

4. $1\frac{6}{10}$ 1.6   one and six tenths

5. $1\frac{15}{100}$ 1.15   one and fifteen hundredths

C. You can write equivalent decimals for the same number.

6. Make a model of each of these numbers: $1\frac{4}{10}$ and $1\frac{40}{100}$. Write the decimal for each number. What do you notice?

7. Model the number 2. Complete this sentence: $2 = \frac{\blacksquare}{10} = \frac{\blacksquare}{100}$ Show two decimals for the number 2.

8. How are fractions and decimals the same? How are they different?

9. Are the decimals 1.7 and 1.07 equivalent? Why or why not?

10. Are the decimals 0.4 and 0.40 equivalent? Why or why not?

PRACTICE

Write the decimal for the part that is shaded.

11.   12.   13.   14.

Write the decimal.

15. $\frac{5}{10}$ 16. $\frac{64}{100}$ 17. $\frac{7}{100}$ 18. $\frac{45}{100}$ 19. $\frac{50}{100}$ 20. $\frac{25}{100}$

21. $\frac{16}{10}$ 22. $8\frac{2}{100}$ 23. $15\frac{7}{10}$ 24. $25\frac{25}{100}$ 25. $100\frac{1}{10}$ 26. $33\frac{3}{100}$

27. thirteen hundredths   28. two and four tenths

29. one tenth   30. sixteen and three hundredths

Write the word name.

31. 0.5   32. 0.09   33. 13.5   34. 0.60   35. 8.03

Tell whether the decimals are equivalent. Write *yes* or *no*.

36. 2.3 and 2.03   37. 2.30 and 2.3   38. 0.20 and 2.00

39. 15.40 and 15.04   40. 15.00 and 15.0   41. 15.4 and 15.40

Mixed Applications

42. Devon prints a report that uses 3 pages and 4 tenths of a page. What decimal shows how many pages he uses?

43. Joni wants to buy software that costs $79.95. She has saved $55.00. How much more money does she need?

44. Kay needs 100 copies of a school newsletter. She prints 45 copies. What decimal shows the part that she has printed?

Comparing and Ordering Decimals

A. Carla uses a pedometer to measure how far she runs. Carla ran 1.8 km this morning and 1.6 km this afternoon. When did she run the greater distance?

You can use a number line to compare 1.8 and 1.6.

| 1.0 | 1.1 | 1.2 | 1.3 | 1.4 | 1.5 | 1.6 | 1.7 | 1.8 | 1.9 | 2.0 |

Think: 1.6 comes **before** 1.8.
 1.6 is **less than** 1.8.

Think: 1.8 comes **after** 1.6.
 1.8 is **greater than** 1.6.

Write: 1.6 < 1.8

Write: 1.8 > 1.6

Carla ran the greater distance this morning.

B. You can also compare decimals digit by digit.

Step 1	Step 2	Step 3
Line up the decimal points.	Begin at the left. Compare to find the first place where the digits are different.	Compare the digits.
1 . 8 **1 . 6**	**1 . 8** **1 . 6**	**8 > 6 or 6 < 8** ***Think:*** 0.8 > 0.6; 0.6 < 0.8

So 1.8 > 1.6 or 1.6 < 1.8

1. How is comparing decimals like comparing whole numbers?

C. You can compare 0.73, 2.78, and 2.76 to order them.

Step 1	Step 2	Step 3
Line up the decimal points.	Compare the other decimals.	Order the decimals.
0.73 **2.78** **2.76** The number without ones is the least.	2.78 2.76 ***Think:*** 0.06 < 0.08 So 2.76 < 2.78.	From least to greatest: 0.73, 2.76, 2.78 From greatest to least: 2.78, 2.76, 0.73

TRY OUT

Compare. Use >, <, or =.

2. 0.4 ● 0.40   **3.** 2.34 ● 2.23

Write in order from greatest to least.

4. 8.81, 18.18, 18.8   **5.** 1.4, 1.1, 1.7

PRACTICE

Compare. Write >, <, or =.

6. 0.6 ● 0.60   **7.** 2.4 ● 2.5   **8.** 0.51 ● 0.52   **9.** 2.6 ● 1.8

10. 1.7 ● 1.9   **11.** 0.75 ● 0.74   **12.** 4.26 ● 4.62   **13.** 3.52 ● 3.25

14. 6.78 ● 6.87   **15.** 9.27 ● 9.27   **16.** 10.10 ● 10.01   **17.** 9.09 ● 9.90

Write in order from greatest to least.

18. 0.25, 0.52, 0.50   **19.** 1.3, 1.4, 1.1   **20.** 0.88, 0.08, 0.80

Write in order from least to greatest.

21. 1.1, 0.7, 1.6   **22.** 3.61, 3.15, 3.09   **23.** 0.99, 1.09, 0.09

Mixed Applications

Solve. You may need to use the Databank on page 522.

24. What was the fastest time in the men's 100-meter freestyle? In what year was the race?

25. In which year was the women's 100-meter freestyle completed in a shorter time, 1980 or 1988?

CALCULATOR

You can compare fractions by changing them to decimals.

$\frac{3}{4}$ = ③ ÷ ④ = 0.75 $\frac{4}{5}$ = ④ ÷ ⑤ = 0.8

0.75 < 0.8, so $\frac{3}{4} < \frac{4}{5}$

Compare. Write >, <, or =. Use a calculator to change fractions to decimals.

1. $\frac{2}{5}$ ● $\frac{12}{25}$ **2.** $\frac{16}{20}$ ● $\frac{4}{5}$ **3.** $\frac{18}{50}$ ● $\frac{7}{20}$ **4.** $\frac{15}{20}$ ● $\frac{19}{25}$

PROBLEM SOLVING

Strategy: Making an Organized List

Eve is playing the electronic game Colorumber. The game uses the colors red, yellow, and green and the numbers 1 and 2. She must choose one color and one number. In how many different ways can she choose a color and a number?

Eve plans to use a tree diagram to help her make an organized list of the color-number pairs.

If Eve chooses the color red, she can make two color-number pairs: red-1 and red-2.

1. If Eve chooses yellow, what color-number pairs can she make?

2. Make a tree diagram for the third color. What color-number pairs can she make?

3. In how many different ways can she choose a color and a number?

Tree Diagram   **List**

red ⟨ 1 _____ red-1
2 _____ red-2

yellow ⟨ 1 _____ ■
2 _____ ■

green ⟨ ■ _____ ■
■ _____ ■

4. **What if** the game had a third number to choose from? In how many different ways could Eve choose a color and a number? Make a tree diagram and an organized list of all color-number combinations.

5. When is it useful to make a tree diagram and an organized list to solve a problem?

PRACTICE

Use a tree diagram to
make an organized list.
Then solve the problem.

6. When Lola works at Electro City,
she wears a skirt and a blouse.
She has 3 skirts and 4 blouses.
How many different outfits can
she wear?

7. Rob plans to watch TV at 8:00
and listen to music at 9:00. He
will watch channel 2, 5, or 13 and
then listen to a symphony or a
concerto. How many different
choices does Rob have?

8. At the Computer Corner each
computer desk comes in a choice
of oak or cherry wood. The desk
can come with a shelf that pulls
out or with one that does not
move. How many kinds of desks
does the store have?

9. Maria is ordering pizza for the
people at the video store. She
can order thin crust or thick crust
and choose one topping from
mushroom, pepper, zucchini, or
tuna. What are the different kinds
of pizza that Maria can order?

Strategies and Skills Review

Solve. Use mental math, a calculator, or paper and pencil.

10. Greg is setting the timer on his VCR to go on at 2:55 P.M.
What other information do you need in order to find
how long the tape will be running?

11. Beth is going to watch one comedy and then one news
show. There are comedies on channels 2, 5, and 9. There
are news shows on channels 2, 5, 7, and 9. In how many
different ways can Beth choose which shows to watch?

12. Di's calculator has 4 rows of keys with 6 keys in each row.
There are 10 digit keys. How many keys are not digit keys?

13. *Write a problem* that can be solved by making an organized
list. Solve the problem. Ask others to solve your problem.

ACTIVITY
Adding and Subtracting Decimals

You can use place-value models to explore
adding and subtracting decimals.

WORKING TOGETHER

Make two sets of cards with the
digits 0 to 9. Shuffle the cards and
place them facedown in a pile.

Step 1 Pick four cards. Use the
digits to make an addition sentence,
such as 0.7 + 2.3.

$$\boxed{0}.\boxed{7} + \boxed{2}.\boxed{3}$$

Step 2 Use place-value models to
make a model of each decimal.

Step 3 Find the sum and record it.
Repeat this activity three more times.

0.7	+	2.3	=	■

Step 4 Now pick six cards and make
a sentence, such as 1.79 + 2.63.
Use your place-value models to
find the sum. Record it. Repeat
this activity three more times.

1. Use your models to find the sum.

   a. 2.5 + 1.8   **b.** 1.8 + 2.5   **c.** 3.45 + 0

   d. 1.3 + 2.5 + 0.9   **e.** 2.5 + 0.9 + 1.3

2. Repeat Steps 1 to 4 for subtraction sentences,
   such as 3.5 − 1.7. Record your results.

$$\boxed{3}.\boxed{5} - \boxed{1}.\boxed{7}$$

3. Use your models to find the difference.

   a. 3.7 − 3.7   **b.** 1.25 − 0

3.5	−	1.7	=	■

SHARING IDEAS

4. How is regrouping in addition of decimals like regrouping in addition of whole numbers?

5. How is regrouping in subtraction of decimals like regrouping in subtraction of whole numbers?

6. Do you think the properties of addition and subtraction apply to decimals? Give examples.

7. Do you think the relationship between addition and subtraction applies to decimals? Give an example.

ON YOUR OWN

Solve. Use place-value models if needed.

8. A new portable VCR has a mass of only 2.81 kg. A small TV set has a mass of 1.67 kg. What is the mass of both of these items together?

9. Jan's computer screen measures 3.15 dm long. Her TV screen measures 4.74 dm long. How much longer is her TV screen?

10. Sal ordered 3 tapes priced at $5.95, $6.99, and $9.89. How much will the tapes cost in all?

11. ***Write a problem*** involving addition or subtraction of decimals. Solve your problem. Ask others to solve it.

Estimating Decimal Sums and Differences

A. Dionne rode the bicycle her father invented 4.57 km from home to the library, 6.69 km from the library to the park, and 2.8 km from the park to home. About how far did she ride all together?

Here are two ways to estimate to solve the problem.

Estimate: 4.57 + 6.69 + 2.8

Rounding	Front-End Estimation	
Round to the nearest whole number.	**Add the front digits.**	**Then adjust the estimate.**

Rounding:

$$4.57 \longrightarrow 5$$
$$6.69 \longrightarrow 7$$
$$+ 2.8 \longrightarrow \underline{+\ 3}$$
$$15$$

Front-End Estimation — Add the front digits:

$$4.57$$
$$6.69$$
$$\underline{+\ 2.8}$$
$$12$$

Then adjust the estimate:

$$\left. \begin{array}{r} 4.57 \\ 6.69 \end{array} \right\} \text{\textit{Think:} about 1}$$
$$\underline{+\ 2.8} \ \} \text{ about 1}$$
$$14$$

Dionne rode about 14 or 15 km.

1. How will the exact answer compare with the estimate found by rounding?

2. How will the exact answer compare with the front-end estimate?

B. You can use two methods to estimate differences.

Rounding	Front-End Estimation	
Round to the nearest whole number.	**Subtract the front digits.**	**Then adjust the estimate.**

Rounding:

$$7.64 \longrightarrow 8$$
$$- 3.7 \longrightarrow \underline{-\ 4}$$
$$4$$

Front-End Estimation — Subtract the front digits:

$$7.64$$
$$\underline{-\ 3.7}$$
$$4$$

Then adjust the estimate:

$$7.64$$
$$\underline{-\ 3.7}$$
less than 4

\textit{Think:} 6 < 7
The exact answer is less than 4.

3. Will the exact answer be greater than or less than the estimate found by rounding? How can you tell?

4. How would you estimate 5.4 − 3.28 using front-end estimation with adjusting? What is your estimate?

TRY OUT

Estimate by rounding to the nearest whole number.

5. 3.4 + 7.58 + 2.91

6. 4.39 − 2.2

Estimate. Use the front digits and adjust.

7. 5.67 + 1.35 + 4.43

8. 5.83 − 2.9

PRACTICE

Estimate by rounding to the nearest whole number.

9. 3.7	**10.** 6.35	**11.** 3.37	**12.** 6.19	**13.** 3.75
4.3	− 1.92	6.49	− 2.9	4.13
+ 2.5		+ 1.8		+ 6.7

14. 5.39 − 2.85   **15.** 8.4 − 3.97   **16.** 6.52 − 3.7

17. 3.7 + 2.14 + 7.3   **18.** 6.2 + 1.35 + 4.9   **19.** 3 − 2.86

Estimate. Use the front digits and adjust.

20. 3.45	**21.** 3.56	**22.** 8.16	**23.** 3.37	**24.** 6.59
1.98	− 1.5	2.3	2.67	3.6
+ 4.2		+ 1.27	+ 4	+ 2.98

25. 7.74 − 2.47   **26.** 6.4 − 2.85   **27.** 8.13 − 4.2

28. 3.17 + 3.9 + 4.1   **29.** 4.75 − 1.5   **30.** 2.9 + 3.01 + 5.16

Mixed Applications

31. Ali rides his bike 2.8 km each way to and from work. About how far does he ride in all?

32. Blank tapes cost $5.29 each. Sandy bought 4 of them. About how much did all of them cost?

Mixed Review

Find the answer. Which method did you use?

33. $35.87	**34.** 390	**35.** 7)490	**36.** 354
+ 76.95	− 240		× 8

MENTAL MATH
CALCULATOR
PAPER/PENCIL

Adding Decimals

A. Tara wants to buy a desk for her computer. The desk must be as wide as the combined width of the tables she uses now. Tara's computer table is 1.5 m wide. Her printer table is 0.65 m wide. What is the combined width of the two tables?

Estimate first. Then find the exact answer.

Tara used place-value models to find the sum.

Add: 1.5 + 0.65

1. What is the combined width of the tables?

2. How did Tara combine the models to find the sum?

3. When did Tara have to regroup? Why?

B. You can add using paper and pencil.

Step 1	Step 2	Step 3
Line up the decimal points. Write an equivalent decimal if necessary.	Add the hundredths. Add the tenths. Regroup if necessary.	Add the ones. Regroup if necessary. Write the decimal point.
$\begin{array}{r} \mathbf{1.50} \\ \mathbf{+\ 0.65} \\ \hline \end{array}$ *Think:* 1.5 = 1.50	$\begin{array}{r} 1 \\ \mathbf{1.50} \\ \mathbf{+\ 0.65} \\ \hline 15 \end{array}$	$\begin{array}{r} 1 \\ \mathbf{1.50} \\ \mathbf{+\ 0.65} \\ \hline \mathbf{2.15} \end{array}$

4. Is the answer reasonable? How do you know?

5. How is using models to find the sum the same as using paper and pencil? How is it different?

6. How is adding decimals similar to adding whole numbers? How is it different?

PRACTICE

Find the sum.

7. 6.4 + 3.2	**8.** 3.45 + 2.31	**9.** 5.17 + 2.81	**10.** 5.4 + 3.7	**11.** 6.23 + 1.82
12. 3.4 + 2.45	**13.** 7.16 + 3.8	**14.** 1.43 + 2.75	**15.** 3.9 + 1.25	**16.** 6.27 + 2.8
17. 3.1 4.7 + 2.4	**18.** 3.25 1.6 + 4.81	**19.** 1.36 2.05 + 0.92	**20.** 8.5 1.36 + 3.54	**21.** 2.9 3.2 + 5.88

22. 5.3 + 2.83 **23.** 7.50 + 2.25 **24.** 6.8 + 4.29 **25.** 3.14 + 2.99 + 0.7

26. 6.33 + 3.9 **27.** 8.9 + 4.07 **28.** 7.85 + 4.11 **29.** 2.73 + 4.3 + 5.4

Critical Thinking

30. Tara writes 20 + 4 + 0.7 + 0.08. What decimal is this? How do you know?

Mixed Applications Solve. Which method did you use?

**ESTIMATION
MENTAL MATH
CALCULATOR
PAPER/PENCIL**

31. Tara made a chart by taping together 2 sheets of paper. Each sheet was 21.6 cm wide. How wide was her chart?

32. Tara bought office supplies for $8.45. She gave the clerk $10.00. What was Tara's change?

33. Tara's study is 3.8 m long and 2.6 m wide. Is the perimeter of the room more than 10 m?

34. *Write a problem* that can be solved by adding decimals. Give it to another student to solve.

Subtracting Decimals

A. The swim team coach uses a stopwatch to time Zach, Ty, and Angel in a race. Zach is the winner. He is 0.45 seconds faster than Angel and 1.6 seconds faster than Ty. How much faster than Ty is Angel?

Estimate first. Then find the exact answer.

Angel used place-value models to find the difference.

Subtract: 1.6 − 0.45

1. How much faster than Ty is Angel?

2. How does Angel use the models to find the difference? Does he regroup? Why?

B. You can use paper and pencil to subtract.

Step 1	Step 2	Step 3	Step 4
Line up the decimal points. Write an equivalent decimal if necessary.	Regroup if necessary. Subtract the hundredths.	Regroup if necessary. Subtract the tenths.	Subtract the ones. Write the decimal point.
1.60 − 0.45	5 10 1.6 0 − 0.4 5 5	5 10 1.6 0 − 0.4 5 1 5	5 10 1.6 0 − 0.4 5 1.1 5

Think: 1.6 = 1.60

3. Is the answer reasonable? How do you know?

4. How would you subtract 9.68 − 2.9? What is the difference?

5. How is using models to find the difference the same as using paper and pencil? How is it different?

6. How is subtracting decimals similar to subtracting whole numbers?

PRACTICE

Find the difference.

7. 0.9
   − 0.3

8. 6.7
   − 2.4

9. 8
   − 4.7

10. 7.1
    − 2.1

11. 5.3
    − 4.6

12. 6.75
    − 1.29

13. 7.13
    − 2.11

14. 8.3
    − 1.45

15. 9.11
    − 7.04

16. 3.06
    − 2.78

17. 7.8 − 5.4   18. 3.7 − 1.9   19. 5.75 − 1.63   20. 8.03 − 7.47

21. 7.04 − 6.3   22. 6.2 − 5.43   23. 7 − 2.51   24. 3 − 1.09

Mixed Applications

Solve. You may need to use the Databank on page 522.

25. In June, Roma could swim to the float in 45.3 seconds. By the end of August it took her 26.8 seconds. How much faster was her time in August?

26. How much faster was the women's winning time in the 100-meter freestyle race in 1988 than in 1984?

27. **Write a problem** comparing two winning times in the freestyle races. Have others solve your problem.

Mixed Review

Find the answer. Which method did you use?

28.   340
    + 510

29. $10.06
    −   9.68

30.   105
    ×   3

31. 8)702

MENTAL MATH
CALCULATOR
PAPER/PENCIL

ALL THE RIGHT MOVES

Logical Reasoning

A. Here is a puzzle for you to solve. First, get three slips of paper. Label them A, B, and C. Then make a stack of coins that has a quarter on the bottom, a nickel in the middle, and a penny on top. Place the stack of coins on paper slip A. Now try to move the stack to C. Follow these rules:

- You can move only one coin at a time.
- You can place coins on slip B.
- You cannot place a larger coin on a smaller coin.

1. Try the puzzle a few times. Write down the total number of moves you use each time. What was your least number of moves?

The shortest solution for this puzzle is 7 moves. These pictures show how it is done. Notice the way the moves are recorded.

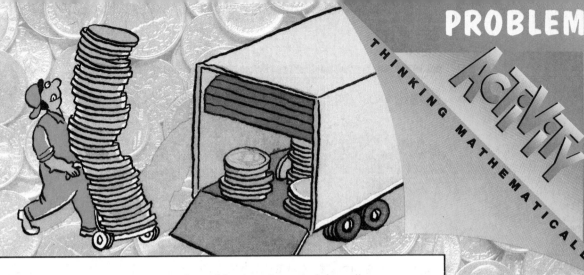

2. Now try the same puzzle with 4 coins. Add a dime to the top of the beginning stack on slip A; the dime now becomes the smallest coin in the stack. How many moves will it take? Record your moves in the manner shown on page 448.

B. When you play with 4 coins, the shortest solution takes 15 moves. If you needed more, try the puzzle again. This table shows the number of moves for the shortest solutions depending on how many coins are used.

Number of Coins	Number of Moves (Shortest Solution)	Pattern
3	7	$(2 \times 2 \times 2) - 1$
4	15	$(2 \times 2 \times 2 \times 2) - 1$
5		
6		

This table shows how the number of coins is related to the number of moves in the shortest solution. Can you find the pattern?

3. Look at the 3-coin puzzle in the table. How many times is 2 used as a factor in the last column? Now look at the 4-coin puzzle. How many times is 2 used as a factor in the last column?

4. What pattern do you see? What do you think the shortest solutions for 5 and 6 coins would be? Copy and complete the chart, following the pattern. Use a calculator to help you.

PROBLEM SOLVING

Strategy: Conducting an Experiment

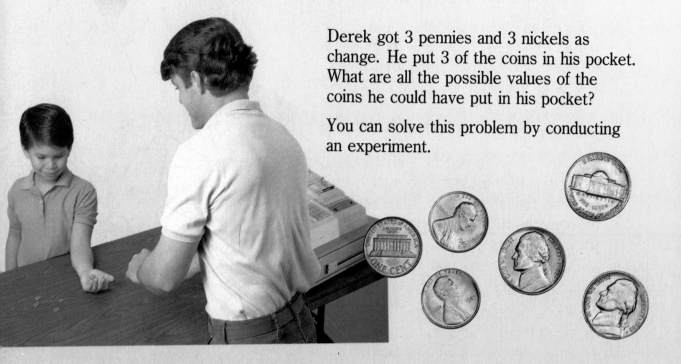

Derek got 3 pennies and 3 nickels as change. He put 3 of the coins in his pocket. What are all the possible values of the coins he could have put in his pocket?

You can solve this problem by conducting an experiment.

Plan your strategy.

Experiment with coins to find all of the possible values.

Try your plan.

Start with 3 pennies. Record their total value. Replace one of the pennies with a nickel. Then record the total value of this new group of coins. Repeat these steps until you have made all the possible combinations of 3 coins.

1. What are all the possible values of coins Derek could have put in his pocket?

2. Why is it better to start with 3 of the same type of coin rather than any 3 coins?

3. What other strategy could you have used to solve the problem?

PRACTICE

Do an experiment to solve the problem.

4. Louise has 1 nickel, 1 dime, and 1 quarter. She puts 2 coins in the jukebox. What are all the possible values of the coins she used?

5. Ollie has a record, a CD, and a cassette in a bag. He pulls 2 items out of the bag. How many different pairs of items could he have pulled out?

6. Rich just bought 4 CDs. One CD is dance music, 1 CD is rock, another is classical, and the last is folk. He shows Zelda 3 of the CDs. How many different sets of CDs could he show her?

7. Lee won the "guess the song" game. She can choose 1 CD from each of 2 groups. Each group has 3 different CDs. How many different pairs of CDs can she choose?

Strategies and Skills Review

Solve. Use mental math, a calculator, or paper and pencil.

8. Janet had $12.70. She spent $6.98 on a tape. Then her father gave her $9.00 for her birthday. How much does Janet have now?

9. Ned has 2 dimes and 3 pennies in his pocket. He pulls out 3 coins. What are all the possible values of these coins?

10. Zeke has 23 albums to put in boxes. Each box holds 6 albums. How many boxes will Zeke need?

11. *Write a problem* that can be solved by doing an experiment. Ask others to solve it.

ACTIVITY Probability

If you were to spin this spinner, what is the likelihood it would stop on blue? **Probability** is the likelihood that something will happen.

WORKING TOGETHER

You can use the spinner to do an experiment to explore probability.

1. How many colors are on the spinner? These are the **possible outcomes.**

2. How many parts of the spinner are blue? This is the **favorable outcome.**

3. Complete: The probability of the spinner stopping on blue is ■ chance out of ■.

4. Is each possible outcome equally likely? Why?

You can write the probability as a fraction.

$$\text{Probability} = \frac{\text{favorable outcomes}}{\text{possible outcomes}}$$

Write the probability as a fraction.

5. spinning blue 6. spinning red 7. spinning green 8. spinning yellow

9. Make a chart like the one to the right. Spin the 4-color spinner 20 times. Use tally marks to record how many times it stops on each color.

Red	
Green	
Blue	
Yellow	

10. How many colors are on the spinner to the right? What part of the spinner is each color? Are all of the outcomes equally likely? Why or why not?

11. What is the probability of spinning blue? spinning green? spinning red?

12. Spin the spinner 20 times. Use tally marks to record how many times it stops on each color.

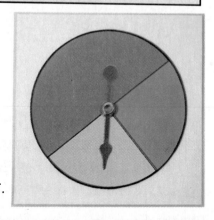

13. Compare the outcomes from each experiment to the probabilities. Are the results close to what you expected?

14. How do you know whether the outcomes of a probability experiment are equally likely?

15. If you spin the spinner you used in the first experiment, what is the probability of it stopping on one of the four colors? Why?

16. What is the probability of spinning orange? Why?

PRACTICE

Use a number cube numbered from 1 to 6. Find the probability of tossing:

17. 1.   **18.** 5.   **19.** 8.   **20.** 1 to 6.

21. Are the possible outcomes equally likely?

Find the probability of picking the color from the bag to the right.

22. yellow   **23.** red   **24.** blue

25. Are the outcomes equally likely?

Critical Thinking

26. Ken spins the 4-color spinner. What is the probability of the spinner landing on blue or green? How do you know?

Mixed Applications

27. Lex has a penny, a nickel, and 3 dimes in his pocket. Which type of coin is he most likely to pull out of his pocket?

28. There are 2 white shirts and 1 red shirt in Ken's closet. What fraction of the shirts are white?

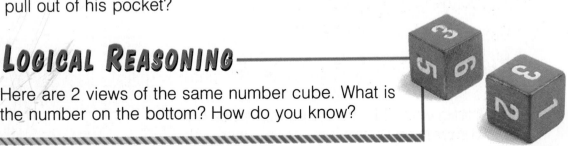

LOGICAL REASONING

Here are 2 views of the same number cube. What is the number on the bottom? How do you know?

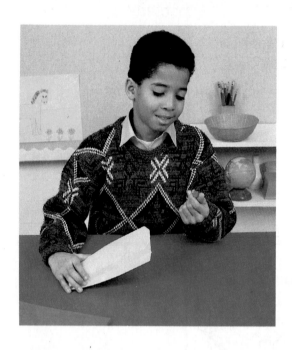

Yaseff puts 3 red cubes, 2 blue cubes, and 1 yellow cube in a bag. He picks a cube from the bag without looking, then returns it. If he does this 24 times, about how many times will he pick each color?

You can use probability to predict about how many times something will happen.

1. What is the probability of his picking a red cube? a blue cube? a yellow cube?

2. How many times do you think he will pick each color?

WORKING TOGETHER

You can do an experiment to test your prediction.

Step 1 Put 3 red cubes, 2 blue cubes, and 1 yellow cube in a bag.

Step 2 Without looking, pick a cube from the bag. Record the outcome in a tally chart.

Step 3 Put the cube back in the bag. Shake it, then pick again. Do this 24 times.

Red	
Blue	
Yellow	

3. How many times did you pick a red cube? a blue cube? a yellow cube?

4. How do the outcomes compare to your predictions?

5. Suppose someone puts 6 cubes in a bag. You know that there are 3 of one color, 2 of another color, and 1 of a third color. This chart shows the outcomes of 24 picks. How can you predict what is in the bag without looking? Try your method.

Red	///
Blue	𝓣𝓗𝓛 𝓣𝓗𝓛 //
Yellow	𝓣𝓗𝓛 ////

SHARING IDEAS

6. What is $\frac{1}{2}$ of 24? $\frac{1}{3}$ of 24? $\frac{1}{6}$ of 24? How do these numbers compare with the results of your first experiment?

7. Tell how you can use probability to predict outcomes.

PRACTICE

Look at the bag of colored cubes to the right. Find the probability of picking the color. Predict how many times you will pick it in 40 tries.

8. yellow

9. red

10. blue

11. green

Find the probability of spinning the number. Predict how many times you will spin it in 30 tries.

12. 2

13. 8

14. one number 0 to 9

15. Marc puts 8 cubes in a bag. He puts in blue, red, and green cubes. There are 4 of one color, 3 of another color, and 1 of the third color. He picks cubes from the bag 40 times and graphs the outcomes. How many of each color are in the bag?

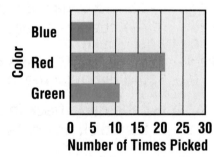

Mixed Review

Find the missing number.

16. $27 \div \blacksquare = 9$

17. A square's area is 16 sq. ft. Length of 1 side = $\blacksquare$

18. $\blacksquare + 237 = 638$

19. $\frac{3}{4} - \blacksquare = \frac{1}{2}$

20. $9)\overline{1,798}$

21. $2 \times \blacksquare = 860$

22. $3 \times \$1.27 = \blacksquare$

23. $312 + (192 - 44) = (192 + \blacksquare) - 44$

24. $3 + 1\frac{2}{3} = \blacksquare$

25. $\frac{4}{\blacksquare} = \frac{16}{36}$

Independent Events

Peggy has 2 bags. She puts 1 red cube and 1 blue cube in each bag. What is the probability of Peggy picking a blue cube from each bag?

The color of the cube Peggy picks from the second bag does not depend on the color of the cube she picks from the first bag. The two events are **independent** of each other.

WORKING TOGETHER

You can do an experiment to find the probability.

Step 1 Take 2 bags. Place 1 red cube and 1 blue cube in each bag.

Step 2 Pick 1 cube from each bag. Record each outcome in a table to make an organized list. Use tally marks to record how many times each outcome occurs.

Step 3 Place the cubes back in their bags. Shake the bags and pick again. Do this 40 times.

1st Bag	2nd Bag	Tally
Red	Blue	/

1. Look at your table. What are all of the possible outcomes?

2. What is the probability of picking a blue cube from both bags? How do you know?

3. How many times did you pick 2 blue cubes? Is this close to what you would have predicted based on the probability?

4. What are the probabilities of the other outcomes? How many times did each occur?

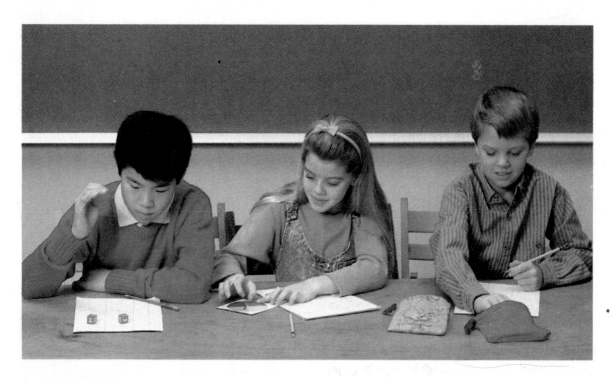

SHARING IDEAS

5. Look at your organized list of possible outcomes. Can you think of another way of finding what the possible outcomes are?

6. Are the possible outcomes of the experiment equally likely? How do you know?

ON YOUR OWN

7. What if you placed a yellow cube in each bag with the red and blue cubes? What are the possible outcomes if you still pick only 1 cube from each bag? What is the probability of each outcome?

8. Predict how many times 1 of the outcomes will occur if you pick 36 times. Then do the experiment to test your prediction.

9. *Make up* your own probability experiment with independent events. Find all of the possible outcomes and their probabilities. Predict how many times 1 of the outcomes will occur if you pick 40 times. Then do the experiment to test your prediction.

DECISION MAKING

Problem Solving: Choosing the Right Gift

SITUATION

Jamal has $20.00 to buy a birthday present for his sister, Miriam. Jamal goes to Murray's Musicland to buy the present.

PROBLEM

Should Jamal buy a record, a cassette, or a CD for Miriam?

DATA

CONSUMER NEWS

Records, Tapes, CD's–What's the Difference?

RECORDS
- Sound quality varies with sound system
- Easy to scratch or break
- Harder to clean
- Wear out more quickly than tapes
- Must turn over to hear whole record
- Cannot be played on a portable player
- Take up a lot of storage space

TAPES
- Sound quality varies with sound system
- Can be erased by contact with magnet
- Do not need cleaning
- Will wear out with use
- Must turn over to hear whole tape
- Can be played on a portable player
- Easy to store

CD'S
- Highest sound quality
- Very hard to damage
- Easy to clean Do not wear out
- No need to turn over to hear whole CD
- Can be played on a portable player
- Easiest to store

Miriam's favorite artists	CD (prices for new releases)	Record	Cassette
Jam Master Z	$13.99	$8.99	$8.99
Rap King Rapp	13.99	8.99	8.99
Winona	13.99	8.99	8.99
Johnny Morgan's X-rays	13.99	8.99	8.99

Record, cassette, or CD? Old or new release?

USING THE DATA

1. How much would two CD's cost?

2. How much would two records or two cassettes cost?

3. How much would three records or cassettes cost?

4. How much would one CD and one record or cassette cost?

MAKING DECISIONS

5. Cassettes and records are less expensive than CD's. Will Jamal really get more for his money buying the cheaper item? What other factors should he consider in making his decision?

6. Miriam has Winona's new release, but not her first album. The first album is on sale for $5.99. How might that affect Jamal's decision?

7. ***What if*** Miriam has a cassette deck and turntable in her room, but the CD player is in the living room? How might it affect Jamal's decision?

8. There is a poster inside Rap King Rapp's new record, but not inside the cassette or CD. The CD has two songs that are not on the record or cassette. Which should Jamal buy?

9. ***What if*** Jamal knows that his parents are buying Miriam a portable CD player for her birthday? How would that help him to make up his mind?

10. Which format do you think Jamal should buy? Why?

11. If you were buying music for yourself, would you buy a record, a tape, or a CD? Why?

Math and Science

Electricity is the power that runs most household appliances. The amount of electricity that an appliance uses is measured in units called **kilowatt-hours.** A kilowatt-hour is the amount of electric energy needed to light ten 100-watt light bulbs for one hour.

Different appliances need different amounts of electricity to run properly. The table shows some common appliances and the amount of electricity they use in one hour.

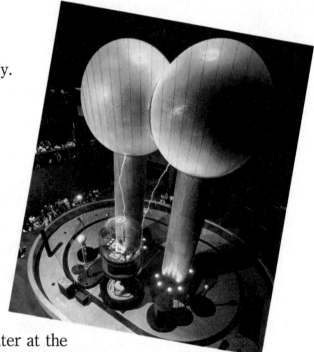

Appliance	Kilowatt Usage
Stereo	0.1
Washing machine	0.25
Computer	0.08
Television	0.2
VCR	0.07
Dishwasher	1.0

What if you ran a stereo and computer at the same time? Would you use more electricity than if you used a television and VCR at the same time?

Think: Stereo and computer–0.1 + 0.08 = 0.18
Television and VCR–0.2 + 0.07 = 0.27
0.18 < 0.27

The stereo and computer would use less electricity than the television and VCR.

ACTIVITIES

1. Find out about one of the scientists who contributed to the development of electricity. Share your information with the class.

2. Many forms of energy use up limited natural resources. List some ways of saving energy, such as turning off lights when they are not in use.

Computer Simulation: Probability

Put 3 red marbles and 3 blue marbles in a bag. Without looking, reach into the bag and pick a marble. Then return it to the bag. **What if** you picked and returned marbles 100 times? Predict how many of each color marble you would pick.

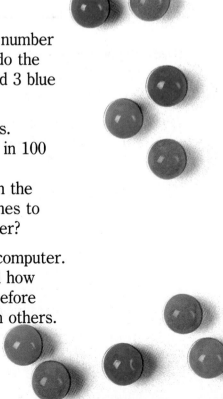

To test your prediction, you can use a computer to re-create, or **simulate**, the experiment. Just enter the number of red and blue marbles in the bag and the number of times you will pick a marble.

AT THE COMPUTER

Run the computer simulation program called MARBLES.

1. Enter 3 red and 3 blue marbles. Enter 100 for the number of trials. How do the outcomes compare with your prediction?

2. Repeat the simulation in Question 1 four more times. What do you notice about the outcomes?

3. Enter 4 red and 2 blue marbles. Enter 100 for the number of trials. Run this new simulation five times. How do the outcomes compare with the simulation for 3 red and 3 blue marbles?

4. Run a new simulation with 1 red and 5 blue marbles. Predict how many times you would pick each color in 100 trials. Run the simulation five times. Make a new prediction based on the simulation results. Now run the simulation five more times and compare the outcomes to your new prediction. Was your new prediction closer?

5. Make up your own experiment to simulate on the computer. Choose how many red and blue marbles to use and how many trials there should be. Predict the outcome before running the simulation. Share your experiment with others.

6. How can a computer help you do probability experiments?

EXTRA PRACTICE

Tenths and Hundredths, page 435..

Write the decimal for the part that is shaded.

1.   **2.**   **3.**   **4.**

5.   **6.**

Write the decimal.

7. $\frac{3}{10}$ **8.** $\frac{24}{100}$ **9.** $\frac{15}{100}$ **10.** $\frac{4}{100}$ **11.** $\frac{2}{100}$

12. $1\frac{5}{10}$ **13.** $12\frac{7}{10}$ **14.** $4\frac{6}{100}$ **15.** $11\frac{78}{100}$ **16.** $7\frac{3}{10}$

17. ten and four tenths **18.** nine tenths

19. fifteen and six hundredths **20.** two and eleven hundredths

Write the word name.

21. 0.5 **22.** 1.3 **23.** 0.32 **24.** 13.5 **25.** 0.09

Comparing and Ordering Decimals, page 437.....................................

Compare. Use >, <, or =.

1. 4.6 ● 4.2 **2.** 3.9 ● 5.1 **3.** 6.5 ● 5.6

4. 2.30 ● 2.3 **5.** 0.43 ● 0.48 **6.** 7.26 ● 7.62

7. ten and four tenths ● thirty-three hundredths

8. five and seven tenths ● six and seven tenths

9. thirty-two hundredths ● three and nine tenths

10. thirty-nine and seven tenths ● ninety-four and two tenths

Problem Solving Strategy: Making an Organized List, page 439...............

Make an organized list. Then solve the problem.

1. Gail has 4 sweaters and 3 skirts. How many different outfits can she wear using these sweaters and skirts?

2. Kevin wants to order a plate of pasta with sauce for dinner. He can choose from 2 types of pasta and 3 types of sauce. How many different dinners can Kevin order?

3. Aisha makes ceramic bowls in 4 shapes. She can coat them with 2 different glazes. How many different bowls can Aisha make?

4. Lars buys a red balloon, a blue balloon, and a yellow balloon. He also buys 3 different pennants. He wants to give his sister a balloon and a pennant. How many different combinations can he make?

Estimating Decimal Sums and Differences, page 443.........................

Estimate by rounding to the nearest whole number.

1.	2.	3.	4.	5.
4.6	2.77	6.8	7.25	4.27
+ 3.1	+ 3.98	+ 4.3	+ 5.19	+ 2.79

6.	7.	8.	9.	10.
5.98	4.07	9.40	7.40	1.98
− 3.26	− 2.8	− 1.95	− 3.28	− .90

Estimate. Use the front digits and adjust.

11.	12.	13.	14.	15.
4.26	6.13	6.96	7.98	9.07
+ 1.96	+ 3.87	+ 8.89	+ 7.14	+ 5.25

16.	17.	18.	19.	20.
4.25	9.36	3.13	8.00	7.16
− 0.09	− 9.27	− 1.05	− 5.84	− 1.92

EXTRA PRACTICE

Adding Decimals, page 445 ....

Find the sum.

1. 1.4 + 8.5	**2.** 42.5 + 20.5	**3.** 10.4 + 6.7	**4.** 19.6 + 5.8	**5.** 6.3 + 9.4
6. 6.81 + 9.63	**7.** 8.52 + 5.87	**8.** 1.49 + 6.14	**9.** 0.37 + 0.90	**10.** 8.64 + 0.20

11. 12.5 + 13.8   **12.** 6.9 + 5.9   **13.** 9.8 + 40.9

14. 16.81 + 24.64   **15.** 8.73 + 9.86   **16.** 14.09 + 13.67

Subtracting Decimals, page 447 ....

Find the difference.

1. 57.3 − 10.3	**2.** 26.6 − 8.2	**3.** 35.0 − 15.8	**4.** 4.1 − 2.4	**5.** 9.2 − 6.9
6. 0.94 − 0.71	**7.** 3.52 − 0.26	**8.** 7.3 − 5.13	**9.** 9.61 − 1.82	**10.** 6.0 − 0.43

11. 3.5 − 2.9   **12.** 51.7 − 9.8   **13.** 84.8 − 83.9

14. 0.84 − 0.68   **15.** 9 − 3.76   **16.** 7.1 − 3.86

Problem Solving Strategy: Conducting an Experiment, page 451 ....

Use models to solve the problem.

1. Alan has 3 different shirts and 3 different pairs of slacks. How many different outfits can he make?

2. Sara makes sandwiches with tuna, egg salad, or cheese. She has whole wheat and white bread. How many different kinds of sandwiches can she make?

Probability, page 453..

Find the probability of the spinner landing on

1. A.

2. B.

3. C.

4. D.

5. A, B, or C?

6. Which letter is most likely?

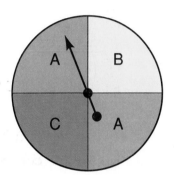

Write the probability.

7. A jar contains 4 balls. One is red, one is blue, one is white and one is green. What is the probability of picking a red ball?

8. What if a yellow ball is added to the jar. what is the probability of picking the yellow ball?

Prediction, page 455 ....

Use the following data for Questions 1 and 2.

Olivia put 7 marbles in a sack. Some were blue and some were green. There were 4 of one color and 3 of the other color. She picked marbles 21 times. These tally marks show the results.

Outcomes

blue	⊬⊬ℋ	⊬⊬ℋ	////
green	⊬⊬ℋ	//	

1. Predict how many marbles of each color there are in the sack.

2. What is the probability of picking a blue marble? a green marble?

Practice *PLUS*

KEY SKILL: Subtracting Decimals (Use after page 447.)

Level A

Find the difference.

1. 7.28	**2.** 24.6	**3.** 44.86	**4.** 5.81
− 3.15	− 13.7	− 13.23	− 2.63

5. 64.86	**6.** $35.64	**7.** 72.3	**8.** 36.4
− 22.94	− 10.72	− 28.5	− 19.5

9. Chris jumped 4.27 m. Evan jumped 3.25 m.
How much farther did Chris jump?

Level B

Find the difference.

10. 92.72	**11.** 51.15	**12.** 63.37	**13.** 9.17
− 31.35	− 20.08	− 29.29	− 3.03

14. $3.05	**15.** 11.84	**16.** 20.0	**17.** 7.37
− 1.12	− 10.5	− 2.76	− 4.91

18. Penny ran a race in 63.8 seconds. Audrey ran it in
59.45 seconds. How much faster was Audrey's time.

Level C

Find the difference.

19. 7 − 4.19   **20.** 13.47 − 3.22   **21.** 6.28 − 4.84

22. 7.49 − 2.99   **23.** 10.15 − 8.97   **24.** 5 − 1.15

25. 6.9 − 1.78   **26.** 7.99 − 3.23   **27.** 5.4 − 3.91

28. Mike rode a total of 37.65 km in 2 hours. He rode
20.9 km the first hour. How many kilometers did he
ride the second hour?

PRACTICE *PLUS*

KEY SKILL: Probability (Use after page 453.)

Level A

Find the probability of spinning:

1. X.

2. Y.

3. Q.

4. A basket contains 2 blue and 3 green balls. What is the probability of picking a blue ball?

Level B

Find the probability of picking:

5. a red crayon.

6. a blue crayon.

7. a yellow crayon.

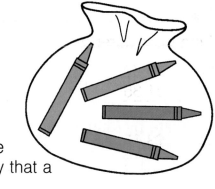

8. A spelling group has 4 boys and 5 girls. One student is chosen. How many possible outcomes are there? What is the probability that a girl will be chosen?

Level C

Find the probability of spinning:

9. 2.

10. 4.

11. 8.

12. 10.

13. A box contains 13 marbles. Two of them are black. What is the probability of choosing a marble that is *not* black?

CHAPTER REVIEW/TEST

LANGUAGE AND MATHEMATICS

Complete the sentences. Use the words in the chart.

VOCABULARY

hundredth
probability
fractions
decimal
equivalent

1. ■ decimals name the same number.

2. $\frac{25}{100}$ written as a ■ is 0.25.

3. A penny is one ■ of a dollar.

4. ■ is the chance that something will happen.

CONCEPTS AND SKILLS

Write the decimal or the word name.

5. $\frac{19}{100}$ **6.** $4\frac{3}{10}$ **7.** six hundredths   **8.** 7.09

Compare. Write >, <, or =.

9. 8.7 ● 8.07 **10.** 9.32 ● 9.23

Order from greatest to least.

11. 4.41; 4.05; 4.5

Estimate by rounding to the nearest whole number.

12.	7.7	**13.**	7.92
	3.9		− 2.4
	+ 1.2		

Estimate. Use the front digits and adjust.

14.	1.02	**15.**	8.42
	3.34		− 3.01
	+ 4.95		

Find the sum or difference.

16.	8.9	**17.**	8.3
	+ 4.76		− 2.75

18. 3.76 + 9.4 + 0.81   **19.** 7 − 2.93

Use a number cube labeled 1–6. Find the probability of tossing:

20. 4   **21.** 9

22. Predict how many times you will toss a 5 if you toss the cube 18 times.

Critical Thinking

Write *true* or *false*. Tell how you made your choice.

23. If 2 decimals are both less than 0.5, then their sum is greater than 1.

Mixed Applications

24. The lumber yard has oak, cedar, and pine. Ned wants to make a table. He has 4 models to choose from. How many choices does he have for the table?

25. Mike has 4 dimes and 3 nickels. He gives three coins to his sister. What are all the possible values of the 3 coins?

PERFORMANCE ASSESSMENT

Work with your group to solve this problem.

Imagine that you and your group have found and measured the length of six different creatures. This table shows the length (in centimeters) of each creature.

Name of Creature	Length
Tree toad	3.8 cm
Spider	0.85 cm
Salamander	4.5 cm
Centipede	2.25 cm
Beetle	1.75 cm
Ladybug	0.65 cm

Rearrange the information to list the lengths in order from greatest to least. Write three statements you can make based on the data.

1. ***Think about:***
   - how to order the lengths
   - how you can use addition and subtraction to compare the lengths

2. Write a paragraph explaining how you ordered and compared the lengths. Then write a number sentence showing how you used addition or subtraction to compare the information.

CUMULATIVE REVIEW

Choose the letter of the correct answer.

1. Which figure is a polygon?

   a. curve   **c.** triangle

   b. angle   **d.** circle

2. Which is eight hundredths?

   a. 0.8   **c.** 0.80

   b. 0.08   **d.** 800

3. Which is 0.20?

   a. two tenths   **c.** twenty tenths

   b. twenty   **d.** two hundredths

4. What is 8.26 plus 4.08?

   a. 13.24   **c.** 12.36

   b. 12.34   **d.** not given

5. Compare: 3.9 ● 3.90

   a. <   **c.** =

   b. >   **d.** not given

6.

What figure is shown?

   a. square   **c.** cube

   b. rectangle   **d.** not given

7. Estimate by rounding:
6.2 + 3.81

   a. 10   **c.** 14

   b. 12   **d.** 15

8. What is 3.76 less than 5?

   a. 1.24   **c.** 2.24

   b. 2.76   **d.** not given

9. Compare: $5\frac{1}{2}$ ● $5\frac{1}{5}$

   a. <   **c.** =

   b. >   **d.** not given

10. What is $\frac{3}{8}$ of 40?

   a. 5   **c.** 18

   b. 12   **d.** not given

11. 9.2 − 5.63

   a. 3.57   **c.** 4.63

   b. 3.67   **d.** not given

12. Add $\frac{3}{4} + \frac{3}{4}$.

   a. $\frac{6}{8}$ **c.** $1\frac{1}{2}$

   b. $1\frac{3}{4}$ **d.** not given

13. Find the perimeter of a square with 8-in. sides.

   a. 16 in.   **c.** 64 in.

   b. 32 in.   **d.** not given

14. Rename: $\frac{18}{4}$

   a. $3\frac{1}{2}$ **c.** $4\frac{1}{2}$

   b. 4   **d.** not given

ODDS

The odds of picking a card marked with a *B* are 2 to 9, or $\frac{2}{9}$.

$$\textbf{ODDS} = \frac{\textbf{NUMBER OF FAVORABLE OUTCOMES}}{\textbf{NUMBER OF UNFAVORABLE OUTCOMES}}$$

1. Why are there two favorable outcomes?

2. Why are there nine unfavorable outcomes?

3. How many possible outcomes are there?

4. What do you notice about the sum of the numbers in the ratio?

What if you wanted to find the odds of picking a card not marked with a *B*?

5. How many favorable outcomes are there?

6. How many unfavorable outcomes are there?

7. What are the odds of picking a card not marked with a *B*?

Find the odds of spinning the color.

8. green

9. not red

10. red, yellow, or green

11. not blue and not green

12. Make your own experiment. You find the probability of each outcome. Have another student find the odds.

YNES MEXIA
An Adventurous Botanist

American-born Ynes Mexia (ee-NES meh-HEE-uh) was 50 years old when she began to study botany. Botany is the science of studying and classifying plants and plant groups. Botanists use math in their work in many ways. They measure the growth of plants. They figure out the number of seeds a plant produces. They record how long it takes for a seed to sprout.

In 1926, Mexia went on her first collecting trip to Mexico. She gathered plant specimens and also took photographs of the plants in their natural environment. During part of her trip, Mexia stayed at the homes of local people and gathered information on the common names and uses of various plants. She collected 33,000 specimens; 50 were new species.

Mexia also traveled to Brazil, where she spent almost two years collecting plants. During this expedition, she made a 3,000-mile journey up the Amazon River to Peru. She traveled part of the trip by canoe, then hired guides and horses to explore a river area that feeds into the Amazon. During her two years in Brazil and Peru, Mexia gathered over 65,000 plant specimens.

In the twelve years that Ynes Mexia spent as a botanist, she collected over 100,000 plant specimens. To honor Mexia's discoveries, some of these plants were named after her.

1. Why is it important for botanists to know the common names and uses that people give to plants that grow in their surroundings?

2. What details about plants do you think might be important to a botanist?

3. If you were a botanist, how would you estimate the number of plants in a given area?

Ynes Mexia
1870-1936

Mental Math: Multiply 10s; 100s; 1,000s

Naima and Miles organize a drive to collect newspapers for a recycling project. This chart shows their goal for collecting papers. How many newspapers will they collect each month?

Month	Number of Newspapers Collected
June	30 newspapers from 80 homes
July	30 newspapers from 800 homes
August	30 newspapers from 8,000 homes

You can find out how many by multiplying.

June: $30 \times 80 = 2{,}400$
July: $30 \times 800 = 24{,}000$
August: $30 \times 8{,}000 = 240{,}000$

So they will collect 2,400 newspapers in June, 24,000 newspapers in July, and 240,000 newspapers in August.

1. Compare the number of zeros in each product with the number of zeros in the factors. What pattern do you see?

2. Does the pattern work for these products? Why or why not?

   $50 \times 60 = 3{,}000$
   $500 \times 60 = 30{,}000$

TRY OUT Write the letter of the correct answer.
Multiply mentally.

3. 80×90 **a.** 720   **b.** 7,200   **c.** 72,000   **d.** 720,000

4. 30×60 **a.** 180   **b.** 1,800   **c.** 18,000   **d.** 180,000

5. 80×500 **a.** 400   **b.** 4,000   **c.** 40,000   **d.** 400,000

6. $50 \times 2{,}000$ **a.** 100   **b.** 1,000   **c.** 10,000   **d.** 100,000

PRACTICE

Multiply mentally.

7. 10 $\times$ 10	8. 100 $\times$ 10	9. 1,000 $\times$ 10	10. 50 $\times$ 10	11. 60 $\times$ 10

12. 70 $\times$ 10	13. 40 $\times$ 20	14. 60 $\times$ 40	15. 200 $\times$ 70	16. 3,000 $\times$ 50

17. 80 $\times$ 10   **18.** 100 $\times$ 70   **19.** 50 $\times$ 1,000   **20.** 30 $\times$ 90

21. 50 $\times$ 20   **22.** 70 $\times$ 70   **23.** 80 $\times$ 100   **24.** 800 $\times$ 50

25. 400 $\times$ 80   **26.** 60 $\times$ 2,000   **27.** 5,000 $\times$ 60   **28.** 2,000 $\times$ 70

29. Multiply by 20.

30	40	50	60	70	80	90
■	■	■	■	■	■	■

30. Multiply by 50.

30	40	50	60	70	80	90
■	■	■	■	■	■	■

Compare. Write >, <, or =.

31. 90 $\times$ 600 ● 900 $\times$ 600   **32.** 40 $\times$ 50 ● 10 $\times$ 100

33. 30 $\times$ 700 ● 300 $\times$ 700   **34.** 40 $\times$ 400 ● 4 $\times$ 4,000

Tell which pair of products are the same in the row.

35. a. 50 $\times$ 4,000   **b.** 90 $\times$ 400   **c.** 80 $\times$ 40   **d.** 60 $\times$ 600

36. a. 80 $\times$ 30   **b.** 40 $\times$ 600   **c.** 60 $\times$ 40,000   **d.** 300 $\times$ 8

2400

Mixed Applications

37. In May Naima and Miles collect 40 newspapers from 90 homes. How many newspapers do they collect in May?

38. Glenn collects from 10 homes. Each home gives her 400 sheets of newspaper. How many sheets does Glenn get?

39. The students collect 300 lb of newspapers in March, 500 lb in April, and 250 lb in May. How many lb of newspapers do they collect in three months?

40. Harvey collects 30 papers from Morgan St. and 400 papers from Third St. How many more papers does he collect from Third St.?

Estimating Products

The booklets for the summer sports program will be passed out by 47 students. If each student passes out 88 booklets, about how many booklets will be passed out in all?

You can estimate to find the answer.

Rounding	Front-End Estimation
Round each factor to its greatest place.	**Use the front digits.**
47 × 88	47 × 88
↓ ↓	↓ ↓
Think: 50 × 90 = 4,500	*Think:* 40 × 80 = 3,200
The estimate is 4,500.	The estimate is 3,200.

Between 3,200 and 4,500 booklets will be passed out.

1. Is the estimate found by rounding greater than or less than the exact answer? How do you know?

2. Is the estimate found by using the front digits greater than or less than the exact answer? How do you know?

3. Estimate 62 × 739 by rounding and front-end estimation. How do the estimates compare? Why?

TRY OUT   Write the letter of the correct answer.

Estimate. Use rounding.

4. 78 × 25   **a.** 160   **b.** 240   **c.** 1,400   **d.** 2,400

5. 53 × $663   **a.** $3,000   **b.** $3,500   **c.** $35,000   **d.** $350,000

Estimate. Use the front digits.

6. 38 × $94   **a.** $2,700   **b.** $270   **c.** $3,600   **d.** $4,000

7. 77 × 852   **a.** 7,200   **b.** 56,000   **c.** 72,000   **d.** 560,000

PRACTICE

Estimate by rounding.

8.	38 × 41	**9.**	93 × 37	**10.**	56 × 66	**11.**	$82 × 74	**12.**	58 × 52

13.	705 × 48	**14.**	593 × 23	**15.**	457 × 81	**16.**	915 × 77	**17.**	$629 × 43

18. 69 × 84 **19.** 93 × $32 **20.** 88 × $405 **21.** 94 × 516

Estimate by using the front digits.

22.	83 × 52	**23.**	71 × 67	**24.**	$45 × 57	**25.**	91 × 65	**26.**	67 × 63

27.	625 × 48	**28.**	$904 × 87	**29.**	290 × 31	**30.**	565 × 96	**31.**	718 × 61

32. 56 × $48 **33.** 83 × 62 **34.** 74 × $525 **35.** 26 × 546

Compare the products. Write >, <, or =.

36. 45 × 362 ● 61 × 346   **37.** 77 × 566 ● 68 × 487

38. 55 × 306 ● 62 × 317   **39.** 88 × 11 ● 66 × 33

40. 93 × 216 ● 142 × 85   **41.** 649 × 58 ● 584 × 69

Mixed Applications

42. Each school can have 175 students in its summer sports program. There are 12 schools. About how many students can be in the program?

43. The sports program runs from 8:15 A.M. until 12 noon each day. How long does the program last each day?

Mixed Review

Find the missing number.

44. ■ × 9 = 72   **45.** $\frac{4}{8} = \frac{■}{2}$ **46.** $\frac{3}{4} + \frac{■}{4} = \frac{3}{4}$ **47.** 48 ÷ ■ = 8

Multiplying by Multiples of Ten

A. The Valley Baseball Boosters are selling season tickets to their team's games. If each of the 20 members sells 35 tickets, how many tickets will the Boosters sell?

Multiply: 20×35

Step 1	Step 2
Multiply by the ones.	**Multiply by the tens.**

Step 1:
$$\begin{array}{r} 35 \\ \times\ 20 \\ \hline 0 \end{array}$$
Think: $0 \times 35 = 0$

Step 2:
$$\begin{array}{r} \overset{1}{3}5 \\ \times\ 20 \\ \hline 700 \end{array}$$
Think: 2 tens $\times$ 35 = 70 tens

The Boosters will sell 700 season tickets.

1. What if each member sells 86 tickets? How many season tickets would be sold?

B. You can multiply larger numbers by multiples of ten.

Multiply: 30×246

Step 1	Step 2
Multiply by the ones.	**Multiply by the tens.**

Step 1:
$$\begin{array}{r} 246 \\ \times\ 30 \\ \hline 0 \end{array}$$
Think: $0 \times 246 = 0$

Step 2:
$$\begin{array}{r} \overset{1}{2}\overset{1}{4}6 \\ \times\ 30 \\ \hline 7{,}380 \end{array}$$
Think: 3 tens $\times$ 246 = 738 tens

TRY OUT   Write the letter of the correct answer.

2. 20×56 **a.** 112   **b.** 1,020   **c.** 1,120   **d.** 11,200

3. 80×41 **a.** 328   **b.** 3,280   **c.** 3,281   **d.** 32,800

4. 30×124 **a.** 372   **b.** 462   **c.** 3,720   **d.** 3,724

5. 50×245 **a.** 25   **b.** 125   **c.** 1,225   **d.** 12,250

PRACTICE

Multiply.

6.	41 × 40	7.	83 × 30	8.	92 × 40	9.	81 × 90	10.	64 × 20

11.	406 × 70	12.	314 × 20	13.	911 × 90	14.	703 × 30	15.	625 × 40

16. 60 × 45   17. 50 × 18   18. 60 × 37   19. 30 × 115

20. 20 × 347   21. 60 × 419   22. 20 × 73   23. 30 × 42

24. 70 × 68   25. 250 × 60   26. 340 × 40   27. 50 × 440

Mixed Applications   Solve. Which method did you use?

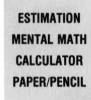

ESTIMATION
MENTAL MATH
CALCULATOR
PAPER/PENCIL

28. The Boosters want to raise money to buy 40 baseball bats. Each bat costs $15. How much money will they need?

29. Derek sells $80 worth of tickets. Carol sells $212 worth of tickets. Who sells more? How much more?

30. Sam sells 50 season tickets. Each ticket costs $25. Does Sam sell over $1,000 worth of tickets?

MENTAL MATH

You can use the properties of multiplication to help you find products mentally.

$$5 \times (18 \times 2) = 5 \times (2 \times 18)$$
$$= (5 \times 2) \times 18$$
$$= 10 \times 18$$
$$= 180$$

Multiply.

1. 4 × 12 × 5   **2.** 20 × 17 × 5   **3.** 25 × 4 × 22

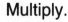

PROBLEM SOLVING

Strategies Review

Use these problem-solving strategies to solve the problems. Remember that some problems can be solved using more than one strategy.

- Using Number Sense
- Choosing the Operation
- Drawing a Diagram
- Solving a Two-Step Problem
- Using Estimation
- Making an Organized List
- Conducting an Experiment
- Finding a Pattern
- Solving a Multistep Problem
- Working Backward
- Guess, Test, and Revise
- Solving a Simpler Problem
- Making a Table

**Solve. Tell which strategy you used.
Use mental math, a calculator, or paper and pencil.**

1. Every student in Mrs. Rose's class is on one of three fund-raising teams. The book-fair team has 12 fewer students than the bake-sale team. The bake-sale team has twice as many students as the movie team. The movie team has 8 students. How many students are in Mrs. Rose's class?

2. The books for the fair are stacked in piles. There are 16 books in the first pile, 14 in the second pile, and 12 in the third pile. If this pattern continues, how many books will be in the next two piles?

3. The movie team sold 320 tickets. The tickets come in books of 9 tickets. How many complete books did the team sell?

4. At the book fair packages of 5 paperbacks and 2 hardcovers are sold at a discount. One woman bought enough packages to have 35 paperbacks. How many books did she buy?

5. The book-fair team hopes that 2,000 books will be donated by the end of May. The team received 450 books in March and 970 books in April. Will it meet its goal if 700 books are donated in May?

6. For the bake sale the team plans to bake chocolate and vanilla cupcakes with a topping of nuts, sprinkles, or chocolate chips. How many different kinds of cupcakes will they bake?

7. Louise, Lester, Larry, and Lulu each bought a different kind of book. They bought books on sports, fairy tales, poetry, and short stories. A boy bought a book of poetry. Lulu did not buy a book of fairy tales. Lester bought a book of short stories. Who bought the book on sports?

8. The bake-sale team meets every fourth day, and the book-fair team meets every third day. This week the bake-sale team meets on Monday, and the book-fair team meets on Tuesday. What is the next day on which both teams will meet on the same day?

9. The Rosas family is going to the movies. They pay for 2 adults' tickets and 2 children's tickets. Adults' tickets cost $1.00. Children's tickets cost $.50. How much does it cost them to go to the movies?

10. There are 10 clowns at the school fair. Some are on bicycles, and the rest are on tricycles. If there are 24 wheels in all, how many bicycles and tricycles are there?

11. One parent bought 6 muffins for $.45 each and 6 brownies for $.35 each. How much did she pay?

12. *Write a problem* that can be solved by using one of the strategies. Solve the problem. Ask others to solve it.

ACTIVITY

Multiplying by 2-Digit Factors

Mrs. Mack is donating a large quilt to a charity auction. The quilt is made of colored squares sewn together. It is shaped like a rectangle that is 36 squares long and 24 squares wide. How many squares are in the quilt?

Estimate. Then draw a diagram to solve the problem.

WORKING TOGETHER

Step 1 On graph paper draw a rectangle that is 36 squares long and 24 squares wide.

Step 2 Separate the rectangle into 4 sections like this:

Section A: 6 squares long by 4 squares wide

Section B: 6 squares long by 20 squares wide

Section C: 30 squares long by 4 squares wide

Section D: 30 squares long by 20 squares wide

How many squares are in each section?

1. A   **2.** B   **3.** C   **4.** D

5. How many squares are there in the diagram?

6. How many squares are there in the quilt?

SHARING IDEAS

7. How did you find the number of squares in each section?

8. Write a multiplication sentence to show how to find the number of squares in each section.

9. How did separating the entire rectangle into smaller rectangular sections make it easier to find the total number of squares?

ON YOUR OWN

Draw a diagram to solve. Write multiplication sentences to show the number of squares in each section.

10. David and his mother are working on a quilt that is 21 squares long and 23 squares wide. How many squares are in their quilt?

11. Mrs. Henderson's quilt won an award at the quilting bee. Her quilt is 42 squares long and 56 squares wide. How many squares are in her quilt?

12. *Write a problem* that involves multiplying two 2-digit numbers. Solve your problem. Ask others to solve it.

ACTIVITY

Multiplying 2-Digit Numbers

A. Janet is selling tickets to the talent show. The theater has 24 rows of seats. There are 32 seats in each row. How many tickets can Janet sell for the show?

You can draw a diagram. Then write multiplication sentences to find the area of each section. Add to find the total.

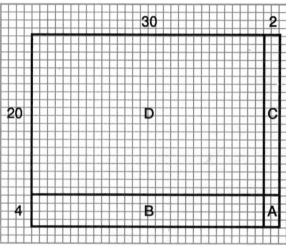

```
    32
  × 24
     8  ← 4 × 2
   120  ← 4 × 30
    40  ← 20 × 2
+ 600  ← 20 × 30
   768
```

1. What part of the diagram does each multiplication sentence show?

Janet can sell 768 tickets.

B. Here is another way to multiply to find the answer.

Step 1	Step 2	Step 3
Multiply by the ones.	**Multiply by the tens.**	**Add the products.**
32	32	32
× 24	× 24	× 24
128 ← 4 × 32	128	128
	640 ← 20 × 32	+ 640
		768

SHARING IDEAS

2. In the first method, why do you add 4 numbers to find the total?

3. In the second method, why do you add 2 numbers to find the total?

PRACTICE

Multiply.

4. $\begin{array}{r} 19 \\ \times\ 11 \end{array}$	**5.** $\begin{array}{r} 42 \\ \times\ 21 \end{array}$	**6.** $\begin{array}{r} 33 \\ \times\ 13 \end{array}$	**7.** $\begin{array}{r} 21 \\ \times\ 24 \end{array}$	**8.** $\begin{array}{r} 32 \\ \times\ 22 \end{array}$
9. $\begin{array}{r} 12 \\ \times\ 12 \end{array}$	**10.** $\begin{array}{r} 31 \\ \times\ 15 \end{array}$	**11.** $\begin{array}{r} 58 \\ \times\ 11 \end{array}$	**12.** $\begin{array}{r} 81 \\ \times\ 32 \end{array}$	**13.** $\begin{array}{r} 71 \\ \times\ 62 \end{array}$

14. 22×51 **15.** 13×62 **16.** 44×22 **17.** 13×13

18. 72×11 **19.** 12×24 **20.** 32×23 **21.** 53×21

22. 13×43 **23.** 42×22 **24.** 33×33 **25.** 41×12

26. What is the product of thirty-four times twelve?

Mixed Applications

27. The Lark Theater has 12 rows of seats. There are 21 seats in each row. How many seats are in the theater?

28. The Computer Club bought tickets worth $75.25. The Crafts Club spent $123.75 on tickets. How much did the two clubs spend on tickets?

29. During the first week of sales 12 of the students sold 20 tickets each. How many tickets did they sell?

30. *Write a problem* that can be solved by multiplying 2-digit numbers. Solve your problem. Ask others to solve it.

Mixed Review

Find the answer. Which method did you use?

31. $4,001 - 1,999$ **32.** $7,896 + 6,947$ **33.** $578 \div 4$

MENTAL MATH
CALCULATOR
PAPER/PENCIL

More Multiplying 2-Digit Numbers

A. To raise money for a track meet, Sarah's track team sold 24 cartons of light bulbs. Each carton contained 58 light bulbs. How many light bulbs did her team sell?

Multiply: 24 × 58
Estimate first. Then multiply.

Step 1

Multiply by the ones.

$$\begin{array}{r} \overset{3}{5}\,8 \\ \times\,2\,4 \\ \hline 2\,3\,2 \end{array} \leftarrow 4 \times 58$$

Step 2

Multiply by the tens.

$$\begin{array}{r} \overset{1}{\overset{3}{}} \\ 5\,8 \\ \times\,2\,4 \\ \hline 2\,3\,2 \\ 1\,1\,6\,0 \end{array} \leftarrow 20 \times 58$$

Step 3

Add the products.

$$\begin{array}{r} \overset{1}{\overset{3}{}} \\ 5\,8 \\ \times\,2\,4 \\ \hline 2\,3\,2 \\ +\,1\,1\,6\,0 \\ \hline 1{,}3\,9\,2 \end{array}$$

Sarah's team sold 1,392 light bulbs.

1. Is this answer reasonable? How do you know?

2. *What if* you multiply 58 × 24? How would Steps 1 and 2 be different? Would the product in Step 3 be the same?

B. You can multiply money amounts the same way you multiply whole numbers.

Multiply: 24 × $.89

Step 1

Multiply as you would whole numbers.

$$\begin{array}{r} \overset{1}{\overset{3}{}} \\ \$.8\,9 \\ \times2\,4 \\ \hline 3\,5\,6 \\ +\,1\,7\,8\,0 \\ \hline 2\,1\,3\,6 \end{array}$$

Step 2

Write a dollar sign and decimal point in the answer.

$$\begin{array}{r} \overset{1}{\overset{3}{}} \\ \$.8\,9 \\ \times2\,4 \\ \hline 3\,5\,6 \\ +\,1\,7\,8\,0 \\ \hline \$2\,1.3\,6 \end{array}$$

3. 36 × 24   **a.** 764   **b.** 816   **c.** 864   **d.** 1,344

4. 75 × $.42   **a.** $4.50   **b.** $4.50   **c.** $29.40   **d.** $31.50

5. 41 × 18   **a.** 369   **b.** 738   **c.** 7,380   **d.** 3,150

6. 23 × $.31   **a.** $.92   **b.** $6.13   **c.** $7.13   **d.** $69.23

P RACTICE

Multiply.

7.   52
     × 41

8.   31
     × 26

9.   45
     × 91

10. $.76
       ×   18

11.   98
       × 52

12.   58
       × 12

13. $.85
       ×   22

14.   25
       × 33

15.   64
       × 53

16.   48
       × 45

17. 57 × 35   **18.** 48 × $.48   **19.** 83 × 99   **20.** 87 × 37

21. 72 × 66   **22.** 75 × 75   **23.** 85 × 89   **24.** 38 × $.19

Mixed Applications

Solve. Which method did you use?

ESTIMATION
MENTAL MATH
CALCULATOR
PAPER/PENCIL

25. The members of the archery team bring their own arrows to the National Archery Finals. They can fit 18 cases of arrows into the team van. Each case holds 32 arrows. How many arrows can they bring to the contest?

26. At the track meet, Dar runs in a 100-meter race, a 500-meter race, and a 1,000-meter race. How many meters does he run?

27. The swim team had a goal of selling 3,000 buttons. They sold 27 cases of buttons that had 80 buttons in each case. Did they meet their goal?

28. There were 1,289 fans at the first meet, 2,378 fans at the second meet, and 3,897 fans at the third. What was the total attendance at the meets?

OUT OF THIS WORLD

Logical Reasoning

A. These problems are truly out in orbit! But with careful reasoning you will be able to solve them all.

1. Ada, Byron, and Clare wrote reports about constellations. Each wrote about one of the following: the Big Dipper, Canis Major, and Orion. Can you look at the clues and decide which constellation each student wrote about?

	Big Dipper	Canis Major	Orion
Ada			
Byron			
Clare			

- Byron's constellation has only one word in its name.
- Ada did not write about the Big Dipper.

Use the chart to organize what you know. Look at the first clue. Which constellation must Byron have written about? Put a ✔ for "yes" in the box where Byron and that constellation meet.

2. Why can you put Xs for "no" in the boxes where Byron and the other constellations meet? Where else can you put Xs? Why?

3. Look at the second clue. Which constellation must Ada have written about? How do you know? What did Clare write about? Complete the chart.

B. Solve the puzzles.

4. Lars, Bruto, and Weptune are creatures from other planets. Which creature comes from which planet?

	Mars	Pluto	Neptune
Lars			
Bruto			
Weptune			

- No creature has a name that rhymes with its home planet.
- Lars and the creature from Neptune are both purple.

5. Quatron, Baxiol-6, and Plim are newly discovered planets. One of the planets has 1 moon. One planet has 2 moons. One planet has 3 moons. How many moons does each planet have?

	1 Moon	2 Moons	3 Moons
Quatron			
Baxiol-6			
Plim			

- Plim has more moons than Quatron.
- Baxiol-6 has an even number of moons.

6. The Acme Spaceship company sells four different models. The brands and prices are shown in the chart. All prices are in interplanetary money—zix. What is the cost of each spaceship?

- The Astro Rocket and the Planet Rover are the most expensive ships.
- The Stellar Flyer is more expensive than the Star Car.
- The Astro Rocket costs more than three times as much as the Star Car.

	6,000 zix	10,000 zix	15,000 zix	20,000 zix
Astro Rocket				
Star Car				
Stellar Flyer				
Planet Rover				

Multiplying 3-Digit Numbers

A. The families on Oak Street are having a street fair. They can use a space 63 feet long and 329 feet wide in the Oak Street Park for their fair. How many square feet of space will they have?

Multiply: 63 × 329

Step 1	Step 2	Step 3
Multiply by the ones.	**Multiply by the tens.**	**Add the products.**

Step 1:
$$
\begin{array}{r}
{\scriptstyle 2} \\
3\,2\,9 \\
\times\ \ 6\,3 \\
\hline
9\,8\,7
\end{array}
\ \leftarrow 3 \times 329
$$

Step 2:
$$
\begin{array}{r}
{\scriptstyle 1\,5} \\
{\scriptstyle 2} \\
3\,2\,9 \\
\times\ \ 6\,3 \\
\hline
9\,8\,7 \\
1\,9\,7\,4\,0
\end{array}
\ \leftarrow 60 \times 329
$$

Step 3:
$$
\begin{array}{r}
{\scriptstyle 1\,5} \\
{\scriptstyle 2} \\
3\,2\,9 \\
\times\ \ 6\,3 \\
\hline
9\,8\,7 \\
+\,1\,9\,7\,4\,0 \\
\hline
2\,0{,}7\,2\,7
\end{array}
$$

The Oak Street families will have 20,727 square feet of space.

1. If 63 × 329 = 20,727, what does 63 × $3.29 equal?

B. You must be careful when there is a zero in a factor.

Multiply: 47 × 507

$$
\begin{array}{r}
{\scriptstyle 2} \\
{\scriptstyle 4} \\
5\,0\,7 \\
\times\ \ 4\,7 \\
\hline
3\,5\,4\,9 \\
+\,2\,0\,2\,8\,0 \\
\hline
2\,3{,}8\,2\,9
\end{array}
$$

2. Tell how the multiplication was done.

3. *What if* you need to find 507 × 47? How could you more easily find the product?

4. 47 × $6.72   **a.** $31.38   **b.** $73.92   **c.** $315.84   **d.** $3,138.40

5. 52 × 508   **a.** 2,606   **b.** 3,556   **c.** 26,416   **d.** 264,160

6. 36 × $8.03   **a.** $289.08   **b.** $73.08   **c.** $298.18   **d.** $730.80

PRACTICE

Multiply.

7. 132
    × 13

8. $2.05
    ×   42

9. 312
    × 32

10. 407
    × 41

11. $3.22
    ×   14

12. 306
    × 78

13. $4.92
    ×   47

14. 860
    × 73

15. 804
    × $.49

16. 384
    × 80

17. $5.35
    ×   44

18. 647
    × 65

19. 507
    × $.36

20. 770
    × 16

21. 908
    × 75

22. 72 × 345   **23.** 16 × $8.02   **24.** 41 × 527   **25.** 65 × 526

26. 329 × 29   **27.** 486 × 53   **28.** 704 × $.49   **29.** 84 × 708

Critical Thinking

30. Miguel made $123.67 by selling sandwiches at the fair. He sold 83 sandwiches for $1.49 each. How many sandwiches would Miguel need to sell at $.83 a sandwich in order to make the same amount of money? How can you find the answer without multiplying?

Mixed Applications

31. Meg sold 262 glasses of apple juice, 92 glasses of grape juice, and 354 glasses of orange juice. How many glasses of juice did she sell?

32. If 875 people come to the street fair and each person spends $16, how much money will be spent?

33. At the fair 108 people paid $.75 each to ride on Kevin's old "bicycle built for two." How much did Kevin earn?

ACTiViTY
Multiplying Larger Numbers

The Highland Helpers want to buy 12 computers for the volunteer fire department. The computers will cost $1,123 each. How much must they raise to buy the computers?

WORKING TOGETHER

You can use mental math, paper and pencil, or a calculator to find the answer. Work with a group. Have each person in your group use a different method to solve the problem.

1. Can you find the product mentally? Why or why not?

2. Tell how you can use paper and pencil to find the product. What is the product?

3. How can you be sure your product is reasonable?

4. Which method was fastest in finding the product?

5. **What if** the computers cost $1,000 each? Which method would be fastest?

Multiply. Which method did you use?

6. 40 × 4,000   **7.** 58 × 6,978   **8.** 33 × 6,211

SHARING IDEAS

9. How is multiplying 4-digit numbers like multiplying 2-digit or 3-digit numbers?

10. How did you decide which method to use to find the answers for Exercises 6–8?

11. When do you think it is easier to use mental math? paper and pencil? a calculator? Why?

12. How many places can there be when you multiply a 4-digit number by a 5-digit number? How do you know?

ON YOUR OWN

Solve. Which method did you use?

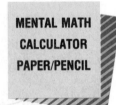

MENTAL MATH
CALCULATOR
PAPER/PENCIL

13. The Highland Helpers use fire trucks and hoses that spout 2,375 liters of water each minute. They spent 35 minutes putting out a fire. How much water did they use?

14. A box of computer diskettes costs $22. Is $500 enough to buy 20 boxes of diskettes?

15. *Write a problem* using large numbers that can be solved by multiplication. Choose which method you think should be used to solve it. Trade problems with other students and compare methods.

Mental Math: Divide 10s; 100s; 1,000s

The 60 members of the Safe Home Society visit 24,000 homes. If each member visits the same number of homes, how many homes does each member visit?

You can use a pattern to find the answer.

$$24 \div 6 = 4$$
$$240 \div 60 = 4$$
$$2,400 \div 60 = 40$$
$$24,000 \div 60 = 400$$

Each member visits 400 homes.

1. Count the number of zeros in the dividend, the divisor, and the quotient. What pattern do you see?

2. Does the pattern work for $2,000 \div 50$? Why or why not?

TRY OUT Write the letter of the correct answer.

3. $80 \div 10$ **a.** 8   **b.** 10   **c.** 80   **d.** 800

4. $4,000 \div 50$ **a.** 8   **b.** 80   **c.** 20,000   **d.** 200,000

5. $36,000 \div 40$ **a.** 9   **b.** 90   **c.** 900   **d.** 9,000

6. $40,000 \div 80$ **a.** 5   **b.** 20   **c.** 200   **d.** 500

PRACTICE

Divide. Use mental math.

7. $20\overline{)20}$ **8.** $70\overline{)140}$ **9.** $50\overline{)3,500}$ **10.** $90\overline{)9,000}$ **11.** $20\overline{)60,000}$

12. $80 \div 40$ **13.** $60 \div 20$ **14.** $60 \div 30$ **15.** $90 \div 30$

16. $250 \div 50$ **17.** $320 \div 40$ **18.** $420 \div 60$ **19.** $640 \div 80$

20. $3,600 \div 90$ **21.** $8,100 \div 90$ **22.** $4,500 \div 50$ **23.** $2,100 \div 30$

24. $12,000 \div 20$ **25.** $18,000 \div 60$ **26.** $64,000 \div 80$ **27.** $40,000 \div 40$

28. Rule: Divide by 20.

100	120	800	1,800	80,000
■	■	■	■	■

29. Find the rule.

150	180	1,200	27,000	30,000
5	6	40	900	1,000

Find the missing number.

30. $50 \times \blacksquare = 35,000$ **31.** $36,000 \div \blacksquare = 90$ **32.** $\blacksquare \div 70 = 0$

33. $\blacksquare \times 300 = 6,000$ **34.** $15,000 \div \blacksquare = 500$ **35.** $\blacksquare \div 20 = 800$

Mixed Applications

36. Claude is mailing 60 boxes of letters on home safety. If each box holds 30 letters, how many letters does Claude mail?

37. Sally ships about 40,000 safety posters to 20 cities. If she ships the same number of posters to each city, how many does each city get?

38. It took 10 hours to print all of the letters to be mailed. Brooke worked for 5 hours. What fraction of the total time did she work?

39. *Write a problem* that can be solved by dividing mentally. Solve your problem. Ask others to solve it.

Mixed Review
Find the answer. Which method did you use?

40. $\frac{3}{8} + \frac{3}{8}$ **41.** 50×50 **42.** $20,304 - 19,458$

MENTAL MATH
CALCULATOR
PAPER/PENCIL

ACTIVITY

Dividing by Multiples of Ten

A. There are 126 students at a meeting about the foreign exchange program. Each classroom holds 40 students. How many classrooms are filled with students? How many students are in an unfilled classroom?

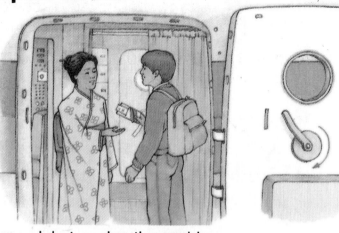

WORKING TOGETHER

Estimate first. Then use place-value models to solve the problem.

1. How many times can you take 40 away from 126? How many groups of 40 can you make?

2. How many models cannot be put in a group?

3. How many classrooms are filled?

4. How many students are in the unfilled classroom?

B. You can divide without using models.

Step 1

Decide where to place the first digit in the quotient.

$$40\overline{)126}$$ ■

Think: 40 > 1 Not enough hundreds
40 > 12 Not enough tens
40 < 126 Divide the ones.

Step 2

Divide the ones.
Write the remainder.

$$40\overline{)126} \quad 3\ R6$$
$$-120$$
$$6$$

Think: $4\overline{)12}$ = 3
Multiply: $3 \times 40 = 120$
Compare: $120 < 126$
Subtract: $126 - 120 = 6$

5. **What if** there were 88 students at a meeting? How would you divide to find how many classrooms would be filled and how many students would be in the unfilled classroom?

SHARING IDEAS

6. How does the method using place-value models compare with the method using numbers?

7. How can you use division facts to help you divide by multiples of ten?

PRACTICE

Divide.

8. $40\overline{)48}$ **9.** $20\overline{)82}$ **10.** $10\overline{)76}$ **11.** $90\overline{)95}$ **12.** $30\overline{)99}$

13. $20\overline{)32}$ **14.** $50\overline{)72}$ **15.** $40\overline{)97}$ **16.** $30\overline{)83}$ **17.** $20\overline{)94}$

18. $70\overline{)143}$ **19.** $50\overline{)158}$ **20.** $60\overline{)184}$ **21.** $90\overline{)725}$ **22.** $80\overline{)647}$

23. $20\overline{)198}$ **24.** $40\overline{)340}$ **25.** $70\overline{)334}$ **26.** $50\overline{)385}$ **27.** $60\overline{)419}$

28. $89 \div 40$ **29.** $62 \div 20$ **30.** $43 \div 30$ **31.** $70 \div 30$

32. $256 \div 50$ **33.** $330 \div 40$ **34.** $527 \div 60$ **35.** $539 \div 90$

Critical Thinking

36. What is the greatest remainder you can have when you are dividing by a 2-digit number? How do you know?

Mixed Applications

Solve. You may need to use the Databank on page 522.

37. Alice is in Spain and exchanges $35 for pesetas. She sees a pair of shoes she likes for 3,780 pesetas. Does she have enough money to buy the shoes?

38. In France, Jessica has 360 francs to buy souvenirs for 20 classmates. If she buys the same thing for each friend, how much can each present cost?

39. If Sean has 440 Belgian francs, how many U.S. dollars can he get in exchange?

40. *Write a problem* using the information in the Databank. Ask others to solve it.

✓ UNDERSTAND
✓ PLAN
✓ TRY
CHECK
✓ EXTEND

Strategy: Choosing the Operation

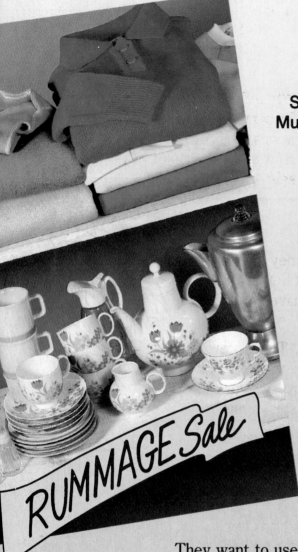

In order to plan which operation to choose to solve a problem you have to understand what is happening in the problem.

Addition: Combine unequal groups.
Subtraction: Separate into unequal groups.
Multiplication: Combine equal groups.
Division: Separate into equal groups.

The students in Mrs. Cruz's class held a rummage sale to raise money for some local charities. They made $103.25 on clothes, $55.35 on books, and $85.40 on household items. How much money did they make in all?

1. Which operation can you use to solve the problem? How much money did they make in all?

They plan to give $45 to each of 4 charities. How much money will they give to charities?

2. Which operation can you use to solve the problem? How much money will they give to charities?

They want to use the rest of the money to buy books for the class library. How much will they spend on books for the library?

3. Which operation can you use to solve the problem? How much will they spend on books?

What if they had given all the money to the 4 charities, in equal amounts? How much would each charity get?

4. Which operation can you use to solve the problem? How much would each charity get?

PRACTICE

**Decide which operation to use. Then solve the problem.
Use mental math, a calculator, or paper and pencil.**

5. Joan bought a plant for $1.35, a poster for $2.50, and a dress for $4.80. How much did she spend in all?

6. At the rummage sale Pat bought a box of 12 tapes. If each tape cost $.35, how much did she pay?

7. The school is using the money earned at the rummage sale to buy a computer for $430. It will be paid for in 10 installments. How much is each installment?

8. When the sale started David had 24 quarts of punch to sell. When it was over he had 5 quarts left. How many quarts of punch did he sell?

Strategies and Skills Review

9. Bob's class is putting on a play to raise money for playground equipment. If Bob sells 6 tickets a day and Seth sells 4 tickets a day, how many tickets will Seth have sold when Bob has sold 36?

10. They had 5 performances of the class play. There were 90 tickets for each performance. All tickets were sold for the first 4 performances. All but 27 tickets were sold for the last performance. How many tickets were sold in all?

11. The students are making posters for the rummage sale. They will use 10 feet of streamers on each poster. They have 160 feet of streamers. How many posters can they make?

12. The parents of the students in Mrs. Cruz's class held a dinner as a fund-raiser. The dinner cost $12 a person. There were 125 people at the dinner. How much money did they raise?

13. At the rummage sale David, Edie, and 5 of their friends bought 63 records. If each bought the same number of records, how many records did each one buy?

14. *Write a problem* that can be solved by addition, subtraction, multiplication, or division. Solve the problem. Ask others to solve your problem.

ACTIVITY

Dividing by 2-Digit Divisors

There are 167 tickets left for the summer sports festival. Hector wants to send 52 tickets to each of the local gyms. How many gyms can Hector send tickets to? How many tickets will be left?

You can divide to find the number of gyms.

WORKING TOGETHER

Estimate. Then solve the problem using place-value models.

Step 1 Make a model of the number of tickets.

Step 2 Separate your model into groups of 52.

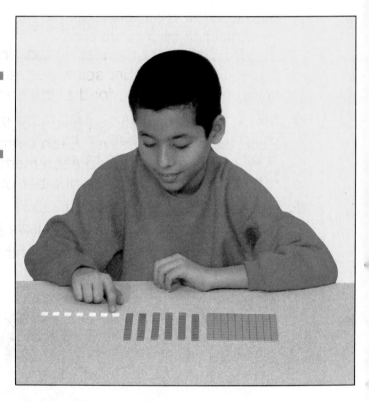

1. How did you model the number of tickets?

2. Did you have to regroup before you could make the groups? Why or why not?

3. How many groups of 52 did you make? How many models were left?

4. How many gyms can Hector send tickets to? How many tickets will be left?

Use models to find each quotient and remainder.

5. 53 ÷ 12   6. 94 ÷ 14

7. 96 ÷ 26   8. 159 ÷ 42

9. 226 ÷ 22   10. 564 ÷ 46

SHARING IDEAS

11. How is dividing by a 2-digit divisor like dividing by a 1-digit divisor? How is it different?

12. Is the quotient always a 1-digit number when you divide a larger 2-digit number by a 2-digit number? Why or why not?

13. Is the quotient always a 1-digit number when you divide a 3-digit number by a 2-digit number? Why or why not?

ON YOUR OWN

Use place-value models to solve the problem.

14. The food stand at the festival took in $384 in one hour. If the average amount spent per person was $16, how many people bought food at the stand?

15. There are 140 tickets set aside for the members of each team at the festival. Each team has 25 members. How many tickets should each member get so that they each have the same number of tickets? How many tickets will be left?

16. *Write a problem* that can be solved by dividing by a 2-digit divisor. Solve your problem. Ask others to solve it.

DECISION MAKING

Problem Solving: Planning a Car Wash

SITUATION

The students of Greenvale Elementary School are planning a car-wash fund-raiser. They want to plant sapling maple trees in the new East City Park. Each tree is $39. Their goal is to plant at least five trees.

PROBLEM

How should the class organize the car wash?

DATA

Car Wash
Day/Time: Saturday 8:00-5:00
Steps: ① Wash
② Rinse with hose
③ Dry
Location: School parking lot
(2 outdoor faucets)
School provides water
and hoses
Teacher supervisors provide
cash box and change

BIG AL'S AUTO SUPPLY

Softee car soap
5 lb for
$5.75
Enough for
60 washes!

Window squeegees
$2.75 each

Bucket
$2.50 each

Wheel scrubber
$2.50 each

Softee car sponge
$1.25 each

Drying/finishing cloth
$4.50 each

USING THE DATA

How much will these supplies cost?

1. 4 buckets

2. 4 sponges

3. 4 drying towels

4. 2 boxes of soap

5. 2 squeegees

6. 2 wheel scrubbers

7. If they buy all the items listed above, how much will the students spend on supplies?

8. How much must they make to buy 5 saplings and cover the cost of the supplies?

9. If they expect 50 customers, how much should they charge each customer to reach their goal? If they expect 100 customers, how much should they charge?

10. If a team of students takes 10 minutes to wash a car, how many cars can the team wash in an hour? How many can the team wash in one 9-hour day?

MAKING DECISIONS

11. What kinds of jobs are there in each washing crew? Which of the supplies are needed to do each job?

12. How many students should be in each washing crew? How many washing crews should there be? Why?

13. What other jobs are there besides the washing crews?

14. *What if* the students work 3-hour shifts? How many students are needed to work a 9-hour day? Why?

15. *What if* one worker uses the hose and works with two crews? How would this change the planning for the car wash?

16. *Write a plan* for a fund-raising car wash. List how you would organize it, how many students you would have, and how much you would charge for each car.

Math and Social Studies

Since 1851 the cost of sending a letter has been based on weight. Back in 1860 it could cost you $10 to send a 1-oz letter—if you sent it by Pony Express from Missouri to California. In 1863 it cost 6¢ to mail a 1-oz letter by first-class mail. Rates fell to 2¢ in 1885, but they have been rising ever since.

The chart shows the cost from 1863 to 1988 of mailing a 1-oz first-class letter anywhere in the United States. In about 100 years the cost of mailing a 1-oz first-class letter rose only 23¢. Rates rose the most in the 1970s and 1980s.

COST OF MAILING A FIRST-CLASS LETTER

Year	Amount	Year	Amount
1863	6¢	1971	8¢
1885	2¢	1974	10¢
1932	3¢	1981	20¢
1963	5¢	1988	25¢

How much more did it cost to mail 25 letters in 1988 than it did in 1963?

Think: In 1963 each letter cost 5¢ to mail.
25 × 5 cents = 125¢ or $1.25

In 1988 each letter cost 25¢ to mail.
25 × 25 cents = 625¢ or $6.25

$6.25 − $1.25 = $5.00

It cost $5.00 more to mail 25 letters in 1988 than it did in 1963.

ACTIVITY

1. Find out about one of the following: the postal service in Colonial times, the Pony Express, or rare stamps. Share this information with your class.

Calculator: Missing Digits

You can use a calculator to help improve your number sense.

In each exercise below, four digits are provided. Fill in each blank with one of the digits to arrive at the quotient shown. Use estimation to choose combinations of digits that might work. Use your calculator to try out your guesses.

1. | 2, 3, 0, 7 | ___)___ ___ ___   → 2 9

(*Hint:* There are no tens in the dividend.)

2. | 8, 2, 2, 6 | ___)___ ___ ___   → 4 7

(*Hint:* The dividend has the same number of ones as hundreds.)

3. | 8, 8, 2, 8 | ___)___ ___ ___   → 3 6

4. | 7, 1, 4, 4 | ___)___ ___ ___   → 6 3

5. | 5, 2, 2, 4 | ___)___ ___ ___   → 6 3

6. | 6, 4, 8, 9 | ___)___ ___ ___   → 9 4

7. | 5, 3, 8, 7 | ___)___ ___ ___   → 5 5

8. | 2, 8, 9, 8 | ___)___ ___ ___   → 9 2

USING THE CALCULATOR

9. Tell how you chose the dividends and divisors. How did using a calculator help?

EXTRA PRACTICE

Mental Math: Multiply 10s; 100s; 1,000s, page 475 ....

Multiply mentally.

1. 70 × 10 **2.** 30 × 100 **3.** 40 × 20 **4.** 30 × 400

5. 30 × 800 **6.** 300 × 50 **7.** 800 × 40 **8.** 200 × 50

Compare. Write >, <, or =.

9. 20 × 400 ● 60 × 300 **10.** 90 × 300 ● 50 × 500

Estimating Products, page 477 ....

Estimate. Use rounding.

| **1.** 543 | **2.** 38 | **3.** 496 | **4.** 312 | **5.** 449 |
| × 64 | × 24 | × 56 | × 72 | × 26 |

6. 705 × 42 **7.** 550 × 35 **8.** 29 × 68 **9.** 31 × 77

Estimate. Use the front digits.

| **10.** 625 | **11.** 12 | **12.** 68 | **13.** 45 | **14.** 47 |
| × 52 | × 23 | × 19 | × 88 | × 24 |

15. 71 × 67 **16.** 20 × 24 **17.** 47 × 56 **18.** 32 × 422

Multiplying by Multiples of Ten, page 479 ....

Multiply.

| **1.** 81 | **2.** 65 | **3.** 46 | **4.** 73 | **5.** 54 |
| × 90 | × 20 | × 20 | × 30 | × 30 |

| **6.** 911 | **7.** 314 | **8.** 406 | **9.** 604 | **10.** 917 |
| × 90 | × 20 | × 70 | × 40 | × 20 |

11. 30 × 115 **12.** 60 × 27 **13.** 40 × 16 **14.** 50 × 45

15. 342 × 20 **16.** 348 × 30 **17.** 409 × 70 **18.** 90 × 312

Problem Solving: Strategies Review, page 481 ....

Solve. Tell which strategy you used.

1. Book labels are sold in packages of 12 or 16. Nancy bought 5 packages and got 76 labels. How many labels were in each package?

2. Mark made some cookies. He gave 24 to Tina and 12 to Ariel. He had 24 left. How many cookies did he make?

3. Ray bought 3 books for $2.95 each. He bought a poster for $5.95. He paid with a $20 bill. What was his change?

4. Gloria buys 6 flowers at the flower booth. They are either red or white. How many different combinations could she have?

Multiplying 2-Digit Numbers, page 485 ....

Multiply.

1. 52×13	**2.** 64×12	**3.** 81×18	**4.** 32×14	**5.** 43×13
6. 74×21	**7.** 31×31	**8.** 61×58	**9.** 52×34	**10.** 91×12
11. 64×22	**12.** 15×11	**13.** 22×24	**14.** 31×13	**15.** 72×34

16. 74×81 17. 34×91 18. 25×31 19. 22×32

20. 44×62 21. 37×81 22. 32×53 23. 22×74

24. 33×33 25. 42×92 26. 43×71 27. 23×52

EXTRA PRACTICE

More Multiplying 2-Digit Numbers, page 487 ....

Multiply.

1. 87 ×20	**2.** 73 ×59	**3.** 41 ×70	**4.** 48 ×73	**5.** 79 ×45

6. 56 ×47	**7.** $.72 × 25	**8.** 81 ×29	**9.** 63 ×53	**10.** 52 ×72

11. 27 × 52　　　**12.** 26 × 38　　　**13.** 39 × 23　　　**14.** 37 × 85

15. 39 × 61　　　**16.** $.38 × 17　　　**17.** 26 × 36　　　**18.** 65 × 92

Multiplying 3-Digit Numbers, page 491 ....

Multiply.

1. 352 × 14	**2.** 423 × 15	**3.** 179 × 46	**4.** 346 × 16	**5.** 664 × 73

6. 243 × 24	**7.** 327 × 19	**8.** 256 × 85	**9.** 727 × 17	**10.** $7.43 × 56

11. 558 × 63	**12.** 652 × 95	**13.** 567 × 15	**14.** 347 × 36	**15.** 465 × 44

16. 35 × 146　　**17.** 24 × 308　　**18.** 72 × 716　　**19.** $.45 × 320

20. 18 × 651　　**21.** 83 × 429　　**22.** 57 × 601　　**23.** 67 × 562

Mental Math: Divide 10s; 100s; 1,000s, page 495 ....

Divide. Use mental math.

1. 80 ÷ 20　　　**2.** 48,000 ÷ 80　　**3.** 450 ÷ 50　　　**4.** 360 ÷ 90

5. 630 ÷ 70　　　**6.** 56,000 ÷ 80　　**7.** 80 ÷ 40　　　**8.** 18,000 ÷ 30

9. 2,400 ÷ 30　　**10.** 4,500 ÷ 90　　**11.** 40 ÷ 20　　　**12.** 12,000 ÷ 60

Dividing by Multiples of Ten, page 497 ....

Divide.

1. $20\overline{)480}$ 2. $60\overline{)668}$ 3. $40\overline{)860}$ 4. $50\overline{)750}$ 5. $30\overline{)659}$

6. $20\overline{)23}$ 7. $30\overline{)62}$ 8. $20\overline{)86}$ 9. $40\overline{)85}$ 10. $30\overline{)95}$

11. $50\overline{)79}$ 12. $30\overline{)243}$ 13. $20\overline{)165}$ 14. $40\overline{)280}$ 15. $80\overline{)666}$

16. $376 \div 40$ 17. $630 \div 20$ 18. $538 \div 50$ 19. $886 \div 60$

20. $254 \div 30$ 21. $429 \div 70$ 22. $716 \div 80$ 23. $679 \div 30$

24. $927 \div 40$ 25. $608 \div 30$ 26. $751 \div 50$ 27. $840 \div 60$

Problem Solving Strategy: Choosing the Operation, page 499 ....

Decide which operation to use. Then solve the problem.

1. The fourth grade class has 125 students. All but 7 of them helped work on the class project. How many worked on the project?

2. The cafeteria can serve 5 people in one minute. How many minutes does it take to serve 45 people?

3. Eric eats 3 meals each day. How many meals does he eat in one week?

4. Amy spent 37¢ on supplies for the project. Joe spent $1.97. How much did they spend all together?

5. The School Store made a profit of $520 this year. The school wants to use this money to buy some new bushes for their garden. Each bush costs $40. How many bushes can they buy?

6. The school is 12 km from Brian's home. The library is 9 km away. How much further is the school than the library?

Practice PLUS

KEY SKILL: Multiplying 3-Digit Numbers (Use after page 491.)

Level A
Multiply.

1. 537 × 42	**2.** 328 × 43	**3.** 234 × 54	**4.** 314 × 81	**5.** 706 × 36
6. 109 × 69	**7.** 444 × 23	**8.** 482 × 34	**9.** 824 × 72	**10.** 680 × 59

11. The Book Club sold 12 books for $2.25 each. How much did they make?

Level B
Multiply.

12. 426 × 43	**13.** 952 × 47	**14.** 667 × 23	**15.** 235 × 47	**16.** 926 × 42
17. 564 × 33	**18.** $182 × 74	**19.** 343 × 34	**20.** 486 × 42	**21.** 251 × 96

22. 84 × 602   **23.** 39 × 648   **24.** 365 × 74   **25.** 520 × 58

26. Jake made 14 long-distance calls. Each call cost $1.90. How much did he spend?

Level C
Multiply.

27. 38 × 725   **28.** 64 × 977   **29.** 42 × 814   **30.** 18 × 473

31. 647 × 60   **32.** 753 × 45   **33.** 469 × 52   **34.** 308 × 75

35. Alice sold 83 sandwiches for $2.95 each. How much did she make?

KEY SKILL: Dividing by Multiples of Ten (Use after page 497.)

Level A ....

Divide.

1. $30\overline{)65}$ **2.** $70\overline{)97}$ **3.** $10\overline{)88}$ **4.** $40\overline{)91}$ **5.** $20\overline{)79}$

6. $50\overline{)85}$ **7.** $60\overline{)96}$ **8.** $80\overline{)84}$ **9.** $20\overline{)55}$ **10.** $30\overline{)48}$

11. $129 \div 40$ **12.** $890 \div 90$ **13.** $685 \div 50$ **14.** $555 \div 20$ **15.** $798 \div 70$

16. Eric had 86 books to pack. He put 20 in each box. How many boxes did he fill? How many books were left?

Level B ....

Divide.

17. $40\overline{)86}$ **18.** $30\overline{)55}$ **19.** $20\overline{)48}$ **20.** $50\overline{)71}$ **21.** $10\overline{)29}$

22. $419 \div 40$ **23.** $760 \div 50$ **24.** $377 \div 40$ **25.** $351 \div 10$ **26.** $569 \div 20$

27. $761 \div 30$ **28.** $805 \div 60$ **29.** $901 \div 70$ **30.** $387 \div 30$ **31.** $686 \div 40$

32. Margie had 342 marbles. She put them in groups of 30 each. How many groups did she have? How many marbles were left?

Level C ....

Divide.

33. $858 \div 60$ **34.** $679 \div 40$ **35.** $458 \div 30$ **36.** $915 \div 70$ **37.** $333 \div 10$

38. $654 \div 90$ **39.** $469 \div 50$ **40.** $578 \div 80$ **41.** $190 \div 20$ **42.** $451 \div 50$

43. $572 \div 60$ **44.** $308 \div 70$ **45.** $250 \div 50$ **46.** $278 \div 40$ **47.** $555 \div 30$

48. Oliver saved 427 stamps. He kept them in envelopes of 20 stamps each. How many envelopes did he have? How many stamps were left?

CHAPTER REVIEW/TEST

LANGUAGE AND MATHEMATICS

Complete the sentences. Use the words in the chart.

1. When multiplying 2-digit numbers, multiply by the ones and then by the ■.

2. When you multiply by 1,000, the number of zeros in the ■ equals the number of zeros in both factors.

3. You can use ■ to estimate a product.

4. When dividing 72,000 by 90, the number of zeros in the ■ is less than the number of zeros in the dividend.

CONCEPTS AND SKILLS

Multiply.

5. 30×50

6. 400×60

7. $20 \times 9,000$

8. $30 \times 4,000$

Estimate. Use rounding.

9. $\begin{array}{r} 53 \\ \times\ 47 \\ \end{array}$

10. $\begin{array}{r} \$572 \\ \times\ \ \ 33 \\ \end{array}$

11. 811×39

12. 49×669

Estimate. Use the front digits.

13. $\begin{array}{r} 31 \\ \times\ 47 \\ \end{array}$

14. $\begin{array}{r} 461 \\ \times\ \ 57 \\ \end{array}$

15. 460×83

16. $22 \times \$927$

Multiply.

17. 782×19

18. $28 \times \$6.37$

19. $59 \times \$4.32$

20. 16×92

Divide.

21. $560 \div 70$

22. $3,600 \div 60$

23. $450 \div 50$

24. $8,000 \div 20$

25. $40\overline{)327}$

26. $70\overline{)633}$

27. $30\overline{)241}$

28. $40\overline{)288}$

Critical Thinking

29. Ian estimates that the product of two 2-digit factors is 4,000. What are the greatest factors possible?

30. If you divide a 3-digit number by a multiple of ten, what is the greatest number of digits you can have in the quotient?

Mixed Applications

31. Kim bought 15 daisies. If each daisy cost 65¢, how much did he pay? Which operation did you choose?

32. Jon's uncle owns a sock store and gives Jon 15 pairs of new socks every month. How many pairs of socks does Jon receive from his uncle in a year?

33. Steve has to put 130 shingles on his roof. If the shingles are sold in boxes of 8, how many boxes does he need to buy?

PERFORMANCE ASSESSMENT

Work with your group to solve this problem.

A group of 20 students decides to sell greeting cards to help raise money for charity. Each box has 32 cards. If the group sells 440 boxes, they will receive a prize.

Use this information to write word problems using multiplication and division. You can write separate problems for each operation, or a multi-step problem using both multiplication and division.

1. *Think about:*
   - how to write a problem using multiplication
   - how to write a problem using division

2. Write a paragraph explaining how you wrote your problems, and how you solved them.

CUMULATIVE REVIEW

Choose the letter of the correct answer.

1. What is 60 times 90?

   a. 540   **c.** 54,000

   b. 5,400   **d.** not given

2. Compare: $\frac{32}{6}$ ● $5\frac{1}{3}$

   a. <   **c.** =

   b. >   **d.** not given

3. What is 28,000 divided by 70?

   a. 40   **c.** 4,000

   b. 400   **d.** not given

4. Subtract 9.06 from 12.

   a. 21.06   **c.** 3.06

   b. 2.94   **d.** not given

5. Find 36 multiplied by 417.

   a. 14,012   **c.** 15,012

   b. 14,912   **d.** not given

6. 63 × $5.49

   a. $345.87   **c.** $49.41

   b. $355.87   **d.** not given

7. Estimate the width of a car.

   a. 6 in.   **c.** 6 yd

   b. 6 ft   **d.** 6 mi

8. Estimate by rounding:
689 × 82.

   a. 56,000   **c.** 48,000

   b. 54,000   **d.** 63,000

9. Find the area of a square with 9-yd sides.

   a. 18 sq yd   **c.** 36 sq yd

   b. 36 yd   **d.** not given

10. 92 × $47

   a. $3,724   **c.** $4,314

   b. $4,224   **d.** not given

11. Divide 86 by 20.

   a. 5   **c.** 4 R6

   b. 4 R16   **d.** not given

12. Estimate the weight of a rake.

   a. 1 oz   **c.** 10 lb

   b. 20 oz   **d.** 20 lb

13. Compare: 1.10 ● 1.01

   a. <   **c.** =

   b. >   **d.** not given

14. Find the product of 80 and 692.

   a. 55,360   **c.** 48,360

   b. 55,260   **d.** not given

CASTING OUT NINES

Tim uses a method called **casting out nines** to check multiplication. He follows these steps.

Step 1

Add the digits of the factors. If the sum is greater than 9, add the digits of the sum. Continue until you get a sum of 9 or less. Then, multiply the results. If necessary, add the digits of the product to get a sum of 9 or less.

Step 2

Add the digits of the product. If the sum is greater than 9, add the digits of the sum. Continue until you get a sum of 9 or less.

$$637 \qquad 6 + 3 + 7 = 16 \rightarrow 1 + 6 = 7 \qquad 4 + 3 + 9 + 5 + 3 = 24$$
$$\times\ 69 \qquad 6 + 9 = 15 \rightarrow 1 + 5 = 6 \qquad\qquad\qquad 2 + 4 = 6$$
$$7 \times 6 = 42 \rightarrow 4 + 2 = 6 \qquad 2 + 4 = 6$$

Compare. The numbers should be the same.
Tim's product is correct. $637 \times 69 = 43{,}953$.

Check each product by casting out nines. Tell if the product checks or not. If it doesn't check, write the correct answer.

1.	**2.**	**3.**	**4.**	**5.**
82	38	677	548	62
× 19	× 72	× 29	× 56	× 46
1,558	2,616	17,503	30,688	2,852

DATABANK

The Databank contains statistics and data similar to what can be found in outside reference books. The charts, graphs, menus, and maps contained here provide the real-world information needed to solve problems throughout the Pupil's Edition.

PROFITS OF FOUR COMPUTER COMPANIES

Statement of Profits		
Company	Year	
	1990	1991
Fina Computers	$486,424,920	$794,806,050
Kane Computers Inc.	$163,725,908	$207,918,420
Mavis Software	$ 23,078,090	$ 39,649,750
Beekman Computersoft	$110,319,998	$119,139,099

YEARLY RAINFALL
(in inches)

San Francisco, CA	35 in.
Moscow, USSR	24 in.
Berlin, Germany	23 in.
Paris, France	22 in.
Fairbanks, AK	13 in.
Phoenix, AZ	10 in.
Los Angeles, CA	8 in.
Cairo, Egypt	1 in.

TALL BUILDINGS IN THE UNITED STATES

City	Building	Height		
		Stories	Feet	Meters
Chicago	Sears Tower	110	1,454	436
New York	World Trade Center	110	1,350	405
New York	Empire State Building	102	1,250	375
Chicago	Amoco	80	1,136	341
Chicago	John Hancock Center	100	1,127	338
New York	Chrysler Building	77	1,046	314
Los Angeles	Library Tower	73	1,017	305
Houston	Texas Commerce Tower	75	1,002	301
Houston	Allied Bank	71	992	298
Seattle	Columbia Seafirst Center	76	954	286

PLUM TREE CAFÉ MENU

Sandwiches
Tuna Salad. $2.35
Tuna Melt. $3.10
Shrimp Salad. $3.55
Chicken Salad. $2.75

Entrées
Roast Chicken. $8.50
Sirloin Steak $9.25
Broiled Fish $9.50
Broiled Pork Chops
   with applesauce. $8.75

Above served with potato, vegetable,
and salad

Side Orders
French Fries $1.10
Cole Slaw . . . . $ .95
Cheese Sticks $2.25

Salads
Lettuce and Tomato $1.75
Chef's Salad $4.50
Health Salad $3.70

Beverages
Orange Juice $1.00
Fruit Punch $1.50
Milk . . . . $ .80
Apple Juice. $1.00
Lemonade. . . . . $ .75
Chocolate Milk. . . . . $ .90

Apple
80 calories
120 Vit. A units

Ice cream (1 cup)
270 calories
540 Vit. A units

Milk (1 cup)
150 calories
310 Vit. A units

Lemonade (1 cup)
105 calorie
10 Vit. A uns

Apple pie (1 piece of pie)
345 calories
40 Vit. A units

Green beans (1 cup)
35 calories
780 Vit. A units

Hamburger
185 calories
20 Vit. A units

Fried egg
85 calories
290 Vit. A units

Bacon (2 slices)
85 calories
0 Vit. A units

Corn (1 ear)
70 calories
310 Vit. A units

Muffin (corn)
125 calories
120 Vit. A units

CALORIES AND VITAMIN A* IN SOME FOODS * International Us

DATES OF SOME INVENTIONS

	1990
	1985
	1980
	1975
HOME COMPUTER ▶	1971
	1965
LASER ▶	1958
SOLAR BATTERY ▶	1954
ELECTRONIC COMPUTER ▶	1946
RADAR ▶	1940
	1935
ROCKET ▶	1926
TELEVISION ▶	1923
	1920
	1915
CELLOPHANE ▶	1908
AIRPLANE ▶	1903
	1900
RADIO ▶	1895
ZIPPER ▶	1891
MOVIE CAMERA ▶	1889
GASOLINE AUTOMOBILE ▶	1887
LIGHT BULB ▶	1879
TELEPHONE ▶	1876
	1870
TYPEWRITER ▶	1867
	1865

GREATEST KNOWN SPEEDS OF VARIOUS ANIMALS

(in miles per hour)

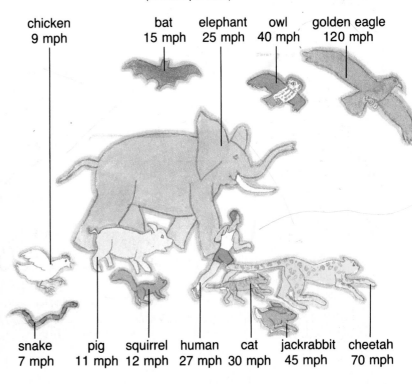

chicken 9 mph

bat 15 mph

elephant 25 mph

owl 40 mph

golden eagle 120 mph

snake 7 mph

pig 11 mph

squirrel 12 mph

human 27 mph

cat 30 mph

jackrabbit 45 mph

cheetah 70 mph

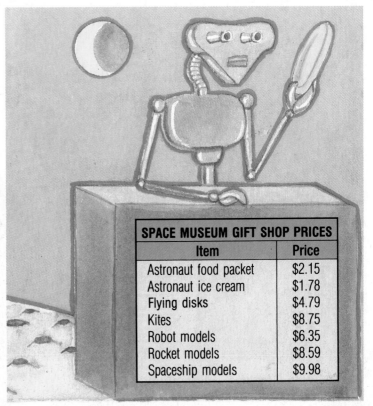

SPACE MUSEUM GIFT SHOP PRICES	
Item	**Price**
Astronaut food packet	$2.15
Astronaut ice cream	$1.78
Flying disks	$4.79
Kites	$8.75
Robot models	$6.35
Rocket models	$8.59
Spaceship models	$9.98

DATABANK

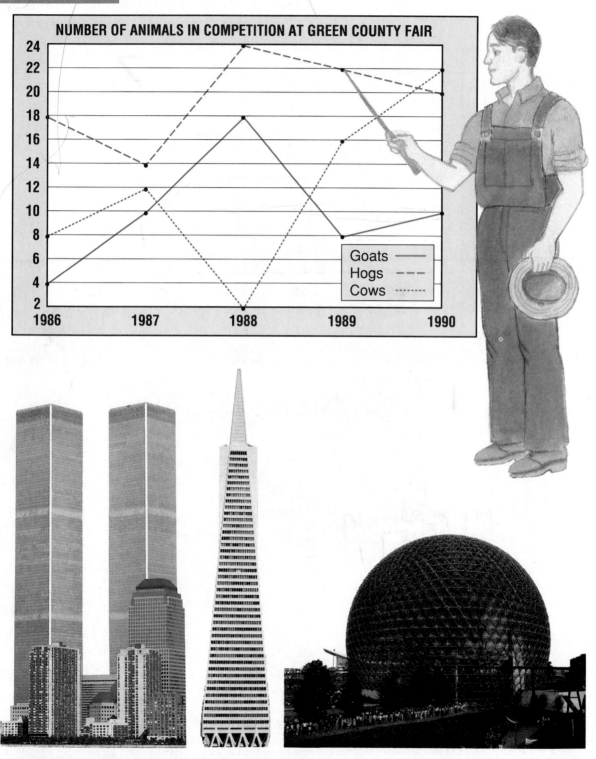

NUMBER OF ANIMALS IN COMPETITION AT GREEN COUNTY FAIR

Goats ——
Hogs – – –
Cows ·······

World Trade Center
(New York City)

TransAmerica Building
(San Francisco)

Expo '67 Dome
(Montreal)

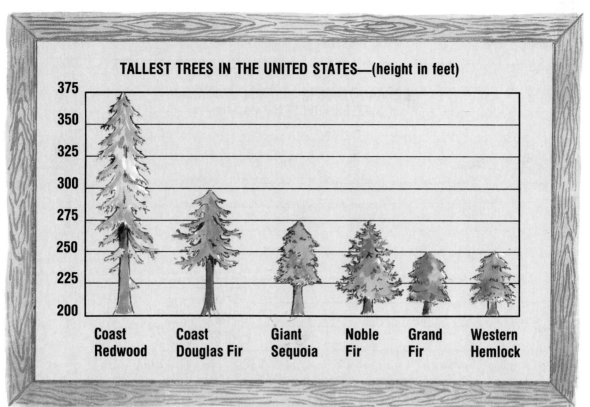

TALLEST TREES IN THE UNITED STATES—(height in feet)

Coast Redwood	Coast Douglas Fir	Giant Sequoia	Noble Fir	Grand Fir	Western Hemlock

375
350
325
300
275
250
225
200

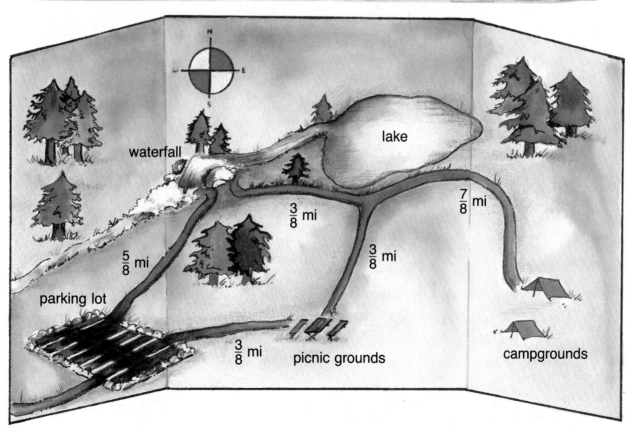

lake

waterfall

$\frac{7}{8}$ mi

$\frac{3}{8}$ mi

$\frac{3}{8}$ mi

$\frac{5}{8}$ mi

parking lot

$\frac{3}{8}$ mi

picnic grounds

campgrounds

DATABANK

WINNING TIMES IN OLYMPIC SWIMMING
100-METER FREESTYLE (in seconds)

Year	Men	Women
1976	49.99	55.65
1980	50.40	54.79
1984	49.50	55.92
1988	48.63	54.93

Turkey
850 lira = 1 U.S. dollar

Senegal
300 francs = 1 U.S. dollar

Belgium
40 francs = 1 U.S. dollar

Japan
145 yen = 1 U.S. dollar

Spain
126 pesetas = 1 U.S. dollar

Chile
200 pesos = 1 U.S. dollar

Greece
137 drachmas = 1 U.S. dollar

Rates subject to change.

GLOSSARY

A

addend A number that is added. In the addition sentence 5 + 4 = 9, 5 and 4 are addends.

addition An operation on two or more numbers that tells *how many in all* or *how much in all*.

$$9 \leftarrow \text{addend}$$
$$\underline{+\ 3} \leftarrow \text{addend}$$
$$12 \leftarrow \text{sum}$$

A.M. A label showing that a time occurs between 12:00 midnight and 12:00 noon.

angle A figure formed by two *rays* with the same endpoint.

area The number of square units it takes to cover the surface of a *plane figure*.

 The area of the square is 9 square units.

average A statistic about two or more numbers found by adding the numbers and dividing their sum by the total number of addends.

B

bar graph A *graph* that displays data using bars of different lengths.

C

capacity The *volume* of a *space figure* expressed as the amount of liquid the figure can hold.

centimeter (cm) A metric unit of length. There are 100 centimeters in a *meter*.

⊢——⊣ 1 centimeter

circle A closed plane figure.

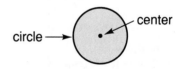

common factor A number that is a factor of two or more numbers. The common factors of 4 and 6 are 1 and 2.

common multiple a number that is a multiple of two or more numbers. A common multiple of 2 and 3 is 6.

composite number A whole number that has factors other than itself and 1.

523

congruent Figures that have the same size and shape, and lines and angles that have the same measure are congruent.

customary system A method of measurement that uses the following units:
Length/Distance: inch, foot, yard, mile
Capacity: cup, pint, quart, gallon
Weight: ounce, pound, ton
Temperature: degree Fahrenheit

D

decimal A number that uses place value and a decimal point to express mixed numbers or fractions with denominators of multiples of ten.

tens	ones	.	tenths	hundredths
2	4	.	7	5

$$24.75 = 24\frac{75}{100}$$
$\uparrow$
decimal point

decimeter (dm) A metric unit of length. A decimeter equals 10 *centimeters*. There are 10 decimeters in a *meter*.

degree Celsius The unit used to measure temperature in the metric system of measurement.

degree Fahrenheit The unit used to measure temperature in the customary system of measurement.

denominator The number beneath the line in a fraction.

$\frac{3}{4}$ ← numerator
← denominator

difference The answer to a subtraction problem. In the subtraction sentence $10 - 6 = 4$, 4 is the difference.

dividend The number that is divided into equal parts in a division problem.

$5\overline{)40}$ ← dividend

division An operation on two numbers that tells *how many groups* or *how many in each group*. Division can also tell *how many are left over*.

$46 \div 5 = 9\,R1$ There are nine 5's in 46 with a *remainder* of 1.

divisor The number that the *dividend* is divided by to find the *quotient* in a division problem.

8 ← quotient
$9\overline{)72}$ ← dividend
$\uparrow$ divisor

E

equivalent decimals Two or more decimals that name the same number. 3.1 and 3.10 are equivalent decimals.

equivalent fractions Two or more fractions that name the same number. $\frac{1}{3}$, $\frac{2}{6}$, and $\frac{3}{9}$ are equivalent fractions.

$$\frac{1}{2} = \frac{2}{4}$$

estimate To find *about how many* or *about how much* by using rounded numbers or only the front digits to compute. Estimating gives an answer that is close to the exact answer.

even number Any whole number that can be divided by 2 evenly. All even numbers have a 0, 2, 4, 6, or 8 in the ones place.

expanded form A method of writing a number as the sum of the values of its digits. Expanded form for 389 is 300 + 80 + 9.

F

fact family A group of related number sentences.

$$2 \times 4 = 8 \quad 4 \times 2 = 8$$
$$8 \div 2 = 4 \quad 8 \div 4 = 2$$

$$3 + 2 = 5 \quad 2 + 3 = 5$$
$$5 - 2 = 3 \quad 5 - 3 = 2$$

factor The numbers that are multiplied in a multiplication problem.

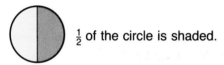

fraction A number that names part of a whole or part of a set.

$\frac{1}{2}$ of the circle is shaded.

front-end estimation A method of finding an answer that is close to the exact answer by computing with only the front digits of numbers.

G

graph A picture that organizes data to make it easy to understand and use. Types of graphs are *bar graph, line graph,* and *pictograph.*

I

intersecting lines Lines or line segments that meet or cross at a common point.

K

kilometer A metric unit of length. There are 1,000 *meters* in a kilometer.

L

line A straight figure that extends in both directions.

line segment A straight figure with two endpoints.

line of symmetry A line on which a figure can be folded so that its two halves match exactly.

M

mass The mass of an object tells how much of it there is.

median The middle number in a series of numbers ordered from the least to the greatest. The median of 4, 5, and 7 is 5.

meter A metric unit of length. There are 100 *centimeters* in a meter.

metric system A method of measurement that uses the following units:
Length/Distance: centimeter, decimeter, meter, kilometer
Capacity: milliliter, liter
Mass: gram, kilogram
Temperature: degree Celsius

mixed number A number made up of a whole number and a fraction. All mixed numbers are greater than 1. $3\frac{1}{2}$ is a mixed number.

multiple The product of a number and any other whole number. Some multiples of 4 are 4, 8, 12, 16, 24, 32, and 48.

multiplication An operation that tells *how many in all* when equal groups are combined.

$$
\begin{array}{r}
8 \leftarrow \text{factor} \\
\times\, 5 \leftarrow \text{factor} \\
\hline
40 \leftarrow \text{product}
\end{array}
$$

N

number sentence A mathematical fact written horizontally with numbers and symbols.

$$4 \times 5 < 23 \qquad 42 \div 7 = 6$$

numerator The number above the line in a fraction.

$$
\frac{3}{5}
\begin{array}{l}
\leftarrow \text{numerator} \\
\leftarrow \text{denominator}
\end{array}
$$

O

odd number Any whole number that has a 1, 3, 5, 7, or a 9 in the ones place.

ordered pair A pair of numbers that describes the location of a point on a graph, map, or grid. The ordered pair (5, 2) describes where the star is located on the grid.

order property A characteristic of addition and multiplication that gives the same result no matter how the addends or factors are positioned.

$$3 + 4 = 7 \qquad 4 \times 5 = 20$$
$$4 + 3 = 7 \qquad 5 \times 4 = 20$$

P

parallel lines Lines in the same plane that never meet.

perimeter The distance around an object. The perimeter of the rectangle is 16.

place value The value of a digit based on its position in a number. In 9,275, the 7 stands for 7 tens, or 70. In 784, the 7 stands for 7 hundreds or 700.

plane A flat surface extending in all directions.

plane figure Any figure that exists on a flat surface. Plane figures have no depth.

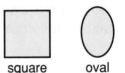

square oval star

P.M. A label showing that a time occurs between 12 noon and 12 midnight.

polygon A closed plane figure formed by line segments.

prime number A whole number greater than 1 with only itself and 1 as factors. 7 is a prime number. 2 is the only even number that is prime.

probability A number from 0 to 1 that measures the likelihood of an event occurring.

product The answer to a multiplication problem.

$$
\begin{array}{r}
5 \\
\times\, 4 \\
\hline
20 \leftarrow \text{product}
\end{array}
$$

Q

quotient The answer to a division problem.

$$7\overline{)35}^{\,5} \leftarrow \text{quotient}$$

R

range The difference between the least number and the greatest number in a set of data.

ray A straight line that has one endpoint and extends in one direction.

regroup To exchange equal amounts, such as 1 ten for 10 ones or 10 tens for 1 hundred, when computing.

remainder The amount left over when a number cannot be divided into equal parts.

$$\begin{array}{r} 6\ R1 \leftarrow \\ 7\overline{)43} \\ \underline{42} \quad \text{remainder} \\ 1 \leftarrow \end{array}$$

Roman numerals Symbols used by the ancient Romans to name whole numbers.

I = 1   V = 5   X = 10   L = 50
C = 100   D = 500   M = 1,000

rounding Replacing the exact number with the nearest multiple of 10, 100, 1,000, and so on. You compute with rounded numbers to find out about how many.

2,648 to the nearest 10 is 2,650
2,648 to the nearest 100 is 2,600
2,648 to the nearest 1,000 is 3,000

S

space figure A figure that exists in more than one plane.

cube   sphere   pyramid

sphere A space figure in the shape of a ball.

subtraction An operation on two numbers that tells *how many are left* when some are taken away. Subtraction is also used to compare two numbers.

$$\begin{array}{r} 14 \\ -\ 8 \\ \hline 6 \leftarrow \text{difference} \end{array}$$

sum The answer to an addition problem. In the addition sentence 9 + 6 = 15, 15 is the sum.

V

vertex The common point of the two rays of an angle or the two sides of a polygon.

volume The number of cubic units a space figure contains. The rectangular prism has 3 cubic units.

W

whole numbers The numbers that tell how many: 0, 1, 2, 3, . . .

TABLE OF MEASURES

TIME

$$
\begin{aligned}
60 \text{ seconds (s)} &= 1 \text{ minute (min)} \\
60 \text{ minutes} &= 1 \text{ hour (hr)} \\
24 \text{ hours} &= 1 \text{ day (d)} \\
7 \text{ days} &= 1 \text{ week (wk)} \\
12 \text{ months (mo)} &= 1 \text{ year (y)} \\
\text{about } 52 \text{ weeks} &= 1 \text{ year} \\
365 \text{ days} &= 1 \text{ year} \\
366 \text{ days} &= 1 \text{ leap year}
\end{aligned}
$$

METRIC UNITS

LENGTH

$$
\begin{aligned}
1 \text{ centimeter (cm)} &= 10 \text{ millimeters (mm)} \\
10 \text{ centimeters} &= 1 \text{ decimeter (dm)} \\
10 \text{ decimeters} &= 1 \text{ meter (m)} \\
1{,}000 \text{ meters} &= 1 \text{ kilometer (km)}
\end{aligned}
$$

MASS   1 kilogram (kg) = 1,000 grams (g)

CAPACITY   1 liter (L) = 1,000 milliliters (mL)

TEMPERATURE   0° Celsius (°C) . . . Water freezes
100° Celsius . . . Water boils

CUSTOMARY UNITS

LENGTH

$$
\begin{aligned}
1 \text{ foot (ft)} &= 12 \text{ inches (in.)} \\
1 \text{ yard (yd)} &= 36 \text{ inches} \\
1 \text{ yard} &= 3 \text{ feet} \\
1 \text{ mile (mi)} &= 5{,}280 \text{ feet} \\
1 \text{ mile} &= 1{,}760 \text{ yards}
\end{aligned}
$$

WEIGHT   1 pound (lb) = 16 ounces (oz)

CAPACITY

$$
\begin{aligned}
1 \text{ cup (c)} &= 8 \text{ fluid ounces} \\
1 \text{ pint (pt)} &= 2 \text{ cups} \\
1 \text{ quart (qt)} &= 2 \text{ pints} \\
1 \text{ gallon (gal)} &= 4 \text{ quarts}
\end{aligned}
$$

TEMPERATURE   32° Fahrenheit (°F) . . . Water freezes
212° Fahrenheit . . . Water boils

SYMBOLS

<	is less than	$\overrightarrow{AB}$	ray AB
>	is greater than	$B \sphericalangle^{A}_{C}$	angle ABC or angle CBA or angle B
=	is equal to	$\overleftrightarrow{LM} \parallel \overleftrightarrow{OP}$	line LM parallel to line OP
°	degree	$\overleftrightarrow{UZ} \perp \overleftrightarrow{WY}$	line UZ perpendicular to line WY
$\overleftrightarrow{AB}$	line AB	(5,3)	ordered pair 5,3
$\overline{AB}$	line segment AB		

INDEX